Beginning Graphics Programming With Processing 3

Edited by Antony Lees

Foreword by Ira Greenberg

Cover Design by Louise Gillard

Written by

Alex Harris	Anabela Greene
Anton Dil	Antonio Bruno
Antony Lees	Ben Notorianni
Boyd Stratton	Bruce Lawley
Bryan Clifton	Charlie Beddoes
Daniel Bergmann	Darragh Buffini
Dušan Ličer	Geoff Riley
Graham Hall	Grant Mankee
Ian Macey	Ian Welch
James Gray	Jannetta Steyn
JeanLuc Brausch	John Wilson
Liam Madden	Mark Miller
Mark Moran	Marshall Heap
Martin Humby	Martin Prout
Mike Richards	Mike Taperell
Neil Keskar	Neil Petrie
Neil Singh	Nigel Parker
Rebecca Ewen	Richard Brown
Rob Martin	Rob Spain
Roberto Vormittag	Rosie Wood
Samir Rabab	Sharon Dawes
Sheep Dalton	Stewart Edwards

CONTENTS

FOREWORD

In 2001, an obscure academic project was initiated by Casey Reas and Ben Fry, graduate students at the MIT Media Lab. The main goal of the project was to create a computer programming language designed especially for artists. They named the project *Processing*. Over the next 10 years Reas and Fry worked on the language – mostly in their spare time and from different locations – and other people began to notice. A web-based and open-source initiative, *Processing*, slowly attracted a nationwide cult following. Traditional artists discovered *Processing* and began teaching themselves how to program; programmers and computer scientists began using *Processing* for rapid prototyping; instructors introduced *Processing* into their classrooms – both in art departments as well as in departments of computer science.

In 2007, I authored the first English language reference on *Processing*, through Friends of ED Press, which was followed shortly by a book by Reas and Fry and then another digital artist/instructor Daniel Shiffman. More books have since followed. To say *Processing* has arrived is an understatement. In addition to the books and finalization of the core language, many users contributed code libraries as we as sister projects, including *Arduino* and *OpenFrameworks*.

In 2008, Professor Darrel Ince, of the Open University, invited me to come lecture at the OU main campus in Milton Keynes, UK. Darrel and I corresponded over the previous year about *Processing* and my book as well as his own radical publishing initiative. Darrel proposed to create a book on *Processing* as an exercise in crowdsourcing, where each chapter of the book would be written by a different author – all OU students and alums. The idea sounded inspiring to me, though I was honestly somewhat sceptical at the time that a project so potentially complex would ever get finished. Having taught for years, I knew how students often started projects with a full head of steam and then slowly got distracted and busy as they moved on to different classes or graduated. During my visit to Milton Keynes, Darrel and some of his students presented their publishing project to me. Numerous students stood up and discussed their chapters – their progress, challenges and excitement about the experience. One of the most interesting challenges the group faced was one of geography. The OU works on a distance model, so the students and alums are scattered around the globe. I wasn't the only visitor Darrel had invited that day, his co-authors were visitors as well. I was blown away by the presentations and, caught up in the fervor, offered to contribute a foreword to the book. (Remember, I thought it would never get finished)

I am now very, very happy to admit that my original scepticism was unfounded and plain wrong. Darrel and his army of students have indeed produced another *Processing* book. And not just *another* book, but a major contribution to the *Processing* literature and community. There is something fitting that perhaps the final and introductory text to be produced on *Processing* was created in the same spirit – with many of the same logistical challenges of remote collaboration and open source fervor – as the language itself. This book is both an anthology of individual thoughts and techniques on learning *Processing* and computer graphics and a unified work on creative coding. The book speaks with many voices, giving it a complexity and richness not quite found in other books. It is certainly less consistent than the other books but also more wonderfully surprising. I look forward to referring to this book for years to come

Happy creative coding!

Ira Greenberg, 2010

PREFACE

This book started as an experiment in crowdsourcing to create a book with a large number of authors about the graphics programming language *Processing*. The result is this book, authored by 45 Open University students and computing academics using only the Internet as a communication medium and compiled together to create a unique piece of work

Processing is a free, open-source, programming language based on the much larger Java language. It focusses on the visual output of computer programs, designed for non-programmers, and those more experienced, to create visual graphics and animation. Processing includes everything needed to create and view graphics including an IDE (Integrated Development Environment) that can be used to create programs and graphics

The book aims to teach the Processing programming language to both non-programmers and experienced programmers alike, allowing those who have not worked on computer programs before to become competent in the language and anyone to create some visually stunning graphics and animation regardless of prior experience. The book does not intend to teach the Java language itself, although the Processing language utilises it and has similar syntax. As such, the detail on aspects such as Object Orientation is only taught to the level required to create *Processing* programs, rather than attempting to teach all of the Java language and related aspects itself. There are many good Java resources online and in print for those who want to learn more of the surrounding language

The book is divided into 3 main sections:

- **Section 1** – for those new to programming. Chapter 3 may be relevant to those new to the Processing language
- **Section 2** – for existing programmers and those who have read section 1
- **Section 3** – advanced Processing concepts suitable for all levels

The final chapter in Section 3 introduces *Processing* in other languages such as JavaScript and Android, demonstrating how widespread the language and its ideas have spread

You will soon discover that there are no real rules to creating graphics in Processing and that minor changes can yield unexpected results. So our best advice is, try stuff out, see what happens, have fun!

SECTION 1: PROGRAMMING PRINCIPLES

Chapter 1: Introduction to Programming
by Mike Taperell and Roberto Vormittag

This chapter introduces you to the idea of computer art and to Java, the programming language that Processing is based upon. You'll also see an example of how Processing can be used to create a simple graphic

Computer Graphics

From the earliest cave paintings, artists were never slow to take advantage of the opportunities new technology offered and this has resulted in a steady progression— both in technique and visual appeal—that can be seen to have matured as the centuries progressed. This evolution exists both in the materials and techniques used as well as in the imaginative way that subjects of paintings can be portrayed.

The advent of computers and computing have provided such a raft of new tools and possibilities that art has exploded onto our screens, impacting all walks of life and touching everyone. Works of art, once displayed only in museums and churches, now present themselves everywhere from the displays on our mobile phones to the ever present advertisements that populate our media. Looking back from their privileged viewpoint a hundred years hence, our progeny will surely identify the years of the computer explosion as the dawn of a new era in exciting and accessible art.

Computers have, through the use of specialised software programs, created the possibility to make adjustments to images that totally transform both the look and the composition of a picture. However, as this book will show, it is in the use of computer programs that excite and produce some of the most unusual and stimulating work that modern technology excels. There is, after all, something rather wonderful about watching a computer produce shapes and colours on the screen as you watch, knowing that this particular work is unique to that occasion and is being produced just for you! This is all the better, of course, when the set of instructions is one that you produced and crafted yourself.

A computer program is simply a list of instructions that the computer takes, processes and which results in a particular output. In a way, it's like writing a shopping list where you enter the items required and the order in which they must be purchased as you walk around the store. The computer, in this case you, then performs the task and at the end there is a result, in this case a basket full of shopping. Specifying these instructions makes you the computer programmer and although each instruction may be simple, the combined effect can produce amazing results. You, the programmer and artist, produce the list of instructions you wish the machine to perform and, at the press of a key, your program runs and output appears on the screen.

13

Using simple computer code it is possible to construct an endless variety of shapes in millions of colours, all of which can be arranged, moved and overlaid to form either a composition, some form of pattern or a representation of an object existing in the real world. Using the *Processing* environment upon which this book is based, it is also possible to easily and quickly make changes to the structure of the program which, when run again, will produce a different result. As you will see later, the changes to the program may be small, but the end-product can be totally different from that produced earlier, a procedure that is notoriously laborious using traditional art methods. The really exciting part is that, by experimenting, you can create unexpected and amazing graphical works

The Java Programming Language

A computer program is simply a set of instructions, written in a programming language, that tells the computer what to do. The Processing language, which essentially tells the computer how to display graphics, is based on a programming language called Java. Just as you don't have to know how a car works to be able to drive one, you also don't need to know how a computer works to write a computer program. However if you do know the basics of combustion engines, transmission systems, braking systems, and tyre grip physics, it will make you a better—and safer—driver. The same applies to programming. So let's start by looking at what is going on under the bonnet of our PC when we run a computer program.

The Computer

For all their wonderful multimedia capabilities of modern day, computers are, at their heart, nothing more than number crunching machines. Inside every PC is the single most important piece of hardware – the microprocessor, also known as the Central Processing Unit, or CPU. The CPU is responsible for executing program instructions and manipulating data. However there is one catch: CPUs understand only binary numbers (sequences of zeroes and ones). Program instructions and data expressed in binary format are commonly known as machine code.

On the same circuit board where the CPU is located, you will find a bunch of silicon chips which make up your PC's Random Access Memory (RAM). It is in the RAM that the machine code is stored for the CPU to fetch and execute. What happens is this: whenever you ask your operating system for example *Windows*, to run a program, say, by double clicking on the program's icon, the operating system reads the relevant file(s) from disk and loads the program into RAM. Once in memory, the operating system can start feeding the machine code to the CPU for execution. The combination of a specific operating system version running on a particular type of hardware is often referred to as a platform.

You now know (almost) everything a programmer needs to know about computer architecture. To write a computer program in machine code that the CPU understands would be a colossal task, even for the geekiest among geeks, because binary numbers don't mean much to humans. Instead, we like to communicate concepts through words and sentences. So we have a problem: computers and people 'speak' two completely different languages.

Translation and Compilers

If you need to communicate with a person who only understands Japanese, and you don't know the first thing about the Japanese language, what do you do? You hire a translator, of course. And that's exactly the solution that computer scientists came up with to solve the computer-human language mismatch: they created programming languages based on symbols that people understand (called high-level programming languages), and then use software to translate these 'human-friendly' program files (the source code) into machine code for the CPU to execute. The translation process from source code to machine code is called compilation. There are two categories of software that perform compilation: source code compilers and source code interpreters.

A compiler translates the source code into binary before the program is run (known as compile-time), storing the resulting machine code on disk as an executable program. When the operating system loads a compiled program into RAM for execution, the CPU can execute it straight away without any delays since it is already in binary format. Compiled programs use the CPU speed to the full; they are said to be *high-performing* programs. The issue with compiled programs is that they aren't portable - for example a program compiled to run on Windows will not run on a Mac without modification.

An interpreter performs source code compilation during execution of the program (at what is called runtime). When you request the execution of an interpreted program, the operating system loads the interpreter in RAM, which, in turn, loads the program source code as-is and then compiles one instruction at a time into machine code on-the-fly before it is passed to the CPU for execution. The resulting machine code is never stored on disk, so every time an interpreted program is executed the compilation has to be performed all over again. This makes them portable but adds extra processing required by the on-the-fly compilation of the source code into machine code at runtime, making them potentially slower than compiled programs

Java takes a different approach: it uses both a compiler and an interpreter. Java source code is firstly processed by a compiler, but the result of the compilation is not machine code as with traditional (native) compilers; the Java compiler produces something called bytecode. Bytecode is the closest you can get to machine code, while still maintaining platform-neutrality. Unlike machine code, bytecode cannot be executed as-is; an interpreter is still required to run the compiled Java program. The Java interpreter is usually known as the Java Virtual Machine, or JVM. Because the bytecode is already pretty close to machine code, the JVM can perform the on-the-fly compilation from bytecode to machine code very quickly—much faster compared to purely interpreted languages.

As the bytecode is platform-neutral, compiled Java programs are entirely portable; you can run your compiled Java program on any platform for which there is a JVM implementation, without changing a single line of code. The JVM runtime execution of bytecode performs to levels close to that of machine code-compiled programs. Java manages to combine portability with high performance. That's quite an achievement.

Java and Processing

Java comes with a large collection of ready-made software components providing a wide range of functionality that you can incorporate into your programs straight out-of-the-box. In computing parlance, such a collection of reusable software components is called a *software library*. And the way you access the functionality provided by a software library is by means of its Application Programming Interface (API).

An API is essentially a well-documented set of component interfaces organized in a structured way. The range of functionality provided by the Java libraries is staggering. It covers the storage of data (collections); utilities to manipulate text; mathematical operations; program input and output; network programming; security; database connectivity; graphical user interfaces; two-dimensional graphics; and a lot more. This rich set of libraries makes a programming language more appealing as it allows programmers to produce complex software faster, with less code and more quality.

The *Processing* development environment, used for computer art, is built using Java. The programming language used in *Processing* is Java, although *Processing* provides an extended graphics API and a simplified programming model that gets you started with graphic programming very quickly, whilst, at the same time allowing you to use more advanced techniques as you gain more experience.

To conclude this introduction, it is worth taking a look at a very simple *Processing* program. You need not understand the detail at this point, but it gives a small view of what a Processing program looks like. It draws the St. George's Cross, in the form of the national flag of England. The output from the program is shown in Figure 1

```
/** St George's Cross - a very simple Processing program.*/
// Calculate and set variables, not that the number represents
// the number of pixels, these are the dots on a computer screen
int flagDimension = 70;
```

```
// The flag width will be 70*5=350
int flagWide = flagDimension * 5;

// The flag height will be 70* 3 pixels =210
int flagHeight = flagDimension * 3;

// The width of the cross will be 210/5 = 42 pixels
int crossWidth = flagHeight / 5;

// Call required Processing API functions
// define sketch window size of 350 by 210 pixels
size(flagWide, flagHeight);

// Set window background to white
// 255 is the integer value for white
background(255);

// Set stroke weight for the cross, this gives a width of 42
strokeWeight(crossWidth);

// set stroke colour to red
stroke(255, 0, 0);

// draw the cross
line(0, flagHeight/2, flagWide, flagHeight/2);
line(flagWide/2, 0, flagWide/2, flagHeight);
```

Figure 1: Drawing of the St George's Cross

Chapter 2: Algorithms

by Alex Harris, Samir Rabab and Stewart Edwards

An algorithm is a description of some process that a computer executes using a programming language. To implement a computer program you need to design an algorithm. This chapter enables you to do this. It is one of the most important chapters in the book as everything else that follows depends on it

What is an Algorithm?

An obvious point to start the chapter with is; what is an algorithm? This might sound like a simple question for some of you but it never hurts to cover the basics so that everyone ends up at the same point. Algorithm sounds like a scary word but it is actually something really quite simple. It is just a set of instructions that can be put together to perform a task. An algorithm is something that you use already in everyday life without even thinking about it. To take a basic example, imagine the steps needed for getting out of bed

Algorithm for getting up in the morning

1. Think 'I need to get up'
2. Throw back the covers
3. Grudgingly take one foot and place it on the floor
4. Heave yourself up
5. Place second foot on floor
6. Rub eyes
7. Stand up

So there you are up out of bed, algorithm done, understood and comprehended. It really is that easy. Let's try another one. You decide that before going for your daily run, you will write an algorithm for it. Give it a try then compare it to our version below

Algorithm for going for a run

1. Put on running clothes and shoes
2. Open door.
3. Go out of door
4. Close door
5. Start jogging to warm up
6. Start running
7. Cool down
8. End run

Let's now try an algorithm more closely related to what you would do with a computer. Computers love algorithms. And every algorithm that you will ever write does exactly what you have already done: it lists the sequences of events that need to take place to make something happen. Computers follow instructions exactly, so it is important that they are told precisely what to do, otherwise they can do unexpected and strange things. Computers do not think like we do, they can only follow orders. This is where algorithms have their power - you can use them to visualise what a computer will do

Let's think about something you probably do without thinking, using a computer application such as playing a game on the computer. Any game will do, we'll use a game of pool:

Algorithm for playing pool on the computer

1. Sit at computer
2. Turn computer on
3. Log in to my desktop
4. Click pool game icon
5. Start playing pool and have fun
6. Stop when I win/lose

Grab a pen and paper and write an algorithm for your favourite computer game or application, it will help you understand the concepts more clearly.

This concept can also be translated to writing a Processing program. Imagine you want to draw a line on the screen. You could delve straight into the programming but it would help to first write an algorithm to help visualise the process.

Algorithm to visualise programming a straight line

1. Open *Processing* tool
2. Write code to draw a straight line on the screen
3. Run the code to draw the line
4. Look at the line with great satisfaction

A bit abstract maybe but all need to do now is exactly the same thing, but in more detail by expanding on the steps needed to write the code: simply listing out the sequence of things that the computer needs to do to draw the line.

Algorithm for actually drawing the line

1. Pick a point on the screen
2. Pick a second point on the screen

3. Draw a line between these two points

The output of our algorithm can be seen in Figure 2.

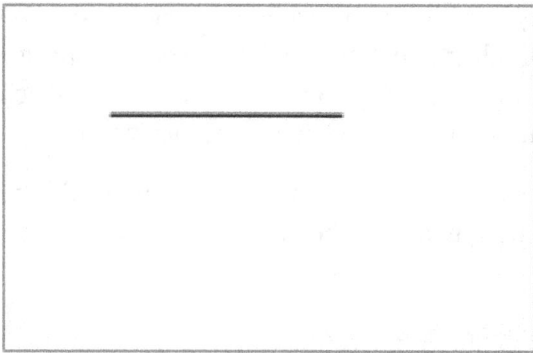

Figure 2: A Line Drawn using an Algorithm

So there you have it. You now know that an algorithm is simply an ordered list that helps you do something. You know that computers do things through using programs, and algorithms are just descriptions of these programs - lists of instructions if you like - and you now know how to write your own algorithms. Easy isn't it? Next we will look at some more complex algorithms.

Parts of an Algorithm

The algorithms we've shown so far have been intentionally simple and not included any repetition or decision-making. It is vital that we use a finite number of steps in our algorithm. Thus, the aim is for our algorithm to terminate when the last step has been executed. *A well designed algorithm is always guaranteed to terminate.*

Think of it as describing the most basics steps needed to accomplish something in minute detail, for example, how to cook a joint of lamb. Imagine trying to tell a robot how to cook lamb. It isn't sufficient to tell the robot to watch the lamb, because that's exactly what it would do, watch it burn on the stove. You would need to tell it when to intervene, in this case when the lamb is sufficiently cooked

As you will see however, having a finite number of steps (although a step in the right direction) does not necessarily guarantee the termination of our algorithm. Let's re-consider the 'running' algorithm:

Algorithm for going for a run

1. Put on running clothes and shoes
2. Open door

3. Go out of door
4. Close door
5. Start jogging to warm up
6. Start running
7. Cool down
8. End run

It seems straight forward enough; it is, under normal circumstances. But, what would happen if you encounter a problem along the way, say in step 2. The door does not open, it is jammed or locked and the key is nowhere to be found. Suddenly, the task of getting out of the door (step 3) does not seem that straight forward.

For a human, this might present a setback, and cause a delay in the time taken to get to the final step within the algorithm. A deviation will become inevitable while we make the necessary arrangements that will help us overcome 'the door problem', making a phone call to the locksmith for instance. A computer on the other hand, faced with such an algorithm, where one of its steps cannot be successfully executed will crash and throw out an error message along with some technical jargon, which is its way of saying 'bad algorithm'.

To overcome this shortfall in our algorithm, we need to introduce a mechanism that allows the algorithm to make 'decisions' along the way to indicate the correct path to follow based on a given set of circumstances.

Algorithms usually incorporate some, or all, of the following features

- Sequence
- Decision
- Repetition

Sequence

The order in which the steps appear within our algorithm can be extremely important. If we further divide step 2 of our algorithm 'Open door' into three separate steps:

1. Unlock door
2. Turn handle
3. Pull handle to open door

We can safely claim that executing step 3 before step 1 makes a large difference to the success of the algorithm. However, the order we put on our running clothes may be less important (putting your shoes on before your t-shirt makes little difference to the end result)

Decision

Decisions help us to find alternative routes based on a given condition, i.e. what to do in the situation where the door does not open, or equally as bad, if it does not close behind you. Do you cancel your run, find another solution, or ignore the problem? Any of those may be acceptable, or unacceptable, to you

Repetition

You can think of step 6 'Start running' as a continuous repetition of the same action, namely that you keep running until it is time for step 7 'Cool down'. This is an example of repetition. Repetition almost always must include a decision, namely when to stop repeating

Going back to our running algorithm, consider the following enhancement:

Algorithm for going on a run (with repetition and decision making)

1. Put on running clothes and shoes
2. Open door
    a. If door can be opened, open door
    b. Else cancel run
3. Go out of door
4. Close door
5. Choose direction
    a. If raining turn left into the undercover running complex
    b. Else turn right into the park
6. Start jogging to warm up
7. Start running
8. Keep running for 30 minutes
9. Cool down
10. End run

You will see that we've enhanced the algorithm by adding in some repetition (how long to keep running for) and some decision making:

- When to stop running
- Which direction to take depending on the weather
- What to do if we can't open the door

As you can see, decisions can be used to enable us to recover from problems that could occur (door not opening, for example) during the execution of our algorithm. However, we can also use decisions to aid us in controlling and selecting the most optimum route for our algorithm to follow, so that our end goal can be achieved in the most efficient way possible.

When making decisions in algorithms it will be your job as a programmer to pick the solution that represents the best alternative, taking into account the various factors that surround your particular project.

This introduction to algorithms underpins all computer programs and being able to understand and write them will form the basis of every computer program you write.

Chapter 3: Introduction to *Processing*
by Charlie Beddoes, John Wilson and Sheep Dalton

This chapter will introduce you to the *Processing*: a Java-based system for computer graphic art. You will see how *Processing* has a number of instructions that allow you to draw simple graphical objects such as lines and learn how to use the *Processing* Integrated Development Environment

The Processing Environment

The *Processing* environment has been designed specifically for artists to create pieces of computational art as easily as possible; this is reflected by the simplicity of the program interface. However, this simplicity does not equal poor output. It is possible to create very complex pieces using this program even if you haven't ever written code before using *Processing*, without months of programming to achieve it.

We will take a closer look at the main components of the *Processing* environment as a way of familiarising yourself before you really get your teeth in to it. This type of environment is referred to as an IDE (Integrated Development Environment) known in *Processing* as the PDE (Processing Development Environment). In the following descriptions it is important to know that *Processing* refers to the created graphic as a *sketch* and the code written to create it as *sketch code*

To install *Processing* head over to the *Processing* website (processing.org) and download it for your operating system (Windows, Mac, Linux etc), unzip the file you downloaded and run the processing application. When you open the program you should be met with a window similar to the one shown in Figure 3

This screen is made up of six main components, shown in Figure 3, which briefly are:

- Toolbar - the basic functions for handling the sketch code and running it
- Tabs - one tab per piece of sketch code
- Text Editor - the editor where you can write and see your code
- Line Numbers – the line numbers for your code with current line highlighted
- Message Area - where *Processing* displays messages to you
- Console - where any text output (including error messages) is displayed
- Console/Error Tabs – Buttons to switch between the Console and Errors tabs

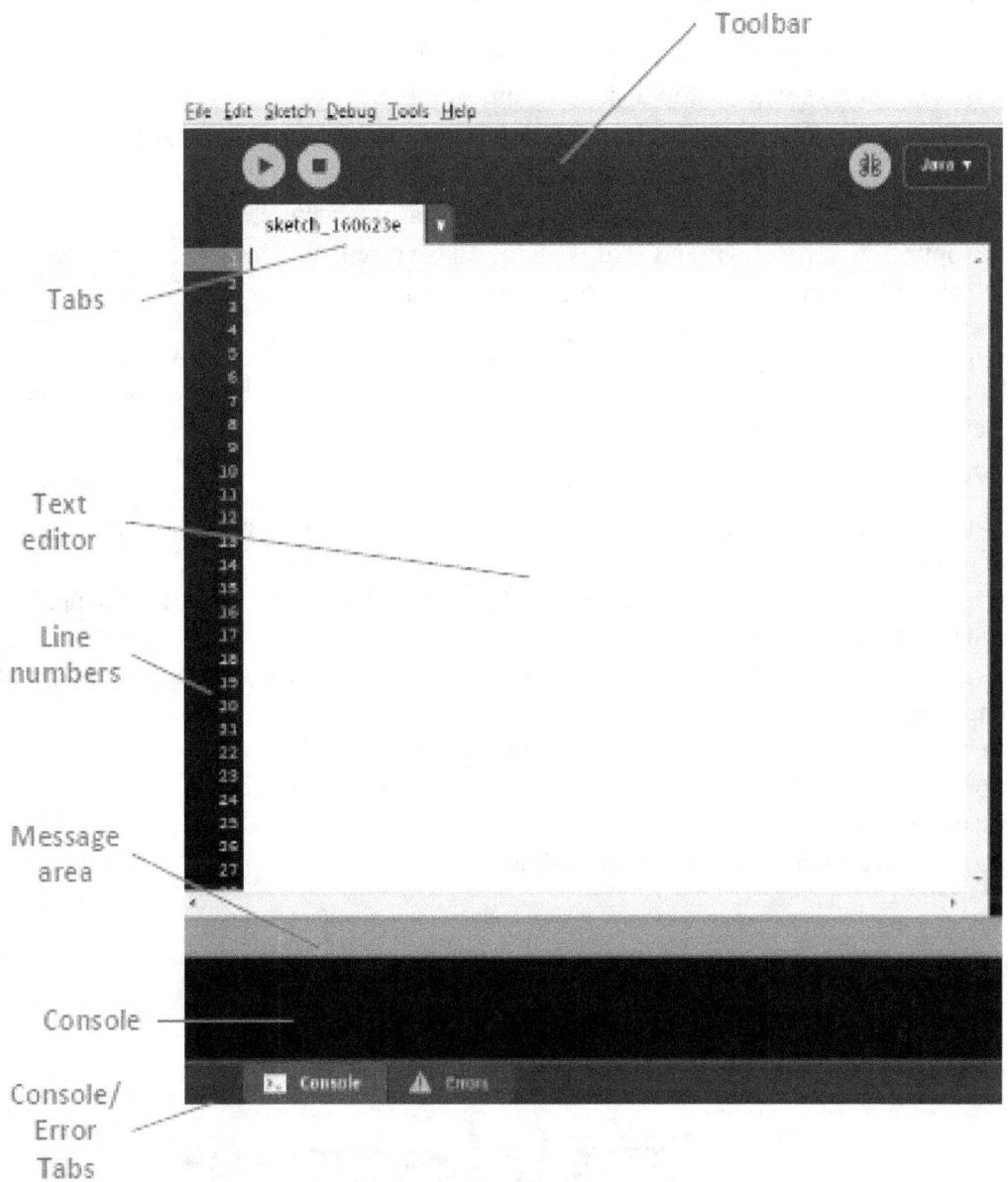

Figure 3: The Processing Environment

The toolbar itself probably bears some additional explanation in case the functions are not obvious. Note that that the top menu may differ on your computer due to the operating system you use (the one shown in the example was produced on a Windows 7 machine). However, it is simply a standard window menu, so the one you see should be similar to the standard one you are used to

The buttons are shown in Figure 4 and briefly explained as:

- Run - allows you to compile your code and execute it
- Stop - allows you to stop a sketch from running
- Debug – starts the debugger for debugging your sketch code. We won't cover debugging here as it is a large topic
- Mode - allows you to change the 'mode' that your sketch will run in. The default option given is Java and that is the mode we will use until we introduce modes much later in the book. Other modes can be added such as JavaScript and Android

The top menu contains a series of useful actions that you may use. We won't provide a full explanation of every menu option, there is a full description on the *Processing* website if you need it, but we will briefly describe each one:

- File. This contains a series of commands that open and file *Processing* sketches. This command set is also used for printing and for setting preferences such as the maximum amount of memory available.
- Edit. This contains a series of commands that manipulate source code, for example cutting chunks of text.
- Sketch. This part of the *Processing* environment is concerned with running sketches and importing libraries.
- Debug. This contains actions used when debugging sketch code.
- Tools. This contains a variety of tools that you will only use infrequently unless you become a hardcore user.
- Help. This contains a series of help facilities.

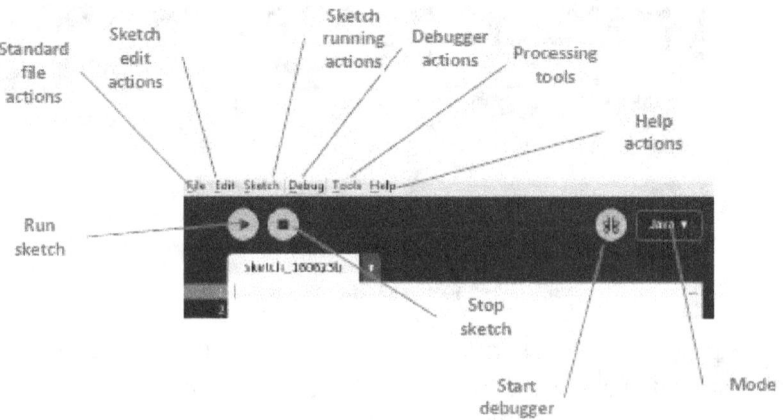

Figure 4: Processing Environment Toolbar

Your First Sketch

Let's now use the *Processing* environment with a real example by creating our first running sketch. We will start by writing one line of what programmers called 'code' or 'source code'.

Start *Processing* and in the white text editor type the following line on its own.

```
println("hello world!");
```

Now press the 'run' button. Assuming you have typed it in exactly as you see it above you should now notice that a small window appears and the message:

```
Hello world!
```

printed in white on the black background beneath the text area, similar to Figure 5. Quit the window that was just created - this is known as the *display window* and is where the graphics you will create are displayed. Currently it is blank because all we did was output some text. Congratulations. You have made your first sketch. Most programmers call this the *hello world moment*. If you can get this to appear on the screen then it shows everything is working correctly.

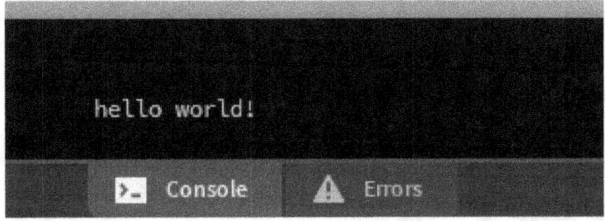

Figure 5: Hello World!

You can now save this sketch using the File > Save menu option. Call it something like hello_world. This will save a file called hello_world.pde. *Processing* uses the .pde extensions to show that the file relates to a *Processing* sketch file

Let us go through the sketch and see what you have just done. It began with the command, or procedure, or message (they are currently synonymous) called `println`. This is short for PRINT LINE, and reaches far, far back into the dawn of computing. Many years ago computers were attached to teletype printers, a sort of computer-controlled electric typewriter. For example, the hot line between America and the USSR during the Cold War was a teletype (literally far-type): a set of wires connecting two teletype machines. Typing the letter H at one end would cause the letter H to be printed on the corresponding remote machine. By typing this way, two people, or presidents perhaps, could have a conversation. Once you had written your message you would press the return button to send it.

Later, during the development of the computer, someone had the idea of hooking up a computer to a teletype machine and then programming it to send text to the printer. This concept, while wildly primitive, does sit at the heart of all programming languages. Being able to print line or `println` a message to yourself is one of the last ditch ways you can check to see how a program is working. So you can see that for most programmers, once they figure out how to do the `println` then they can be sure that everything works as it should.

After the command comes a rounded bracket in which 'arguments' are contained, which are given to the preceding command. So in this case the argument is "Hello world!", some text that we want to print. Old-fashioned quotes are used to show that this is text and not, for example, a number. Finally, the line ends with a semicolon. Some languages assume that the entire line is the line of code. *Processing* takes the semi colon as the end of line marker and missing this will produce an error

Processing will attempt to alert you to errors in your code with a meaningful error message. Missing a semicolon will produce an error stating that you are "Missing a semicolon". You can click on the *Errors* tab at the bottom for a more descriptive version of the error. As you can see in 6 the tab shows the error, the tab on which it is located (as you can have multiple sketches open at a time) and the line on which it occurred. Of course we only have 1 line, but if you had 1000 it would be very useful! Multiple errors can be displayed here if you have more than one error

Figure 6: Error Console Showing Missing Semicolon Error

The 'missing semicolon' error is an easy one to spot and fix. Some errors may not be so easy and require more effort for you to work out where the issue lies. As an example, try changing one of the speech marks (") to an apostrophe (')

```
println('Hello World!");
```

This will generate an error of 'Invalid Character Constant' which is much less obvious. However, as Figure 7 shows, it does tell you on which line the error occurs, and you will have to read over that line of code to work out what the error is and how to fix it. You can try this yourself

Figure 7: Error Console Showing Invalid Character Constant Error

If you would like a bit of practice at studying errors, try spotting the errors in the following lines of code. The *Processing* Error console tab might help you if you copy these into a *Processing* window

```
println("Hello World!");
println("Hello World!")
println("Hello World!");
println("Hello World!');
println"Hello World!");
```

Your Second Sketch

Let's move on to something a bit more interesting. Type the following code into the text window in *Processing* and press the run button. Don't worry about understanding it all at this point

```
println("hello world");
size(640,580);
rect(72,72,405,505 );
ellipseMode(CORNER);
ellipse( 135,135,108,99 );
ellipse( 306,135,108,99);
triangle(279,270,324,358,234,358);
arc(153,405,270,83,0,PI );
```

If *Processing* complains, don't worry, as it is hard to write a long list of code without making a typing error. It can be hard to understand what is going wrong so if *Processing* does complain then make sure that the code is copied down exactly as it is shown here in the book. If you are sure there are no errors on one line then check the line before or after. Generally, make sure that every command ends with a ';' semicolon (this is the most common mistake that people make).

When you run this code you should see the display window being created. Congratulations! This window should show a picture of a face resembling the picture in Figure 8. The face is drawn on what *Processing* calls a 'canvas' which is essentially the area you can draw on inside the display window

So what happened? We will briefly take you through the lines you just typed. The first line of the code is the familiar `println` of 'hello world' left over from the first sketch. As you have already seen with algorithms, the code starts from the top of the list and works its way down the list.

The next line, `size` tells *Processing* how big a window it should be creating. You generally call `size` once and only once; the arguments to `size` are the dimensions in pixels (a dot on the screen) you will ultimately use. If you make the values large (1000000, 100000) then you will get a window bigger than the screen

Figure 8: Picture of a Face

The next few lines draw the face - rectangle for the face, ellipses for the eyes, triangle for the nose and an arc for the mouth.

Now let's save the sketch and change the sketch name by using the *Save* option. Press the *Save* button; a File Dialog window will open, offering you the option of renaming the sketch. Let's rename the sketch by changing the highlighted name to HelloWorld and clicking on the *Save* button. Once this has been done, the *Processing* window should reflect the new name of the sketch along the top bar of the application and above the editing frame.

That is your first *Processing* sketch written and saved. For fun try replacing the arc line with:

```
arc(153,405,270,83,PI,0);
```

and rerun the sketch to get a frown. Have you noticed that all you did was play with the numbers? Why not carry on playing with changing some other numbers?

Chapter 4: Programming Basics

by Alex Harris, Bryan Clifton, Daniel Bergmann, Mike Richards and Sheep Dalton

This chapter will introduce you to the basic programming concepts needed to create a *Processing* sketch. It will introduce you to a number of very important programming concepts such as comments, variables, assignment statements and operators.

Variables

Computer programs need places to store information – these places are called *variables* (because their value may change during the execution of the program). Variables can be likened to pigeon holes in an internal snail mail system, where each employee or department (or whatever) has a pigeon hole in which mail is placed. Essentially the pigeon hole represents the *variable*. This is where important information is stored. Before you can use a variable, you must declare it. This is usually done at the top of a program code. Here is an example of a simple variable declaration:

```
int numberOfWheels;
```

The first word, `int`, tells *Processing* that the variable will hold an integer (whole number) value. *Processing* is an example of a *typed* language—that is variables may belong to one of a number of different *types* such as an integer (don't worry if this seems to be a lot to take in right now, we will return to types below).

The second word `numberOfWheels` is the name we have chosen for the variable. And that's it! You can now use the variable `numberOfWheels` in your sketch code.

Processing allows you to be extremely creative with variable names, so take advantage of that flexibility to choose appropriate names for the ones in your sketches; whilst it is very tempting to call variables `a`, b or `temp`; these names aren't terribly meaningful when you come back to your code many months later. We will give you some guidance below.

One question that might have occurred to you is, what is the value of `numberOfWheels` now we have declared it? The answer is that we can't be sure; although *Processing* can access our new variable, it has not been given an initial value. If you try to run the following sketch:

```
int numberOfWheels;
println(numberOfWheels);
```

which will display the value of the variable `numberOfWheels` you will see a warning in the message area of the *Processing* window along the lines of:

```
The local variable numberOfWheels may not have been initialized
```

To avoid this error, it is good practice to *initialise* a variable at the same time as declaring it. As the name suggests, initialisation sets a starting value for the variable, doing this is a great help when debugging a program—you can track the values of variables from the moment they are created and check that their values are always what you expected. Initialisation is extremely simple, the declaration can be rewritten as shown below to use initialisation:

```
int numberOfWheels = 4;
```

If you rewrite the simple sketch above with this declaration and initialisation, then run it, you should see the number 4 appear in the text area of the *Processing* window. The act of setting a variable to a value is known as 'assigning', so variables must be initialised by assigning a value to them before they can be used by using the = sign (known as an operator, we will cover these in a moment)

So, how do we name variables? *Processing* is a 'case sensitive' language meaning that it treats upper and lower case letters as different characters. So if you declare the variables `myname`, `myName`, `Myname`, `MyName` and `MYNAME` you create five different variables.Most *Processing* programmers use so-called 'camel case' when naming variables. Camel-case is a method of naming where individual words are joined without spaces, the first letter is in lowercase with the first letter of the subsequent words are capitalised; so a variable used to store the number of wheels on a toy car could be named `numberOfWheels`.

Processing does have some simple rules for naming variables:

- Variable names may only contain letters, numbers, hyphens (-) and the underscore character (_);
- You cannot use any of the reserved keywords as a variable name, for example `int`. In addition to these strict rules it is recommended that you don't give variables the same name as any of your functions or objects to avoid confusion (do not worry about what objects and functions are at this stage, we come back to them later)

Finally, although *Processing* is case sensitive and allows you to create two variables with near identical names such as `myName` and `MyName`, we strongly recommend that you do *not* do this as it will inevitably lead to confusion.

As we mentioned before, variables in *Processing* belong to one of several types. *Processing* is a so-called typed language which means it treats different forms of data in different ways—called types. Although types can make life ever-so-slightly more difficult for programmers they do prevent problems when programs are run by preventing the programmer from using inappropriate operations, for example trying to divide a piece of text by 2

In this section we will introduce you to the most common types used in *Processing* and then show you how data can be transformed from one type to another. By the end of this section you should be able to select an appropriate type for your data and use these variables in small sketches.

There are two broad categories of types; the simplest types are known as *primitive types* whilst more complex types of information are not unsurprisingly known as complex types. *Processing*'s primitive types are shown below

Integer

Whole number values (including negative numbers) in the range -2147483648 to 2147483647

Example: `int numberOfWheels = 4;`

Float

Decimal values (including negative numbers) in the range -3.40282347E+38 to 3.40282347E+38

Example: float maximumPrice = 12249.99;

Character

Individual alphanumeric and symbolic characters in the Unicode character range

Example: `char shirtSize = 'L';` (don't forget to use the single quotes)

Boolean

Logical values with only 2 permitted values; true and false

Example: `boolean isFamousArtist = true;`

Colour

Colour values expressed in terms of Red, Green and Blue components. Values must be given in triplets of red, green and blue—in that order. Each component has a minimum value of 0 and a maximum value of 255.

Example: `color canvasColour = (255,0,255);` (sets canvasColour to magenta). Note the American spelling of color

If you're unfamiliar with colour values, a quick explanation is needed. Every possible colour can be produced by combining different brightnesses of the three primary colours red, green and blue (usually abbreviated to R, G and B). If one of the three primaries is completely absent then it is given the value 0, the maximum intensity for one of the primaries is given the value 255.

Fortunately, you don't need to work out these values for yourself. *Processing* includes a Color Selector window which can be opened from the *Tools* menu in the *Processing* system. Use the mouse pointer to find the colour you want to use, the corresponding RGB value is given in the three boxes R, G and B.

Other Types of Declaration

Variables get their name because they can assume different values at different times and places in a program. However, sometimes you will need to refer to a value you don't want to be changed, known as a *constant*. The declaration of a constant is very similar the same as that for a variable except for the addition of the keyword *final* and, by convention, the variable name is written in uppercase to show it is a constant. For example:

```
final int DAYS_IN_A_WEEK = 7;
```

Any attempt to overwrite the value will now result in an error message. *Processing* has a number of pre-defined mathematical constants such as PI, HALF_PI and TWO_PI representing Pi values. You cannot initialise or change the values of these three constants—which is fortunate when you think about it as mathematics wouldn't be the same without it!

Try running the following code and see what happens (you should get an error message)

```
final int DAYS_IN_A_WEEK = 7;
DAYS_IN_A_WEEK = 8; // nobody wants that!
```

Operators

We frequently use operators in programming and have already met some of them. Others we know

from daily life such as addition (+), subtraction (-) and division (/). There are a number of different operators and they fall into distinct categories. We'll go through each of the categories here along with the operators in them.

Operators work by taking values, known as arguments, and applying them to the variable on the left-hand side of the line (known as an operation)

Assignment Operator

We have already met the assignment (=) operator, although we haven't fully explained what it does. An assignment statement takes a value or the result of a calculation and assigns it to a variable. The *assignment operator* is the = (equals) symbol and takes the general form of

```
variable = value;
```

An example we have already used is the assignment

```
int numberOfWheels = 4;
```

The assignment operator here is assigning the number 4 to the variable numberOfWheels. Any time the variable is used it will contain the number 4 unless you change the assignment by, for example, assigning another value.

```
int numberOfWheels = 4;
numberOfWheels = 5; // put the spare wheel in
println(numberOfWheels);
```

If you run the above code you will see that *Processing* displays the number 5 because we altered the assignment for the variable. Notice that we only use the type int once. You only declare a variable once, by declaring its type and name, but you can assign it as often as you want. You can also assign variables to each other, for example

```
int numberOfWheels = 4;
int numberOfTyres = numberOfWheels;
println(numberOfTyres);
```

This assigns the value of numberOfWheels (which is 4) to the variable numberOfTyres, which is now also 4. When working with primitive types this simply copies the value (in this case 4) into the other variable - changing the original has no effect

```
int numberOfWheels = 4;
int numberOfTyres = numberOfWheels;
numberOfWheels = 3;
println(numberOfTyres);
```

Running the code above will still display the numberOfTyres as 4 despite changing the numberOfWheels, all we did was copy the value, the 2 variables are otherwise unconnected;

Mathematical operators

The mathematical operators are perhaps the most familiar as we often see them in daily life

Operator	Description	Example
+	Addition - adds 2 numbers together (can also be used to concatenate 2 strings)	x = x + 1;
-	Subtraction - subtracts one number from another	x = x -1;
/	Division - divides one number by another	x = y / 10;
*	Multiplication - multiplies one number by another	x = y * 2;
%	Modulo/modulus - gives the remainder of one number divided by another	x = y % 2;

Table 1: Basic mathematical operators

As you can see, the multiplication (*) operator uses a slightly different symbol from the more familiar x and the modulo operator uses the usual percentage (%) sign which is not used for percentages. Notice that in some examples you are using the same variable in both the assignment and the operation. For example x = x + 1 is taking the current value of x, adding 1 and re-assigning it back to x

```
int x = 0;
x = x +1;
```

Here the value of x at the end is 1 - you took the value of x (0), added 1 (to make 1) and re-assigned that value to x. You can try some of the examples from Table 1 by first declaring variables x and y, for example

```
int x = 0;
int y = 10;
x = x + 1;
println(x);
```

Be careful not to divide by zero as that will cause an error (dividing by zero results in an infinity answer and *Processing* doesn't know how to deal with infinity!)

The modulo operator (%) is used to provide the remainder from division. This can be especially useful to examine whether a number is exactly divisible by another as this would give a remainder, or modulo, of 0, for example to determine if a number is an even number

```
int x = 10;
println(x % 2); // the remainder of 10 / 2 is zero so x is an even number
```

```
x = 3;
println(x % 2); // the remainder of 3 / 2 is 1, so x is an odd number
```

Shorthand Operators

In addition to these common operators, shorthand operators have similar functions to those above but allow you to write less code when you want to change the current value of the variable. The available operators are shown in Table 2

Operator	Description	Example
++	Add 1 (increment) to the current value	x++;
--	Subtract 1 (decrement) from the current value	x--;
+=	Add the current value to the given value	x += 2;
-=	Subtract the current value from the given value	x -= 2;
*=	Multiply the current value by the given value	x *= 2;
/=	Divide the current value by the given value	x /= 2;

Table 2: Shorthand Operators

The increment and decrement operators (++ and -- respectively) are slightly unusual in that we only provide a variable name and the operator. The operator either increases or decreases the value of the variable by 1 and so:

```
int x = 0;
x ++;
```

would result in x being 1. Likewise if we set x as 1 and then used x-- then x would be set to 0.

Though the increment and decrement functions are useful the fact that they only adjust the value by 1 can be a drawback. The other shorthand notations allow us to adjust a variable by any given amount. We can apply this with addition, subtraction, multiplication and division by using +=, -=, *= or /= respectively. If we wanted to add 5 to the variable counter then we can achieve this by using

```
int x = 0;
x += 5; // x is now 5
```

Relational Operators

Relational operators are used for comparing values or, more commonly, the values of variables. Relational operators work by comparing the left-hand value to the right-hand value and outputting a boolean result (either true or false as mentioned earlier). The available operators are shown in Table 3

Operator	Description	Example
==	Equal to (left-hand value is exactly the same as the left)	x == 10
!= <>	Not equal to (note that <>, technically less-than-or-greater-than) has the same effect (left-hand value is not the same as the right)	x != 10 x <> 10
&lt;	Less than (left-hand value is less than the right)	x < 10
<=	Less than or equal to (left-hand value is less than, or the same as, the right)	x <= 10
&gt;	Greater than (left-hand value is greater than the right)	x > 10
>=	Greater than or equal to (left-hand value is greater than, or the same, the right)	x >= 10

Table 3: Relational Operators

One point worth mentioning is that the = symbol is only used for assigning values, as we've already seen. If we are to compare the contents of two variables then we use == for equality, so 5==5 would equal true whereas 5 = 5 would not make sense

Try experimenting with these with different values of x. For example

```
int x = 5;
println(x < 10);
```

will result in the boolean value true being printed to the screen. Relational operators are commonly used in conjunction with conditional structures which we will meet later and, based on the result, evaluate what to do next.

Logical operators

Logical operators are those that work on boolean values, which we have seen are always either `true` or `false`. These will return true or false values based on the Boolean values of the two input variables. The operators are shown in Table 4

Operator	Description	Example
!	NOT (opposite of the boolean eg NOT true, or NOT false)	!hungry
&&	AND (true if both sides are true, otherwise false)	hungry && thirsty
||	OR (true if one side is true, otherwise false)	hungry || thirsty

Table 4: Logical Operators

Try some examples of these and see what values you get. Can you predict whether they are true or false? For example try:

```
boolean hungry = true;
boolean thirsty = false;
println(hungry && thirsty);
```

Binary operators

Binary, or bitwise, operators are an advanced topic and provide operators such as binary and (&),

binary or (|) along with shift operators such as bit-shift right (>>) and left (<<). These functions aren't used that often and deal with a lower level of detail which we won't cover here but will be covered later in the book.

Precedence and brackets

Though the examples we have used so far have been relatively simple, we can develop long sequences of operators and the computer will evaluate them in accordance with its own rules of precedence. A seemingly ambiguous sequence such as 5*2+3 which could result in either

```
(5 * 2) + 3 which equals 13
5 * (2 + 3) which equals 25
```

In reality, *Processing* uses its own rules, which is to do multiplication before addition, so the answer is 13 but this isn't obvious to the author, or reader, unless you understand the rules of precedence.

These rules can be hard to remember the exact order in which they are applied but a good rule of thumb is to always use brackets to determine which parts you want to be evaluated first as everything within round brackets, (), is evaluated first. Even if you understand these rules, (5 * 2) + 3 is much easier to read than 5*2+3 even though the result is the same. If you actually meant the result to be 25 you would have to write it as 5 * (2 + 3)

Powers

Powers are the means to take a number and multiply it by itself many times, so x to the power 2 (x^2) is x * x, and x to the power 3 (x^3) is x*x*x. This is easy for small powers but can become unwieldy for high powers. Luckily *Processing* has an inbuilt function for dealing with powers, pow(). Here, x^3 becomes pow(x,3), x^5 becomes pow(x,5) and so on.

This can be added into longer expressions. For example the algebraic expression

$3x^4 + 2x^2 - 5$

becomes

```
3*pow(x,4) + 2*pow(x,2) - 5
```

Note that we could still write $2x^2$ as 2*x*x if we wanted to

Comments

Writing code is like learning to draw, and like drawing making code is about learning, thinking and reflecting. With a real sketch it is hard to decide what is going to be important and what will end up being redundant. When you do come to make something, then you find yourself constantly referring to other, previous, sketches to see how you did something last time.

For this reason, it is important to leave yourself clues or messages about what you were thinking about when you made something. If we were making something, we might type it like this

```
ellipse(135,135,108,99); // Left eye.
ellipse(306,135,108,99); // Right eye.
triangle(279,270,324,358,234,358 ); // Nose.
arc(153,405,270,83,0,PI); // smile.
```

The words after the double black slash // are called comments. These are notes that you make in the code. For example, you can label one shape 'nose' which is useful if you come back a month later and want to make the face wink. The comments above follow a double slash and go to the end of the line, they can also be put at the beginning of the line; in this case the whole line becomes the comment.

You can say anything in comments, they are for the reader; the computer ignores it. Comments should add something to the code that will help the reader, whether that is another programmer or yourself at a later date. Comments that add nothing to readability such as:

```
x = x + 1; // adds one to the value of x
```

are simply a waste of time and effort. The reader can see that 1 is added to x. A better comment would be to explain *why* you are adding 1 to it. Our comments above assist the reader in knowing which ellipse is which eye, for example, and so add to readability

Sometimes a single line is not enough. Sometimes you have to express yourself at length. For this, *Processing* uses a begin and end marker. /* or a slash and star indicating the start of a long comment and the */ or star and slash ending it.

```
/* This is an example of a long comment that is longer than
*    a line. It is a tradition to start each new line with an
*    asterisk to show that the comment continues.
*/
```

You can do some very clever things with comments, such as hide junk code from *Processing* or generate automatic documentation for your sketch code but that is outside the remit of this chapter

As an early example of drawing using what we have learned, and some other concepts we will learn later, we have created some code for you to look through below

```
// Create some variables and assign values
int xpos;
int ypos;

// Setup our sketch window and assign a background colour
size (300, 300);
background (255);

xpos = 0;
ypos = 200; // 1/3 of the sketch window

// draw a green rectangle for grass
noStroke();
fill(0, 128, 64);
```

```
rect(xpos, ypos, 300, 100);

// Draw a sun in the sky
ypos = ypos - 150;
xpos = 250;
fill(255, 255, 0);
ellipse(xpos, ypos, 50, 50);

// Now draw our dream home
xpos = 75;
ypos = 100;
stroke(0);          // set the border colour of the house
fill(192, 192, 192);  // set the fill colour of the house
rect(xpos, ypos, 100, 100);

// with a roof
fill (128, 128, 64);    // light brown - sort of
beginShape (TRIANGLES);
vertex(xpos, ypos);
vertex(xpos + 100, ypos);
vertex(xpos + 50, ypos - 50);
endShape();

// and some windows
fill(255, 255, 255);  // white
rect(xpos + 10, ypos + 10, 25, 25);
rect(xpos + 65, ypos + 10, 25, 25);
rect(xpos + 10, ypos + 65, 25, 25);

// and a door
fill(0, 128, 255);
rect(xpos + 65, ypos + 65, 25, 35);
```

Can you see some examples of the assignment operator in action? Initially we assign the value of 0 (zero) to **xpos** and 200 to **ypos**. Once we have used these to draw the rectangle (strictly speaking we DON'T need to – we could just use the values directly), we modify the value of **ypos** by subtracting 150 from it in the assignment statement:

```
ypos = ypos - 150;
```

This statement simply instructs the sketch to subtract 150 from whatever value is currently held in *ypos*. In addition, we reset the value held in *xpos* to 250.

Once you have entered and executed this code you should see an image similar to that shown Figure 9 – *a dream home!*

Figure 9: Dream Home Using Assignments

Chapter 5: Conditional Statements
by JeanLuc Brausch and Samir Rabab

In this chapter we delve into `if` statements and look at some other conditional statements which are used to determine the flow of the sketch by examining conditions and using those to decide the course of action to take

All the *Processing* code we have written so far can be read top-to-bottom so we have been able to surmise what the sketch will do by reading it sequentially. Conditional statements break this top-to-bottom flow by introducing decision making points into the sketch and determining which parts of the code to execute based on conditions.

The if Statement

An `if` statement is a type of conditional statement and uses a boolean to determine the result. Remember that booleans can only be `true` or `false`, so this gives us two possible paths - the one where the condition is true and the one where it is false. A basic `if` statement takes the form

```
if (some boolean is true) {
    // do something
}
```

This means that, if the boolean evaluates to `true`, the code inside the brackets will be executed. If the boolean evaluates to `false`, the code inside the brackets is ignored. Regardless of the result, any code *after* the brackets will be executed. Try these simple examples

```
boolean isConditionTrue = true;
if (isConditionTrue) {
    println(isConditionTrue);
}
println("Code after the brackets");
```

You should see that both `println()` statements are executed. Try changing the value of the boolean variable to `false` and run it again. You should see that the only the `println()` statement after the brackets is executed. Note that you don't need to use the relational operator `==` with booleans as they are already a boolean value

Of course, this only represents a simple case where you perform one action and have one decision to make. More complex statements allow you to represent more complicated scenarios such as:

- Compound statements

- Multiple conditions
- Multiple branches
- Nested if statements

Compound Statements

What if there was code you wanted when the condition was false? In that case you could use the if-else statement we saw earlier. These take the form

```
if (boolean is true) {
   // do something
} else {
   // do something else
}
```

Using an example you can run, you can try this

```
boolean isConditionTrue = true;
if (isConditionTrue) {
   println(isConditionTrue);
} else {
   println(isConditionTrue);
}
println("Code after the brackets");
```

If you change the boolean variable you should see different results. You should now start to see how using conditions can alter how your sketch works. We have used a simple text output, but it might totally change your sketch, by changing the colour scheme for example

Multiple Conditions

In some situations it is necessary to evaluate at least two conditions in order to decide on the path of execution. For example, as well as ensuring that the door is open, we also need to ensure that we have a key for the door before we go out, thus avoiding locking ourselves out.

To facilitate the use of multiple conditions within the if statement, we can use logical or relational operators to determine the result of multiple boolean statements. We can combine boolean variables with operators to make complex conditions such as

```
if (x < 10)
if (x == 25)
if (x == 25 && y < 10)
if (!booleanVariable)
if ((x < 25 && y > 6) && (aVariabe == 75 || booleanVariable))
```

These can become as complicated as you like, but remember that the more complicated you make them, the harder it becomes to read (the last one is becoming too difficult to figure out!)

Multiple Branches

Every `if` statement that we have seen so far had at most two branches, one represented the path to follow if the condition was evaluated to true, while the other was reserved for the path to follow if the condition was evaluated to false. It is possible however to modify the `if` statement to include more branches as demonstrated in the following example:

```
if (x < 5){
   println("x is less than 5");
} else if (x > 10) {
   println("x is greater than 10");
} else {
   println("x is between 5 and 10");
}
```

Here the conditions are tested from top to bottom and, as soon as one of the conditions evaluates to true, its corresponding branch is executed. Again, one and only one branch will be executed as a result of this `if` statement. You can think of the `else` branch as a catch-all branch that will be executed if all of the conditions that precedes it fail to be evaluated to true.

There is no limit to the number of branches that you can include within the `if` statement, however, if you find yourself in a situation where you are using more than three branches, it is worth considering whether you can achieve the same result more eloquently by using a concept known as the `switch` statement; later you will see how to use this

Nested `if` statements

Finally, consider the following simple algorithm which nests (that is, places one `if` statement inside another) `if` statements

```
if (x > 10) {
   if (y > 10) {
     println("x and y are greater than 10");
   } else {
     println("x is > 10 but y is not");
   }
}
```

Here the outer `if` statement determines if x is greater than 10 and the inner `if` statement (having already established that x is greater than 10) determines if y is greater than 10. Of course this could be accomplished with multiple conditions, it is up to you, as the programmer, to decide which is most readable. Too many nested statements could soon render the code unreadable. If this happens, then maybe it is time to look for alternative ways for solving the same problem

The Ternary Operator

The ternary operator is a shortcut way of setting a variable based on the result of a condition. You might think of it as a shorthand alternative to an `if...else` statement and is used as follows:

```
variable = (condition) ? expression_if_true : expression_if_false;
```

If the condition is true, the first value is assigned to the variable otherwise the second value is assigned to the variable.

The ternary operator is derived from early programming languages where storage and memory space was still an issue and this is why it seems a little cryptic and sometimes confusing at first sight. Programmers often need time to get used to it and some even choose not to use it at all opting for the more verbose `if...else` syntax.

Consider the following example:

```
int aNumber = 7;
String aMessage;
if (aNumber % 2 == 0 ){
    aMessage = "The number is even";
} else {
    aMessage = "The number is odd";
}
println(aMessage);
```

Executing the code above will print

```
The number is odd
```

at the bottom of the *Processing* window as the condition `7%2==0` is not met as the remainder when 7 is divided by 2 returns 1; thus the condition is false and the code in the `else` statement is executed.

The equivalent of this statement using the ternary operator is shown below:

```
int aNumber = 7;
String aMessage = (aNumber % 2 == 0)?
```

```
    "The number is even ": "The number is odd";
println (aMessage);
```

Notice that we have spread the ternary operation over two lines since the book has a limited number of characters to a line. You can do this in *Processing* since whitespace and returns are irrelevant and not recognised by the *Processing* system.

First, the condition is tested, in our case, is the modulo 2 of aNumber equal to 0 ? If the condition is true then the value *before* the ":" is returned and assigned to the variable aMessage otherwise the value *after* the ":" is returned and assigned to the variable aMessage.

The condition (7%2==0) evaluates to false as 7 modulo 2 returns 1, thus the String "The number is odd" is assigned to aMessage which is then printed at the bottom of the *Processing* window.

The difference between the ternary operator and the if...else statement is that the if...else syntax *executes a block of code* based on the condition it evaluates; the ternary or conditional operator is an expression which returns a value based on the condition it evaluates.

The advantage of the ternary operator is, that it lets you assign a value to a variable based on a condition with a single line of code; however if you find yourself having trouble in understanding the syntax, you can still use the longer if...else statement to achieve the same thing.

Let us consider another example to demonstrate the effectiveness of the ternary operator; we might want to write a sketch that draws lines with alternating colours. To achieve this with an if...else statement, we could write the code below. The sketch uses a for statement. this will be described in detail later; for now all you need know is that it executes the if statement 100 times with i having a value 0, 1 etc. up 99.

```
// The code below loops around 100 times
for(int i=0;i<100;i++){
  if(i%2==0){
    stroke(0); // Use black for the line.
  } else {
    stroke(255); // Use white for the line.
  }
  line(30, i, 80, i); // Draw a line from x 30 to 80, y is constant.
}
```

The same code, however, can be rewritten much more effectively in only 3 lines of code by using the ternary operator:

```
for(int i = 0; i < 100; i++){
    stroke((i%2==0)?0:255);
    line(30, i, 80, i);
}
```

The output of this can be seen in Figure 10; if variable i is even the stroke is black otherwise i is odd and the stroke is white.

Figure 10: Alternating line colours

As you have seen in the example above the ternary operator seems a little cryptic and difficult to use at first sight; however, once you get used to it, you'll realize that it provides a very short and efficient way to assign a value to a variable based upon a Boolean condition. It should be used sparingly though due to the difficulty in reading the code based on it

Switch Statements

The switch statement, like an if...else statement, is used to control code execution based on the value of a control variable. The value of the control variable is compared to the value of a case selector, which is a constant value and needs to be of the same type as the control variable.

The switch statement is executed from top to bottom comparing the value of the control variable to each case selector. If the value of the control variable matches the value of a case selector, the code will enter a block of statements. The code after the case selector will be executed until a break command causes the execution to terminate the processing of the case block and exit the switch statement. If the value of the control variable does not match any of the case selectors the statements in the default case are executed.

The possible types of the control variable and the case selectors are the primitive types int, char, short or byte. The format of a switch statement is:

```
switch (control variable) {
 case selector:
    statements;
    break;
 case selector:
    statements;
    break;

    ...
 default:
    statements;
    break;
}
```

There can be as many cases as required and each case can contain as many statements as needed.

It is important to stress that the break command is optional, but if you fail to give it, the execution flows through into the next case. Even if the selector and the control variable do not match, the sketch will continue executing the code block for that case too.

The default case at the end is optional and the statements in this block are executed if no case selector matches the value of the control variable. The last break in the default case is unnecessary; but it is considered good practice to write it.

The switch statement is frequently used where a large number of conditions need to be tested; the switch statement is easier to debug, easier to read and easier to maintain than an equivalent series of if...else statements. Let us consider programming a solution using if...else statements. The sketch draws a shape based on a character, for example if s is typed a square is drawn and if c is typed then a circle is drawn.

```
// c for circle, s for square, r for rectangle, t for triangle
char shape = 'c';
switch (shape) {
    case 'c':
        ellipse(50, 50, 25, 25);
        break;
```

```
case 's':
    rect(30, 30, 25, 25);
    break;
case 'r':
    rect(30, 25, 25, 50);
    break;
case 't':
    triangle(30, 70, 30, 30, 75, 70);
    break;
default:
    background(0);
    break;
}
```

You can change the shape by changing the initialisation of the variable. The `switch` statement is executed from top to bottom, comparing the value of the control variable to the constant value of each `case` selector. If the value of the case selector is logically equal to the value of the control value (control variable `==` `case` selector) then the statements after the `case` selector are executed. In our example, the user presses the 'c' key, which causes the following statements to execute:

```
case 'c':
    ellipse(50, 50, 25, 25);
    break;
```

This draws an ellipse, in our case a circle, on the screen. The `break` command causes the sketch to exit the `switch`. You might try deleting the break statement and seeing what happens. If you change the character to one with no associated `case` statement, 'x' for example, the default block is executed

As you have seen from the examples above, the `switch` statement is more structured and more readable than the equivalent `if...else` statement. In general, it is considered good programming practice to use a `switch` statement to replace large series of `if...else` statements whenever possible.

Chapter 6: Arrays and Loops

by Antony Lees, James Gray, Mark Moran and Rosie Wood

This chapter describes the important topics of arrays and loops. Without arrays you would be hard put to do any programming in *Processing*. The chapter introduces single-dimensional arrays: arrays that contain a single list of data. The chapter also describes repetition known as loops, introducing `for`, `while` and `do-while` loops and moves on to two-dimensional arrays and nested loops

Arrays

Imagine a scenario where, being an avid cyclist, you want to record the number of minutes for each ride and work out your average time. One way of doing this is to create a variable for each day's time, and average them, like this:

```
// One variable for each time
int mondayTime = 38;
int tuesdayTime = 37;
int wednesdayTime = 38;
int thursdayTime = 36;
int fridayTime = 35;
int saturdayTime = 39;
int sundayTime = 37;
// Add all the times together, and divide by 7 (the number of days)
int total = mondayTime + tuesdayTime + wednesdayTime +
    thursdayTime + fridayTime + saturdayTime +
    sundayTime;
float average = total/7.0;
// Print average in the message area.
println (average);
```

This works but it's tedious, and would become even more so if we wanted to store times for a month, or a year, rather than a week. It also means we need to count the variables in order to work out the average. Wouldn't it be nice if we could put all those numbers into one variable?

The Array

The answer to our problem is an array. An array is a way of storing lots of things in one variable. Here's one way to store all the times:

```
int times[] = {38,37,38,36,35,39,37};
```

That's less typing! But what's actually happening here? The bit to the left of the equals sign is mostly familiar—we're declaring something of type `int[]`, and what we're declaring is called `times`. The square brackets are important—they are telling the system that the thing we are declaring is an array, so can be read as 'int array'. On the right of the bracket is a quick way of putting some numbers into the array.

So an array is a bit like a list. An integer variable can store one number, but an integer array variable can store lots of numbers. Not just numbers though. We can declare arrays of any data type we like, for example strings are collections of characters enclosed in quotes:

```
// An array of String values...
String[] days = {"Monday", "Tuesday", "Wednesday", "Thursday",
    "Friday", "Saturday", "Sunday"};
```

In order to get the data out of the array again we need to know what position the piece of data is in. To find out what's in a particular position in the array, we can use an *index* in the square brackets:

```
String[] days = {"Monday", "Tuesday", "Wednesday", "Thursday",
    "Friday", "Saturday", "Sunday"};
String myBirthday = days[3];
println(myBirthday);
```

So the variable `myBirthday` will now contain the string that was in position 3 of the array days. But here we have to be very careful! What do you think is in position 3? If you think it's "Wednesday", we suggest you type those lines in and try it.

Although humans tend to count starting at 1, computers have a tendency to start counting at 0. So "Monday" is not stored in `days[1]`—it's really in `days[0]`. "Tuesday" is in `days[1]`. "Wednesday" is `days[2]`, and so on. There are seven *elements* in the array, they are numbered from 0 to 6.

Now, we can produce the code we need to calculate the average time using the array:

```
// Put the times into an array.
int[] times = {38,37,38,36,35,39,37};
// Add all the times together, and divide by 7 (the number of days).
int total = times[0]+times[1]+times[2]+times[3]+
    times[4]+times[5]+times[6] ;
float average = total/7.0;
println (average);
```

The first part of the code is better; but the second part, where we are adding all the times together, still doesn't look too good. Imagine if we had to add data for an entire year! It would be a lot easier if the computer could go through the array adding all the numbers up, rather than us having to type out each one:

```
times[0]+times[1]+times[2]+times[3]+
times[4]+times[5]+times[6]
```

The for statement

Rather than type out every element in the array, what we need to do is *loop* through each element. To do this we can use a programming facility known as a `for` statement. For statements take the form

```
for (counter declaration; termination statement; counter increment) {
    //loop body
}
```

This type of loop allows us to specify the number of times a code block will repeat. We use a number to state the amount of iterations. The loop takes a start value, an exit loop conditional clause and the amount the looping integer will be changed by. These loops can be incremented or decremented. It sounds a lot more complex than it is in practice!

For example

```
for (int count=0; count<7; count=count+1){
    total = total+times[count];
}
```

The various parts of this are:

- counter declaration - declare a counter that will be used inside the loop and incremented each time. In this example we declare an `int` called `count` and initialise it to zero
- termination statement - a boolean statement that determines when the loop should end. Here it will end when `count` reaches 7 ie the loop continues while `count<7`
- counter increment - increment the counter for each iteration. Here we add 1 to `count` each iteration
- loop body - the code that is executed each iteration of the loop. The declared counter variable can be used inside the body. Here we use it to access the element in the array
- We can use this loop in our cycling times example to add together every value in the array

```
// Put the times into an array.
int[] times = {38, 37, 38, 36, 35, 39, 37};
// Set up a variable for the total of all the times.
```

```
int total = 0;
// Loop to count through the array.
for (int count=0; count<7; count=count+1){
   total = total+times[count];
}
float average = total/7.0;
println (average);
```

The loop will now access every element in the array using the `count` variable since `count` starts at 0and ends at 6, and the elements in the array also run from 0 to 6. Each time the loop body is executed, the increment statement will add 1 allowing the next element to be accessed. The value in the array element is added to `total` until the loop ends, at which point we can get the average

We declared a new variable, `count`, as part of the top of the loop. Because it is declared as part of the loop, it will only exist within the loop. We can use it in the loop header, and we can use it in the loop body but, as soon as we exit the loop, it will disappear.

So this won't work:

```
for (int count=0; count<7; count=count+1){
   total = total+times[count];
}
float average = total/count; // This does not work.
```

You will be told by the *Processing* system that it `Cannot find anything named "count"`. This is because `count` was declared as part of the loop, so disappeared immediately the loop ended.

It is also worth saying that you can replace the statement count= count+1 in the `for` statement with the auto increment version you met before; indeed this is almost standard practice when you are moving through an array element by element.

So we can rewrite the top of the loop as:

```
for (int count=0; count<times.length;count++)
```

It is also possible to start at the end of the array and move to the beginning using the auto decrement operator --.

Here's a simple sketch that uses a `for` loop to draw a radiating lines pattern:

```
// Sunburst - radiating lines.
size(300, 300);
for (int position=0; position < width; position += 10){
```

```
    line(width/2, height, position, 0);
}
```

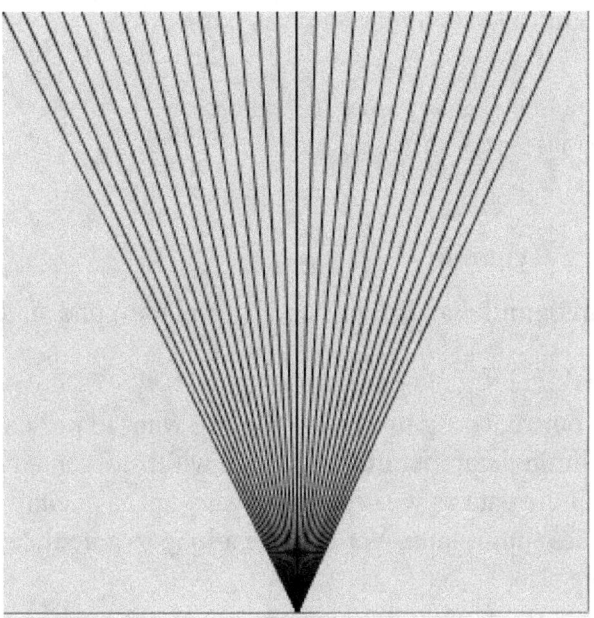

Figure 11: Output from the radiating lines sketch

The first line sets the size of the output window to 300 pixels square. At the start of the loop, a new integer variable, `position`, is declared and set to 0. This will be a position along the top of the window. In the condition we continue while `position` is less than `width`—the width of the window (i.e. 300). At the end of each loop, we will add 10 to `position`—effectively moving it 10 pixels to the right along the top of the screen. The effect of this can be seen in Figure 11

The body of the loop is a statement to draw a line. The `line` command needs to be told four things:

- The horizontal position of the start of the line. This is halfway along in this case.
- The vertical position of the start of the line. This is at the bottom of the screen.
- The horizontal position of the end of the line. This is the value of our `position` variable.
- The vertical position of the end of the line, zero is the top of the screen.

You will meet the line command in more detail later.

If we wanted to use the decrement operator instead we could just as easily start drawing at the maximum horizontal position and decrement until we reach zero. Try this example and you will see that the result is exactly the same as before

```
size(300, 300);
for (int position = width; position > 0; position -= 10){
   line(width/2, height, position, 0);
}
```

Making Arrays More Dynamic

So far, we have declared, initialised and filled an array with one statement, for example:

```
int times[] = {38,37,38,36,35,39,37};
```

Let's imagine that, in our radiating lines example, we want to pre-calculate the position of the line and display a limited number of lines which we'll store in an array. In this instance, rather than initialise all the data as we did above, we want to declare and initialise an array first, and then put values into it later. We can use a loop to calculate the line positions and fill each element of the array.

```
size(300, 300);
int[] coordinates = new int[10];
// calculate and set the coordinates
for (int index = 0; index < coordinates.length ; index++) {
   coordinates[index] = index * 10;
}
// display the lines
for (int position=0; position < coordinates.length; position++){
   line(width/2, height, coordinates[position], 0);
}
```

You will notice some differences from the previous example. We are using 2 for loops here, one to fill the array and one to display the lines. We could have done this in one loop but we have separated them here in order to clearly show what the sketch is doing

The line

```
int[] coordinates = new int[10];
```

creates a variable called coordinates, which will be an array of integers and makes space for ten integers. We haven't filled these spaces yet - it's a bit like drawing up a space for a list in a notebook and numbering the lines ready for the list entries - by default they are filled with zeros.

We use the first `for` loop to calculate the line positions and store them in the array. We set each element in the array using the line

```
coordinates[index] = index * 10;
```

which sets the element numbered `index` to the value we calculate. We can then use these values in the second `for` loop by looping through the values in the array and using them to display the line.

You may also notice that we have changed the `for` loop to use a new termination condition using the array `coordinates.length`

```
for (int index = 0; index < coordinates.length ; index++) {
```

this is accessing the array and pulling out the length (ie the number of elements) in order to make sure we don't loop for longer and try to access an element that doesn't exist. It also prevents us from getting confused about the number of elements (remember that the first element is index 0, so the last is index 9 even though there are 10 elements). If you try to access element 10 you will see *Processing* display an error

`for` loops are not the only type of loops, we will now look at the other types of loop that *Processing* offers

For-Each loops

There is another type of `for` statement known as a for-each loop. This type of loop is a shorter way of creating a `for` loop and accessing every element in an array for example. For-each loops take the form

```
for (type element variable name : array variable) {
```

We can compare the two types of loop by using our previous example using the `for` loop:

```
for (int index = 0; index < coordinates.length ; index++) {
    line(width/2, height, coordinates[position], 0);
}
```

Whereas a for-each loop that does the same thing looks like this:

```
for (int position : coordinates){
    line(width/2, height, position, 0);
}
```

Notice that we no longer need to declare or use an index, nor do we need to access the array element directly, the loop handles this for us by assigning the current element for that loop iteration to the variable we declared as `position`. As you can see, the for-each notation is much simpler and easy to read, but you can use whichever you are most comfortable with

The while statement

The `while` statement, like a `for` statement, repeats a number of times executing the code inside the statement each time. However, whilst `for` statements repeat for a set number of times (iterations), while statements allow us to repeat a section of code until a condition becomes false. In this respect, a `while` statement is a bit like an `if` statement that is repeated *until* the condition is no longer true

To demonstrate `while` statements in *Processing*, we will use the `point` function inside the `draw` function to create dots on the screen. This simply draws a one-pixel point at the coordinates given as arguments to the function in the form

```
point(x,y);
```

where `x` is the number of pixels along the horizontal axis and `y` is the number of pixels down the vertical axis. So, for example

```
point(10,20);
```

will draw a point at the coordinate (10, 20) which is 10 pixels from the left of the window, and 20 pixels from the top. We will print out each coordinate so you can see what the sketch is doing.

A simple example of a `while` statement, shown below, might simply loop until the value of a variable reaches a certain value, in this case 19 (as we are using < 20)

```
// Set the current point as the start point.
int i = 0;
// Loop around while i is less than 20.
while (i<20) {
    // Output the value of i.
    println(i);
    i++;
}
```

Of course, this isn't a very interesting use of *Processing*: it just demonstrates the concept; so a slightly more complicated `while` statement, shown below, will print a line of dots, using the `point` command, and also output the coordinates of the dots so we can see what it is doing

```
background(255);
```

```
// Set the current point as the start point
int currentPoint = 0;
// Loop around while the current point is less
// than the end point.
while (currentPoint < width) {
    // Draw a single pixel point at that point, 20 pixels down.
    point(currentPoint,20);
    println("point:"+currentPoint);
    // Increment by 5 to leave a gap horizontally.
    currentPoint+=5;
}
```

This will produce the output shown in Figure 12: a screen with a lot of dots across it.

Figure 12: Points on the screen

You might try changing the `while` to an `if` to see the difference

```
if (currentPoint < width) {
```

The if statement will create one dot, whereas the while statement kept creating dots until its condition (`currentPoint<width`) was false i.e. when `currentPoint` reaches the width of the window

The loop will exit at the point when the condition is checked and found to be false, not at the point that the condition *becomes* false. Therefore the remainder of the loop iteration will complete and the loop will exit when the condition is evaluated. An analogy for this is a runner having to complete a lap, even though someone has won.

As an example of this, if we increment the `currentPoint` variable *before* we display it, and change the condition to < 40, you will see that the point at 40 is still drawn because the

< 40 condition is not evaluated until the *next* iteration of the loop (at which point it is evaluated as being 40 and the loop ends)

```
background(255);
// Set the current point as the start point
int currentPoint = 0;
// Loop around while the current point is less
// than the end point.
while (currentPoint < 40) {
    // Increment by 5 to leave a gap horizontally.
    currentPoint+=5;
    // Draw a single pixel point at that point, 20 pixels down.
    point(currentPoint,20);
    println("point:"+currentPoint);
}
```

When to use `while` loops and `for` loops

In the above examples, we specify the gap between the points by incrementing the `currentPoint` variable (the x-axis coordinate) by a set value of 5. What if, though, we wanted to vary the gap between each point by an arbitrary value by specifying the x-axis coordinate of each point? This would be possible using the above examples, but the resulting code would be untidy and overly-complicated

As we have seen, as the body of the statement will be executed multiple times, it can be used to access each element of an array in turn, ending when the last element is reached. This provides a convenient method of accessing every element in the array. Using an array, we can change our point sketch to specify the *x*-axis position of the points.

```
background(255);
int i = 0;
// Specify the x-axis coordinates
int[] array = {11,23,35,47,59,67,75,83,91};
// Loop over the array
while (i<array.length) {
    point(array[i], 20);
    i++;
}
```

Using a counter, each element in the array can be accessed in turn and the value given as the x-axis coordinate to the point command. The result is shown in Figure 13.

Figure 13: Variable points using an array

You may be wondering at this point why there is a need for a `for` statement if a `while` statement can do the same thing. If they seem similar it is because they are: a `for` statement provides a simple way of using a counter to define the number of times a statement loops. This means that the number of times the statement runs is known. Although a `while` statement can use a counter, as in the above examples, this need not be (and often isn't) the case. `while` statements with counters tend not to look as neat as for statements. For instance, the example above using a `for` statement would look like:

```
background(255);
// Specify the x-axis coordinate.s
int[] array = {11,23,35,47,59,67,75,83,91};
// Loop over the array.
for(int i = 0; i<array.length;i++) {
    point(array[i], 20);
}
```

The main difference, however, lies in how you know when to exit the loop. The condition for exiting a `while` statement is not usually as straightforward: it is likely that you will not know exactly how many times it will loop when you write it because the value of the condition will be determined *while* the sketch is running. It is also important to remember that it is possible (and a very common error) to accidentally write a `while` statement that will loop forever—an infinite loop—because the condition never becomes false. Have a look at the code below

```
background(255);
// Set the current point as the start point
int currentPoint = 0;
// Loop around while the current point is less
// than the end point.
```

```
while (currentPoint < 40) {
 // Draw a single pixel point at that point, 20 pixels down.
   point(currentPoint,20);
   println("point:"+currentPoint);
   // Removed the currentPoint+=5 so it loops forever
}
```

In the above example, the `while` statement loops forever because we never increment the value of `i`, so the condition will forever be true. If you run this, you will see the value of `i` being printed on the console. You can stop the sketch by pressing the 'stop' button in the *Processing* window. It is therefore necessary to have a well-defined condition that you know will exit at some point. A badly designed condition can result in something known as an infinite loop.

There are various ways of using the condition in a `while` statement to determine how many times the statement will execute. Any statement can be used as the condition, provided it evaluates or returns a Boolean value. This could be:

- a counter that is tested in the condition (such as an `if` statement),
- a variable that is tested for some criteria,
- a Boolean that is set to false in order to exit,
- any code that results in a Boolean.

The do-while Statement

Just as it is possible to have a `while` statement that loops forever, it is also possible to have one that never executes *if* the condition is never met. If the condition never evaluates to true, the loop body will never be executed. However, sometimes you might always want a section of code to be executed even if the condition is not met.

A common use for this is requesting input from the user until they enter an exit character—you would always want to request the input, even if they enter the exit character first time. Using our previous example, you might always want one dot to be drawn on the screen. Using a `while` statement you would have to draw one dot before the loop. For example

```
background(255);
// Set the current point as the start point
int currentPoint = 0;
// always draw a dot at 5,20
point (5, 20);
while (currentPoint < 0) {
   // Increment by 5 to leave a gap horizontally.
   currentPoint+=5;
```

```
    // Draw a single pixel point at that point, 20 pixels down.
    point(currentPoint,20);
    println("point:"+currentPoint);
}
```

In this situation, there is another type of loop statement that can be used: the do-while statement. A do-while statement is like a while statement; however, it evaluates the condition *after* the body of the loop has been executed. This means that the code inside the body is always executed at least once—if the condition is found to be false, the loop will exit at that point having already executed the code. The do-while loop takes the form:

```
do {
    // do something
}
while (condition)
```

We can rewrite our example above using a do-while loop to ensure that the first point, at 5,20, will always get drawn even if the loop condition is false

```
background(255);
// Set the current point as the start point
int currentPoint = 0;
do {
    // Increment by 5 to leave a gap horizontally.
    currentPoint+=5;
    // Draw a single pixel point at that point, 20 pixels down.
    point(currentPoint,20);
    println("point:"+currentPoint);
}
while (currentPoint < 0);
```

Using a while statement, the loop body would never be executed. If there is a chance that the code should never be executed, then a while statement would be more appropriate. do while statements should only be used when you know that you need the loop code to be executed as least once. As such, they are seldom used, but do provide a useful way of eliminating duplicate code.

Two-Dimensional Arrays and Nested Loops

The arrays we have seen up to now have been one-dimensional arrays which are basically a list of items of a similar type and could be represented by Table 5 showing four elements numbered 0 to 3

element(0)
element(1)
element(2)
element(3)

Table 5: Elements in a one-dimensional array

A two-dimensional array is best described as a *table* of items of a similar type. Table 6 shows a two-dimensional array. This has four rows and four columns. The first number refers to the row and the second number refers to the column.

element(0,0)	element(0,1)	element(0,2)	element(0,3)
element(1,0)	element(1,1)	element(1,2)	element(1,3)
element(2,0)	element(2,1)	element(2,2)	element(2,3)
element(3,0)	element(3,1)	element(3,2)	element(3,3)

Table 6: Elements in a two-dimensional array

Employing two-dimensional arrays in computer graphics can be quite useful as a table can be used for storing coordinate data. The use of programming constructs such as loops allows for each element of the array to be processed individually. The difference for a two-dimensional array is that access to the elements needs to move in both directions, i.e. horizontally as well as vertically.

In *Processing* terms you already know that a one-dimensional array is declared as follows:

```
int[] myArray = new int[size];
```

A two dimensional array declaration is shown below

```
int[][] myArray = new int[sizeX][sizeY];
```

The difference here is that the second array has two sets: one to control the *x*-coordinate and another to control the *y*-coordinate. In theory, it doesn't really matter whether the first or second subscript is considered to be the *x* or *y*-coordinate but the convention is to list the x-coordinate first. What is really important though is that any reference to the sets in the code should remain consistent throughout the sketch code.

The example we will develop will involve manipulating each element of the two-dimensional array which will then be drawn on the screen using *Processing*'s `point` function which draws dots on the screen. Writing such a sketch involves thinking of the elements of the array as pixels on the screen. Therefore, it might help to firstly delve further into what a pixel actually is.

A pixel (picture element) is a small dot in an image on a television or computer display which can have its colour varied in order to create the image you see on the screen. The display is made up of these dots so if we create a sketch of `size(200,200);` then there are 200 pixels across (x-coordinates) and 200 pixels down (y-coordinates) making 200 x 200 (40,000) pixels!

To demonstrate how two-dimensional arrays work we will write a *Processing* sketch that randomly sets the corresponding pixel colour to get an interesting effect which displays a large square containing nine different coloured squares within it. The sketch sounds quite simple, but when we break it down into stages, you can see how much computation is involved:

1. Define display area width and height.
2. Declare array `screenArray[][]` to represent the pixels in the display area.
3. Initialise `screenArray` so that each corresponding pixel has a colour
4. Loop through `screenArray` and set the colour of that pixel
5. The first two steps are fairly simple, we set the size of the screen and create our two-dimensional array

```
size(200,200);
int[][] screenArray = new int[200][200];
```

Note that `screenArray` is the 2-dimensional array that holds values representing the pixels in the display area. The contents of `screenArray` are not the pixels themselves. We also haven't initialised any of the contents yet, only created the array with the given size

Next we will need a loop. Since we know in advance what the width and height of the display area will be, thus we know the terminating condition for the loop. Therefore, a `for` loop will be suitable here. In order to loop successfully through all rows and columns of the array and display the area, we need to employ the concept of *nested loops*. Doing this will allow us to access each array element distinctly.

Before we develop the code for our sketch, we need to describe the concept of *outer* and *nested* loops. A loop can be used to populate or process the elements in a one-dimensional array as you will have already seen. When processing a 2-dimensional array, we need to move horizontally across the columns as well as vertically down the rows. This is done by using an outer loop to control the vertical, top-to-bottom processing and a nested loop contained inside the outer loop to control the horizontal, left-to-right processing. For each value of the outer loop, the nested loop does its full range in its entirety. Below is a simple piece of code showing a nested *for* loop:

```
for (int x=0; x <=10; x++){
    println("x ==" + x);
    for (int y=0; y <=10; y++){
        println("y==" + y);
        // do processing here
    }
}
```

The processing inside the nested loop could be anything from a mathematical calculation to some graphical manipulation; The latter will usually be true for sketches in this book. If you run the above code you can see the output from the loops. You should be able to see that for each time the outer loop is run (known as an *iteration*) the nested loop runs through all 10 of its iterations

An easy way to describe what happens in the above code is as follows. When the outer loop sets x to 0, the nested loop runs from 0 to 10. When the outer loop subsequently moves on to 1, the nested loop again runs from 0 to 10. When the outer loop moves on to 2, the nested loop once again runs from 0 to 10. This process of the nested loop running repeatedly through its full range continues until the outer loop reaches the end of its range.

We can now use this to iterate over our `screenArray` and set each element in the array, which corresponds to a pixel on the screen, to a colour that we will later display

```
// for each x coordinate
for (int i = 0; i < screenArray.length; i++) {
    // for each y coordinate
    for (int j = 0; j < screenArray[0].length; j++) {
        // set a colour based on the coordinates
    screenArray[i][j] = color(i, j, i + j);
    }

}
```

The `color` function is used here to generate a colour based on the coordinates. You needn't understand how this function works for the moment, simply concentrate on the array. We are setting a `color` value in each element of the two-dimensional array by iterating over every element in the array

We have set up our outer and nested loops to allow us to distinctly access each element of the array in turn. For each value of the outer loop, the nested loop runs through all of its values. In other words, each time the outer loop changes to its next value, the nested loop runs through its entire range. So we are effectively moving through the array one row at a time, where the nested loop is controlling the horizontal movement from beginning to end, each time the outer loop changes vertically downwards to the next row; where the nested loop subsequently starts over. This process continues until the end of the array is reached (bottom-right element or `screenArray[200][200]`. Figure 14 illustrates the direction of movement through an array as the code runs.

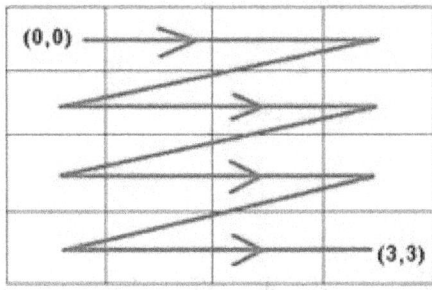

Figure 14: Order in which array elements are processed when using nested loops

We then use the array to access the corresponding colour at the coordinates and draw the dots on the screen

```
// for each x coordinate
for (int i = 0; i < screenArray.length; i++) {
    // for each y coordinate
    for (int j = 0; j < screenArray[0].length; j++) {
        // set the colour
        stroke(screenArray[i][j]);
        // draw a dot at the coordinates
        point(i,j);
    }
}
```

Nested loops are used here again; this time to read the values into the `stroke` function that sets the current colour being used. The `point` function then draws the coloured point to the current pixel on the display area.

The complete sketch should look like the one below

```
size(200,200);
int[][] screenArray = new int[200][200];
// for each x coordinate
for (int i = 0; i < screenArray.length; i++) {
    // for each y coordinate
    for (int j = 0; j < screenArray[0].length; j++) {
        // set a colour based on the coordinates
        screenArray[i][j] = color(i, j, i + j);
    }
}
// for each x coordinate
for (int i = 0; i < screenArray.length; i++) {
    // for each y coordinate
    for (int j = 0; j < screenArray[0].length; j++) {
        // set the colour
        stroke(screenArray[i][j]);
        // draw a dot at the coordinates
        point(i,j);
    }
}
```

If you run this, the result is that we colour every pixel on the screen, as shown in Figure 15, with an interesting gradient

Figure 15: The output from the two-dimensional array Sketch

Chapter 7: Functions

by Bruce Lawley and Geoff Riley

This chapter is a key one for *Processing* programming. In it we describe something called a function. This is a chunk of code that can be reused time and time again. By writing functions you save yourself a lot of time repeating code. The chapter looks at how you write a function and the role of arguments.

An Introduction to Functions

Up to this point all our coding has been linear: that is to say our sketches start at the top and work their way right through until they get to the bottom. There are times when we've almost repeated the same pieces of code within the same sketch. Wouldn't it be great if there was a way that you could just write that bit once and then tell the computer to use it again and again? This is where functions come in.

A function is like a mini piece of sketch that can be used over and over by a main sketch code. Every function has a name and, optionally, has one or more arguments passed to it. The basic structure of a function is:

```
void function_name (argument_list) {
    // function content
}
```

This is made up of several parts:

- the keyword void indicates that the function does not return any value. We cover returns values a bit later, so for now we will always indicate no return value as void
- the function name largely follows the normal naming conventions that you would expect for any identifier except it should start with a verb eg doSomething
- the round brackets enclose any arguments that the function will be expecting, these will be examined shortly
- the curly brackets are used to mark the beginning and end of the code that comprises the function, this can range from a simple statement of just a single line to a complex routine of many lines.
- The round brackets and braces must always be present—even if they have nothing to enclose: that is to say, if there are no arguments, the round brackets are still present but with nothing between them; and if there is no code (if the function is a placeholder to be filled in later for example) then the braces are still present. In the latter case it is usual to insert a comment as a reminder about the empty function!

The argument list allows us to influence the way that the function will operate. Arguments are lists in a similar fashion to the way that variables are declared, except that they are separated by commas: so you would declare a variable type followed by a variable name, and then a comma followed by the same sequence repeated for however many arguments are required. For example, the `ellipse()` function in *Processing* has four arguments of type `float` and looks like this:

```
ellipse(float a, float b, float c, float d);
```

where the a and b are the coordinates, c and d are the width and height respectively.

If you ever find yourself writing a function with more than five or six arguments though, then your function is most likely trying to do too much and should be examined to see if it can be broken down into two or more simpler functions. This is because the more complicated a function is, the harder it is to work out where any issues may arise and the easier it is for an error to slip through unnoticed.

Let us look at writing an example. Let's say we want to simplify the *Processing* `ellipse()` function to always draw circles. In that instance 4 arguments aren't needed because the width and height will always be the same. We will name it 'drawCircle'

We already know what arguments we are going to need; we are mimicking the first two arguments of the ellipse function, but replacing the third and fourth with a single `diameter` argument. So our argument list is going to be

```
float x, float y, float diameter
```

We can pass these arguments straight on to the ellipse routine, passing the `diameter` for both the `width` and `height` arguments, without any additional processing. The function will look like this:

```
void drawCircle(float x, float y, float diameter) {
    ellipse(x,y,diameter,diameter);
}
```

A similar function named `drawSquare` could be created to call the rectangle function as follows:

```
void drawSquare(float x, float y, float width) {
    rect(x,y,width,width);
}
```

We can use this function (known as 'calling') like any other in the *Processing* language. When we do, we tell *Processing* to draw an ellipse, or rectangle, with the arguments given, which will draw a circle or square

Let us write a short sketch to draw a circle on top of a square using the functions that we've just declared. You'll notice that, because we've written our own functions, we also have to use some new *Processing* functions to write our code. This is because functions are only available in what *Processing* calls 'active' mode. We cover this later but for now just notice that we have put our function calls into a new function called setup() which *Processing* executes when the 'run' button is pressed

```
void setup() {
    size(400,400);
    background(255);
    drawSquare(200,200,150);
    drawCircle(200,200,150);
}
```

When we execute this we generate a window looking like Figure 16. The circle draws with the x, y arguments specifying the centre of the circle, whereas the square draws with the x, y arguments specifying the top left corner.

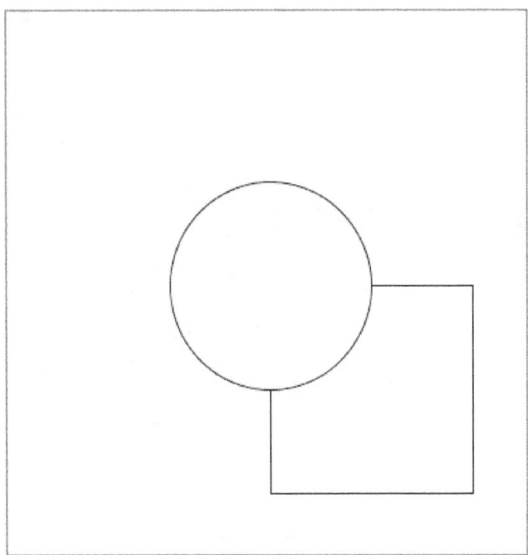

Figure 16: A square and a circle drawn using functions

Notice that the circle is drawn in the middle of the canvas whereas the square is offset. This is because the ellipse() function draws from the centre of the shape but the rect() function draws from the top-left corner. It might be useful to have a further function, say drawSquareCentred that uses the x, y arguments to specify the centre in the same way as the circle.

Now, the only difference between the normal square and the 'centred' square is that an offset is going to be applied to the x and y arguments; so we're going to use the fact that the functions become part of the system to expand on `drawSquare` and not repeat the `rectangle` command.

Our `drawSquareCentred` function is going to use what is known as a 'local' variable. This is a variable that is declared like any other variable, but *within* the function braces, it cannot be accessed outside of the function itself, it is completely self-contained: it is said to have a scope extending to the end of the function.

```
void drawSquareCentred(float x, float y, float width) {
    float halfWidth = width/2;
    drawSquare(x-halfWidth,y-halfWidth,width);
}
```

If we now modify our short test sketch to replace `drawSquare` with `drawSquareCentred` we get the result we originally intended; this is shown in Figure 17.

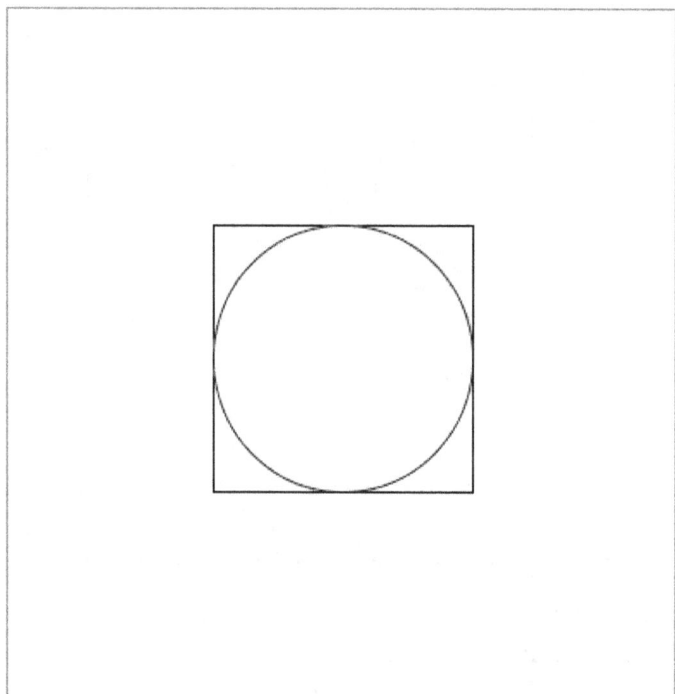

Figure 17: A centred square and circle

So we have two functions that can draw circles and squares, what if we want one function that is capable of drawing either? Well, this is simply a case of providing an argument that tells the function which type of figure to draw: again, the magic is in the function arguments.

Let us create a new function called `drawShape` specifying the type of shape followed by the usual position and size arguments that we've been using above; we'll end up with a function like this:

```
void drawShape(int shapeType, float x, float y, float width){
    // The code to do the drawing
}
```

We'll use `width` as the generic size since it can be the diameter of a circle as well as the width of a square. We come to a slight stumbling block here though—what do we pass as an argument for `shapeType`? The common method for answering this is to define some constant values that are agreed upon and defined globally at the top of the file, so we could have:

```
final int CIRCLE = 1;
final int SQUARE = 2;
```

later in the book we will talk about constants, the only thing to say at this stage is that we normally include a number of upper-case letters in their name. Our function will be:

```
void drawShape(int shapeType, float x, float y, float width) {
    if (shapeType == CIRCLE ) {
        drawCircle(x,y,width);
    }
    if (shapeType == SQUARE ) {
        drawSquareCentred(x,y,width);
    }
}
```

If we then modify the `setup` routine as follows, we find that we get exactly the same result as before.

```
void setup() {
    size(400,400);
    background(255);
    drawShape(SQUARE,200,200,150);
    drawShape(CIRCLE,200,200,150);
}
```

If, at a later date, you were to write a function to draw an octagon, then it would be very simple to add that as a further option to the `drawShape` function by defining a new constant value, e.g. OCTAGON. This would then mean that everywhere that you had used drawShape would immediately be able to take advantage of the extra shape, without a need to modify the code in each place where it was used.

This is a very powerful aspect of functions and the design of the argument list. It should be noted, however, that a single function should be limited to performing *one* specific task— if a function is designed to draw a shape, do not expand it to also calculate some complex mathematical sum: that should be the job for a different function. Sometimes it is all too tempting to add in a bit of extra code because 'it's doing something else with the same data', but this generally just leads to 'difficult to track down errors' and 'very hard to understand code'.

A further useful aspect of functions is their ability to make calls to themselves! This is called 'recursion'. It is a technique that should generally be avoided, but in controlled situations can be very useful. The reason for its avoidance is that is can very quickly use up a lot of processing memory if the number of recursions is not monitored in some way. It's worth saying at this point that if you don't understand this example just ignore it: we will hardly be using recursion in the book.

The example we are going to look at uses a depth system to keep the recursion in check. This example will show a method of drawing a grid of circles specified by a depth argument. The depth indicates how many multiples of two are applied to the grid along each side, so a depth of 1 would give a 2 by 2 square, a depth of 2 would give a (2 x 2) by (2 x 2) square and so on. We'll call this function drawCircles(), and you will see when you enter the function the first check is to see if we need to go any deeper before starting to draw: if we do, then we split the area up into quartiles and make a further call for each of the four quartiles with depth reduced by one, and so on; this goes on until there's no need to go any deeper and so a circle is drawn and the function returns either to the original calling code or to the next place within the drawCircles() function that it had got up to before.

As you can see this function calls the drawCircle() function we already created so you should add this function to the sketch. It can be seen from this function declaration that drawCircles() is called exactly the same as drawCircle(), but with the addition of a depth argument.

```
void drawCircles(float x, float y, float diameter, int depth) {
    if (depth>0) {
        float halfDiameter = diameter / 2 ;
        drawCircles(x - halfDiameter, y-halfDiameter,
        halfDiameter, depth-1) ;
        drawCircles(x+halfDiameter, y-halfDiameter,
```

```
        halfDiameter, depth-1) ;
        drawCircles(x-halfDiameter, y+halfDiameter,
        halfDiameter, depth-1) ;
        drawCircles(x + halfDiameter, y+halfDiameter,
        halfDiameter, depth-1) ;
    }
    else {
        drawCircle(x, y, diameter);
    }
}
```

If you change your `setup` function to that below and run the sketch you will see the amazing geometric pattern as shown in Figure 18

```
void setup() {
    size(400, 400);
    background(255);
    fill(229, 138, 19);
    drawSquareCentred(200, 200, 150);
    fill(229, 19, 19);
    drawCircles(200, 200, 150, 1);
    fill(169, 19, 229);
    drawCircles(200, 200, 150, 2);
    fill(56, 19, 229);
    drawCircles(200, 200, 150, 3);
    fill(19, 229, 227);
    drawCircles(200, 200, 150, 4);
    fill(46, 229, 19);
    drawCircles(200, 200, 150, 5);
}
```

As you can see, by using reusable functions we can create amazing results with very little code. Try creating some of your own functions and calling them.

As programmers we often try to simulate real world situations within our code. Functions represent tasks or processes and, in the real world, we often get some results from a task we complete. We previously saw that the `void` keyword is used to create a function that doesn't return any value. Functions with no return value need to be trusted to perform their desired task but will not offer the programmer any indication on what was done or what the result may be. A real-world example might be trusting a microwave oven to cook your food but never telling you when the timer is finished

Figure 18: The Execution Of drawCircles Sketch

Return Values

Return values are exactly as they sound: they are values that are returned by the function to the calling routine. Practically any type can be returned from a function, from standard primitive types like integers to custom data types that the programmer has created themselves (we will visit this concept later). The possibilities are endless.

The `void` value

In previous examples we haven't had a return value. Or so it seems. The *Processing* system believes we had a return value even if we did not. It believes we had a special kind of return value called the "void return value". Let's quickly look at an example you should recognise

```
void drawCircle(float x, float y, float diameter) {
    ellipse(x,y,diameter,diameter);
}
```

The function that doesn't need to return any values and, initially, it appears that it doesn't return anything. However, in our function declaration we have included the keyword `void`. This is actually a return type. Return types are the type of value that the function expects to return. In this instance, the return type being set to `void` is telling the compiler that the result that's returned will be nothing i.e. no value will be returned. The compiler is implicitly creating a return value even though that return value has no value at all. Void return types are *Processing*'s way of saying "Don't return a value", even though the language is expecting one.

The `return` keyword

As we've discussed, functions that do not return a value are useful, but we also need to create functions that execute a task and then returns some value that's been created within the function. This is achieved by use of return values. We've briefly looked at how we declare the return type but now let's expand on this and look at non-`void` return types. We specify the type of return value in the function declaration. Let's look at a very simple example:

```
int addNumbers(int number1, int number2) {
    return number1+number2;
}
```

In this example, the return value type is `int`, an integer. This means that we expect the function to return an integer value as its result. Once we've declared this it becomes mandatory and the compiler will generate an error if the function doesn't attempt to return an integer value.

To actually return a value from the function we use the `return` keyword. This keyword terminates the function, giving control back to the calling function. When it does so it assigns the overall result of the function as the value specified with the `return` keyword. In our example, the result of `number1+number2` will be the return value and the value that's returned to the calling function. It's important to remember that when the *Processing* system hits a `return` keyword it will cease to execute the rest of function. Any code below the `return` keyword will not be executed and the compiler will warn you that such code will never be hit. The `return` statement closes the execution of the function and returns control to the function that called it.

We can now use this function

```
int myResult = addNumbers(1,3);
```

The integer `myResult` will hold the return value of the function `addNumbers`. In this case that will be 4. This is a simple example that will hopefully give you a feel for how return values work.

Return values aren't limited to simple primitives like integers. They can be set to return almost any return type the programmer requires including strings, Booleans or even complex data types that the programmer has created.

Overloading

Names are everywhere. People have names and so do pets. We use names as a way of identification, a way of knowing who the recipient is. If two people share the same name then it can be confusing. In the world of *Processing*, names have a similar purpose and suffer from similar problems. We use names in *Processing* to identify all parts of sketch code—from simple variables to functions; but if two objects share the same name then the compiler gets confused and doesn't know which object you might be referring to. In real life, two people with the same name can be identified by other characteristics such as hair or eye colour. In *Processing*, we can also use other characteristics of the function to uniquely identify it. These characteristics are known as function signatures.

Functions are normally named after the task they undertake. This is not only good practice, but it might be required as part of a project's naming conventions. But even more crucially, the appropriate naming of functions can quickly identify the purpose of a function without requiring the developer to read the whole function to understand it. But quite often multiple functions will be required to carry out similar tasks.

Within *Processing* it's quite normal to have multiple functions that are only differentiated by the different arguments that each take. The combination of the parameters and the name of the function form what is known as a *function signature*. These signatures are used to uniquely identify a function and consist of the name of the function, the number of parameters and the type of parameters that the function takes. Function signatures form the cornerstone of something known as overloading. But before we get to this, let's consider a problem and how function signatures might help to solve this problem.

For this processing example, we will be looking at a function that draws a shape that's filled in with a background colour. I'll call this function `drawColouredShape`.

```
void setup(){
    size(200,200);
    drawColouredShape(0);
}
void drawColouredShape(color colour){
    fill(colour);
    ellipse(20,20,10,10);
}
```

Here we have a function called `drawColouredShape()`. This function does very little other than it creates a coloured ellipse. By itself, this is perfectly fine. But what happens if the requirements for this sketch change? Let's say we now want to create a function that does the same thing and assume that we can't change the existing function because it is being used already, but allows the programmer to specify the coordinates of the ellipse

We could create a function with a new name that specifies what it does differently, `drawColouredShapeCircleWithCoords` for example. This idea of naming functions based on the parameters certainly works but we sacrifice some degree of readability and clarity. Not only that but it can also be cumbersome and tedious to name functions in this way. Ultimately it's a rather inelegant solution to the problem and it would be much better if we could use the same function name for both functions and allow the compiler to use the correct function depending on its arguments.

Fortunately, *Processing* has a way to solve this kind of problem with the use of function signatures. As we have already established, function signatures are used to uniquely identify a function and consists of the name of the function, the number of parameters and the type of parameters that the function takes. For *Processing* it's the function signature, and not just the name of the function, that helps it to uniquely identify the exact function it requires. So by using a different function signature we can use the same function name multiple times.

It's important to understand that function signatures in *Processing* only consist of the function name and parameters. The accessibility modifier and return value do not form part of the function signature and thus will not help to uniquely identify the function. The use of function signatures in this way is known as *function overloading*.

Although we will concentrate on function overloading, other types of overloading exist, such as operator overloading. An example of this is the + operator which can be used to add numbers, or concatenate Strings, For example

```
int x = 10 + 12;
String words = "Hello " + "World";
```

Using Function Overloading.

Let's now consider an example of overloading. The following two functions are seen as two separate functions by the *Processor* system as they have differing parameter types and thus different function signatures.

```
void drawColouredShape(color colour)
void drawColouredShape(color colour, int xPos, int yPos)
```

If we were to call this function and pass just the colour as a parameter then the first function would be called. However, if we passed a colour as a parameter and the co-ordinates as the other parameters then the second function would be called.

You can try this in your sketch and see that no errors are created and *Processing* knows which function you mean to call, even if you call them both

```
void setup(){
```

```
    size(200,200);
    drawColouredShape(0); // black
    drawColouredShape(255, 50, 50); // white
}
void drawColouredShape(color colour){
    fill(colour);
    ellipse(20,20,10,10);
}
void drawColouredShape(color colour, int xPos, int yPos){
    fill(colour);
    ellipse(xPos,xPos,10,10);
}
```

Chapter 8: Object-Oriented Programming
by Bryan Clifton and Nigel Parker

This chapter deals with a type of programming known as object-oriented programming and introduces you to classes and functions, powerful and important concepts that allow a much larger reuse of code than you previously met using functions

Object-Oriented Programming

Traditional programming languages, such as Pascal, COBOL, C and Visual Basic (amongst others) are *procedural* languages. In a procedural language you develop the code in a *linear* format, like a shopping list for example. You define your function and procedures in terms of a list of instructions, building libraries of functions and procedures that perform specific tasks which allows you (the programmer) to modularise your code.

Object-Oriented Programming (OOP) uses a different paradigm and introduces a whole new plethora of terminology. We will only cover a few of these terms here. The three main terms you will become familiar with are *class*, *function* and *message*. However, we will also discuss *properties*, *instances* and *inheritance*. A few other terms will pop up, but will only be discussed in very basic detail.

OOP uses the concept of objects that describe 'real world' things such as a person, an animal or a shape such as a square. In procedural programming you have variables which allow for such things as counting and storage of data, in OOP these are now termed properties. When a function or procedure was called you would issue a command such as

```
functionName(some argument [,maybe some more arguments])
```

In OOP you achieve similar goals by sending messages to the object. When an object is created from a class (more shortly) you can pass messages to it, the object can perform calculations and pass messages back which can be processed by other objects. A properly programmed class will know about itself. For instance, a class created to store the details of a person may have the facility to answer how tall it is; i.e. it knows its own height.

To interact with the object and call its functions and access it properties you use the objects interface. The interface defines all the functions and properties of the class. that you might need to ask it to do things or find out what it knows. As with procedural languages where you can create libraries of functions and procedures, you may also create libraries of classes that can be used in different programming projects.

Why would we use classes? Once a class is developed and tested it can be used in many different projects. OOP allows something called *inheritance* this means that additional requirements that are specified the class can be extended and new functionality added without modification to the original class. What does this achieve? Fewer errors in your code (known as 'bugs') and a high reusability factor!

Classes

When programming in OOP you begin by creating a description of the object, this is known as a class and this can be likened to a blueprint that describes everything about the object to be created and contains all the necessary functioning components to make the object work. However, classes cannot be directly worked with since they only provide the template - *instances* of the class need to be created. You have to create an *instance* of the class to work on; this is known as *instantiation* and gives us the *object*.

You might think of a class like a cookie cutter. The cookie cutter itself represents the class definition (the shape of a car, or animal, for example), and the resultant piece of cookie dough being an instance of the class of which you can create many. In some sense the act of cooking the dough could be considered a message and the condition of the dough could be considered a property, for example cooked or uncooked. Sending the message *you are being cooked* could change the property from *uncooked* to *cooking*. You could also ask the cookie if it was cooked yet. The cookie cutter can be used to make many cookies just as a class can be used to make many instances

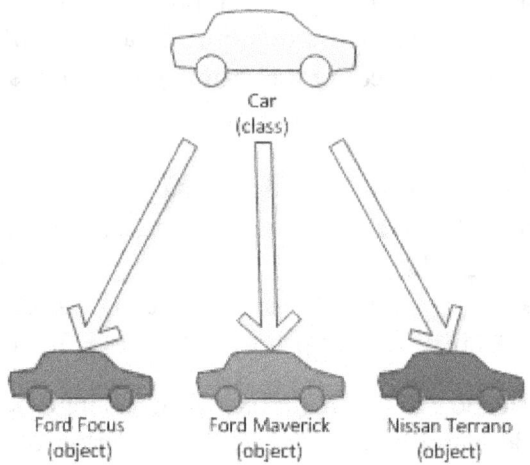

Figure 19: Relationship between classes and objects

Each instance (or object, these terms are interchangeable) can contain a set of properties that describe its characteristics (known as the object's 'state'). Imagine a class that defines a car. Each car is individual in its own right, each is a distinct object if you like, but they all have many characteristics and behaviours in common, and it these commonalities that allow us to group them all together under the heading 'car'

Figure 19 represents the relationship between a class and an object. The "blueprint" image at the top represents the class; this encapsulates all the properties and functions (the interface) of that class, and the images below represent several objects created from the class. It is important to point out that you can create more than one object from a class

Let's try to define a class for cars. The first thing we need to do is to list attributes that are common to cars, or at least the attributes (properties) we need for our purposes. Can you think what properties a car might have? We've made a list below but there are likely others

- Colour
- Make
- Model
- Engine size
- Number of doors

If we define a class for cars with these characteristics then each object we create will also have those characteristics, so we are saying that all cars must have a colour for example. However the specifics of each may be different - not all cars are red, but they all have a colour.

This is a useful process to go through when thinking about classes and objects. Once you've defined something that can be seen as an object, you might try to define what its properties would be.

To define our Car class in *Processing* you use the `class` keyword

```
class Car {
}
```

This can be part of the main sketch code, below `setup()` for example, or you can create your class in a new tab in order to separate the code a little and make it easier to read. Either way, you've now defined a class!

Instances of our class, known as objects, can be created using the `new` keyword

```
Car myCar = new Car();
```

This will create a new instance of Car which we will assign to a variable called `myCar`. Though it won't do much at this point, we can add this into our class

```
void setup() {
    Car myCar = new Car();
}
class Car {
}
```

Let's now add the properties from our list above. We'll need to decide which type represents our properties best. In computing terms properties can take the form of (for example) integers, characters and strings. There are many others to choose from and the type of property chosen obviously depends on the purpose of the property; you wouldn't have a property that holds a name declared as an integer for instance, this would most likely be a string. Careful thought should be given in choosing a type.

Properties are usually given camel-case names, starting with a lowercase letter. We have gone for the types shown in Table 7

Property	Type
colour	String
make	String
model	String
engineSize	int
numberOfDoors	int

Table 7: Properties of a Car

You might also have chosen a `float` type for `engineSize`, in order to represent values such as 2.1 litre cars, but we're choosing to represent the size in cc, so we should probably change the name to reflect that as `engineCC`

We can represent this in our class:

```
class Car {
    String colour;
    String make;
    String model;
    int engineCC;
    int numberOfDoors;
}
```

These properties can be accessed using a 'dot' notation such as `myCar.colour` will access the `colour` property. Setting a property value follows the format

```
<Object>.<Attribute Name> = <Value>;
```

So we can set the colour using

```
myCar.colour = "Red";
```

which assigns the string "Red" to the colour property of our car. We can check this by printing out the property value as shown in the code below

```
void setup() {
    Car myCar = new Car();
    myCar.colour = "Red";
    println(myCar.colour);
}
```

Having done this, we should note that it is considered good never to directly access properties like this. This is because some of the properties may not be suitable for consumption by other pieces of code and are therefore considered *private*. Examples of this might be hiding credit card numbers so someone else can't see them, or people's dates of birth just to prevent them being changed. Of course this does introduce the problem of how to access them if we can't access them directly - this is where functions are used

Functions

Functions can be defined as part of a class and, as such, are only usable by objects of that class. In our previous car example we will need a way to access the car's colour. To do this we would have functions (known as getter and setter functions) that access this property called getColour() and setColour() that allow the colour of the car to be defined and accessed. These functions then access the variables access as shown in our updated class definition below

```
class Car {
    String colour;
    String make;
    String model;
    int engineCC;
    int numberOfDoors;

    void setColour(String newColour) {
        colour = newColour;
    }

    String getColour() {
        return colour;
    }
}
```

We can then change our sketch to use these new functions rather than access the properties

```
void setup() {
    Car myCar = new Car();
    myCar.setColour("Red");
    println(myCar.getColour());
}
```

Generally speaking when defining a property in a class there would be (at least) two functions for accessing this property and this property would be declared as private (it can't be seen outside of the class but can only be accessed using get and set functions); there would be a *get* function for accessing the content of the property and a *set* function for assigning values to the property providing a public way of accessing the property. Together the *get* and *set* functions are known as the *accessor pair*. This technique also allows you to enforce rules on what can (and can't) be done with the property. These functions are known as the object's *interface*

We can also use functions to do more interesting things. We could, for example, create one to tell us if the car is economical by working out if it less than 1200CC (in this illustration, obviously this isn't necessarily an indication of fuel economy!), which might look like this

```
boolean isEconomical() {
    return engineCC < 1200;
}
```

Here we are returning a boolean which will be `true` if the `engineCC` property is less than 1200, otherwise it will return `false`. We don't need to store the result of this calculation, we can simply calculate it each time we need to answer and return the result

One of the important advantages to remember about objects created from a class is that the properties are also created and can differ between each instance of the class; they are not shared amongst all the objects; each object has its own copy. This means that, in our example, the engine size can be different between objects and therefore the `isEconomical()` result can also differ. We might have created one hundred Car objects all with different properties. You should be able to see from this how we no longer necessarily know what our sketch will do when we wrote the code as we have many different, but similar, looking objects

To reinforce your understanding of the concepts explained above we would like you to think about something and how you would model this in OOP terms. The example is a bread toaster. Think what the properties and useful functions would be and carry on reading when you have thought about this some more. Also think about which types would best represent the properties

Table 8 represents our initial thoughts on what properties and functions (representing the interface) would be required to model a toaster in OOP. It may not be exhaustive or indeed accurate and would undoubtedly require additional design considerations before being implemented.

So how did we come up with this list? One way is to think about how you use a toaster and the controls that are on a toasting machine. There is more to it than the controls though - how does the toaster know when the toast is done? It may use a timer based on the controls or it may have a sensor

Properties	Functions
temperature (int)	insertBread
timeToToast (int)	lowerBread
On (boolean - false for off)	eject
overheating (boolean)	changeTemperature
breadInserted (boolean)	changeEjectTime
	isOverheating
	switchOn

Table 8: Properties and functions for a Toaster class

We've represented when the toaster is turned on or off, its current temperature, if there is any bread inserted, how long to cook the bread for before ejecting and whether the toaster is overheating. From an interface point of view, thinking about how a toaster works may provide ideas for potential functions. We would need functions to control the input and output of the toaster (insert Bread, eject toast, etc.) and functions to control the state of the toaster (change temperature, change ejection time, if the toaster is overheating, etc.). You may well think of some more

Try and come up with some other examples; for instance think about an ATM (cash machine) and what properties and functions that would require, or perhaps add to the car example thinking about what properties may be involved (for instance temperature, fuel level, etc.) and functions (accelerate, break, etc.)

Graphical Example

Let's now take a look at a graphical example of using classes and functions.

As *Processing* is all about graphics, let us begin by developing a class that will allow us to describe a simple shape, and for this example we will choose a circle. When we consider a circle there are a number of attributes that are important:

- *Radius*: The length of a straight line extending from the centre of a circle.
- *Diameter*: The length of a straight line passing through the centre of a circle and meeting the circumference at each end.
- *Circumference*: The length of the outer boundary of a circular area.
- *Origin*: The centre point of a circle through which the radius and diameter pass.

We don't need all of these attributes in order to be able to describe our circle, in fact we could calculate the diameter and circumference given the radius. All we really need in order to be able to describe our circle is a radius and an origin.

We begin our class definition using the word `class` followed by the name we want to give to the class, and we would suggest something descriptive of the object itself so that it is obvious from just reading the code what it is we are describing.

```
class Circle { }
```

Any code we write that describes the properties or functions of the class will be enclosed within the braces {}.

The first thing to do is describe the properties that a class has, these are described using variables.

```
class Circle {
    float originX; // The centre of the circle (x axis).
    float originY; // The centre of the circle (y axis).
    float radius;  // The radius of the circle.
}
```

We also need functions to access these properties. We've only created the setter functions since we have no need to access the values once we set them

```
void setOriginX(float x) {
    originX = x;
}

void setOriginY(float y) {
    originY = y;
```

```
}

void setRadius(float r) {
    radius = r;
}
```

Here we have defined our new class and have described its attributes, it has x and y positions and a radius. We can now create new Circle objects

```
void setup() {
    Circle c1 = new Circle();
}
```

If you were to run this code a new instance of the Circle class would be created, named c1, but nothing would be shown on the screen. If you remember from the Car class we defined some additional functions that described the behaviour of a car, and that is what we need to do with the Circle class. Let us start by defining a function that will allow us to see the circle on the screen.

Let's begin by deciding on a name for the function, there is nothing stopping us calling our function anything we like, but something descriptive would be more useful when reading through the code, so we'll define the draw function as

```
void drawCircle() { }
```

We now need to add the code to the function that will perform the function required when called; in this case we want the function to draw the circle on our screen at the position specified in the origin with the radius defined.

```
void drawCircle() {
    ellipse(originX, originY, radius, radius);
}
```

Now all we need to do is set the property values and tell the circle to draw itself

```
void setup() {
    Circle c1 = new Circle();
    c1.setOriginX(30);
    c1.setOriginY(30);
    c1.setRadius(50);
    c1.drawCircle();
}
```

Running this code should result in a circle similar to that shown in Figure 20

You should now start to see why objects are useful - the circle knows how to draw itself, our sketch no longer needs to know how it does that, only that, by calling the `drawCircle()` function, the circle will draw itself

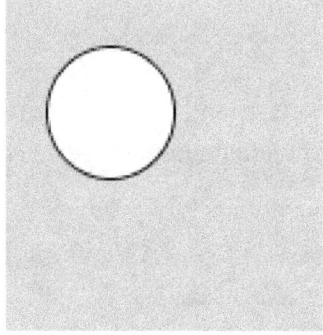

Figure 20: Circle drawn by the Circle class

So now we have a class that will allow us to draw a circle on the screen, which is great provided we want the circle to be white. Let's look at how we can change our class to overcome this limitation. Let's add a new property called `colour` that we can set using a setter function

```
color colour; // the colour of the circle
void setColour(color c) {
    colour = c;
}
```

we can use this to set the colour in the drawCircle()function

```
void drawCircle() {
    fill(colour); //fill the circle with the colour
    ellipse(originX, originY, radius, radius);
}
```

We can now set the colour of the circle before we call the drawCircle()function, for example

```
void setup() {
    Circle c1 = new Circle();
    c1.setOriginX(30);
    c1.setOriginY(30);
    c1.setRadius(50);
    c1.setColour(#ff0000); //red
    c1.drawCircle();
}
```

This will now draw a red circle as we specified in the `setColour()` function as shown in Figure 21

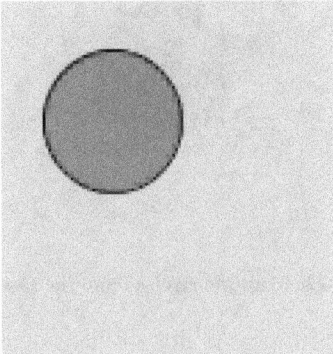

Figure 21: Red circle drawn by the Circle class

Since we created the circle as a class, we can create as many instances of the class we like, with different property values, simply by creating a new circle instance and calling `drawCircle()` on that one too

```
void setup() {
    Circle c1 = new Circle();
    c1.setOriginX(30);
    c1.setOriginY(30);
    c1.setRadius(50);
    c1.setColour(#ff0000); //red
    c1.drawCircle();

    Circle c2 = new Circle();
    c2.setOriginX(50);
    c2.setOriginY(50);
    c2.setRadius(50);
    c2.setColour(#000000); //black
    c2.drawCircle();
}
```

This code, when run, will draw two circles with different colours as demonstrated in Figure 22

Though a fairly simple use of classes and objects, this demonstrates, a powerful use of objects - we can create as many as we like, with different attributes, and we don't need to know how they work, they know themselves! We could create one hundred of these if we wanted to

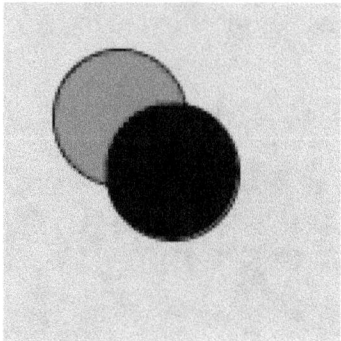

Figure 22: Multiple circles from the same class

You may feel that all the setter functions are quite long-winded, especially if you never want to change the values of the properties. There is a special type of function, known as a *constructor*, that allows you to specify the property values as part of the `new` instance statement

Constructors

Constructors allow you to specify the values for properties as part of the instance creation statement. This simplifies the code you need to write and also allows you to remove any setter functions where you don't want the values to change later (if you provide setter functions then other programmers can use them to change the values after the object is created). An object where you have no setter functions but specify all the values in the constructor is known as an *immutable object* since it cannot have its property values changed.

Constructors look much like other functions with some subtle differences:

- they have no return type
- the function name is the name of the class

So a simple example, with no arguments, would look like

```
Circle() { }
```

We specify the attributes to the constructor in the same way we do for other functions, in the brackets, and we can use those to set our property values

```
Circle(float x, float y, float r, color c) {
    originX = x;
    originY = y;
    radius = r;
    colour = c;
```

94

```
}
```

As you can see, this notation is considerably more compact than our four setter functions but has the same effect of setting the values that will then be used in our drawCircle() function. It also greatly simplifies our main sketch code since, instead of using four different setter functions, we just specify the values in the new statement

```
void setup() {
    Circle c1 = new Circle(30, 30, 50, #ff0000);
    c1.drawCircle();

    Circle c2 = new Circle(50, 50, 50, #000000);
    c2.drawCircle();
}
```

Note that, as with all functions, the values must be in the same order as the argument list of the function. If you re-run your code you should see the exact same output as before but with a lot less code!

Before we end this chapter we will just make a point about argument naming. As you can see from the above we named our arguments differently to our attributes (properties) eg

```
colour = c;
```

Which seems ok, but it would be more readable if we also named the argument colour, rather than c, or had to make up some other name that also meant colour. We could just name them the same eg

```
colour = colour;
```

but this will confuse *Processing* as it won't know which colour variable we mean so will use the one closest to the statement, which is the one in the argument list, thereby setting the argument to itself and never setting the instance variable that we use in drawCircle()!

If you try this example, where we renamed the argument names to the same as the property names

```
Circle(float originX, float originY, float radius, color colour) {
    originX = originX;
    originY = originY;
    radius = radius;
    colour = colour;
}
```

You will see no output as we never set the coordinates, radius or colour. The way around this is to use the `this` keyword. In *Processing* `this` refers to 'this object' and is used like a variable (it is known as a pseudo-variable). So in our example it can be used to denote which `colour` we are referring to, where `colour` refers to the argument and `this.colour` refers to the variable

If you add `this` to each of the variable names in the constructor, as shown below, you will see it all works again even though you've used the same names

```
Circle(float originX, float originY, float radius, color colour) {
    this.originX = originX;
    this.originY = originY;
    this.radius = radius;
    this.colour = colour;
}
```

Chapter 9: Advanced Object-Orientation
by Antony Lees, Ian Macey and Rob Martin

This chapter deals with some advanced Object-Oriented Programming concepts. We delve back into constructors with some advanced examples and cover the advanced concepts of inheritance, composition, overriding and overloading

Frogs

In this chapter we will develop on the Object-Oriented Programming concepts by using classes to create a fun frog graphic as shown in Figure 23

Figure 23: Frog graphic using OOP

We will start with a simple class definition that will draw a single frog

```
void setup() {
    size(300,300);
    Frog frog = new Frog();
    frog.display();
}

class Frog {
    // Properties (attributes)
    int xPos; // Horizontal position
    int yPos; // Vertical position
    // displays the frog
    void display() {
        strokeWeight(2);
        fill(colour); // colour
        // body
        ellipse(xPos, yPos, 90, 45);
        // feet
```

```
        fill(107, 142, 35);
        ellipse(xPos - 30, yPos + 15, 45, 23);
        ellipse(xPos + 30, yPos + 15, 45, 23);
        // Eyes.
        fill(255, 255, 255);
        ellipse(xPos - 15, yPos - 23, 23, 30);
        ellipse(xPos + 15, yPos - 23, 23, 30);
        fill(0, 0, 0);
        ellipse(xPos - 15, yPos - 23, 8, 8);
        ellipse(xPos + 15, yPos - 23, 8, 8);
        // Mouth.
        arc(xPos, yPos - 2, 30, 5, 0, PI);
    }
}
```

By now you should be able to read most of this. We have our sketch code that creates a new Frog object, called frog, and displays it by calling the display() function. The class itself has two instance variables holding the coordinates to draw the frog and a display() function that sets colours and draws shapes at the coordinates

Advanced Constructors

A constructor is automatically invoked when an object is created, using the keyword new, as in:

```
Frog frog = new Frog();
```

As we've seen, a constructor is a function, but it is different to other functions in that it has the same name as the class. Yet if we look at our code for the Frog class we can see that there is not a function with the name Frog, thus no constructor. Why? The answer is the default constructor

Default Constructors

Actually there is a constructor; it's just hidden. If you don't define a constructor then every class you create will have a default constructor that when invoked assigns default values to the instance properties of the object (the general rule is that numbers will be zero, strings will be an empty string ""). The default constructor has no arguments and this is why calling new Frog() still works even though we haven't written a constructor

For our Frog class we haven't set any values for the coordinates, so these will be given the default values of zero.

```
int xPos; // Horizontal position
```

```
int yPos; // Vertical position
```

If we want to set these to something other than zero we have a number of choices. We can set the values in a number of ways. We could initialise them inline, for example

```
int xPos = 80; // Horizontal position
int yPos = 60; // Vertical position
```

Or we could create our own no-argument constructor, for example

```
Frog() {
    xPos = 80;
    yPos = 60;
}
```

Either of these options mean we don't need to alter our code that creates new frogs as the no-argument constructor, be it the default one or the one we just wrote, still exists and so `new Frog()` is still valid. You should note that writing a constructor, any constructor, removes the default one since *Processing* deems you not to need it because you wrote one yourself.

There is a problem with what we have discussed so far, in that every instance of the `Frog` class that we create will have the same initial values for its instance variables. This means that every `Frog` object will have a horizontal position of 80 and a vertical position of 60. Now actually we might require each `Frog` object to start in different horizontal and vertical positions on the screen. We could do this in the constructor

```
Frog(int xPos, int yPos) {
    this.xPos = xPos;
    this.yPos = yPos;
}
```

As we previously said, creating a constructor means that the default constructor is removed, so we now have no no-argument constructor. This means our `new Frog()` code is no longer valid and we need to specify the coordinates in the creation statement, for example

```
Frog frog = new Frog(80, 60);
```

If you've made these changes as you went along your code should now look similar to that below

```
void setup() {
    size(300,300);
    Frog frog = new Frog(80, 60);
    frog.display();
}
```

```
class Frog {
   // Properties (attributes).
   int xPos = 80; // Horizontal position
   int yPos = 60; // Vertical position

   Frog(int xPos, int yPos) {
      this.xPos = xPos;
      this.yPos = yPos;
   }
// displays the frog
   void display() {
      strokeWeight(2);
      fill(colour); // colour
      // body
      ellipse(xPos, yPos, 90, 45);
      // feet
      fill(107, 142, 35);
      ellipse(xPos - 30, yPos + 15, 45, 23);
      ellipse(xPos + 30, yPos + 15, 45, 23);
      // Eyes.
      fill(255, 255, 255);
      ellipse(xPos - 15, yPos - 23, 23, 30);
      ellipse(xPos + 15, yPos - 23, 23, 30);
      fill(0, 0, 0);
      ellipse(xPos - 15, yPos - 23, 8, 8);
      ellipse(xPos + 15, yPos - 23, 8, 8);
      // Mouth.
      arc(xPos, yPos - 2, 30, 5, 0, PI);
   }
}
```

If you run this, you will still see the frog displayed on the screen. The values we pass to the new constructor will override the default values we set on the instance variables. What happens though, if you really did want a no-argument constructor *as well*? Maybe you want frogs to be displayed in a default position unless you specify it. There is a way of doing this using *overloading*

Overloading Constructors

We previously looked at how overloading is when you create more than one function with the same name but a different set of arguments (known as the *function signature*). Since constructors are just special types of functions, you can overload those too

We can add the no-argument constructor as well as the constructor we already created so that we have two constructors

```
Frog(int xPos, int yPos) {
    this.xPos = xPos;
    this.yPos = yPos;
}


Frog() {
    // use defaults
}
```

These two constructors can live happily together in the same class as they have different signatures in the form of different argument lists, one has two int arguments and one has no arguments. You should note that only the types and their order of the arguments make up the signature, you can't create another constructor with two int arguments even if their names are different.

If we now create another frog instance using the default constructor you will see that both constructors work and display frogs

```
void setup() {
    size(300,300);
    Frog frog = new Frog(120, 120);
    frog.display();
    Frog frog2 = new Frog();
    frog2.display();
}
```

We could also do this for specifying the colour of the frog by creating a third constructor that allows us to change the colour. For this we would need a new instance variable, which we will call colour

```
color colour;
```

We will assume that people will always want to set both the position and the colour, so we will create a new constructor with three arguments

```
Frog(int xPos, int yPos, color colour) {
    this.xPos = xPos;
    this.yPos = yPos;
    this.colour = colour;
}
```

We could also, if we wished, create another that allowed the specification of the colour but also used the default position, or one that only allowed the horizontal (x) coordinate to be changed, there are many possibilities.

To use our new constructor we need to create a third Frog instance and pass the colour to it, for example

```
color frog3Colour = color(0, 0, 0);
Frog frog3 = new Frog(160, 180, frog3Colour);
frog3.display();
```

This will create and display three frog instances as shown in Figure 24. Cute little fellas aren't they?

Figure 24: Three frogs with different positions and colours

Imagine now that we want to create a new type of frog, one that shares all the same attributes of our Frog class, but adds to it. This type of frog will look exactly the same but be able to fly, we will call them hover frogs. This could mean creating a new class, called HoverFrog, and copying all of the Frog code into it, then adding our additional code to display them differently. This seems like a waste of effort and also introduces a problem in terms of ongoing maintenance of your code - you now have two copies of the same code that, if you wanted to change, you would have to change twice! Fortunately *Processing* has a mechanism to handle this known as *inheritance*

Inheritance and Overriding

Inheritance is where you base one class off another such that the new class, known as a *subclass*, has access to all the code of the other, known as the *superclass*. The subclass is said to *inherit* all of the behaviour of the superclass. This makes our job easier as we don't need to duplicate the Frog code, and any changes we make to the Frog class will also be inherited by our new HoverFrog class

When considering subclasses it is appropriate to consider whether the subclass represents a specialisation of the superclass, that is, can it be considered the same thing but the superclass is a more general form? This is known as an *is a* relationship. You can see if a subclass relationship is appropriate by saying 'x class is a y class' and deciding if that makes sense. For example, a picture is a work of art, a car is a vehicle, a cat is an animal, or in our case a hoverfrog is a frog. If it sounds wrong, for example, 'cat is a vehicle' then it probably is wrong. In object-oriented programming we would say that the subclass extends, specialises or inherits from the superclass

Let's go ahead and create our new class. This follows the same notation as before with one small difference, we use the extends keyword

```
class HoverFrog extends Frog {
}
```

Amazingly, this is all the code you need to create a subclass! If you create a new instance of this class and display it, it will work exactly the same as before. If you run this you will see two frogs

```
void setup() {
    size(300,300);
    Frog frog = new Frog(200, 200);
    frog.display();
    HoverFrog hoverFrog = new HoverFrog();
    hoverFrog.display();
}
```

The HoverFrog class has inherited all of the abilities of the Frog class including the ability to display itself. The constructors, though, are not inherited, so we only have the default constructor at this point, but you can add them if needed. Of course we haven't made it any different so our hoverfrog looks identical to our frog, so let's do that next by creating a display() function for our hoverfrog

```
void display() {
    super.display();
    // rotor blades
```

```
    line(xPos, yPos - 22, xPos, yPos - 50);
    line(xPos - 30, yPos - 63, xPos + 30, yPos - 35);
    line(xPos - 30, yPos - 35, xPos + 30, yPos - 63);
}
```

If you run this code you should see a hoverfrog, complete with rotor blades, as you can see in Figure 25

Figure 25: Frog and Hoverfrog

There are a few things here that may confuse or surprise you,. We mentioned before that the subclass inherits the functions from the superclass but we have created a new `display()` function and you may recall that the hoverfrog was still displayed before we added this function. Before we added this, the inherited function from Frog was used, but once we create one in the subclass, that is the one that is used when we call `hoverFrog.display()`. This means that we can redefine the function to do what we want when a hoverfrog instance is used, but the original frog displays as before. Creating a new function with the same signature (recall that this is the function name and arguments) in the subclass is known as *overriding* and means we can add to, or completely change, the behaviour of that function in the subclass. In this case we have added rotor blades to the hoverfrog and *Processing* knows which `display()` function to use

You may also see a new keyword being used, `super`. Like `this`, `super` is a pseudo variable that allows you to specify which instance you mean. The `this` keyword refers to the current instance, so can be used to show that you mean the object, rather than the variable from the function signature, for example. The `super` keyword is used to refer to the superclass and can be used to specify that you mean the function or variable from that class. In this case we are using it to show we mean the `display()` function from the Frog superclass and so the line `super.display()` means 'call the `display()` function from the superclass' which is how we display the frog, then draw the rotor blades. You might try removing, or commenting out, this line and see what happens. You should see that you *only* get the rotor blades because the code for drawing the frog, in the Frog class, is never called. You may wonder how this worked before we created a `display()` function - that is due to overriding. Once we overrode the function by creating one in hoverfrog, the superclass function was no longer automatically inherited and we have to call it explicitly to run that function. Note also that we have access to the coordinate variables from the Frog superclass, `xPos` and `yPos`, and we can use them in our code for displaying the rotor blades

Composition

The last OOP concept we'll discuss is composition which is where an object of one class consists of objects of other classes. Although this sounds complicated, you have seen it before when we used a String object as a variable. Anywhere we declare an object variable we are composing our object of another object. Unlike inheritance these objects need not be conceptually related to each other so inheritance is not the appropriate technique. We can model this relationship in object oriented programming by saying that an object *has a* other object. Examples are that a picture has a frame, a frog has a leg, a car has a wheel. However if we try to model these using inheritance they don't make sense - a wheel is not a car and a leg is not a frog.

Suffice it to say that variables need not just be primitive types such as `int` or `color`. Variables can hold any type, primitive types or objects, and where a variable is an object we call this composition

Object-orientation is a huge subject which we can't hope to cover in a book about *Processing*. If you want to learn more about object-oriented programming or the Java language that *Processing* is based on then we recommend getting a book on these subjects which will cover OOP in considerably more detail. For example we haven't touched upon interfaces, abstract classes, inner classes, polymorphism or any number of Java classes that you could use when creating *Processing* sketches. However these chapters should provide you with enough knowledge on object-oriented programming to enable you to proceed to the next sections and learn about *Processing* with which you will be able to create some fun and visually stunning graphics

SECTION 2: BEGINNING PROCESSING

Chapter 10: Programming with Processing
by Antony Lees and Graham Hall

This chapter introduces you to programming in *Processing* and explains the concepts needed to start writing graphics programs. We will look at the types of facilities available in *Processing* and explain the basic structure of a *Processing* sketch

Processing is a programming language and integrated programming environment (IDE) aimed at creating graphically-rich computer programs and provides an API (application programming interface) for creating graphics such as lines, curves, shapes and colours.

When you create and run a *Processing* sketch (which is what *Processing* calls a program) a display window is created that will display the graphics you specified in your code. *Processing* provides functions and variables that enable you to interact with the display window and these form the core of any *Processing* sketch you are likely to write

Controlling the Processing Environment

Processing provides function and variables for controlling and accessing the size of the display window. The `size()` function allows you to set the size of the display window, in pixels, for example

```
size(200, 300);
```

which would set the size to 200 pixels wide (x-axis) and 300 pixels high (y-axis). You would normally set the size of the window at the start of the sketch. If you don't set the size at all, *Processing* will use a default size of 100 x 100. You can access the size of the window in your sketches using the `width` and `height` variables which are automatically set. So in our example above they would be 200 and 300 respectively.

You can also set the size to be the same as the screen, such as your computer screen, by using the `displayWidth` and `displayHeight` variables. This means that

```
size(displayWidth, displayHeight);
```

would set the size of the window to be the same size as the screen. This would also set the `width` and `height` variables to the values of the screen size.

We can also control the background colour using the `background()` function. For example

```
background(0, 0, 0);
```

will set a black background. We can use this in a simple sketch that sets a random background colour and draws a line using the window size

```
size(200, 200);
background(random(255), random(255), random(255));
line(0, 0, width, height);
```

You needn't completely understand the `line()` and `random()` functions for now except to know that we are selecting a random colour up to 255 in order to set the background colour, and drawing a line from the top left (coordinates 0,0) to the top right (coordinates width, height) as can be seen in Figure 26

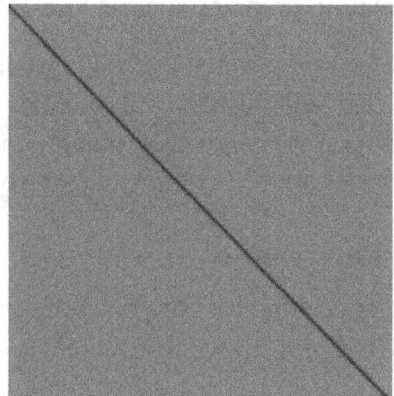

Figure 26: Random background colour and line

Static and Active Mode

You may have noticed that, up to this point, all of our graphics sketches have been stationary. This is because all the code we have written so far has been in *static mode* which is one mode that *Processing* can run in.

Static Mode

When we use static mode *Processing* (known in previous versions of *Processing* as 'basic mode') will display the graphics we have specified once and then stop drawing any longer, leaving the graphics in the display window. This is the simpler of the two modes as we don't need to think about what happens when the graphics are redisplayed

You can tell *Processing* to use static mode simply by writing our code as we have done. This differs from the other mode, active mode, in which you place your code inside the `draw()` function

Active Mode

Active mode (known in previous version of *Processing* as 'continuous mode') differs from static mode in that there are two built in functions; they are `setup()` and `draw()`.

When designing an animation sketch, it is necessary to separate the things which happen before the animation begins from the things which happen during the animation. This is the role of the setup() function, which allows you to initialise and setup various arguments for a sketch, for example the size of a window.

```
void setup() {
    // put anything here that you want to
    // happen once at the start of the sketch
}
```

Notice the word `void()` which appears before the name `setup()` which indicates that *Processing* is not expecting any value to be returned from the function.

The role of the function `draw` is to loop around executing the code that is contained in the function. It repeatedly executes all the code within its body. This means that any code you put inside the function will be displayed and redisplayed (known as 'drawing') over and over until you stop the sketch. This means that you can vary the way the graphics are drawn each time in order to change them. Each time the graphics are drawn is known as a *frame*, in a similar way to cartoons are displayed in frames

```
void draw() {
    // Put anything here that you want to happen
    // once every time the frame is refreshed
}
```

If we create a draw() function that alters the graphics each time, we have created an animation. We can recreate our sketch that changes the background colour in active mode in order to show how the `draw()` function is called continuously.

```
void setup() {
    size(200, 200);
}

void draw() {
    background(random(255), random(255), random(255));
    line(0, 0, width, height);
}
```

Running this sketch will show you that the background colour is changing rapidly; each time the a frame is drawn, the background colour changes to a random colour. The `draw()` function is run automatically by *Processing* you wouldn't ordinarily call the function yourself. You may notice that we draw the line exactly the same each time and wonder why, if we are never going to change it, why not put it in the `setup()` function. The reason for this is that, when we change the background we are effectively clearing the window, so we need to redraw the line. The background() function is often used for this in *Processing* and you'll often see background() as the first function inside the draw() function for this reason, otherwise the graphics will be drawn on top of the ones from the last frame

Active Mode Controls

Processing provides some functions and variables that allow you to control how graphics are drawn in active mode. Firstly you can control continuous drawing by stopping and starting the looping using loop() and noLoop(). The noLoop() function will stop the draw() function from being executed and the loop() function will start it again. If you add a noLoop() call into our background sketch you will see that the background colour no longer changes, similar to static mode

You can also control the speed at which the frames are displayed using the frameRate() function. The default frame rate (that is, number of frames per second) is 30. You can try adding this into the sketch, for example

```
void setup() {
    size(200, 200);
    frameRate(5);
}
```

will reduce the number of frames per second to 5. If you run the sketch you will see the background colours changing much more slowly. You can also access the frame rate in your sketch, if you need to, using the frameRate variable. If you want to know how *many* frames have been displayed so far there is the frameCount variable which will tell you that value. If you add the following line into your draw() function it will print the current frame number to the console

```
println(frameCount);
```

We will now look at a more advanced animation, just to show you how these concepts can be put together

Animation

Our objective is to create an animation of a bouncing ball which will bounce off the sides of the window as shown in Figure 27. We need to start with a setup() function

```
void setup(){
    size (400,450);
    background(255);
}
```

This sets the size of the display window and sets the background colour, in this case white. You can run this if you wish, you will see the appropriately sized and coloured window

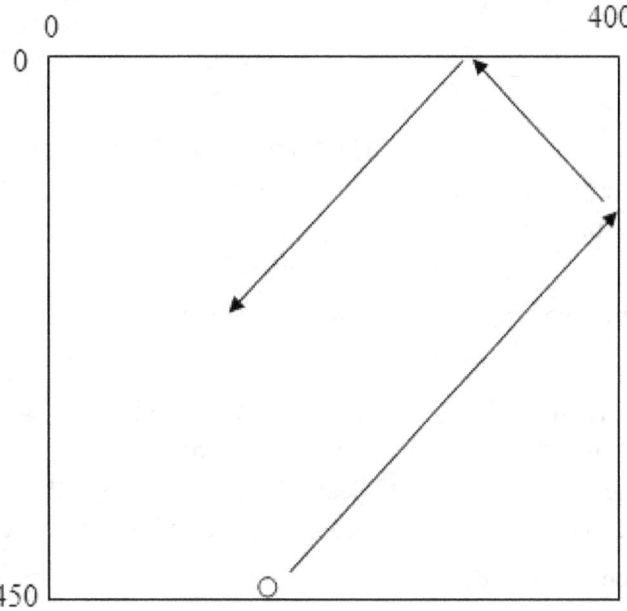

Figure 27: Bouncing ball animation

Before we do any animation code, we also need some variables to control the direction and location of the ball

```
int xPosition;
int yPosition;
final int ballSize = 8;
int xSpeed;
int ySpeed;
```

Here we have created variables to hold the x- and y-coordinates position of the ball and the 'speed' (the number of coordinate positions to move per frame). We also created a `final` variable to hold the size of the ball. We don't need to change the ball size during the sketch, so it is appropriate to declare it as `final`.

We can initialise the position and speed variables in the `setup()` function. We will start with the ball in the middle of the bottom edge of the screen

```
void setup() {
    size (400,450);
    background(255);
    // initialise position
```

```
    xPosition = width/2;
    yPosition = height;
    // initialise speed
    xSpeed = 6;
    ySpeed = 6;
}
```

Now we are ready to do some animation. The things which happen each time the screen is refreshed are put inside the `draw()` function. We begin by drawing the ball as a circle, making use of the variables which specify its position and size.

```
void draw(){
    ellipse(xPosition, yPosition, ballSize, ballSize);
}
```

Running this will display the ball at the bottom of the screen but the ball won't move. This is because we are drawing the ball in the same place each frame so, even though we are running in active mode, every frame is the same! We can change the values of xPosition and yPosition slightly, so the ball will appear to have moved when the next frame is drawn:

```
xPosition = xPosition + xSpeed;
yPosition = yPosition - ySpeed;
```

The amount by which the ball moves is determined by the speed variables. The coordinate system measures downwards from the top of the window, so we need to reduce the yPosition value if the ball moves upwards.

The sketch at the moment would work for a few frames, with the ball travelling diagonally upwards to the right from its starting position, but it would soon disappear off the edge of the screen. We need to find a way of making it bounce back. The key to making the ball bounce is to detect when it reaches the edge of the container, then reverse its movement direction. We can do this using `if` statements

```
if (xPosition > width){
    xSpeed = -xSpeed;
}
```

The above statement detects if the x-position goes beyond the edge of the screen (the `width`) and reverses the speed by setting `xSpeed` to its negative value so as soon as the horizontal position of the ball goes beyond the right-hand wall, the horizontal component of the speed will be reversed and the ball will start to move back into the container

Figure 28: Bouncing ball animation with trail

We can use a similar conditional statement to detect the ball escaping through the left-hand wall, and reverse its horizontal speed again to bounce it back:

```
if (xPosition < 0){
    xSpeed = -xSpeed;
}
```

Two more conditionals are needed to bounce the ball back from the bottom and top walls of the container:

```
if (yPosition > height){
    ySpeed = -ySpeed;
}
if (yPosition < 0){
    ySpeed = -ySpeed;
}
```

If we now put all of this together and run it. the ball begins from the bottom of the window and bounces as it encounters each of the walls. A trail is left behind to show its motion as shown in Figure 28

Recall that each frame is drawn on top of the last, so each time we change the coordinates and draw the ball we are also seeing the balls drawn in the previous frames. It is easy to change the sketch to show the single bouncing ball without leaving a trail behind. We just add a background() command as the first line of the draw() function. The final code is shown below

```
int xPosition;
int yPosition;
final int ballSize = 8;
int xSpeed;
int ySpeed;

void setup() {
   size (400,450);
   // initialise position
   xPosition = width/2;
   yPosition = height;
   // initialise speed
   xSpeed = 6;
   ySpeed = 6;
}

void draw() {
   // clear the screen
   background(255);
   // add speed to location
   xPosition = xPosition + xSpeed;
   yPosition = yPosition - ySpeed;
   // draw ball
   ellipse(xPosition, yPosition, ballSize, ballSize);
   // reverse speed if we reach the edges
   if (xPosition > width){
      xSpeed = -xSpeed;
   }
   if (xPosition < 0){
      xSpeed = -xSpeed;
   }
   if (yPosition > height){
      ySpeed = -ySpeed;
```

```
    }
    if (yPosition < 0){
        ySpeed = -ySpeed;
    }
}
```

Chapter 11: Coordinates, Pixels and Points
by Anton Dil and Antony Lees

The basic element of a computer graphic is the pixel; this is a single point on a screen. This chapter examines the role that pixels have in computer graphics and describes some of the facilities in *Processing* that allow the programmer to manipulate pixels and how coordinates work in the *Processing* environment

Coordinate Systems and Pixels

We have previously seen that the *Processing* display window is created with a given size using the `size()` function which defines the number of pixels along the x and y axes, so a size of 600, 400 will create a window 600 pixels wide and 400 pixels high.

The displayable area is like a grid, with the number of pixels measured from the top-left point, position (0, 0) and increasing along each axis. As shown in Figure 29 the coordinates of any single pixel can determined by providing the x and y coordinates in relation to the starting point at position (0, 0). As examples, the bottom right of a 600 x 400 display is at position (600, 400) and the middle is at position (300, 200).

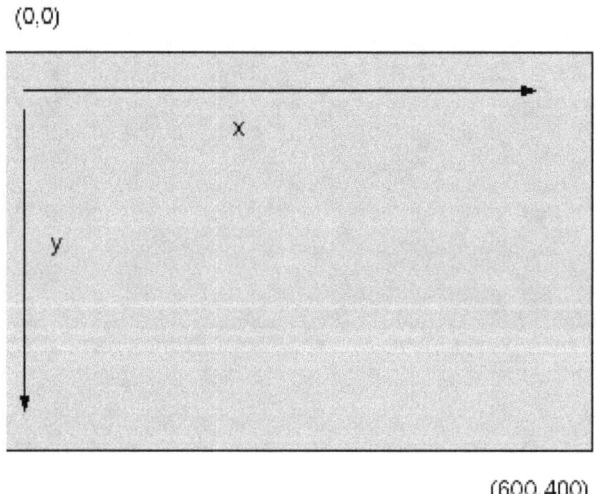

Figure 29: Coordinates of the Processing screen

We can use the coordinates to draw a point by providing them as the arguments to the `point` function in the form `point(x, y)`. For example, the code

```
size(600, 400);
point(300, 200);
```

will draw a point in the middle of the screen. Any set of coordinates can be used to draw a point. Provided the coordinates are within the range of those of the screen, then the point will be visible. If coordinates are used that are not within that range, for example a negative number or a number greater than the greatest x or y position, the point will not be visible. *Processing*'s built-in variables `height` and `width` can be used find out what the limit of the coordinates are. Therefore the point

```
point(width, height);
```

is at the bottom-right of the screen. We can demonstrate this with a small sketch to draw random points on the screen

```
void draw() {
    // create random values, converted to int
    int pointX = int(random(width));
    int pointY = int(random(height));
    // draw the point
    point(pointX, pointY);
    // print the coordinates
    println(pointX + ", " + pointY);
}
```

There are a few things going on here that we will explain:

- We used the `random()` function which generates a random `float` between zero and the number given, in our case the width or height of the screen. The `random()` function is overloaded and can also take a lower number, which is zero if not given
- We converted the `float` created by the `random()` function using the `int()` function. We didn't technically need to do this as we could use the `float`, but it doesn't look as nice in the console output. The `int()` function just truncates (that is removes everything after the decimal point) the `float` number created by the `random()` function
- We drew a point at the coordinates
- We printed out the coordinates

If you run this, you will see something similar to Figure30. Since the coordinates are randomly generated the points will not be in exactly the same place

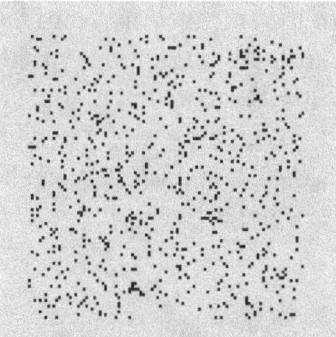

Figure 30: Points drawn at random coordinates

You can also achieve this same effect using the `set()` function which will set the pixel at the given coordinate to a specified colour, for example

```
color c = color(0); // black
// draw the point
set(pointX, pointY, c);
```

If you change your code to the above you will see the same effect. The difference lies in the intention of the code. The `point()` function is for drawing dots whereas the `set()` function is for setting pixel colour. Points don't *have* to be a single pixel in size, though they are by default. You can change the size of the point using the `strokeWeight()` function. You might try adding `strokeWeight(5)` to your sketch and seeing what happens - the points drawn should be much larger!

You will see coordinates are often used in *Processing,* for example for drawing lines, shapes, manipulating images, as you will usually need to know where you are drawing and where the confines of the screen are. A line, for example, is drawn with two sets of x and y coordinates, one to determine the start point and one for the end point.

```
line(x1, y1, x2, y2);
```

We will cover lines a bit later, now we will do something a little more interesting with points and show how little effort it can take to produce really interesting and pretty pictures!

Random Walker Sketch

The key to achieving something interesting when constructing a picture out of points alone is to get the computer to do the mindless repetitive work of plotting one point after another, leaving us free to be creative and exploit the kinds of functions we have at our disposal for varying colour or width of stroke. Enter the random walker.

We can instruct *Processing* to plot points in a random 'walking' pattern like someone who can't find their way home, by moving a defined distance in a random direction like someone who is lost. The effect of each 'step' is to draw a random path which may look something like that shown in Figure 31

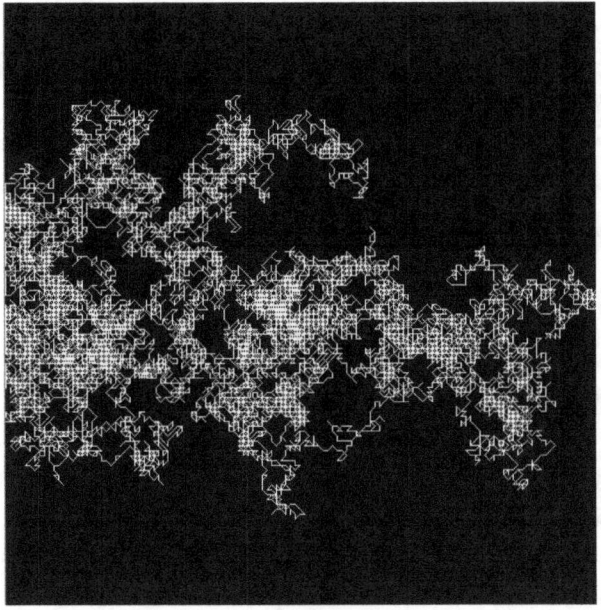

Figure 31: A random walker

First of all, it's nothing but points. So, we will show you how you can plot one point after another, following a direction that can vary radically from one moment to the next. One thing we will certainly have to incorporate is rules for what to do when our walker reaches a boundary. By boundary, we mean the edge of the area that we have decided to show, such as a 500 x 500 display area. There's no point wandering off beyond this area and plotting where the walker is, because the point will no longer be visible. To remain visible we have to keep our walker in our area. We will use a 'bouncing' option to return the walker the way it came, but you can easily adapt the code to try another approach.

```
if (x > width){
    --x;
}
else
    if (x < 0){
    ++x;
}
```

This rule does not attempt to take into account a current direction of travel; it merely prevents the *x* value from becoming negative or greater than the width of the display area. A similar rule could be written to prevent the y coordinate from being greater than the height of the area

Walking

So how might we randomly walk? Since a pixel is located in a grid, each pixel has a certain number of neighbours, which it more-or-less touches. This is known as *connectedness*. There are two traditional notions connectedness and they are sometimes known as 4-connectivity (4-c) and 8-connectivity (8-c), shown in Figures 32 and 33.

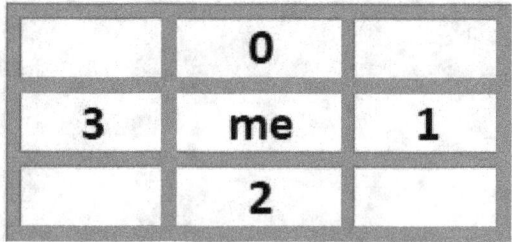

Figure 32: 4-connectivity

4-connectivity works on connecting up, down, left and right so the walker could go in any of these directions. 8-connectivity also allows connections on the diagonals so our walker could go in eight directions

7	0	4
3	me	1
6	2	5

Figure 33: 8-connectivity

Now, suppose that we plot where you are, and then plot every pixel you proceed to, on your random walk in our `width x height` area. We will need to be able to randomly pick a direction to go, which can be represented by numbers. We can code that very easily as follows by creating a function that randomly selects one of four numbers:

```
int newDirection4(){
    return (int) random(4);
}
```

This will returns 0, 1, 2 or 3 which corresponds to our numbering. We could just as easily choose from eight directions using a function like this:

```
int newDirection8() {
```

```
    return (int) random(8);
}
```

Given that the walker's current position is (x,y), we can map the relative coordinates we can go as shown in Figure 34 based on a graphical coordinate system, in which x increases to the right, and y increases as you go down

7 (x-1,y-1)	0 (x,y-1)	4 (x+1,y-1)
3 (x-1,y)	(x,y)	1 (x+1,y)
6 (x-1,y+1)	2 (x,y+1)	5 (x+1,y+1)

Figure 34: The coordinates of the 8-connected neighbours

We can use these coordinates with the direction-number we already obtained from the random generated function to choose a new x-coordinate value by creating a new function to provide us with a new value for x:

```
int newX(int x, int direction){
   switch(direction){
      case 1: case 4: case 5:{ //E, NE, SE
         ++x;
         break;
      }
      case 3: case 6: case 7:{ //W, SW, NW
         --x;
         break;
      }
   }
   // bounce off the boundaries of the grid
   if (x > width){
      --x;
   }
```

```
    else
    if (x < 0){
        ++x;
    }
    return x;
}
```

We can do the same with the y-coordinate

```
int newY(int y, int direction){
    switch(direction){
        case 0: case 4: case 7:{ //N, NE, NW
            --y;
            break;
        }
        case 2: case 5: case 6:{ //S, SE, SW
            ++y;
            break;
        }
    }
    if (y > height){
      --y;
    }
    else
    if (y < 0){
        ++y;
    }
    return y;
}
```

We have used a switch statement, but you could have achieved the same thing using an if statement There are several cases for each action. For example, if the direction is 2, 5 or 6, y is incremented.

The nice thing about using a switch statement is that it easily and clearly accommodates both a newDirection4 function and a newDirection8 function, because of the order in which we arranged the cases. You can choose which kind of connectedness you want to use.

Also notice that the last thing we did in these functions was to use the rules to ensure that our walker doesn't get to wander off our grid. Once we've got a new point, we plot it! That's almost all we need, we just need to connect all our code together to create a sketch

```
// Number of points to plot before you change direction.
```

```
final int STRIDE = 4;

void setup(){
    size(500, 500);
    background(0);
    stroke(#ff00ff); // Colour used to plot
    strokeWeight(1); // pixel size
    walk(50000);
}

// Plot points for a number of iterations.
void walk(int steps){
    // Start at middle of the grid.
    int x = width/2;
    int y = height/2;
    int direction = newDirection4(); // Random direction.

    for(int i = 0; i < steps; i++){
        if(i % STRIDE == 0){ //time to change direction (maybe)
            // You can use newDirection4() or newDirection8() here.
            direction = newDirection8();
        }
        x = newX(x, direction);
        y = newY(y, direction);
        point(x,y); // Plot that point.
    } // Repeat for value of steps variable
}
```

The sketch plots points the number of times specified in the walk() function, in our case 50,000! The effect of this can be seen in Figure 35. We have done this in static mode, so the graphics appear already 'walked'. You might try changing the code so you can see the walking by adding a draw() function

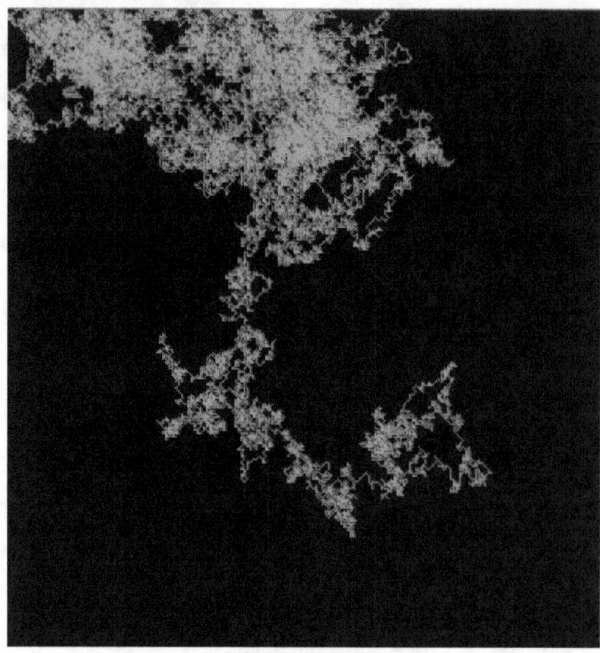

Figure 35: Random walking with stride 2, connectedness 8

If you add the above code to the functions we already created for calculating direction and coordinates you will be able to run the sketch and see the results of the random walking. Try changing some of the variables such as colour, stride length and connectedness

Chapter 12: Colour

by Richard Brown and Rob Spain

This chapter looks at how colour is perceived by humans, how it is displayed on a hardware device such as an LCD screen and then shows how *Processing* can be used to display coloured pixels. We will explore the various functions in *Processing* that allow you to control and manipulate colour

Light and Colour

We see light due to the tissue on the retina, inside the back of our eyes, being stimulated by the arrival of light energy. Through the nervous response of those retinal cell structures, called rods and cones, we perceive the radiated energy in the visible frequency band as light.

Light is emitted over many frequencies from various sources such as the sun, lightning or fire and maybe reflected by objects before it hits our eyes. Our eyes have developed to pick up different frequencies of light by developing three types of cones that can detect different wavelengths; short (blue), medium (green) and long (yellow-red) wavelengths. The frequency is interpreted by our brains as colour and, due to this, colour images can be produced by varying the levels of these wavelengths. Computer and video screens make use of this effect and modulate the output from only pure red, green and blue pixels to create a full spectrum of colour.

Computer monitors, televisions and digital projector systems all display very small patterns of pure red, green and blue light. The response in our eyes and brains work together to mix those fine arrays of red, green and blue, producing a wide spectrum of colour. Each pixel on the screen can be individually switched on or off and adjusted to have a range of brightness in between. The mechanism differs for different screen types (for example between LED and LCD) but the effect is the same. These don't represent the full visible range but are sufficient to give a range of colour that they can simulate the original, for example with digital photographs.

Since our eyes have sensitive cones centred roughly in the wavelength bands we call red, green and blue and since the monitor will use pure red, blue and green illumination to stimulate them, it is perfectly reasonable to also store and process digitised colour values within a computer in terms of their red, green and blue sub-components. Modern computers can process and store data in variations of each of red, green and blue that has been found to provide enough resolution to satisfy the human eye's colour acuity.

Processing and Colour

Processing uses a primitive data type called color (note the American spelling) to store the subcomponents of each of red, green and blue (this colour system is known as RGB- Red, Green, Blue) and a further subcomponent to store a value called alpha that represents the opacity (or transparency) of the RGB colour.

color datatypes are declared using any of the following syntax variations:

```
color(greyvalue);
color(greyvalue, alpha);
color(redvalue, greenvalue, bluevalue);
color(redvalue, greenvalue, bluevalue, alpha);
color(hex);
color(hex, alpha);
```

All of the values are integers but values outside the range of 0 to 255 will be clipped at those limits (so entering 500 will end up as 255 for example). The color() function will create and return a color type that can be used in arguments to other functions such as background()

If the three values of RGB are equal in value the resultant "colour" is a shade of grey. *Processing* allows a shorthand argument form where the value for all of RGB is presented just once. In the list above greyvalue can range from 0 (black) to 255 (white). To specify ranges of colours outside this range you have to give the three arguments for RBG. Some examples are shown in Table 9

hex is a string format presented using the 6 digit hexadecimal format of #rrggbb (the same pattern as specifying HTML or CSS colours) or, alternatively, the hexadecimal formatted 8 digit string syntax: 0xaarrggbb where alpha is represented by the first two hex characters.

Each of the syntax types has a variant that allows the alpha to be specified. The default alpha value is 255 or fully opaque. Lower values allow some background or lower layers to be visible through this object when graphics are placed on top of each other

Red	Green	Blue	Colour
0	0	0	Black
0	0	255	Blue
0	255	0	Green
0	255	255	Cyan
255	0	0	Red
255	0	255	Magenta
255	255	0	Yellow
255	255	255	White

Table 9: Simple RGB colours

Since each of the three RGB components can be varied from 0 to 255 giving each 256 or 2^8 variations. The RGB model can therefore represent 256 x 256 x 256 or 2^{24} possible colours. That gives more than 16 million individually specifiable colours. This exceeds the ability of the eye/brain to distinguish colour variations.

You might like to try some colour variations by setting them as a background() argument, for example:

```
color c = color(255, 255, 0);
background(c);
```

Some more colours you might try are shown in Table 10

Red	Green	Blue	Colour
128	128	128	Mid Grey
100	100	250	Mid Blue
20	60	20	Olive Green
255	100	0	Orange
0	0	40	Navy Blue
160	240	230	Eggshell Blue
70	0	10	Crimson
255	210	210	Pink

Table 10 More RGB colours

Alpha Transparency

As mentioned, as part of the colour you can set the alpha transparency which determines how transparent (or opaque, depending on how you look at it) the colour is. The value is relative to the range of the colour so for the RGB model, where the maximum value is 255, then 255/2 (127.5) is 50% opaque, so 255 is totally opaque and 0 is totally transparent

Colour Modes

Though the RGB colour scheme is more widely known, *Processing* allows colours to be described using two quite distinct numerical models: RGB and HSB (Hue, Saturation, Brightness) using the colorMode() function which takes the forms

```
colorMode(mode);
colorMode(mode, max);
colorMode(mode, max1, max2, max3);
colorMode(mode, max1, max2, max3, maxA);
```

The first argument, mode, is one of the colour mode variables given by *Processing* RGB or HSB. The max variables refer to the maximum value you can specify (the default is 255 as you previously saw with RGB). This means you can set a higher or lower value for hue, saturation and brightness (or red, green blue if using RGB) if you wish. The maxA argument refers to the alpha transparency value. Examples of setting colour mode are

```
colorMode(RGB);
colorMode(HSB, 100);
colorMode(HSB, 360, 100, 100);
```

Once the colour mode is set, you use the color function as usual. However HSB is a very different way of looking at colours. Instead of specifying in color(red, green, blue) you have to think in terms of color(hue, saturation, brightness)

The hue by convention ranges from 0 to 360 degrees. Hue is the 'colour' of the colour. For example, red and yellow are different hues, but red and pink are the same hue. Each hue represents a distinct color. The HSB hue range is from 0 (red), 120 (yellow), 180 (green) to 240 (blue).

The saturation represents the strength of colour and is commonly referred to as a percentage value scale where 0 represents no colour, and 100 represents the full colour. All greyscales 'colours' have zero colour. A pastel colour such as rose pink has a low saturation, whereas a bold colour such as fire engine red has a high saturation.

Brightness again normally specified on a scale from 0 to 100. White has maximum brightness (value = 100) while black has minimum brightness (value = 0). In the HSB model, hue and saturation values have little or no visible effect at extreme levels, either black or white.

You can, if you need to extract the components of a colour. The six functions below called with a color datatype as an argument will return the value of that component.

```
red(color);
green(color);
blue(color);
hue(color);
saturation(color);
brightness(color);
```

For example

```
colorMode(RGB);
color c = color(255, 0, 0);
float redValue = red(c);
println(redValue);
```

will result in the value 255.0 (the decimal point is because it is a float type). You could use these in a sketch to, for example, increase brightness. The code below accesses the hue, saturation and brightness of the current background colour and increases the brightness. If you run this you should see the background progressively get brighter

```
color c;
void setup() {
    colorMode(HSB);
    c = color(0);
}

void draw() {
    background(c);
    float hue = hue(c);
    float saturation = saturation(c);
    float brightness = brightness(c) + 1;
    c = color(hue, saturation, brightness);
}
```

In order to show you how the colour mode can affect a sketch, you can try changing the colour mode on the following code which simply draws points with differing colours based on the coordinates

```
size(200,200);
colorMode(RGB); // try changing to HSB
// for each x coordinate
for (int i = 0; i < 200; i++) {
    // for each y coordinate
    for (int j = 0; j < 200; j++) {
        // set the colour
        stroke(color(i, j, i + j));
        // draw a dot at the coordinates
        point(i,j);
    }
}
```

The output from this, as shown in Figure 36, in RGB colour mode is very different from the HSB colour mode output with no changes to the code other than colour mode

Figure 36: Colours in RGB colour mode (left) and HSB colour mode (right)

Colour Functions

We will now look at some of the functions that *Processing* provides for manipulating colours - blendColor() and lerpColor()

Blending Colour

Blending colour, using the blendColor() function, provides a simple method of combing two colours to create a new one. For example if we add together red and green we will see yellow as you would expect. The function takes the form

```
blendColor(colour, colour2, mode);
```

where the mode is how you want to manipulate the colours. We will use ADD which adds the two colours together to create a new colour as in this example

```
color red = color(255,0,0);
color green = color(0,255,0);
color redAddGreen = blendColor(red,green,ADD);
```

The example code below demonstrates this by colouring points

```
size(300, 300);
color red = color(255,0,0);
color green = color(0,255,0);
color redAddGreen = blendColor(red,green,ADD);
// for each x coordinate
for (int i = 0; i < 300; i++) {
 // for each y coordinate
 for (int j = 0; j < 300; j++) {
 // set the colour
 if (i < 100) {
  stroke(red);
```

```
 } else if (i < 200) {
  stroke(green);
 } else if (i < 300) {
  stroke(redAddGreen);
 }
 // draw a dot at the coordinates
 point(i,j);
 }
}
```

To understand exactly how this works to create a new colour, consider the way colours are defined.

When we write

```
color red = color(255,0,0);
```

We're creating a colour with a red component of 255, a green component of 0 and a blue component of 0.

Not surprisingly the colour is pure red. When we use blendColor() to ADD a colour, it adds each of the components to create a new colour with those components. So in our example, adding red and green, we are adding components (255,0,0) and (0,255,0). blendColor() combines these to form a new colour with the components (255,255,0) which corresponds to yellow. These can be seen in Figure 37

As well as the ADD blending we used, there are also other blend modes that allow you to create new colours from existing ones including SUBTRACT, MULTIPLY, LIGHTEST and DARKEST

Figure 37: Pixels coloured by blending red and green

Linear Interpolation

Linear interpolation is the means to find a point between two other points at a defined increment. So linear interpolation, in the strangely named lerpColor() function, is the means to find the colour between two other colours. The function takes the form

```
lerpColor(colour1, colour2, interpolationAmount);
```

where the `interpolationAmount` is a float between 0.0 and 1.0, with 0.5 as the midway point between the two, for example

```
color black = color(0);
color white = color(255);
float interpolationAmount = 0.5;
```

The code below demonstrates the function by calculating the points in order to display a graduation between the two colours

```
size(300, 300);
color black = color(0);
color white = color(255);
float interpolationAmount = 1.0 / height;
// for each x coordinate
for (int i = 0; i < 300; i++) {
   // for each y coordinate
   for (int j = 0; j < 300; j++) {
      // set the colour
```

```
      stroke(lerpColor(black,white,interpolationAmount*i));
      // draw a dot at the coordinates
      point(i,j);
   }
}
```

Here each iteration of the loop advances the interpolation on a little by using the loop counter, so the colour gradually changes and moves from one colour to the other giving a graduated effect as shown in Figure 38

Figure 38: Graduated effect using lerpColor()

Chapter 13: Lines
by Martin Humby and Rosie Wood

This Chapter examines the nature of lines and how they can be used to create graphics using the line drawing facilities provided by *Processing*. We will look at traditional straight lines and also examine how lines can be used to create more complex graphics such as curves

Lines and Pixels

Drawing a line may seem very simple, and it can be using the facilities of *Processing*, but *Processing* hides from us the complexity of line drawing in computer displays so first we will look at how lines are drawn

As we have seen, pixels are arranged in grids and the smallest part of any display we can draw in is a single pixel. This is fine for lines drawn parallel to the x and y axes, straight up-and-down or left-to-right lines, but for lines with any other angle, diagonal lines, this represents a problem.

Since pixels are largely square, drawing a diagonal line means choosing which pixels best represents a line with the required angle, as shown in Figure 39. Imagine if you, as the programmer, had to decide which pixels to fill in to create the line; you would need a lot of pixels and also have the task of working out how to best represent the line. Luckily Jack Bresenham already solved these problems (in 1962) and most line drawing methods either incorporate Bresenham's line algorithm or owe something to it. Even luckier for us, *Processing* hides the complexity of the algorithm from us with a simple `line()` function

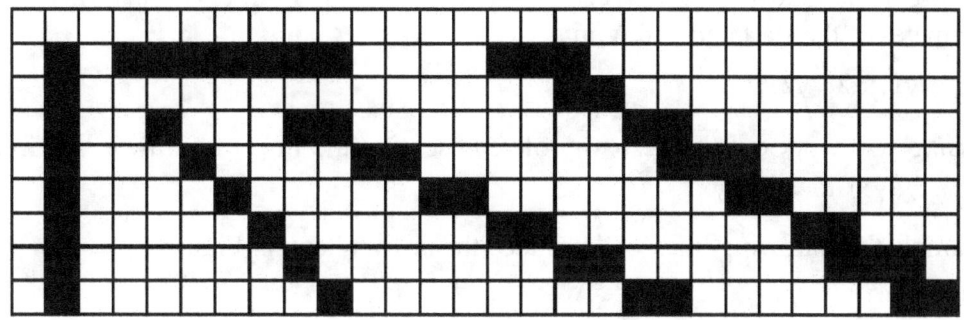

Figure 39: Lines drawn over pixels at different angles

Lines in *Processing* are represented by two sets of coordinates. Figure 40 shows a line that joins the coordinates (1,3) and (3,5). The two points specify the line. They show that it's a short line and has two end points in that it does not continue on past the two end points.

135

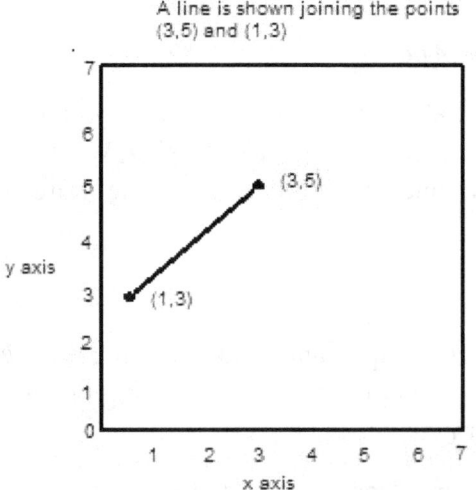

Figure 40: A line within the coordinate system

When drawing lines you should remember that *Processing* has a coordinate system which is completely different to those in use in mathematics. The point (0,0) does not start at the bottom left-hand corner but at the top left-hand corner.

You can specify any coordinates for a line, it will stretch infinitely though specifying coordinates beyond the confines of the screen means you won't see anything that goes past the edge of the screen

The line() Function

Processing's line function is relatively simple; it takes four arguments specifying the x and y coordinates of the start and end points

```
line(x1, y1, x2, y2);
```

Processing will work out the best way of representing the line and draw a line from the point `(x1, y1)` to `(x2, y2)`.

For example the following lines will produce the arrow shape in Figure 41

```
size(300,300);
line(50, 50, 200, 50); // horizontal
line(50, 50, 50, 200); // vertical
line(50, 50, 200, 200); // diagonal
```

Figure 41: Arrow shape made from lines

Line Style

There are three functions that set the 'style' of the line that will be drawn by the next and subsequent calls to `line()`. The effect of calling any one of these functions remains in place until the same function is called again. These functions allow you to set the line colour, line thickness and determine the shape of the end of the line. We will look at these in turn

Line Colour

Line colour can be set by using the `stroke()` function. The function takes as arguments the colour you want the line to be, either by using the `color` type itself, or by using the RGB/HSB values as previously seen, for example

```
stroke(0); // black
line(10, 10, 90, 10);
stroke(255, 0, 0); // red
line(10, 50, 90, 50);
color green = color(0, 255, 0);
stroke(green);
line(10, 90, 90, 90);
```

Line Thickness

Line thickness can be controlled using the strokeWeight() function which sets the 'weight' of the line

```
strokeWeight(1); // thin
line(10, 10, 90, 10);
strokeWeight(5); // thicker
line(10, 50, 90, 50);
strokeWeight(10); // even thicker
line(10, 90, 90, 90);
```

The weight is set in pixels with a default weight of 1, using a float, so it is technically possible to have a line half a pixel wide. Figure 42 shows the difference in line weights created by the sketch code

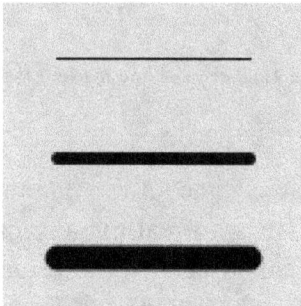

Figure 42: Line weights

Line Shape

You can also change the way lines are displayed by specifying what the ends of the lines look like using the strokeCap() function.

```
strokeWeight(15);
strokeCap(ROUND);
line(10, 10, 90, 10);
strokeCap(SQUARE);
line(10, 50, 90, 50);
strokeCap(PROJECT);
line(10, 90, 90, 90);
```

This function sets what the end of the line should look like with a choice of ROUND (rounded ends, the default), SQUARE (square ends) or PROJECT (ends that project beyond the end of the line). The different line endings can be seen in Figure 43

Figure 43: Line ends

Drawing Lines

A simple example of line drawing is to create a sketch that uses the line drawing facilities within *Processing* to produce an animation that involves the continual drawing of a series of random lines. Each line will have two sets of random end-points, a random colour and a random thickness or stroke.

```
int startX;
int finishX;
int startY;
int finishY;
int lineColour;

void setup(){
 //set up a white window background and size 400x400
 size(400,400);
 background(255);
}

void draw(){
    //Draw a set of random lines
    startX = round(random(400));
    startY = round(random(400));
    finishX = round(random(400));
    finishY = round(random(400));
    strokeWeight(random(10));
    stroke(random(255),random(255),random(255));
    line(startX, startY,finishX, finishY);
}
```

Here the endpoints of the lines are randomly generated (the maximum values are 400; this matches the size of the window) and then the width (stroke) of the line is set followed by a random value of colour for the line. Finally the line is drawn using the `line()` function. The output of your sketch might look something like that shown in Figure 44

Figure 44: Lines with random length, colour and thickness

Drawing Grids

The effect of drawing a single line tends to be minimal and it is more likely that many lines will be needed to produce a required effect. As a practical example of drawing lines we will now create a sketch that draws a grid as shown in Figure 45. This can be achieved fairly simply by drawing lines at given intervals to create a grid-like structure

We will firstly need to work out how far apart to draw the lines by calculating the width of each cell in the grid.

```
float xCells = 13; // number of cells horizontally
float yCells = 19; // number of cells vertically
// compute cell width
float cellWidth = width / xCells;
// compute cell height
float cellHeight = height / yCells;
```

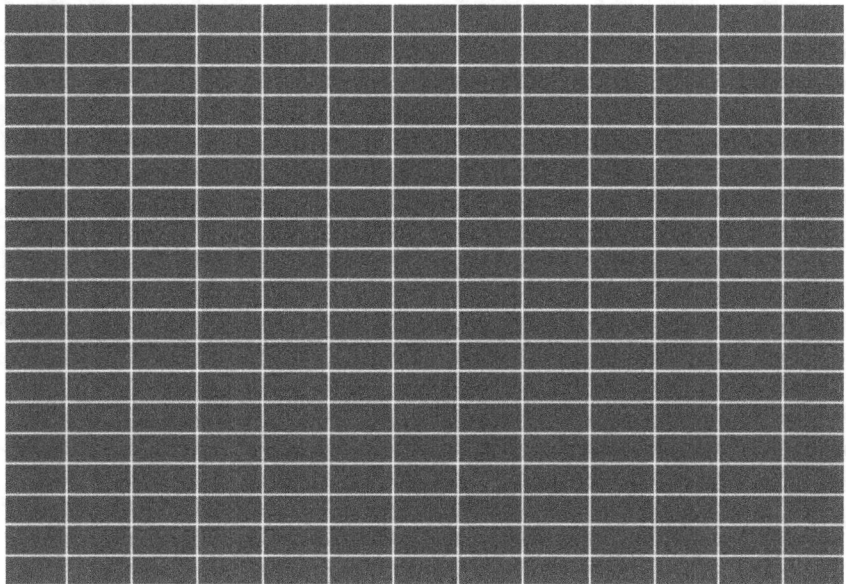

Figure 45: Grid drawn using lines

This code calculates the width and height of each cell given the number of cells we want to draw, which are held in variables so we can change them later if we wish. So the width of each cell is the width divided by the number we want to display, and similarly with the height.

We then need to draw all the lines and, since this is a repetitive call to draw each line, we can use loops to work out the location of each one and call the line() function. The loop to draw the vertical lines might look like the code below

```
// draw the vertical lines
for (float x = cellWidth; x < width; x += cellWidth) {
    // x is the x-coordinate of the vertical line drawn in the window
    line(x, 0, x, height);
}
```

We start the loop at the left of the grid so the loop variable x is declared and initialised to draw the first line at cellWidth. We end the loop when the width is reached so we don't continue to draw lines beyond the border of the displayable area, so the loop continues while x < width. For each loop iteration we add cellWidth to the loop variable using the shorthand += operator to take it to the coordinate of the next grid line so the value of x is now cellWidth larger than before meaning we can draw the line there. The function that draws horizontal grid lines is similar.

```
float xCells = 13; // number of cells horizontally
float yCells = 19; // number of cells vertically
```

```
void setup() {
    size(900, 600);
    background(0.25 * 255); // charcoal grey
    stroke(255); // white grid lines
    strokeWeight(2);
    // draw a grid with number of cells xCells * yCells
    drawGrid();
}

// all the grid drawing code is in here
void drawGrid() {
    // compute cell width
    float cellWidth = width / xCells;
    // compute cell height
    float cellHeight = height / yCells;

    // draw the vertical lines
    for (float x = cellWidth; x < width; x += cellWidth) {
        // x is the x-coordinate of the vertical line drawn in the window
        line(x, 0, x, height);
    }

    // draw the horizontal lines
    for (float y = cellHeight; y < height; y += cellHeight) {
        // y is the y-coordinate of the horizontal line drawn in the window
        line(0, y, width, y);
    }
}
```

You might try changing the variables that determine how many cells are drawn and you should see that the sketch calculates the optimum cell size to fit them onto the screen

Curved Lines

You may remember from Geometry lessons at school that placing lines correctly on squared paper produces curves. To jog your memory, we will repeat the lesson and place lines along the x and y axes of a grid but we will be using *Processing*, instead of squared paper and a sharp pencil. Figure 46 was created by drawing straight lines with each at a greater angle than the next, the effect of which is the appearance of a curve

Some fairly simple code is all that is needed to draw this as shown below

```
int n=0;
```

```
void setup() {
    size(400, 400);
    strokeWeight(1);
    background(255);
    frameRate(5);
}

void draw() {
    line(0, n, n+10, height);
    // move where the line is drawn
    n+=10;
}
```

As you can see, there is very little effort needed to draw this which shows the power of computer-generated graphics over traditional paper and pen methods. All we do is incrementally increase the angle of the lines by adding 10 pixels to n, and drawing the line from the left of the screen. We specified a slower frame rate so you can see what is going on

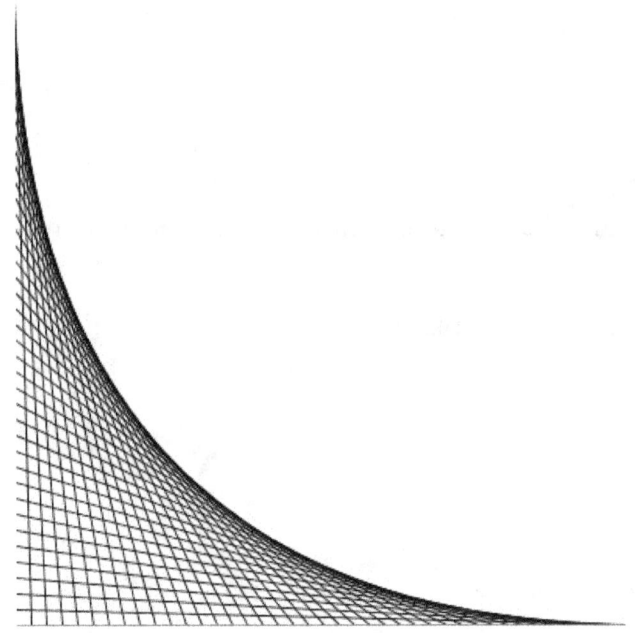

Figure 46: Curve drawn from straight lines

We might now decide to repeat the exercise, in the other three corners of our screen. Fortunately we have a pattern to guide us, in the code we just created

```
line(0, n, n+10, height);
```

We can see that the pattern starts at zero across and a variable n down, which increases by ten each time the draw function is executed. The line-end coordinate is the value of n+10 and is always the height of the screen downwards. To make our next pattern at the bottom right corner we know the first coordinate should start at the width of the screen across and have n pixels down. On each iteration, the point should have a variable number across and a fixed value equal to the height of the screen. If we are careful not to hardcode (that is, set to a specific value rather than letting the code calculate it) any of the integers used to draw our sketch, this will mean our code can run in any size of window.

Try to calculate the statements needed to draw the other three patterns to achieve an effect like that in Figure 47 (our new draw() function includes them below if you need them). You might also add a function to change the stroke colour each time the draw loop repeats

```
void draw() {
    // random colour
    stroke(random(255), random(255), random(255));
    line(0, n, n+10, height); // bottom left
    line(width, n, width-n+10, height); // bottom right
    line(0, n, width-n+10, 0); // top left
    line(width, n, n+10, 0); // top right
    // move where the line is drawn
    n+=10;
}
```

Symmetrical Patterns

We can use a minor modification to our curved lines sketch to produce some interesting effects using just lines

The basis for our symmetric patterns code looks like the one below

```
int lineSpacing = 20;

void setup() {
    size(400, 400);
    strokeWeight(1);
    background(255);
    stroke(random(255), random(255), random(255));
}

void draw() {
    for (int x=0;x < width+1;x+=lineSpacing) {
        for (int y=0;y < height+1;y+=lineSpacing) {
            drawLine(x, y);
```

```
      }
    }
}

void drawLine(int x, int y) {
}
```

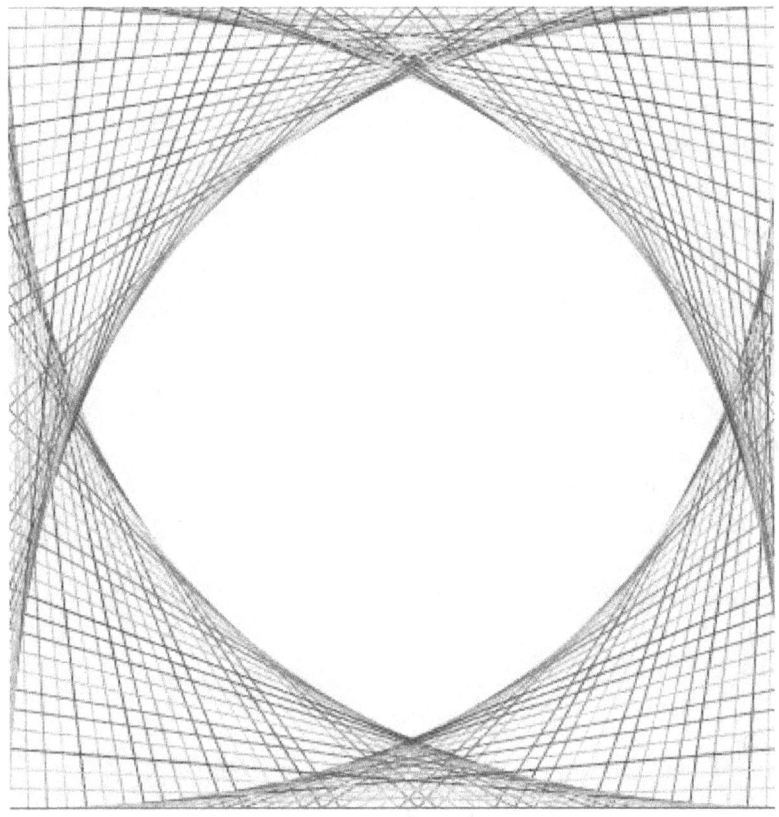

Figure 47: Curves in all four corners

As you can see, this is similar to the curved line sketch we created but we have added a nested loop with separate x and y coordinates and the ability to change the spacing between lines with the lineSpacing and lineSpacing variables. We've also extracted the actual line drawing into a new function, drawLine(), which is currently empty but we will place the calls to line() in here. There is no technical reason to do this, it is simply to make the code more readable by creating a single place that the line code can go

The simplest symmetrical pattern would use a single line which, when run, will produce a star-like effect as shown in Figure 48

```
void drawLine(int x, int y) {
```

```
    line(x, y, width-x, height-y);//star
}
```

You can also add extra lines and alter the line spacing to achieve different effects. Try any of the examples or try altering the line spacing and adding your own lines to see what effects you can create just using lines

```
int lineSpacing = 10;
// radiating star effect
line(x,height,width-x,0);
line(0,y,width,height-y);
```

produces a radiating star effect

```
int lineSpacing = 50;
 // stitched effect
line(x, height, y, 0);
line(height, height-y, 0, x);
```

produces a stitched effect

```
int lineSpacing = 20;
// flower effect
line(0, height-y, y, y);
line(0, y, y, height-y);
line(width, height-y, y, y);
line(width, y, y, height-y);
line(x, 0, width-x, x);
line(x, height, width-x, x);
line(width-x, 0, x, x);
line(width-x, height, x, x);
```

produces a flower effect

All of these effects can be seen in Figure 48

Figure 48: Symmetric patterns using lines

Chapter 14: Shapes
by Boyd Stratton, Dušan Ličer and Sharon Dawes

This Chapter introduces *Processing*'s built-in shape functions for creating rectangles, quadrilaterals, ellipses, arcs and triangles, and looks at how they can be used for creating computer graphics. We then look at how *Processing* can be used to transform shapes including moving, rotating and resizing them

One of the easiest ways to create a shape in *Processing* is to use the basic 2D shape drawing functions. *Processing* has built-in functions for creating rectangles, quadrilaterals, ellipses, arcs and triangles

Rectangles

Rectangles are created in *Processing* using the rect() function. The basic function requires four arguments to draw a rectangle which define the start coordinates, the width and the height in pixels. You can create an equilateral rectangle (a square) by using the same width and height

```
rect(x, y, a, b);
```

The way the values are interpreted depends on the current mode of the rectangle which, by default is CORNER, which specifies that the first two arguments passed to rect() are the top-left corner and the next two arguments are the width and height, in pixels, respectively. The below code will therefore draw a rectangle starting at point (10, 10) with a width of 70 pixels and a height of 50 pixels as shown in Figure 49

```
rect(10, 10, 70, 50);
```

Figure 49: A Rectangle

The mode is changed using the rectMode() function for which there are four possible values:

- CORNER - x and y are the top-left corner coordinates, a and b are the width and height
- CENTER - x and y are the centre coordinates, a and b are the width and height

- CORNERS - x and y are the top-left coordinates, a and b are the bottom-right coordinates
- RADIUS - x and y are the centre coordinates, a and b are the width and height

The code below draws four rectangles, passing the same arguments to each rect() call, but changing the rectMode() each time to show the effect a prior call to rectMode() has on a subsequent call to rect().

```
int x = 300;
int y = 200;
int a = 150;
int b = 100;
size(600,400);

noStroke(); // remove borders
fill(255); //The white rectangle
rectMode(RADIUS);
rect(x, y, a, b);

fill(0,0,255,150); //The blue rectangle
rectMode(CORNER);
rect(x, y, a, b);

stroke(0); // add border
fill(0,255,0,150); //The green rectangle
rectMode(CENTER);
rect(x, y, a, b);

strokeWeight(2); // increase border size
fill(255,0,0,150); //The red rectangle
rectMode(CORNERS);
rect(x, y, a, b);
```

Figure 50 shows the rectangle function responding to the fill() function which specifies the fill colour of the rectangle; we have also specified some transparency in the fill() function calls to make it clear in the diagram where each rectangle overlaps. The noStroke() function removes the boundary of the rectangle entirely. The colour of the border can be specified with the stroke() function, and the weight (thickness) of the border can be increased by using the strokeWeight() function, the default is 1 pixel

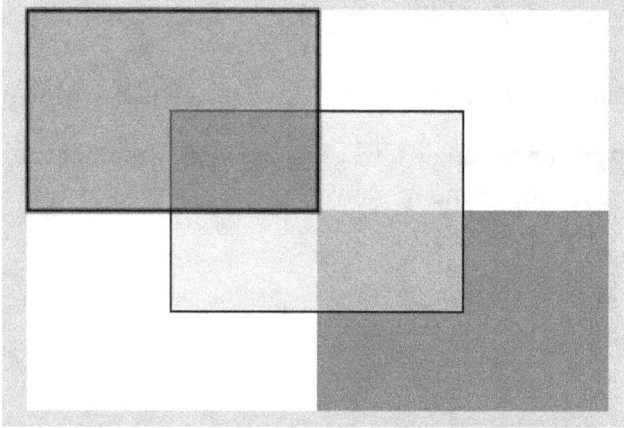

Figure 50: Rectangles with different modes and borders

Rectangle Corners

Processing also has overloaded `rect()` functions that allow you to create rounded rectangles which can be used on rectangles in any rectangle mode

```
rect(x, y, a, b, r);
rect(x, y, a, b, r1, r2, r3, r4);
```

The first function allowed you to specify the radius r of the rounded corner, in pixels, which is applied to all four corners. The second allows you to specify the radius of *each* corner so that you can have differently shaped corners if you wish

To demonstrate this we can apply this to a version of our previous code

```
int x = 300;
int y = 200;
int a = 150;
int b = 100;
size(600,400);

fill(0,0,255,150); //The blue rectangle
rectMode(CORNER);
rect(x, y, a, b, 10);

stroke(0); // add border
fill(0,255,0,150); //The green rectangle
rectMode(CENTER);
rect(x, y, a, b, 20, 30, 40, 50);

fill(255,0,0,150); //The red rectangle
```

```
rectMode(CORNERS);
rect(x, y, a, b);
```

In Figure 51 you should be able to see the rounded corners; the red rectangle has perpendicular corners as before, the blue rectangle has symmetrical corners and the green rectangle has corners with different radii

Figure 51: Rectangles with rounded corners

Quadrilaterals

While the rect() function is useful, it is only able to draw rectangles (or squares if you have symmetrical dimensions) but not any other quadrilaterals such as rhombus, kite or any custom 4-sided shape you might want to draw. This is where the quad() function is used

```
quad(x1, y1, x2, y2, x3, y3, x4, y4);
```

This function can draw any quadrilateral shape by specifying the coordinates of the corners where the lines intersect (known as a *vertex*, plural *vertices*). The coordinates start with the top-left (x1, y1) and proceed in sequence (either clockwise or anti-clockwise depending on whether they are to the left or right of the first coordinates). The code below will draw a parallelogram as shown in Figure 52

```
quad(10, 10, 70, 10, 90, 50, 30, 50);
```

Using coordinates you can create any quadrilateral you require including rectangles! You may wonder why *Processing* has the rect() function if quad() can be used. Rectangles are a specific type of quadrilateral and probably the most frequently used, so they represents a specialisation of the quad() function. The rect() function is simplified in that you only

151

need specify one or two sets of coordinates, so it is easier to use. It also allows *Processing* to provide specialised features such as the rounded corners

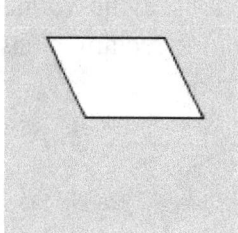

Figure 52: A Parallelogram

Ellipses

Ellipses can be thought of as ovals, where an equilateral ellipse is a circle, and are drawn using the `ellipse()` function which is similar to the `rect()` function, except of course it draw ellipses

```
ellipse(x, y, a, b);
```

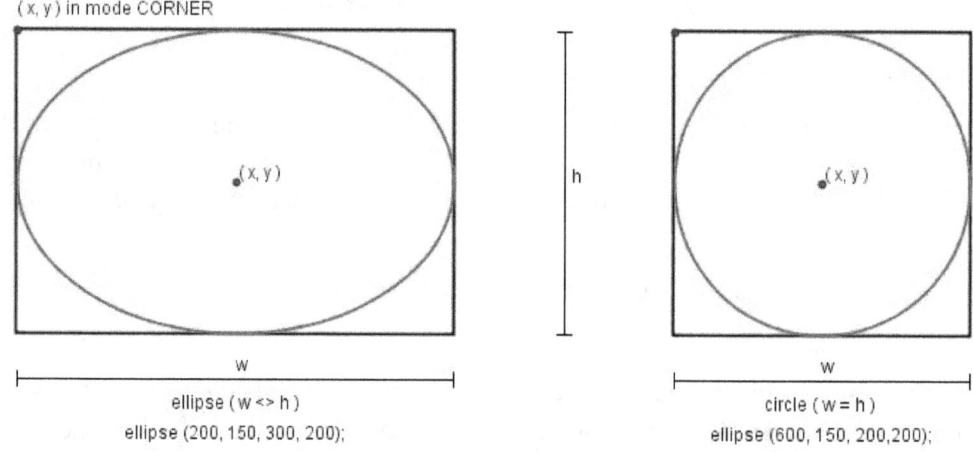

Figure 53: Ellipses Examples

The ellipse and the circle in Figure 53 can be drawn by the following sequence of statements in *Processing*

```
size(800,400);
background(255);
smooth();
```

```
noFill();
strokeWeight(2);
stroke(255,0,0); //use red colour
ellipse (200, 150, 300, 200); //draw ellipse
ellipse (600, 150, 200,200); //draw circle
```

We can observe that a circle is just a special case of an ellipse, with equal width and height. Furthermore, w and h represent the width and the height of the rectangle bounding the ellipse. An ellipse can be drawn in different modes that can be altered by the ellipseMode() function, similarly to the rectMode() we have already seen. The default mode is CENTER. All possible modes are:

- CENTER - x and y are the centre coordinates of the ellipse, a and b are the width and height diameter
- RADIUS - x and y are the centre coordinates of the ellipse, a and b are the width and height radius
- CORNER - x and y are the top-left coordinates of the bounding rectangle, a and b are the width and height diameter
- CORNERS - x and y are the top-left coordinates of the bounding rectangle, a and b are the bottom-right coordinates of the bounding rectangle

To demonstrate we can take our rectangle code and simply change rect() to ellipse(), and rectMode() to ellipseMode() with no other modifications

```
int x = 300;
int y = 200;
int a = 150;
int b = 100;
size(600,400);

noStroke(); // remove borders
fill(255); //The white rectangle
ellipseMode(RADIUS);
ellipse(x, y, a, b);

fill(0,0,255,150); //The blue rectangle
ellipseMode(CORNER);
ellipse(x, y, a, b);

stroke(0); // add border
fill(0,255,0,150); //The green rectangle
ellipseMode(CENTER);
ellipse(x, y, a, b);
```

```
strokeWeight(2); // increase border size
fill(255,0,0,150); //The red rectangle
ellipseMode(CORNERS);
ellipse(x, y, a, b);
```

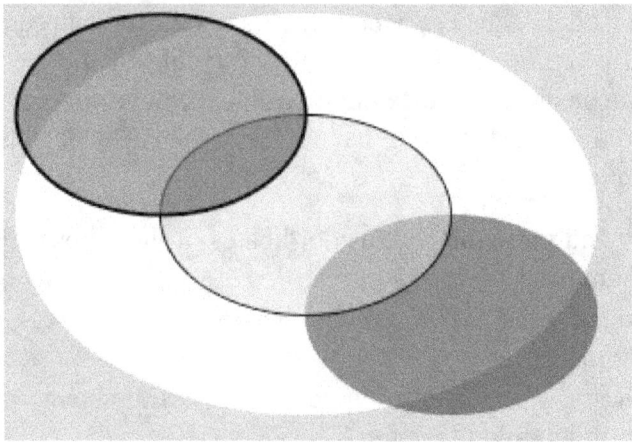

Figure 54: Ellipses with different ellipse modes

The notion of there being a corner (and corners) mode for an ellipse function may sound a little strange, so as an example we can draw a rectangle around a couple of the circles from our previous example

```
int x = 300;
int y = 200;
int a = 150;
int b = 100;
size(600,400);

fill(255); //The white rectangle
ellipseMode(RADIUS);
ellipse(x, y, a, b);
noFill();
rectMode(RADIUS);
rect(x, y, a, b);

fill(255,0,0,150); //The red rectangle
ellipseMode(CORNERS);
ellipse(x, y, a, b);
noFill();
rectMode(CORNERS);
rect(x, y, a, b);
```

As you can see from Figure 55, drawing a rectangle at the same coordinates as the ellipse creates a rectangular boundary that fits neatly around the ellipse. This is known as the *bounding rectangle*. Since this rectangle has corners, these are the corners referred to in the ellipse modes

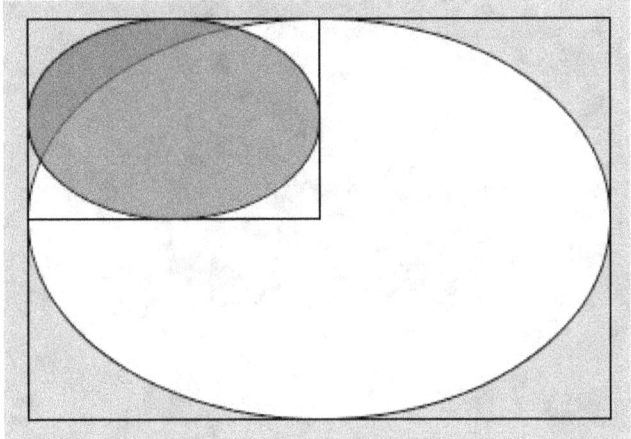

Figure 55: Ellipses and their bounding rectangles

We can use the coloured ellipses to create an interesting gradient effect, shown in Figure 56, by drawing a number of concentric circles with decreasing radii.

```
int numberOfShapes = 6; // The number of ellipses to draw
int startRadius = 45; // The radius multiplier between neighbouring ellipses

void setup() {
    size(800,600);
    ellipseMode(RADIUS); // Set the ellipse mode to be RADIUS
    noStroke(); // no borders
}

void draw() {
    //Loop through the shapes
    for(int i = numberOfShapes; i > 0; i--) {
        // scale the red channel from full red (255) to black (0)
        float redAmount = (i-1)*(float)255/(numberOfShapes-1);
        fill(redAmount, 0, 0);
        // shrink the radius
        float radius = i*startRadius;
        ellipse(width/2, height/2, radius, radius);
    }
}
```

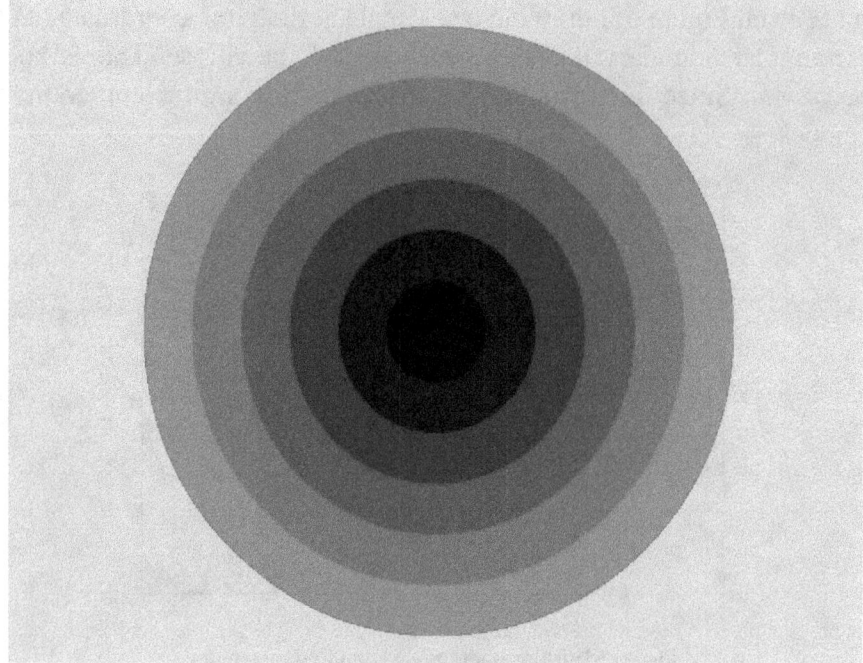

Figure 56: Concentric circles

The colour change is achieved by calculating how much red to use. The calculation `redAmount` divides full red (255) by `numberOfsShapes-1` to give us the linear amount of red we will change by on each iteration. The '-1' is required since the first iteration through the loop *(when i=0)* will give a redAmount of 0, so we must scale the rest of the red channel across `numberOfsShapes-1`, rather than `numberOfShapes`.

As the loop iterates the colour change is multiplied by i-1 to adjust the colour on each iteration. As we want to get to zero by the end of the loop we use i-1 rather than i.

To demonstrate a more subtle gradient change, a simple change of the two variables `numberOfShapes` and `startRadius` as follows, give the result in the image shown in Figure 57.

```
int NUMSHAPES = 90;   // The number of ellipses to draw
int startRadius = 3; // The radius multiplier between neighbouring ellipses
```

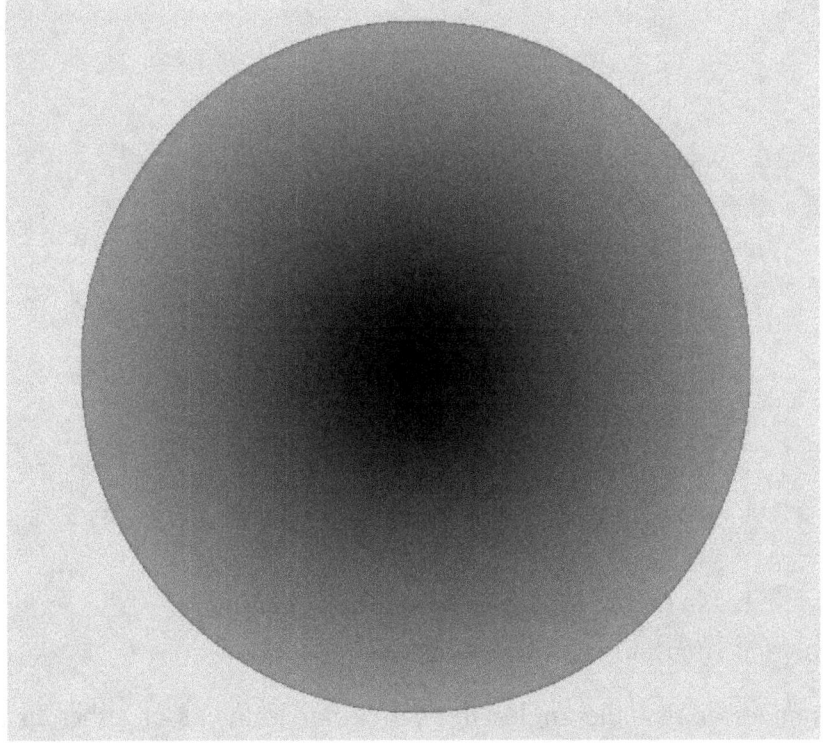

Figure 57: Gradient effect using concentric circles

Arcs

An arc is like a slice of a circle drawn along the outer edge of an ellipse determined by the arguments (x, y, a, b) as we saw when drawing ellipses. The `arc()` function also has additional arguments that determine the start and end point to specify the start and end angle that the arc covers. *Processing* uses radians for angles; a full circle covers 2π radians, a semi-circle is π radians, a quarter circle $\pi/2$, etc.

```
arc(x, y, a, b, start, end);
arc(x, y, a, b, start, end, mode);
```

The first four parameters are the same as for an ellipse. Start is the angle from which the arc starts to draw and stop is the angle where it stops. The angles are expressed in radians and counted in a clockwise direction. Basically, we give an arc an ellipse and tell it which part of it to draw. All parameters can be either of int or float type. Predefined constants PI, TWO_PI, HALF_PI and QUARTER_PI can be used for an easier manipulation of the angles

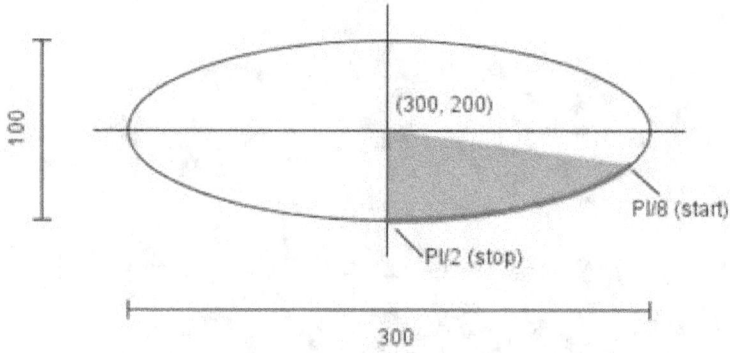

Figure 58: Drawing an Arc

The arc shown in red in Figure 58 can be produced by calling

```
arc(300, 200, 300, 100, PI/8.0, HALF_PI);
```

We should remember that the angles in *Processing* follow each other in a clockwise direction and that start should always be at a lower position than stop. Greater values of the whole round trip (2*PI) will also work. It means that we shouldn't start at PI/2 and stop at PI/8 in our example. However, if we start at (9/8)*PI and end at (5/2)*PI, we will get the same result.

The optional mode argument determines how the arc is drawn and filled. The options are:

- OPEN - arc filled with border on the outside edge but no border on the inside. This is the default mode
- CHORD - arc filled with border all the way around that cuts straight across
- PIE - arc filled with a border all the way around but cuts back into the centre (like a pie with a slice cut out)

This is best demonstrated with an example, the output of which can be seen in Figure 59

```
size(300, 300);
arc(50, 50, 90, 90, 0, PI+HALF_PI, OPEN);
arc(130, 130, 90, 90, 0, PI+HALF_PI, CHORD);
arc(210, 210, 90, 90, 0, PI+HALF_PI, PIE);
```

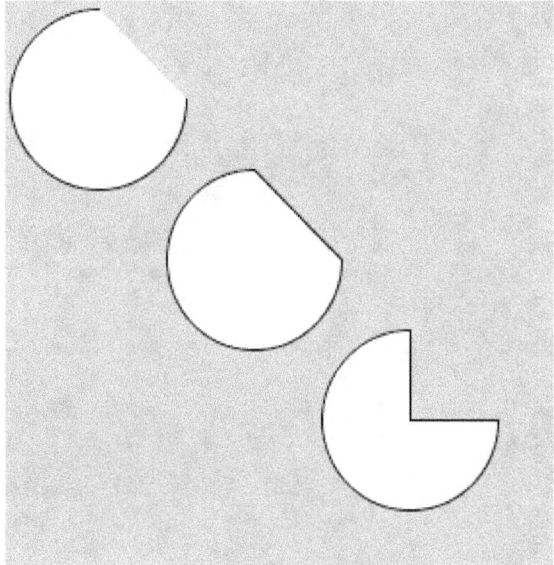

Figure 59: Arc Modes

Confusingly, the `arc()` function also uses the `ellipseMode()` function in a similar way to the `ellipse()` function to allow users to specify how the coordinates for the origin of the arc are interpreted.

To do a little more with arcs, we can use the arc() function to create pictures as shown in Figure 60

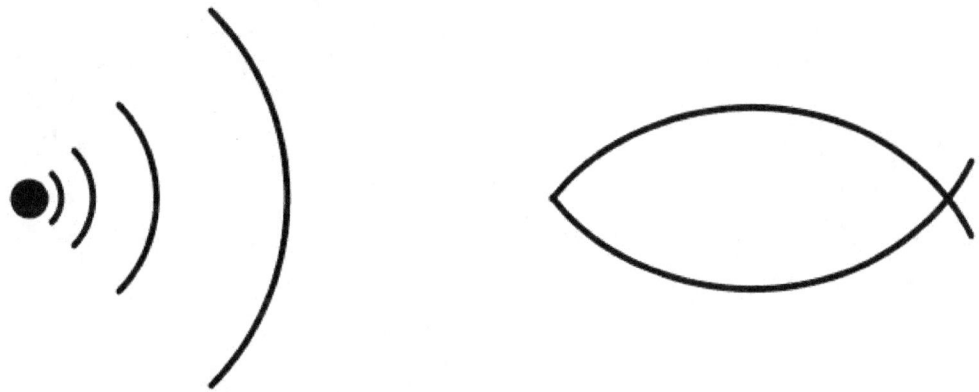

Figure 60: Using Arcs to Create Pictures

As you can see from Figure 60, we have used a simple set of arcs to create a picture of a radar and a fish, the code for which is shown below. As you can see, this required very little code to produce

```
size(800,400);
background(255);
smooth();
stroke(0);
strokeWeight(4);
int x = 100;
int y = 200;
//draw radar
fill(0);
ellipse(x,y,20,20);
noFill();
arc(x,y, 40, 40, -PI/4.0, PI/4.0);
arc(x,y, 80, 80, -PI/4.0, PI/4.0);
arc(x,y, 160, 160, -PI/4.0, PI/4.0);
arc(x,y, 320, 320, -PI/4.0, PI/4.0);
// draw fish
x=550;
arc(x, 270, 300, 250, (-13/16.0)*PI, -PI/8.0);
arc(x, 130, 300, 250, PI/8.0, (13/16.0)*PI);
```

We can extend this concept to create some slightly more complicated shapes that involve joining arcs together (Figure 61).

Figure 61: Joining Arcs To Create Pictures

It is not trivial to connect the arcs without the proper paths support. On the other hand, we can see that an ellipse has four contact points with its bounding rectangle - at angles 0, PI/2, PI and (3/2)*PI. These points are intuitively easy to see and can be used to draw simple shapes. The arcs shown in Figure 62Error! Reference source not found. are actually

160

connected at the multiplier of PI/2 for angles. The drawing can be produced by the following code

```
size (800,400);
noFill();
background(255);
smooth();
stroke(0);
strokeWeight(2);
// draw moon outline
arc(100,200,200,200, -PI/2.0, PI/2.0);
arc(100,200,100,200, (3/2.0)*PI, (5/2.0)*PI);
//draw ladle outline
ellipse(400, 250, 100, 30);
arc(400, 250, 100, 100, 0, PI);
arc(300, 250, 100, 300, -(5/8.0)*PI, 0);
// draw wings outline
arc (700, 200, 200, 80, PI, (3/2.0)*PI);
arc (700, 250, 200, 180, PI, (3/2.0)*PI);
arc (500, 200, 200, 80, -PI/2, 0);
arc (500, 250, 200, 180, -PI/2, 0);
```

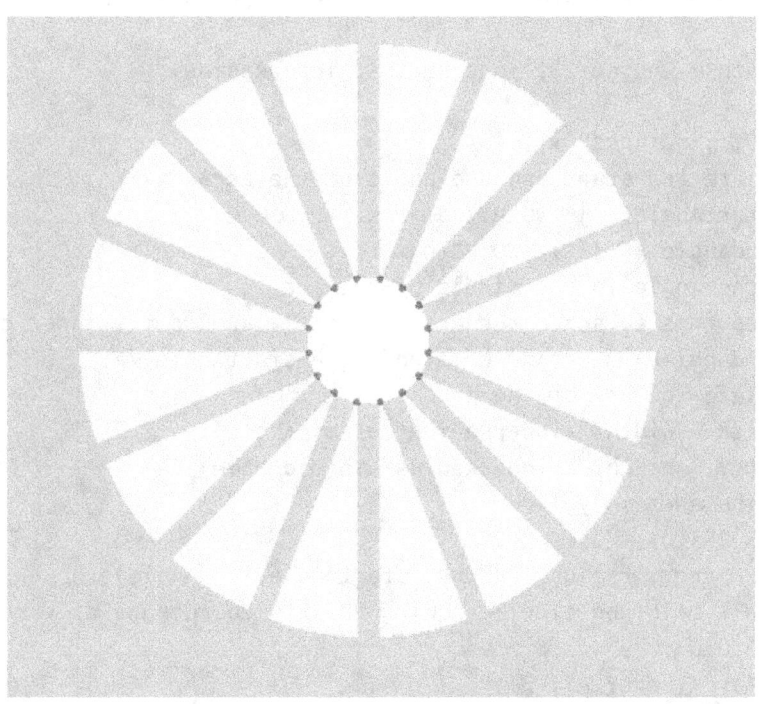

Figure 62: Flower Graphics Made From Arcs

This joining of arcs can now be used in a loop to create the graphics shown in the Figure 62

The code loops around the inner circle drawing however many arcs are specified by numArcs. This is done to space the arcs out a little so the arc can be seen. Without the inner circle the sketch would just show a large yellow circle! (albeit made up of individual arcs).

To align the arcs correctly in relation to the centre of the circle the sketch calculates the angle of the midpoint of each arc and uses that angle to calculate the arc origin on the circumference of the inner circle.

```
int radius = 150; // The radius multiplier between neighbouring ellipses
int numArcs = 16; // The number of arcs to draw
int innerRadius = 40; // The radius of the circle we draw the arcs around

void setup() {
    size(700,500);
    ellipseMode(RADIUS); // Set the ellipse mode to be RADIUS
    noStroke();
}

void draw() {
    //Draw the inner circle to show how the arcs are positioned
    fill(255);
    ellipse(width/2, height/2, innerRadius, innerRadius);

    for(int j=0; j<numArcs;j++) {
        //Calculate the start and end angle of the arcs
        float startAngle = j*TWO_PI/numArcs;
        float endAngle = (j+1)*TWO_PI/numArcs;
        //Find the angle in the middle of the arc
        //We need this to space the arcs correctly around the inner circle
        float midAngle = startAngle + (endAngle-startAngle)/2;
        //Calculate the x,y of the arc
        float arcX = width/2+innerRadius*cos(midAngle);
        float arcY = height/2+innerRadius*sin(midAngle);
        //Draw the arcs in yellow
        fill(255,255,0);
        arc(arcX, arcY, radius, radius, startAngle, endAngle);
        //Draw a little red circle showing the x,y coordinate of each arc
        fill(255,0,0);
        ellipse(arcX, arcY, 2, 2);
    }
```

```
}
```

Triangles

The final shape we will look at is drawing triangles using the `triangle()` function. The triangle function is a little different from the shape functions we have looked at so far. There is no `triangleMode()` function, instead `triangle()` takes six arguments that specify the three coordinate pairs of the three corners of the triangle.

```
triangle(x1, y1, x2, y2, x3, y3);
```

For example, the following small piece of code draws a green triangle (Figure 63)

```
size(500,300);
fill(0,255,0);
// Point 1 at 200,200
// Point 2 at 50, 50
// Point 3 at 400, 200
triangle(200,200, 50,50, 400,200);
```

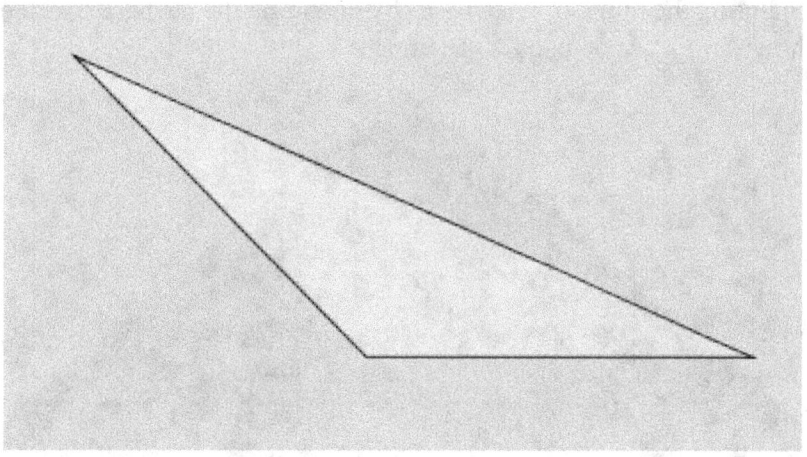

Figure 63: A green triangle

Processing will draw lines between the three sets of coordinates making a triangle. Drawing triangles doesn't really get any more complicated than that so the following, slightly longer, example is intended to show a little more of what can be done with basic triangles

```
int numberOfTriangles = 10;

void setup() {
   size(800,600);
   stroke(0);
```

```
    drawTriangles(width/2, height/2, width, height/2);
}

//Draw the nested triangles shaded black to white
void drawTriangles(float x, float y, float w, float h) {
    for(int i=0; i < numberOfTriangles; i++){
        //Scale the color
        fill(((float)255/(numberOfTriangles-1))*i);
        //Divide the height by the number of triangles
        float hStep = h/numberOfTriangles;
        //Scale the width step by the same ratio as the height
        //...and divide by 2 since we adjust both ends of the triangle
        float wStep = ((hStep/h)*w)/2;
        // remember x,y is the centre of the base line in triangle
        triangle((x-w/2)+wStep*i,y,x,(y-h)+i*hStep,(x+w/2)-wStep*i,y);
    }
}
```

You can try changing the number of triangles by changing the `numberOfTriangles` variable. The sketch shown in Figure 64 used 10 triangles

Figure 64: Nested triangles

Transforming Shapes

Processing has a number of functions which can be used to transform shapes. The three functions that can be used for transforming shapes are

- `translate()` – displays the shape at a given location in relation to its current coordinates

164

- scale() – displays the shape at a given size in relation to its current size
- rotate() – displays the shape at a given rotation in relation to its current rotation

You may have noted the wording in the descriptions. Rather than 'resizes the shape' we said 'displays the shape at a given size'. This is because these functions don't merely take a shape and relocate or resize it; they alter how the shape is displayed, so some understanding of how this works is necessary first of all

Translating

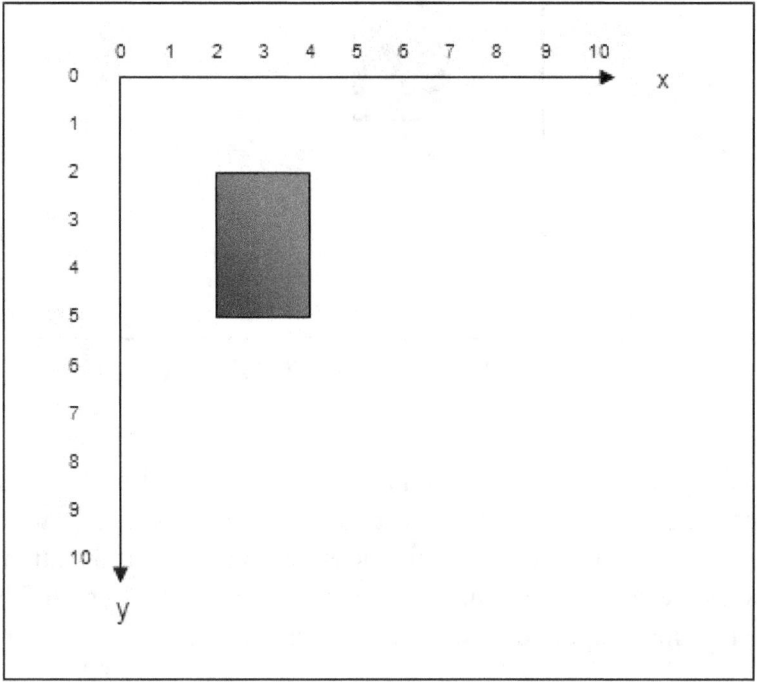

Figure 65: Rectangle displayed against the coordinate axes

Figure 65 shows a rectangle of width 2 and height 3 positioned with its top left hand corner at the point (2,2). Suppose we want to shift it, where xShift and yShift are the amounts the x and y axes respectively are to be shifted by in the positive x and y directions. If the function:

```
translate(xShift, yShift);
```

is used then the rectangle appears to be positioned on a different part of the screen. What is actually happening is that the coordinate system has changed and the origin of the shape has moved. So, for example, if translate(2,3) is applied, then the shape's origin will move 2 units in the direction of the positive x axis and 3 units in the direction of the positive y axis, so that when the rectangle is drawn, its position will be that in Figure 66

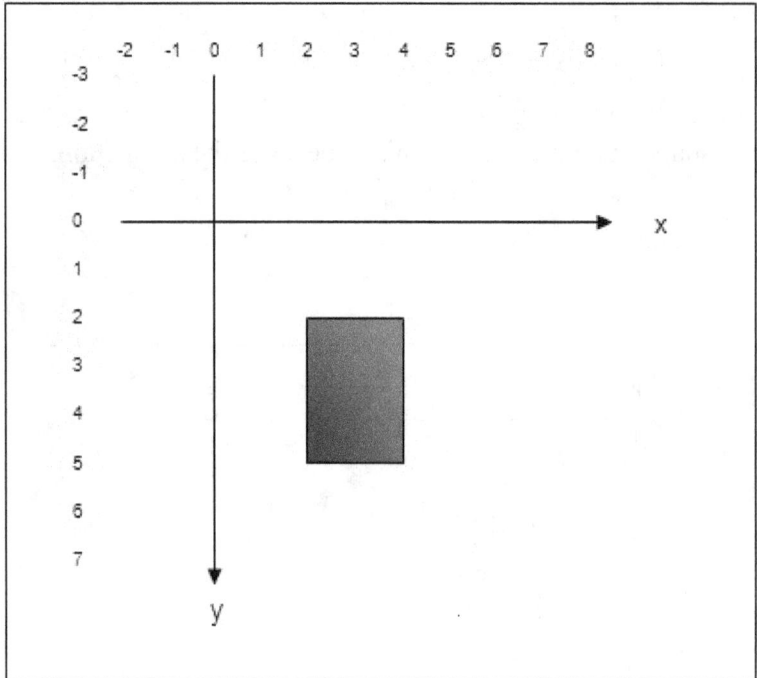

Figure 66: Translated rectangle

The rectangle will appear to be in a different place but the coordinates of its bounding box remain the same. The coordinates of the rectangle haven't changed, only the coordinates of where it is displayed. It is of course quite possible to apply a translation which is large enough that shapes are no longer displayed on a visible part of the screen. This will become a problem once rotation is applied as will be explained later.

Scaling

The effects of applying a scaling are similar. If xScaleFactor and yScaleFactor are the amounts by which the x and y axes are to be scaled, then applying the function:

```
scale(xScaleFactor, yScaleFactor);
```

will have the effect of making shapes drawn on it appear bigger or smaller, depending on the size of the scale factor. Figure 67 shows what happens when scale(2,2) is applied before drawing the rectangle. It appears to be twice its original width and height and positioned further away from the origin, but in fact the coordinates of its bounding box have remained unchanged.

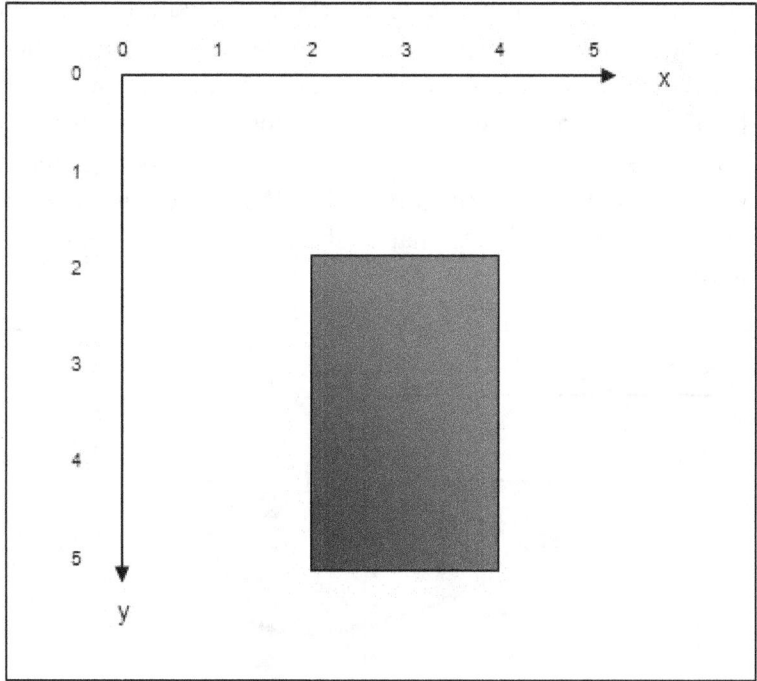

Figure 67: Scaled rectangle

Rotation

The `rotate()` function rotates the graphics context clockwise through the number of radians given by its argument

```
rotate(QUARTER_PI);
```

Constant	Radians	(Degrees)
TWO_PI	2π	($360°$)
PI	π	($180°$)
HALF_PI	$\pi/2$	($90°$)
QUARTER_PI	$\pi/4$	($45°$)

Table 11: Constants available for rotation in radians

The rotation is in radians, as we previously saw with arcs, so you can use the built-in constants which are shown in Table 11

Similarly, with rotation, using the `rotate()` function applied a rotation that doesn't alter the origin of the shape but alters how it is displayed. However there is an added complication here in that the centre of rotation is the origin. This means that, for example, if you rotated the axes about $\pi/2$, then the entire sketch would be outside the visible area. To understand why this is so, look at what appears to happen to the rectangle when `rotate(HALF_PI)` is applied. Figure 68 shows that the coordinate axes rotate clockwise through $90°$, so that its new position is that of the rectangle outside the visible area so it won't be seen at all!

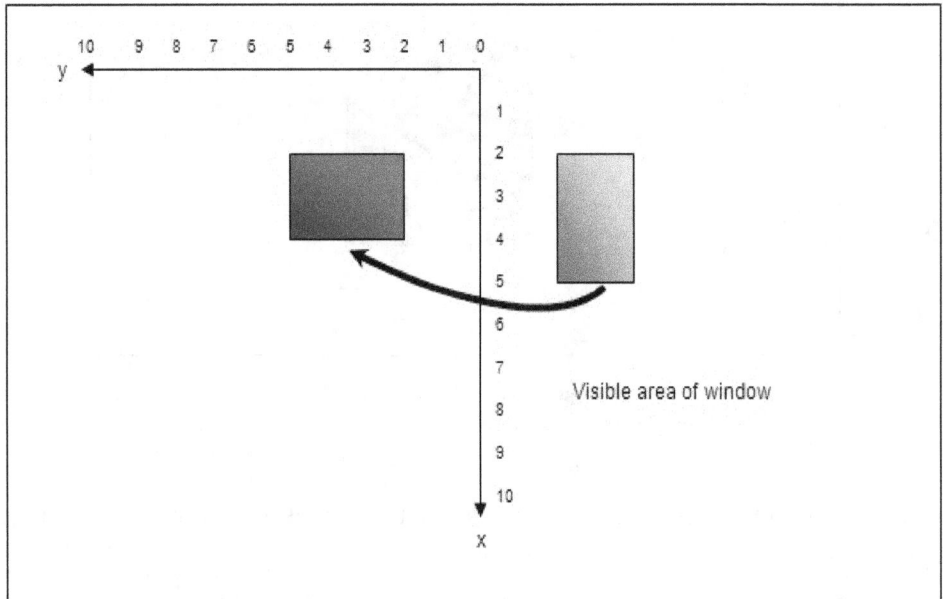

Figure 68: Rectangle rotated HALF_PI radians

What is needed to rotate a shape around a different point, for example the centre of the window, is first to translate the origin to the centre of the window, then perform the rotation, and then translate the origin back again in the direction of the new axes, by the same amounts as the original translation. Thus the following lines of code would rotate the shape through `HALF_PI` about the point (`xShift, yShift`)

```
translate(xShift, yShift);
rotate(HALF_PI);
translate(-xShift, -yShift);
```

Rotation about the centre of the screen could be achieved by setting `xShift` to `width/2` and `yShift` to `height/2`. Rotation about any other point can be achieved in the same way. Figure 69 shows the effect of rotating the graphics context about the point (5,5) before drawing the same rectangle as before.

168

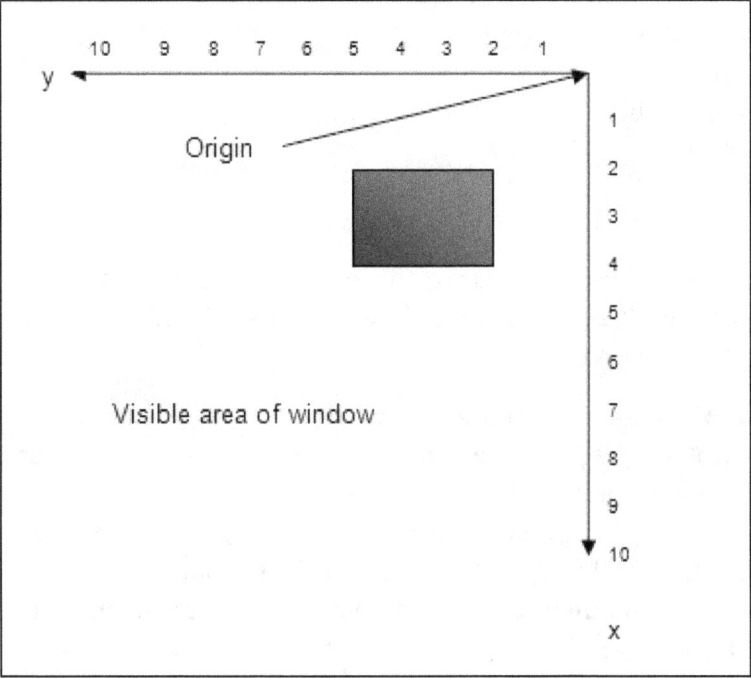

Figure 69: Translated and rotated rectangle

The coordinate axes are still rotated through 90°, but the origin has been translated first to the centre of the window and then to the top right hand corner, so that the area bounded by the positive x and y axes is now visible.

The code below draws a spiral of overlapping circles as shown in Figure 70. This positions the first circle near the centre of the display window and gradually rotates the graphics context while moving the centre of the next circle nearer to the origin using the rotated axes.

```
void setup(){
   size(300,300);
   collapsingBubbles();
}

void collapsingBubbles(){
   float diameter = 20;
   float startX = (width / 2) - diameter;
   float startY = height / 2;
   float rotation = 0.1;
   float totalRotation = 0;
   while (totalRotation < 50) {
      ellipse(startX - totalRotation,
```

169

```
        startY - totalRotation, diameter, diameter);
        translate(width / 2 , height / 2);
        rotate(rotation);
        translate(- width / 2, - height / 2);
        totalRotation += rotation;
    }
}
```

Two variables, rotation and totalRotation, are declared and initialised. rotation holds the angle in radians for each successive rotation. This is set to 0.1. totalRotation holds the cumulative angle of rotation.

The loop uses the variable totalRotation as an offset to the starting coordinates of the circle's centres. Rotation is performed about the centre of the display screen by the angle in the variable rotation, ready for the next iteration, first translating the origin to the centre of the display window, the point (width/2, height/2), and resetting it back after the rotation by translating backwards by the same values along the rotated coordinate axes. The loop ends when cumulative angle of rotation, as incremented at the end of each iteration, is $> 10\,\pi$.

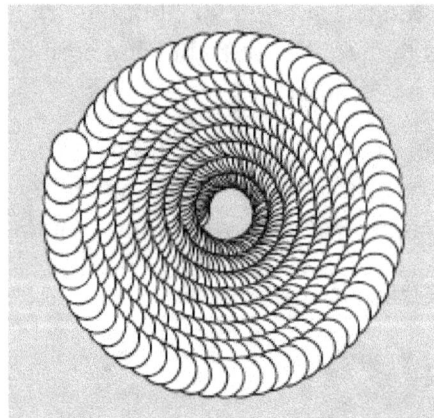

Figure 70: Collapsing bubbles using rotate() and translate()

The Transformation Matrix

The effects of the transformation functions are cumulative – they are applied to an underlying affine matrix which stores the transformations. This means that if you applied both scale() and translate() before drawing a shape then the coordinate axes would be scaled as well as the origin being translated. If you scaled them by 3 and then scaled them by 3 again, in both x and y directions, then the result would be to scale them by 3 * 3 = 9. A function resetMatrix() can be applied between transformations if this is not the intended effect. This changes the underlying affine transformation matrix back to its original settings.

There is just one further consideration before we look at some examples of these functions in action. If the code to draw the shapes is placed in a draw() function, then on each iteration of the code within this, the affine transformation matrix will have been reset. This is equivalent to having performed resetMatrix() in each iteration of a loop. If you want to build up transformations cumulatively using draw(), then you will need a way to store the current transformation and restore it next time draw() is called. This is achieved using a matrix stack in *Processing*, as shown in Figure 71

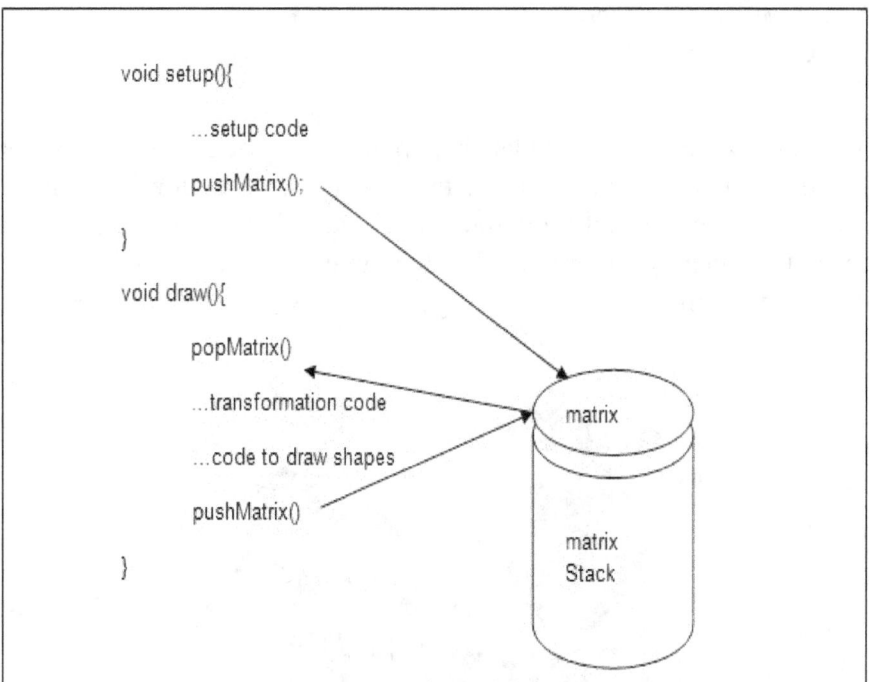

Figure 71: The Processing transformation matrix stack

A call to popMatrix() at the start of the draw() function restores the affine transformation matrix by removing the top matrix from the stack and a call to pushMatrix() at the end of the function places the new affine transformation matrix at the top of the stack. A word of warning though; there has to be a matrix on the stack before you call popMatrix(), so setup() would also need a pushMatrix() call.

The code below preserves the affine transformation matrix where iteration is achieved using the draw() function rather than a loop.

```
float rotation = 0.1;
```

```
void setup(){
    size(300,300);
    pushMatrix();
}

void draw(){
    popMatrix();
    translate(width/2+random(4),height/2+random(4));
    rotate(rotation);
    translate(-width/2-random(4),-height/2-random(4));
    fill(random(255), random(255), random(255));
    rect(90+random(3),90-random(3),40,40);
    pushMatrix();
}
```

This sketch is similar to the previous example which used ellipses except that the coordinates of the bounding box, as well as the shift values used for the translations, have a slight random variation on each iteration (Figure 72). The default rectMode(CORNER) is implied here, which you may remember is not the same default as for an ellipse. The results of successive transformations are saved using pushMatrix() and popMatrix().

Figure 72: Preserving the transformation matrix

Chapter 15: Vertices

by Antony Lees, Ben Notorianni, Ian Welch, Martin Prout and Neil Keskar

In this chapter we look at vertices (singular: vertex) and how they can be used in *Processing* to create continuous lines and simple shapes such as triangles and rectangles. We then move on to see how vertices can be used to create custom shapes using the `vertex()` default mode and how the function can be used to fill in the gaps in continuous lines by automatically joining vertices together

Points

A vertex is basically another word for a point. However, whereas a point can stand alone (it is just a point), a vertex is a point in a shape so the syntax of a `vertex()` function is notably different to that of the `point()` function.

In order to draw two points on a display screen (Figure 73) using the `point()` function you could create similar code to that shown below

```
size(200,200);
background(0);
strokeWeight(10);
stroke(255);
point((width*0.2),height/2);
point((width*0.8),height/2);
```

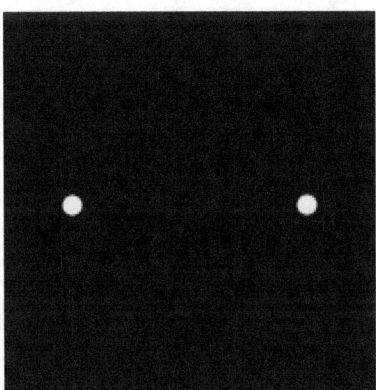

Figure 73: Points drawn using vertices

The code below shows how the use of a `vertex()` function would produce the same outcome as using the `point()` function.

```
size(200,200);
```

```
background(0);
strokeWeight(10);
stroke(255);
beginShape(POINTS);
vertex((width*0.2), height/2);
vertex((width*0.8), height/2);
endShape();
```

You will likely have noticed that there is an inclusion of beginShape() function, and endShape() function, which the vertex() function can be found inside. The beginShape() function essentially begins the recording of the drawing instructions and endShape() stops the recording. The benefit of this is that the data can be plotted based on different drawing algorithms

The beginShape() function has predefined mode arguments, these are POINTS, LINES, TRIANGLES, TRIANGLE_STRIP, TRIANGLE_FAN, QUADS, and QUAD_STRIP. We will look at all of these modes in turn. If no mode is defined the shape can be used to create custom shapes, the topic of the next chapter

Lines

Previously we have created lines using the line() function, however if want to link these lines together then you should use the vertex LINES drawing mode. You can think of this method of drawing as when you join up the dots drawing you probably did as a child where the dots are joined sequentially to reveal a shape. For example joining the dots in Figure 74 will produce a step-like line

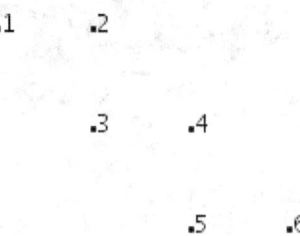

Figure 74: Joining the dots

The dots to be joined up are defined as a series of vertex() functions, that define the (x, y) coordinates of the points on the sketch. Using the beginShape(LINES) mode a line is drawn between each set of vertices in the order they are called, so we draw a line from point 1 to point 2, a line from point 2 to point 3, and so on (Figure 75).

```
void setup(){
   size(250, 200);
```

```
  background(255);
  doLines(); // draw lines
  doText(); // draw numbers
}

void doLines() {
  stroke(255,0,0);
  strokeWeight(6);
  beginShape(LINES); // Start recording vertices
  // line from point 1 to point 2
  vertex(50, 50); // 1
  vertex(100, 50); // 2
  // line from point 2 to point 3
  vertex(100, 50); // 2
  vertex(100, 100); // 3
  // line from point 3 to point 4
  vertex(100, 100); // 3
  vertex(150, 100); // 4
  // line from point 4 to point 5
  vertex(150, 100); // 4
  vertex(150, 150); // 5
  // line from point 5 to point 6
  vertex(150, 150); // 5
  vertex(200, 150); // 6
  endShape(); // Stop recording vertices
}

void doText() {
  fill(0);
  textSize(12);
  text("1", 50, 50);
  text("2", 100, 50);
  text("3", 100, 100);
  text("4", 150, 100);
  text("5", 150, 150);
  text("6", 200, 150);
}
```

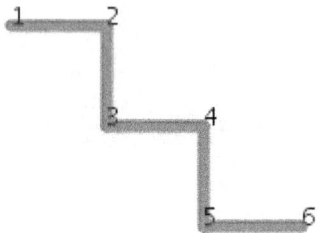

Figure 75: Steps drawn using vertices

Notice our use of the text() function to display the numbers. This simply draws the text in the string between the inverted commas, eg "1", at the (x, y) point given. The textSize() function changes the size of the text. Notice also that these vertices are in pairs, so the first two vertices defines the first line. These need not be interconnected; if the second pair of vertices are not started from the end of the previous one, we remove the interconnecting vertical lines (Figure 76)

```
void setup(){
    size(250, 200);
    background(255);
    doLines(); // draw lines
    doText(); // draw numbers
}


void doLines() {
    stroke(255,0,0);
    strokeWeight(6);
    beginShape(LINES); // Start recording vertices
    // line from point 1 to point 2
    vertex(50, 50); // 1
    vertex(100, 50); // 2
    // line from point 3 to point 4
    vertex(100, 100); // 3
    vertex(150, 100); // 4
    // line from point 5 to point 6
    vertex(150, 150); // 5
    vertex(200, 150); // 6
    endShape(); // Stop recording vertices
}
```

```
void doText() {
    fill(0);
    textSize(12);
    text("1", 50, 50);
    text("2", 100, 50);
    text("3", 100, 100);
    text("4", 150, 100);
    text("5", 150, 150);
    text("6", 200, 150);
}
```

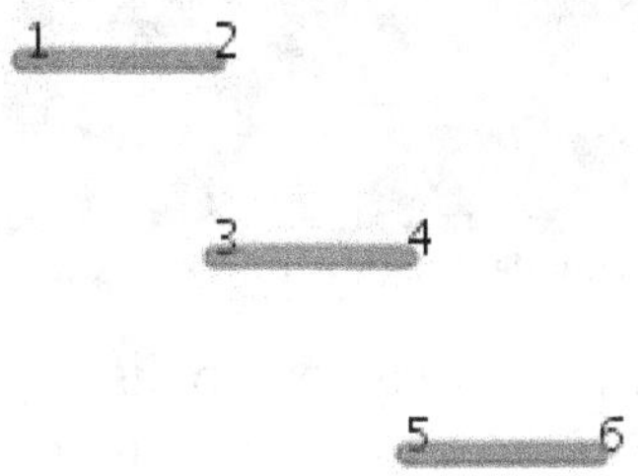

Figure 76: Unconnected lines drawn with vertices

Triangles

The triangles functions allow you to draw triangles, as you'd expect, using vertices. Similarly to the LINES mode, the TRIANGLES mode draws lines between vertices, but this time *Processing* will draw a triangle

```
size(200, 200);
background(0);
stroke(255);
strokeWeight(4);
noFill();
beginShape(TRIANGLES);
strokeJoin(ROUND);
vertex((width*0.2), height*0.8);
vertex((width*0.8), height*0.8);
vertex(width/2, (height*0.2));
endShape();
```

This code will draw a triangle in the centre of the screen as shown in Figure 77. The `noFill()`

function specifies that we don't want the triangle to be filled with colour, we could equally omit it, allowing it to be filled with the default colour, or specify a fill colour using the fill() function. As you might expect, since triangles have three sides, *Processing* draws triangles between each set of three vertices in the order written in the code. Any additional vertices that cannot be grouped into three, eg four, will be ignored, but six will draw two triangles

Figure 77: Triangle drawn with vertices with rounded joins

The strokeJoin() function tells *Processing* how to display the joins between vertices. It can take three different options, ROUND (rounded corners), BEVEL (flattened), and MITER (angular) which is the default option. We used ROUND in the sketch above, you should be able to see that the points of the triangle are slightly rounded. We will use the others to show you the difference. These joins can also be applied to lines where vertices form a join

As well as the TRIANGLES mode, there are also two other triangle modes, TRIANGLE_STRIP and TRIANGLE_FAN

Triangle Strips

TRIANGLE_STRIP mode indicates how multiple triangles are displayed together, in this instance by displaying them next to each other in a 'strip'. We can see the difference if we draw two triangles using TRIANGLES mode then change it to TRIANGLE_STRIP

```
size(200, 200);
background(255);
stroke(0);
strokeWeight(4);
beginShape(TRIANGLES);
strokeJoin(BEVEL);
// triangle 1
vertex(20, 150);
vertex(50, 20);
vertex(80, 150);
// triangle 2
vertex(110, 20);
```

```
vertex(80, 150);
vertex(140, 150);
endShape();
```

This code will draw two triangles next to each other as shown in Figure 78. Note that we have used the BEVEL join, you should be able to see that the corners are flattened

Figure 78: Triangles drawn using vertices with bevel joins

If we change the mode to TRIANGLE_STRIP you should see that the triangles are now joined together like a strip of triangles (Figure 79)

Figure 79: A triangle strip

Triangle Fans

Similar to TRIANGLE_STRIP, the TRIANGLE_FAN mode also specifies how multiple triangles should be displayed. In this case *Processing* will attempt to 'fan' the triangles by using the first vertex as an anchor point from which to display the triangles. Again we can demonstrate this by comparing it to a TRIANGLES sketch

We can code similar to before to create two triangles in TRIANGLES mode. Note that we have used the MITER join, you should be able to see that the corners are now pointed (Figure 80)

```
size(200, 200);
background(255);
```

```
stroke(0);
strokeWeight(4);
beginShape(TRIANGLES);
strokeJoin(MITER);
// triangle 1
vertex(20, 150);
vertex(50, 20);
vertex(80, 150);
// triangle 2
vertex(110, 20);
vertex(80, 150);
vertex(50, 20);
endShape();
```

Figure 80: Triangles drawn using vertices with miter joins

If we change the mode to TRIANGLE_FAN you should see that the triangles are now 'fanned' using the first vertex (bottom-right of the initial triangle) as the anchor point (Figure 81)

Figure 81: Triangle fan

Quadrilaterals

Drawing quadrilaterals using vertices is very similar to drawing triangles, except there must be four vertices. Similarly to triangles, sets of four vertices will be drawn as a quadrilateral whereas any vertices not in sets of four will be ignored. *Processing* will draw lines between the vertices in order to form a four-sided shape as can be seen in Figure 82

```
size(200, 200);
background(255);
stroke(0);
strokeWeight(4);
beginShape(QUADS);
vertex(20, 20);
vertex(20, 50);
vertex(100, 50);
vertex(100, 20);
endShape();
```

The same strokeJoin() types apply with quadrilaterals as they did with triangles and lines

Figure 82: Quadrilateral using vertices

Quadrilateral Strips

Quadrilaterals also have a strip mode, called QUAD_STRIP, that works in a similar way to TRIANGLE_STRIP (there is no fan mode for quads though). You can probably guess how it works by now, it creates a strip of quads as shown in Figure 83

```
size(200, 200);
background(255);
stroke(0);
strokeWeight(4);
beginShape(QUAD_STRIP);
// quad 1
vertex(20, 20);
vertex(100, 20);
vertex(20, 50);
vertex(100, 50);
// quad 2
vertex(20, 80);
```

```
vertex(100, 80);
vertex(20, 110);
vertex(100, 110);
endShape();
```

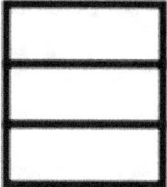

Figure 83: Quad strip using vertices

Triangle Explosion

As a practical example of what can be achieved using vertices, try this sketch that draws forty triangles in a loop with random vertices and grey shades. The loop simply chooses random colours and vertices, the TRIANGLES mode means that a triangle is drawn for every three vertices. You should see something like the effect shown in Figure 84

```
size(300, 300);
background(0);
strokeWeight(1);
smooth();
beginShape(TRIANGLES);
//Draw Triangles
for (int i = 0; i < 120; i++) {
   // randomise the edges colour
   stroke(random(0, 200));
   // Randomize the colouring of the shapes
   fill(random(225, 255), 150);
   // create random vertices
   vertex(random(0, width), random(0, height));
}
endShape();
```

You could try changing the mode to TRIANGLE_STRIP, TRIANGLE_FAN or even QUADS to see what the effect is

Figure 84: Triangle explosion

Continuous Lines

As well as having modes for creating lines and shapes, the vertex() function has a default mode that can be used for drawing any polygon shape. We can use it to define any number of vertices and join them together to make a shape, or we can use it to create continuous lines where *Processing* fills in the gaps between vertices

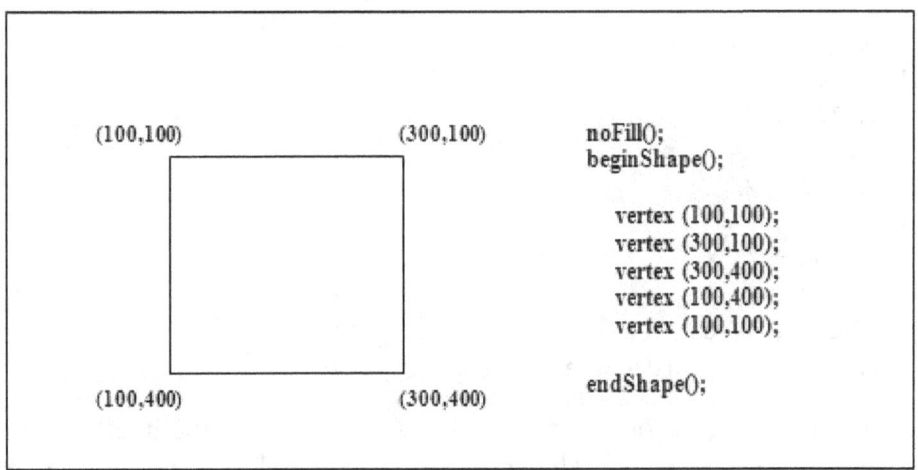

Figure 85: Using Vertices To Draw Shapes

We previously looked at how the LINE mode can be used to create lines. The default mode produces any shape defined by the vertices. As an example, Figure 85 shows an example of drawing a square using vertices

We previously saw how we could draw a line between each of the dots, as in Figure 86, to make a staircase effect.

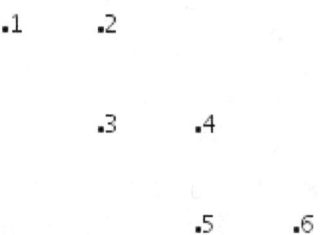

Figure 86: Joining the dots again

When we drew this previously we had to create two sets of vertices for each line in order to tell *Processing* to draw the line between them

```
beginShape(LINES); // Start recording vertices
// line from point 1 to point 2
vertex(50, 50); // 1
vertex(100, 50); // 2
// line from point 2 to point 3
vertex(100, 50); // 2
vertex(100, 100); // 3
// line from point 3 to point 4
vertex(100, 100); // 3
vertex(150, 100); // 4
// line from point 4 to point 5
vertex(150, 100); // 4
vertex(150, 150); // 5
// line from point 5 to point 6
vertex(150, 150); // 5
vertex(200, 150); // 6
endShape(); // Stop recording vertices
```

Using the default mode, we only need specify the vertices, *not* the lines, and *Processing* will draw the lines between them. This means much less code to achieve a similar result

```
noFill();
beginShape(); // Start recording vertices
// line from point 1 to point 2
```

```
vertex(50, 50); // 1
vertex(100, 50); // 2
vertex(100, 100); // 3
vertex(150, 100); // 4
vertex(150, 150); // 5
vertex(200, 150); // 6
endShape(); // Stop recording vertices
```

As you can see from Figure 87, we have only specified one vertex per point and removed the LINES mode from the vertex() function but the output is the same. There is one other difference which is the addition of the noFill() function. This is to tell *Processing* that we don't want to fill the shape in with colour but rather we just want to draw the lines

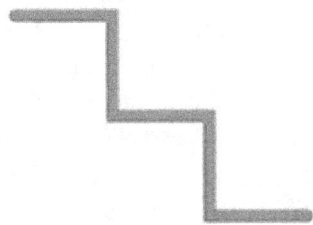

Figure 87: Staircase using default vertex() mode

This mode can be used to create some complex graphics with only a few vertices since we can rely on *Processing* to fill the lines in.

Here is another fairly simple example of an expanding maze based on a dynamically created Fibonacci series, also known as the 'golden ratio'. As the Fibonacci series progresses the ratio of the current Fibonacci number to the previous Fibonacci number approximates to the Golden Ratio (φ). This ratio is approximately equal to 1,618 and occurs in many areas of art and science, from the branching of plants, to arrangement of seeds etc

```
int MAX_FIBONACCI_LEVEL = 14; // maximum level to draw
float PHI = (1 + sqrt(5))/2; // golden ratio

void setup() {
    // calculate Fibonacci numbers
    int[] fibonacci = calculateFibonacci(MAX_FIBONACCI_LEVEL);
    // get the maximum calculated number
    int maxFibonacci = fibonacci[fibonacci.length-1];
    // set the size based on the numbers
    size(maxFibonacci * 2, maxFibonacci * 2);
    // draw the series
```

```
      drawFibonacci(fibonacci);
}

void drawFibonacci(int[] fibonacci) {
   float offsetX = width/PHI; // center spiral using the golden ratio
   float offsetY = height/2;  // center of spiral at middle of frame
   background(255);
   stroke(0);
   noFill();
   strokeWeight(2);
   beginShape();
   print("Fibonacci Series:-\n");
   // loop over the numbers
   for (int i = 0; i < fibonacci.length-1; i++) {
      print(String.format(" %d, ", fibonacci[i]));
      // draw the vertices in relation to the offset
      vertex(offsetX - fibonacci[i], offsetY - fibonacci[i]) ; // top right
      vertex(offsetX + fibonacci[i], offsetY - fibonacci[i]) ; // top left
      vertex(offsetX + fibonacci[i], offsetY + fibonacci[i]) ; // bottom left
      vertex(offsetX - fibonacci[i+1], offsetY + fibonacci[i]) ; // bottom right
   }
   endShape();
}

int[] calculateFibonacci(int level) {
   int[] fibonacci = new int[level];
   // fibonacci always starts with 0 and 1
   fibonacci[0] = 0;
   fibonacci[1] = 1;
   for (int i = 2; i < level; i++) {
      // the number is the sum of the previous 2 numbers
     fibonacci[i] = fibonacci[i-2] + fibonacci[i-1];
   }
   // return the array
   return fibonacci;
}
```

The values of the vertices are calculated using an algorithm whereby the current number is always the sum of the previous two numbers. We have included a print statement in the loop that prints the current value to the console, such statements can be included in your sketches to confirm that the algorithm behaves the way you intend it to

The output from the code should look like that shown in Figure 88

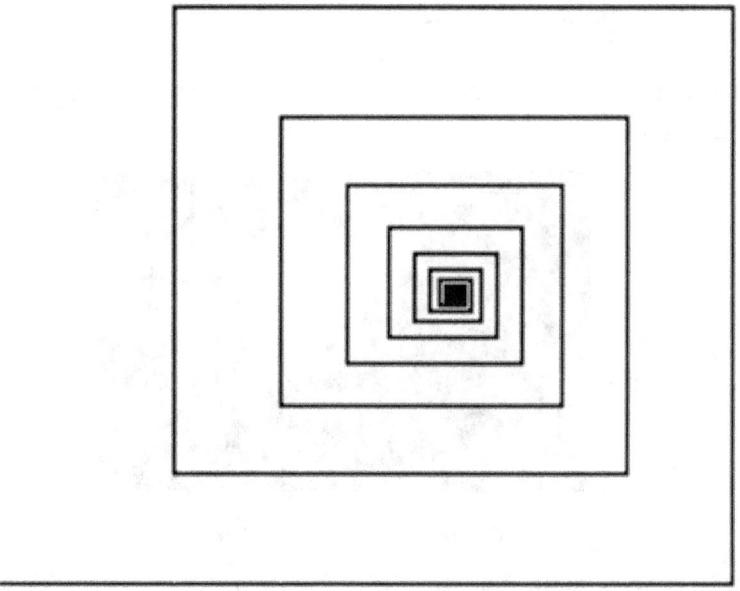

Figure 88: An expanding maze based on the Fibonacci series

We pre-calculate the numbers and store them in an array for ease of drawing. Note that we have offset the vertices to shift the drawing from the origin so that it is all visible within the sketch frame. The size of the sketch window is based on the number of levels we want to draw, so you can try changing this number to see different levels of maze if you wish

Turning Lines into Shapes

Moving from drawing lines using vertices to drawing shapes is very easy. Firstly, we can fill the shape in with colour by omitting the noFill() function. This will colour the shape in white, by default, though you can specify the colour using the fill() function and providing RBG colours as the arguments

```
size(250, 200);
background(0);
stroke(255,0,0);
strokeWeight(6);
fill(0, 255, 0); // green
beginShape(); // Start recording vertices
// line from point 1 to point 2
vertex(50, 50); // 1
vertex(100, 50); // 2
vertex(100, 100); // 3
```

```
endShape(); // Stop recording vertices
```

You should see from this code that the shape is coloured green (Figure 89). However you might also notice that the final line hasn't been drawn, so the shape looks 'open'. This is the same behaviour we saw when we were drawing lines using vertices, this hasn't changed, we just coloured in the space

Figure 89: Shape coloured green

We can finish off the shape by 'closing' it if we wish. We do this by providing a CLOSE argument to the endShape() function which tells *Processing* to draw a final line between the first and last vertices. You can try this yourself by adding CLOSE to the code above. It should look like the triangle shown in Figure 90

Figure 90: Closed shape coloured green

Custom Shapes

Drawing a shape in *Processing* is easy once we know the vertices of the shape's outline. Finding the coordinates of the vertices for precise, geometric objects is usually a straight forward, and sometimes, simple exercise. For example, *Processing* does not have a command for drawing a hexagon but we can easily substitute our own. The code below will draw a hexagon like the one shown in Figure 91

```
void setup() {
```

```
    size(640, 480);
    strokeWeight(9);
    stroke(100);
    drawHexagon(width/2, height/2, height/2.1);
}

void drawHexagon(int x, int y, float radius) {
    beginShape() ;
    for (int i = 0 ; i < 6 ; i++) { // 6 sides
        vertex(x + radius*cos(2.0*PI*i/6), y + radius*sin(2.0*PI*i/6));
    }
    endShape(CLOSE) ;
}
```

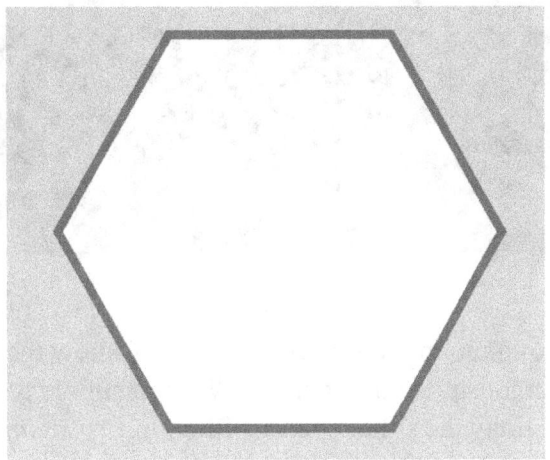

Figure 91: Custom hexagon shape

This process can be followed to create and draw any shapes you can think of

Complex Shapes

Some shapes though are a little bit more tricky, especially natural looking objects. A cloud for example doesn't have well defined edges. Clouds also look the same at different scales – a small part of a cloud will look very much like the whole cloud. This feature of *self-similarity* at different scales crops up often in nature and if you try hard enough you'll see it practically everywhere you look – the branching of trees, the structure of ferns, the crystal patterns of snowflakes, the rugged outline of a mountain and even the broccoli on your dinner plate. We'll continue drawing with the vertex() function and see how it can be used to draw more natural looking shapes. Specifically, we'll develop a sketch that draws a mountain scene similar to the one in Figure 92.

Figure 92: Vertex mountain scene

Drawing the silhouette of a mountain is pretty easy if we know the height of the mountain at regular intervals as demonstrated in Figure 93. We can simple pass the height data to the vertex() command and draw the silhouette as a filled in *Processing* shape. The basic idea is shown in the code fragment below

```
beginShape();
vertex(0, 0);
for (int x = 0 ; x < width ; x++) {
    vertex( x, mountainHeight(x));
}
vertex(x, 0);
endShape(CLOSE);
```

The first vertex() command marks the bottom left corner of the mountain shape. Subsequent vertex() commands inside the for loop trace the outline of the mountain. The final vertex() command marks the bottom right corner of the mountain shape so that when the shape is closed *Processing* fills the mountain shape in correctly. We could of course use predefined vertex data for the mountain, but we are aiming to create a sketch that can generate its own scenes.

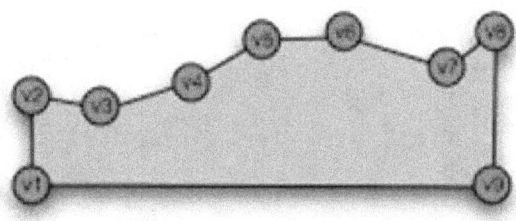

Figure 93: Vertices on a mountain shape

Our first attempt at implementing mountainHeight() might be to use the random() function – given the horizontal position of a vertex we simply return a random value for the height of the vertex in pixels.

```
void setup() {
    size(480, 320);
    colorMode(RGB, 1.0);
    smooth();
    drawMountain();
}

void drawMountain() {
    background(1.0);
    noStroke();
    fill(0.3);
    // Draw the mountain. height is measured from top edge of screen.
    beginShape();
    vertex(0, height);
    for (int x = 0 ; x < width ; x++){
        vertex(x, height - random(0, height));
    }
    vertex(width, height);
    endShape(CLOSE);
}
```

The calculation height-random(0, x) might seem a bit strange at first but remember that the y-coordinate runs down the screen. So, in order to draw the mountain relative to the ground we need to subtract the height of the mountain from the height of the screen. The results from the sketch are shown in Figure 94. Unsurprisingly the output doesn't look anything like a mountain – after all we are using the random() function and by definition it produces a sequence of completely unrelated numbers.

Figure 94: Random mountain height

What we really need is a sequence of semi-random numbers such that neighbouring points are related and vary smoothly. Take a look at the diagram in Figure 95, it shows the type of outline we are trying to achieve. The mountain peak A and the valley B stand out because they set the scale of the mountain. In-between A and B we have a line that varies in a semi -random way with more peaks and valleys. However these peaks and valleys are *dominated* by A and B and so they set the scale for the local area in-between A and B.

Figure 95: Peak and valley in a mountain

Noise

Fortunately *Processing* has another function which fits our needs perfectly – the `noise()` function. `noise()` is different from `random()` in several keys ways.

- `random()` is dimensionless whereas `noise()` works in 1, 2 or 3 dimensions. This might seem a bit strange but it's easy to see – `random()` takes no parameters and each call returns a random number. `noise()` on the other hand takes a floating point value as a parameter (or two or three when working in higher dimensions) and returns a random number based on this value.
- it doesn't matter how many times you call `noise()`, it will always return the same value if passed the same parameter value (or parameter values).
- if you change the parameter value by a small amount then the value that `noise()` returns will also change by a small amount. Put another way, the output value of `noise()` varies smoothly with respect to the input parameter.

These three features are just what we need for drawing a mountain scene and to see why let's dive straight into the complete code

```
void setup() {
   size(480, 320);
   colorMode(RGB, 1.0);
   smooth() ;
}

void draw() {
   background(1.0);
```

```
float startY = height;
float hrzScale = 0.005;
float vrtScale = height;
float whiteness = 0.5;

noStroke();
fill(whiteness);

// Bottom left corner.
beginShape();
vertex(0, startY);

// Outline of mountain ridge from left to right.
for (int i = 0; i < width; i++) {
    vertex(i, vrtScale * noise(i*hrzScale));
}

// Bottom right corner.
vertex(width, startY);
endShape();
}
```

Running the sketch should draw something that looks more like a mountain (Figure 96). The sketch works as before by drawing the ridge as a filled in polygon shape with the bottom left and right corners of the screen as the first and last vertices of the shape. The ridge is drawn from left to right as a sequence of vertices with one vertex at each horizontal pixel position.

Figure 96: Mountain drawn with noise

Even though it is the most important part of the sketch the actual calculation for a ridge vertex is only one line. Let's examine it in detail.

```
vertex(i, vrtScale * noise(i*hrzScale));
```

As you can see, the noise() function is used to calculate the height of the vertex, we simply use the horizontal coordinate of the vertex (specified by the variable *i*) as the parameter to noise() and the return value is used as the height of the vertex. There are a couple of scaling issues to deal with. The return value of noise() is a number between 0.0 and 1.0, so we need to scale it up by roughly the height of the screen. We also need to scale the horizontal coordinate otherwise the output of noise() changes to *fast* and our mountain ridge will be squashed up horizontally and be unrecognizable. Choosing the right horizontal scale is a matter of trial and error and taste. Try experimenting with the value of hrzScale to see the effect it has on the final output.

Our sketch is beginning to shape up now but there is still plenty of room for improvement. For example, we can make our mountain scene more convincing if we add a sense of depth to the drawing. We can do this in a few lines of code by layering several mountain ranges on top of each other. We need to take a little care however and ensure distant mountains are corrected for perspective. Adding perspective to a scene can be a complex task but we will appeal to our artistic license and implement something that is simple and looks *right* rather than being mathematically perfect. One way is to fade them into the colour of the horizon. In our sketch the mountain ranges are grey and the sky is white, so all we have to do is fade successive layers of mountains from dark gray to white. Below is a modified draw() function that draws layers of mountains along with perspective and colour depth cueing.

```
void draw() {
    background(1.0);
    noStroke();

    int kLayers = 8;
    int kBaseLine = height/3;

    for ( int j = 1; j <= kLayers; j++) {

        float startY = height;
        float hrzScale = 0.002 * kLayers/j;
        float vrtScale = height * j/kLayers;
        float whiteness = 0.95 - (0.95 - 0.2) * (j - 1) / (kLayers - 1);

        // Draw mountain range j
        fill(whiteness);

        beginShape() ;
        vertex(0, startY);

        for (int i = 0 ; i < width ; i++) {
            vertex(i, vrtScale * noise(i*hrzScale, j*1.5));
        }

        vertex(width, startY);
        endShape();
    }
}
```

The scene is layered by drawing the most distant mountain range first and the nearest last. Layers are drawn by iteration of the outer for loop, with the number of layers defined by the variable kLayers. Mountains are drawn in much the same way as before except we take into account the layer number when calculating the horizontal and vertical scaling factors (mountains in the background should look smaller and more squashed up than mountains in the foreground). The layer number is also used when calculating the fill colour of the mountains. The biggest change however is the extra parameter to noise().

```
vertex(i, vrtScale * noise(i*hrzScale, j*1.5));
```

Figure 97: Variations in scaling factor, from clockwise top-left 1.5, 1.0, 0.5, 0.1

Previously we were only drawing a single mountain range so we only needed to use the one dimensional version of noise(). However, with the addition of the extra layers the value of the height of any particular vertex now depends on two variables: the horizontal position of the vertex and the layer number of the vertex. noise() works in two dimensions much the same way as it does in one only this time both parameters are taken into account when calculating the return value. In addition, a small change in *either* parameter produces a small change in the return value. You can see the effect of the second parameter by changing the scaling value from 1.5 to smaller values, eg 0.5 or 0.1. As the scaling value decreases the smaller the difference becomes between successive mountain ranges. Figure 97 shows the effect of varying the second scaling factor

As it stands our sketch will draw a different static mountain scene each time it is run. If you prefer you can change this behaviour by explicitly setting the noise seed value by adding the following line to setUp().

```
noiseSeed(3);
```

Each time the sketch is run it will now generate the same scene. You can change which scene is drawn by changing the value of the parameter from 3 to some other number.

We have managed to achieve quite a lot in a few lines of code, all thanks to *Processing*'s vertex() and noise() functions! By leveraging the power of these functions we have been able to generate and draw mountains as polygon shapes. We could also animate our scene by scrolling the mountains across the screen (as though we were looking out of the window of a train). This might sound like a difficult change but it couldn't really be simpler as it's only one extra line of code and a small change to noise(). So, let's have a look at the code one last time along with the change for animating the scene.

```
void setup() {
    size(480, 320);
    colorMode(RGB, 1.0);
    smooth();
}

void draw() {
    background(1.0);
    noStroke();

    int kLayers = 8;
    int kBaseLine = height/3;

    for (int j = 1; j <= kLayers; j++) {

        float startY = kBaseLine + height * j / kLayers;
        float hrzScale = 0.002 * kLayers / j;
        float vrtScale = height * j / kLayers;
        float whiteness = 0.95 - (0.95 - 0.2) * (j - 1) / (kLayers - 1);
        float t = frameCount * j * 0.3;

        fill(whiteness);

        // Bottom left corner.
        beginShape();
        vertex(0, startY);

        // Outline of mountain ridge from left to right.
        for (int i = 0; i < width; i ++) {
            vertex(i, vrtScale * noise((i + t)*hrzScale, (kLayers - j)*1.5));
        }

        // Bottom right corner.
        vertex(width, startY);
```

```
        endShape() ;
    }
}
```

The scene is animated simply by adding a time dependent offset to the horizontal coordinate of the mountain vertices. The following line calculates this offset,

```
float t = frameCount * j * 0.3;
```

The variable `frameCount` is an internal *Processing* variable and is automatically incremented each time the scene is drawn (depending on how fast your PC runs this could happen up to 30 times a second). The scaling factor j * 0.3 ensures that mountains in the foreground scroll faster than mountains in the distance (an effect which will be familiar from looking out the side window of a car or train).

Chapter 16: Event Handling
by Antony Lees, Grant Mankee and Jannetta Steyn

So far nothing you have drawn has been interactive - the sketches are drawn on the screen and are either static or animate themselves without any intervention from you, the user. In this Chapter we introduce event handling by looking at how your animations can become interactive by taking directions from the keyboard or mouse

Events

Events are an important part of any programming language. An event, in programming terms is something detected by the program that can then be handled by the program itself in order to influence the way it runs. The important word here is *detected* - *Processing* will automatically detect that an event has occurred, but how it is handled is up to you as the programmer.

For our sketches to be interactive we need to manage a user's actions and do something in response. Interactive programs allow the user to feel part of the application by giving them some way of manipulating their environment and making the experience unique to themselves. Events in *Processing* are focussed around detecting user's actions from *user interface* devices such as the keyboard or mouse

Keyboard Events

Keyboard events capture anything that is typed on the keyboard. Examples when this might be used are to echo what a user types onto the screen or to use key presses as a means of controlling the program such as a game where the player's character is controlled by arrow keys

Processing provides two methods of detecting if a key has been pressed, one is by means of an *event handler* function and another is by checking a system (pre-defined) variable. We will describe their use before explaining why there is a need for them both

Key Event Actions

keyPressed
The keyPressed variable is a boolean that has the value *true* if a keypress event is currently detected, or the value *false* if there is no key press event detected. This means it can be used in the draw() function to determine if a key is currently pressed. Each time the draw() function is run, the boolean will be evaluated, which means that keeping the key pressed will continue to run the corresponding code each time the draw() function is called.

We can demonstrate this with a small sketch that animates a spaceship (Figure 98). Each time the draw function is called, the keyPressed boolean variable is evaluated and the ship moves up the screen

```
float x = 350;
float y = 400;

void setup() {
   size(800, 600);
}

void draw() {
   background(0); // black
   fill(0, 0, 255); // blue
   ellipse(x, y, 25, 25);
   triangle(x, y-18, x-20, y+10, x+20, y+10);

   if (keyPressed) {
      // move up the screen
      y--;
   }
}
```

You will see that, with a key held down, the ship moves until the key is released – at that point the background ship stops. It might seem that many key events are being generated if the key is held. However a single event is detected when the key is pressed, which sets the keyPressed variable to true. It remains true until the key button is released, when it reverts to being false.

Figure 98: Key controlled spaceship

keyPressed()

In addition to the keyPressed variable, *Processing* provides the keyPressed() function. This function can be defined in your code and is called whenever a mouse press event is detected. This type of function is called an *event handler*. An example of this is shown below

```
float x = 350;
float y = 400;
color shipColour = color(0, 0, 255); // blue

void setup() {
   size(800, 600);
}

void draw() {
   background(0); // black
   fill(shipColour);
   ellipse(x, y, 25, 25);
   triangle(x, y-18, x-20, y+10, x+20, y+10);
   fill(255,255,0);
   ellipse(x-10, y+10, 5, 5);
   ellipse(x+10, y+10, 5, 5);
}

void keyPressed() {
   // move up the screen
   y--;
}
```

You will see that the behaviour is the same as using the keyPressed variable. This might seem strange because we never call the *keyPressed()* function ourselves. When *Processing* detects a key press event the event handler function is called and the spaceship moves up the screen as before

The reason both the variable and function exist is because the code corresponding to the event are run at subtly different times. When a key is pressed the keyPressed variable is set to *true* and the corresponding code is run only if it is still *true* **when** the if statement is reached. The keyPressed() function, however, is run *every time* a keypress event is detected. Generally this won't make much difference to the way your sketch runs unless you are relying on the corresponding event code being run immediately, or if you had an intensive sketch that meant the *if* statement was reached infrequently. Key events are also only useful in active mode since *Processing's* static mode runs only once and stops listening for keys

Processing also provides two other key event functions, keyTyped() and keyReleased() which allow you to further refine what actions to take when keys are pressed

keyTyped()

The keyTyped() function is very similar to keyPressed() with one small difference; keyTyped() ignores any keys that cannot be typed onto the screen so, for example, ignores the Alt, Ctrl, Shift and arrow keys. but works the same as keyPressed() for keys that can be typed such as Enter, Space and any alphanumeric keys. We can demonstrate this by changing our spaceship sketch to use keyTyped() instead of keyPressed()

```
void keyTyped() {
   // move up the screen
   y--;
}
```

If you try this, you will see that the spaceship now only moves when you use typeable keys rather than action keys

keyReleased()

You might be able to guess by now what the keyReleased() function is for - it detects when a key is released (having already been pressed). We might, for example, want our spaceship to change colour when we release a key

```
void keyReleased() {
   shipColour = color(random(255), random(255), random(255));
}
```

Now every time we release the key to stop our spaceship moving it will change to a randomly selected colour. You may notice that, if we keep the key pressed, although *Processing* detects multiple key presses, the key release event is only detected when we actually let go of the key. This is due to the key being repeated, like when you keep a key pressed down when typing, but we only release it once

Key Event Variables

So far our spaceship animation can only move in one direction - up. If we wanted to be able to make it do anything else we would need to define actions that have different controls. *Processing* allows us to detect *which* key has been pressed by using some system variables

key

This variable will always contain the value of the most recent key pressed, typed or released. This will be in the form of an ASCII (American Standard Code for Information Interchange) value. ASCII is a standard that assigns integer numbers to key values, for example 'a' is 97, 'A' is 65 and Space is 32. This value can be used to determine which key was pressed. So we don't have to look these up we can cheat and compare the character directly, for example

```
if (key = 'z')
```

We might use this to rotate our ship, using the z (rotate left) and x (rotate right) keys

```
float x = 400;
float y = 400;
color shipColour = color(0, 0, 255); // blue
float rotation = 0.0;

void setup() {
    size(800, 600);
}

void draw() {
    background(0); // black
    // only rotate this bit
    pushMatrix();
    // rotate round centre of triangle
    translate(x, y);
    rotate(rotation);
    translate(-x, -y);
    // ship
    fill(shipColour);
    ellipse(x, y, 25, 25);
    triangle(x, y-18, x-20, y+10, x+20, y+10);
    // thrusters
    fill(255,255,0);
    ellipse(x-10, y+10, 5, 5);
    ellipse(x+10, y+10, 5, 5);
    popMatrix();
    // end rotate
}

void keyPressed() {
    if (key == 'z') {
```

```
    // rotate clockwise
    rotation -= 0.1;
} else if (key == 'x') {
    // rotate anti-clockwise
    rotation += 0.1;
    }
}
```

Here we have added an if-else statement to check the key pressed is either 'z' or 'x' and increase or decrease the rotation respectively. Notice the changes to the draw() function to rotate the ship. We have used translate() and rotate() to rotate the ship and enclosed them in pushMatrix() and popMatrix() functions. You may recall that translate() is needed to rotate the triangle around its centre, rather than the centre of the screen. We needn't necessarily use pushMatrix() and popMatrix() as the ship will rotate without them, but using them means we *only* rotate the ship (Figure 99); without them the entire sketch would rotate, which is fine for now but not if we wanted to add other detail!

Figure 99: Rotated spaceship

keyCode

Some keys are not specified in the ASCII standard, so *Processing* provides the keyCode variable. This is a useful variable that, like the key variable, can be used to check a key is pressed or released but stores the key in a code so you can access whether the user has pressed an action key such as Delete, Shift, Control, Alt or the arrow keys. *Processing* also provides variables for these keys so don't need to find the codes each time, DELETE, SHIFT, CONTROL, ALT, UP, DOWN etc. For example

```
if (keyCode == UP)
```

By using this variable for keys the code can be easier to read and understand. You should first check that the key is coded using

```
if (key == CODED)
```

We can use this to take more control of our spaceship by adding controls that will move it using the UP, DOWN, LEFT and RIGHT key variables

```
if (key == CODED) {
    if (keyCode == UP) {
        y--; // up
    } else if (keyCode == DOWN) {
        y++; // down
    } else if (keyCode == LEFT) {
        x--; // left
    } else if (keyCode == RIGHT) {
        x++; // right
    }
}
```

If you add this into the code you should now be able to control the direction and rotation of the ship

Mouse Events

Mouse events are the detection of mouse movements, button presses and releases. *Processing* provides event handlers for mouse presses, releases, clicks, movements and dragging.

Mouse Event Actions

The simplest mouse event that *Processing* caters for is when a mouse button is pressed. This event detects any mouse button press – that is when the mouse button is pressed, not released. Similarly to key presses, to enable you to use these events, *Processing* provides both a mousePressed variable, and a mousePressed() function.

mousePressed

The mousePressed variable is similar to keyPressed and is set to *true* when a mouse button is pressed and *false* when no mouse button is pressed. This can be *any* mouse button, the button press is detected regardless. To demonstrate we can extend our spaceship sketch to add a second, mouse-controlled, ship (Figure 100)

We need to add new x, y and colour variables to the top. Let's also imagine that this ship has a cloaking device that makes it invisible. The cloaking device starts off *false* so we can see it

```
float x2 = 100;
float y2 = 100;
color mouseShipColour = color(255, 69, 0); // orangey
boolean cloaked = false;
```

and add the code to draw the new ship

```
if (!cloaked) {
    // mouse ship
    fill(mouseShipColour);
    ellipse(x2, y2, 25, 25);
    triangle(x2, y2 + 18, x2 - 20, y2 - 10, x2 + 20, y2 - 10);
    // thrusters
    fill(255, 255, 0);
    ellipse(x2+10, y2-10, 5, 5);
    ellipse(x2-10, y2-10, 5, 5);
}
```

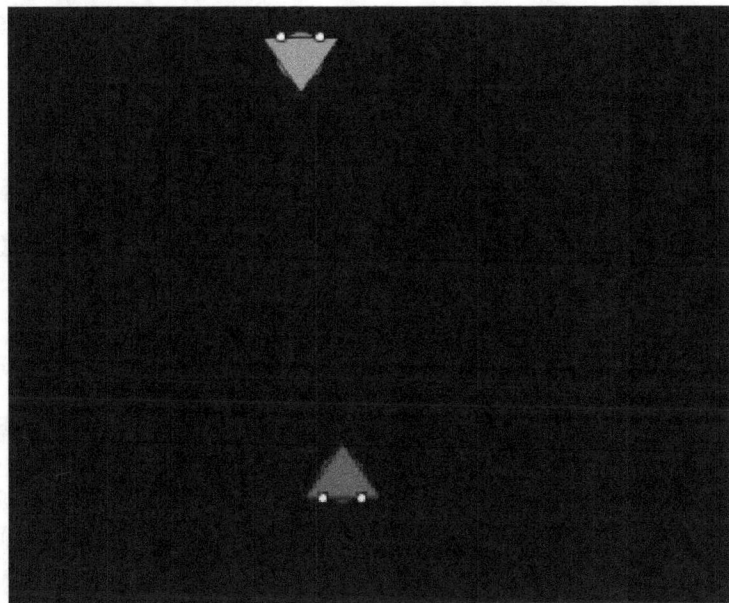

Figure 100: Two spaceships

When we press a mouse button the ship goes into cloaking mode and we can no longer see it

```
void mousePressed() {
    cloaked = true;
}
```

mousePressed()

As you might expect, mousePressed() is very similar to the keyPressed() function. We can replace the use of the mousePressed variable with the event handler function and achieve the same effect

```
void mousePressed() {
    cloaked = true;
}
```

Of course, since we have changed the variable that cloaks the ship, it stays cloaked even when we release the mouse button. What we need is the mouseReleased() function

mouseReleased()

The mouseReleased() function is the opposite of the mousePressed() function. This mouse event is detected when a mouse button is released after being pressed. As with mousePressed(), it doesn't matter which mouse button is released, the event is detected for any button release.

```
void mouseReleased() {
    cloaked = false;
}
```

Running this will show you how the mousePressed() and mouseReleased() functions are detected independently. When a mouse button is pressed, the ship disappears, and reappears when the mouse button is released

mouseClicked()

The mouseClicked() function is like a combination of mousePressed() and mouseReleased(). This event is detected when a mouse button is pressed and then released. Again, the event is detected for any mouse button clicked. We can replace our mousePressed() and mouseReleased() functions with the mouseClicked() function

```
void mouseClicked() {
    cloaked = !cloaked;
}
```

This acts more like a toggle, so we set the cloaked boolean to the opposite of its current value (shown as !cloaked). This has the advantage of not having to keep our finger on the mouse button to keep the ship cloaked

The mouseClicked() function is overloaded with a MouseEvent object which allows you to access various attributes about the event such as the number of times the mouse button was clicked. This could be useful if you wanted to detect double clicks for example, using the getCount() function

```
void mouseClicked(MouseEvent event) {
    println(event.getCount());
}
```

You can use the overloaded function even if you don't want to use the event object, it is entirely up to you

Mouse Event Variables

In addition to the mousePressed variable, *Processing* provides other variables that can be used when programming mouse events

mouseButton

When we looked at mouseClicked it didn't matter which button we pressed. However, if you wanted to know which button was pressed, *Processing* provides the mouseButton variable which can be compared to three predefined variables - LEFT, RIGHT and CENTER. We might alter our code so that different mouse buttons cloak or uncloak the ship

```
void mouseClicked(MouseEvent event) {
    if (mouseButton == LEFT) {
        cloaked = true;
    } else if (mouseButton == RIGHT) {
        cloaked = false;
    }
}
```

We could, if we wished, do this using the MouseEvent object by calling the getButton() function, but the effect is the same

```
void mouseClicked(MouseEvent event) {
    if (event.getButton() == LEFT) {
        cloaked = true;
    } else if (event.getButton() == RIGHT) {
        cloaked = false;
    }
}
```

mouseWheel()

The mouseWheel() function is called when the mouse wheel is used and always has a MouseEvent argument that can be used to determine the use of the wheel. The getCount() function from the MouseEvent object returns positive values or negative values depending on which way the wheel is turned. We could use this to move our ship by adding (or subtracting depending on the value) values from the y2 coordinate

```
void mouseWheel(MouseEvent event) {
    y2 += event.getCount();
}
```

This will move the ship up or down the screen depending on which direction the wheel is turned

mouseX and mouseY

The `mouseX` and `mouseY` variables provide a means of knowing where the mouse pointer is at any given time by assigning the x and y coordinate values respectively when a mouse event is detected. When used with the `mouseClicked()` function, for example, the exact coordinates of the mouse press can be obtained by accessing these variables

```
void mouseClicked() {
    println("x:" + mouseX + " Y:" + mouseY);
}
```

The same effect can be achieved using `getX()` and `getY()` functions from the `MouseEvent` object

```
void mouseClicked(MouseEvent event) {
    println("x: " + event.getX() + " Y:" + event.getY());
}
```

The `mouseX` and `mouseY` variables can be used anywhere, not just in mouse event functions. As an example, you might print out the values of the variables in the `draw()` function, which would continuously print the coordinates of the mouse pointer

```
void draw() {
// output the coordinates to the console
    println(mouseX + " " + mouseY);
}
```

If you run this you will see that '0 0' is printed out unless you move the mouse pointer over the *Processing* window, when the mouse pointer coordinates will be printed

pmouseX and pmouseY

The `pmouseX` and `pmouseY` variables are similar to the `mouseX` and `mouseY` variables in that they hold the coordinates of the mouse pointer. However, the `pmouse` variables hold the previous coordinates, whilst the `mouse` variables hold the current coordinates. This can be demonstrated simply by drawing a line from the previous to the current mouse coordinates, as shown below:

```
void setup() {
    // black background
    background(0);
```

```
}

void draw() {
    // draw a line from the previous mouse coordinates
    stroke(255);
    line(pmouseX, pmouseY, mouseX, mouseY);
}
```

If you run this, you will see that, as you move the mouse, a line will be drawn wherever you move (Figure 101). All that is happening is that a line is being drawn from the previous mouse coordinate pmouseX and pMouseY to the current mouse coordinates mouseX and mouseY. As the draw() function is run continuously, every mouse move will draw a line

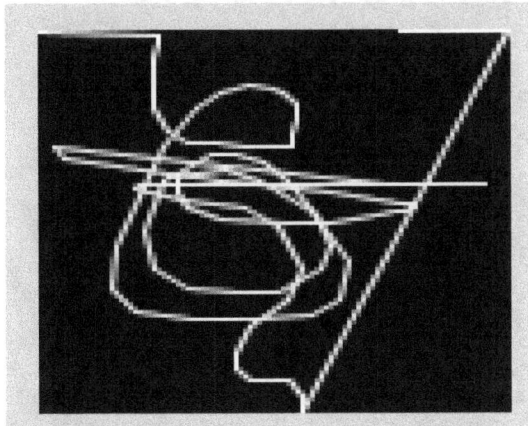

Figure 101: Drawing lines with mouse coordinates

Mouse Movement Functions

mouseMoved()
The mouseMoved() function detects events whenever the mouse pointer is moved. This means that anything in the mouseMoved() function will run every time the mouse is moved so you should be careful what you put in here; anything too intensive could slow your sketch down too much if the mouse is moved often

We can use it, combined with the mouseX and mouseY variables, to move our ship in a much freer manner than using the mouse wheel

```
void mouseMoved() {
    x2 = mouseX;
    y2 = mouseY;
}
```

We could of course use the MouseEvent for this if we wished

```
void mouseMoved(MouseEvent event) {
    x2 = event.getX();
    y2 = event.getY();
}
```

This will set the xy and y2 coordinates if our ship to the current mouse coordinates. Now, whenever we use the mouse, the ship will follow the mouse pointer!

mouseDragged()

The mouseDragged() function is the last mouse function provided by *Processing*. It can be thought of as a combination of the mouseMoved() and mousePressed() functions. Like the mouseMoved() function, the code inside the function is only run if the mouse is moving and, like the mousePressed() function, a mouse button must be pressed but it doesn't matter which button.

We could use this, in combination with some mouse variables, to provide rotation for our ship

```
void mouseDragged() {
    if (pmouseX < mouseX) {
        rotation2 += 0.1;
    } else {
        rotation2 -= 0.1;
    }
}
```

We have used the pmouseX and mouseX variables here to determine if the direction the mouse is being moved and rotate the ship accordingly. We will need to add rotation variables four our mouse-controlled ship and include the relevant translate() and rotate() function calls. The full code is shown below

```
float x = 400;
float y = 400;
color shipColour = color(0, 0, 255); // blue
float rotation = 0.0;

float x2 = 100;
float y2 = 100;
color mouseShipColour = color(255, 69, 0); // orangey
boolean cloaked = false;
float rotation2 = 0.0;
```

```
void setup() {
    size(800, 600);
}

void draw() {
    background(0); // black
    // only rotate this bit
    pushMatrix();
    // rotate round centre of triangle
    translate(x, y);
    rotate(rotation);
    translate(-x, -y);
    // ship
    fill(shipColour);
    ellipse(x, y, 25, 25);
    triangle(x, y-18, x-20, y+10, x+20, y+10);
    // thrusters
    fill(255, 255, 0);
    ellipse(x-10, y+10, 5, 5);
    ellipse(x+10, y+10, 5, 5);
    popMatrix();
    // end rotate

    if (!cloaked) {
        // only rotate this bit
        pushMatrix();
        // rotate round centre of triangle
        translate(x2, y2);
        rotate(rotation2);
        translate(-x2, -y2);
        // mouse ship
        fill(mouseShipColour);
        ellipse(x2, y2, 25, 25);
        triangle(x2, y2 + 18, x2 - 20, y2 - 10, x2 + 20, y2 - 10);
        // thrusters
        fill(255, 255, 0);
        ellipse(x2+10, y2-10, 5, 5);
        ellipse(x2-10, y2-10, 5, 5);
        popMatrix();
    }
}

void keyPressed() {
```

```
    if (key == 'z') {
       // rotate clockwise
       rotation -= 0.1;
    }
    else if (key == 'x') {
       // rotate anti-clockwise
       rotation += 0.1;
    }

    if (key == CODED) {
       if (keyCode == UP) {
          y--; // up
       }
       else if (keyCode == DOWN) {
          y++; // down
       }
       else if (keyCode == LEFT) {
          x--; // left
       }
       else if (keyCode == RIGHT) {
          x++; // right
       }
    }
}

void mouseClicked(MouseEvent event) {
    if (event.getButton() == LEFT) {
       cloaked = true;
    } else if (event.getButton() == RIGHT) {
       cloaked = false;
    }
}

void mouseDragged() {
    if (pmouseX < mouseX) {
       rotation2 += 0.1;
    } else {
       rotation2 -= 0.1;
    }
}

void mouseMoved(MouseEvent event) {
    x2 = event.getX();
```

```
    y2 = event.getY();
}

void mouseWheel(MouseEvent event) {
    y2 += event.getCount();
}
```

Buttons

Buttons and other graphical user interface (GUI) elements such as sliders, list boxes and spinners are usually referred to as widgets. These are used to enhance the user's experience of an application and allows them to interact with it. A button executes or launches an action such as allowing the user to select a file for opening

Unlike some more extensive languages such as Java, *Processing* does not provide libraries with ready-made widgets. The process of creating buttons is not complex, but it is quite painstaking. To create a button we need to define an area on the screen that will serve as a button. This is usually done by:

1. drawing some shape, such as a square or a circle in that area
2. determining whether the mouse button was pressed and if so, whether it was pressed in the button area
3. executing a process that we determine.

We have already covered all the processes and skills required to complete these steps. All that is now required is to put it into practice. We can demonstrate these techniques by creating a sketch with one button that will switch on a light bulb if it is off, or switch it off if it is on

Step one can be accomplished with the following few lines of code

```
final int BUTTON_TOP_LEFT_X = 10;
final int BUTTON_TOP_LEFT_Y = 10;
final int BUTTON_WIDTH = 20;
int buttonColour = color(0);

void setup() {
    // Draw window of 200 pixels wide by 200 pixels high
    size(200,200);
}

void draw() {
    // draw the button
    fill(buttonColour);
```

```
    rect(BUTTON_TOP_LEFT_X, BUTTON_TOP_LEFT_Y, BUTTON_WIDTH, BUTTON_WIDTH);
}
```

This creates a screen with a black square, our button, in the top-left corner as shown in Figure 102

Figure 102: Black square button

We can use mouse events to accomplish the next steps. Firstly we need to determine whether the mouse button is pressed. This is done by adding the mousePressed() function to our sketch code. Secondly we need to determine whether the mouse is being pressed over the square we drew that serves as our button. Our sketch can now be extended with the following code

```
// Handle mouse event
void mousePressed() {
    if (mouseX >= BUTTON_TOP_LEFT_X &&
        mouseX <= (BUTTON_TOP_LEFT_X + BUTTON_WIDTH) &&
        mouseY >= BUTTON_TOP_LEFT_Y &&
        mouseY <= (BUTTON_TOP_LEFT_Y + BUTTON_WIDTH)) {
        // Code to be executed when the mouse button is pressed in this area
    }
}
```

Since we want to switch the bulb on and off we will need to maintain the state of the bulb. A Boolean variable seems most appropriate as there are only two states the bulb can be in (on or off)

```
boolean isBulbOn = false;
```

This can be altered in our mousePressed() function which will change the state of the bulb when the button is pressed

```
// Code to be executed when the mouse button is pressed in this area
```

```
if (isBulbOn) {
    isBulbOn = false;
} else {
    isBulbOn = true;
}
```

This will reverse the state of the bulb depending on its state. However there is an easier way to do this where we always want to reverse the state (since there are only two states) using the ! not operator

```
isBulbOn = !isBulbOn;
```

This simply sets the isBulbOn variable to the opposite of its current value

We now need to reflect the state of the light bulb. To do this the draw function can be extended to draw the light bulb in one of its two states. We will keep things very simple so we are going to draw the light bulb using a grey square for the base and a white circle when the bulb is switched off or a yellow circle when the bulb is switched on.

```
// draw bulb
fill(64,64,64);
rect(93,90,15,20);
// draw a circle for the light bulb
if (isBulbOn) {
    fill(255, 204, 51); // an orange fill when the bulb is on
} else {
    fill(255); // a white fill when the bulb is off
}
ellipse(100,80,30,30);
```

You can now try this sketch. You should see that pressing the button switches the lightbulb on and off (Figure 103)

Figure 103: Using a button to change lightbulb state

Button State

I'm sure you will agree that this is not a very exciting button we have created. Nowadays, in the graphical environments we are used to, we can see when a button has focus. This means that buttons display differently when they are pressed, unpressed or when the mouse hovers over it by, for example, changing colour

To mimic this behaviour we need to code behaviours for the mouse when it is pressed, released or moved. The three functions, you might recall, that we need to use are `mousePressed()`, `mouseReleased()` and `mouseMoved()`

The button's normal colour will be black as before. To show the differences we will use totally different colours so if the mouse is pressed down while inside the button area we will make the button red and if the mouse is only hovering above the button we will use blue (Figure 104)

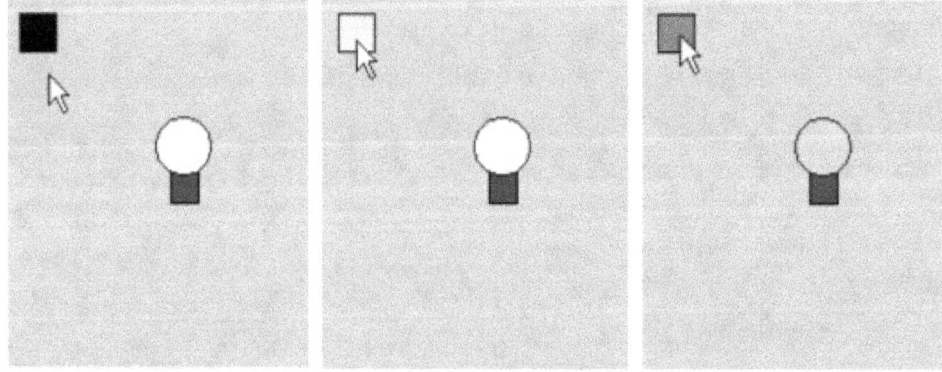

Figure 104: Button focus (from left: Unpressed, hovering, pressed)

We need to define three new variables to hold the colours for the three different states. To do this the following lines are added to the declarations at the beginning of the sketch code

```
// Define the colours for the button in its various states
int BUTTON_COLOUR_UP = color(0);
int BUTTON_COLOUR_DOWN = color(255, 0, 0);
int BUTTON_COLOUR_OVER = color(99, 255, 255);
int buttonColour = BUTTON_COLOUR_UP;
```

Note we have set the initial colour of the buttonColour variable. We can start by changing the button colour when the mouse is pressed inside the button area since we already have a function for pressing the mouse in our sketch. The mousePressed() function can be enhanced to do this by adding one line (shown in bold)

```
void mousePressed() {
    if (mouseX >= button_top_left_x &&
        mouseX <= button_top_left_x + button_width &&
        mouseY >= button_top_left_y &&
        mouseY <= (button_top_left_y + button_width)) {
        // change button colour
        buttonColour = BUTTON_COLOUR_DOWN;
        isBulbOn = !isBulbOn;
    }
}
```

In order to change the button colour when the mouse pointer hovers over the button we can use the mouseMoved() function to set the colour if the mouse is within the button coordinates.

```
void mouseMoved() {
    if (mouseX >= BUTTON_TOP_LEFT_X &&
        mouseX <= (BUTTON_TOP_LEFT_X + BUTTON_WIDTH) &&
        mouseY >= BUTTON_TOP_LEFT_Y &&
        mouseY <= (BUTTON_TOP_LEFT_Y + BUTTON_WIDTH)) {
        button_colour = button_over_colour;
        buttonColour = BUTTON_COLOUR_OVER;
    } else {
        buttonColour = BUTTON_COLOUR_UP;
    }
}
```

You may notice that you have seen this if statement before – we used it in our mousePressed() function. In order to not duplicate code, and have a single place we need to maintain it if we needed to change, we could *refactor* this out into a new function (refactoring is when you change existing code to do the same job but in a different way). We will call this function `buttonIsInFocus()` and have it return a boolean true if the mouse is over the button, false if it is not

```
boolean buttonIsInFocus() {
    return (mouseX >= BUTTON_TOP_LEFT_X &&
        mouseX <= (BUTTON_TOP_LEFT_X + BUTTON_WIDTH) &&
        mouseY >= BUTTON_TOP_LEFT_Y &&
        mouseY <= (BUTTON_TOP_LEFT_Y + BUTTON_WIDTH));
}
```

We can now replace our mouse functions to use the new function. We hope you agree that is much neater

```
void mouseMoved() {
    if (buttonIsInFocus()) {
        buttonColour = BUTTON_COLOUR_OVER;
    } else {
        buttonColour = BUTTON_COLOUR_UP;
    }
}
```

The only thing left to do now is to create a `mouseReleased()` function so the button returns colour when the mouse button is released. We can use our `buttonIsInFocus()` function again

```
void mouseReleased() {
    if (buttonIsInFocus()) {
        buttonColour = BUTTON_COLOUR_OVER;
    } else {
        buttonColour = BUTTON_COLOUR_UP;
    }
}
```

More Realistic Buttons

Rather than using just a square for a button, we can create a more realistic-looking button using triangles, a line and rectangles. We can create the illusion of a 3D button that moves up and down, when clicked, by drawing a bevel that is shaded in one corner which gives the impression of light shining on the button from the left. When the button is clicked, the two colours are switched around so that opposite corner is the darker colour giving the impression that the button is being pressed down. This effect can be seen in Figure 105

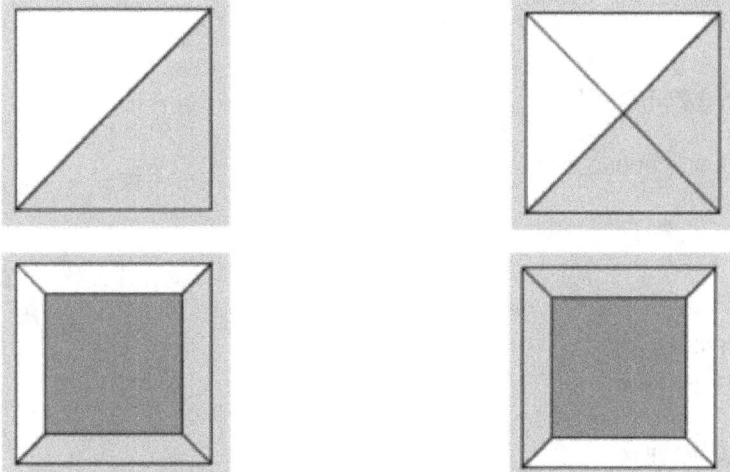

Figure 105: Steps to create a realistic button

This can be broken down into 4 steps which will show how this illusion is created:

1. Draw two triangles, the one on the left white and the one on the right grey
2. Draw a line from top left to bottom right. These diagonal lines help to create the illusion of a bevel
3. Draw a smaller darker square on top
4. To give the appearance of the button being depressed merely switch the colours of the two triangles

We can then combine this effect with our lightbulb sketch by adding the button drawing code into our draw() function and mouse event functions

```
final int BUTTON_TOP_LEFT_X = 10;
final int BUTTON_TOP_LEFT_Y = 10;
final int BUTTON_WIDTH = 20;
final int BEVEL_WIDTH = 3;

// Define the colours for the button in its various states
int BUTTON_COLOUR_TOP = color(128);
int BUTTON_COLOUR_UP = color(192);
int BUTTON_COLOUR_DOWN = color(255);
int BUTTON_COLOUR_OVER = color(128);

int BUTTON_LEFT_COLOUR = BUTTON_COLOUR_DOWN;
int BUTTON_RIGHT_COLOUR = BUTTON_COLOUR_UP;
```

```
int BACKGROUND_COLOUR = color(192);
int HOVER_COLOUR = BACKGROUND_COLOUR;

boolean isBulbOn = false;
void setup() {
    background(BACKGROUND_COLOUR);
    size(200,200);
}

void draw() {
    rectMode(CORNER);
    // highlight square
    noStroke();
    fill(HOVER_COLOUR);
    rect(BUTTON_TOP_LEFT_X - BEVEL_WIDTH, BUTTON_TOP_LEFT_Y - BEVEL_WIDTH,
        BUTTON_WIDTH + (BEVEL_WIDTH*2), BUTTON_WIDTH + (BEVEL_WIDTH*2));
    // draw the button
    stroke(0);
    fill(BUTTON_RIGHT_COLOUR);
    triangle(BUTTON_TOP_LEFT_X + BUTTON_WIDTH, BUTTON_TOP_LEFT_Y,
        BUTTON_TOP_LEFT_X + BUTTON_WIDTH, BUTTON_TOP_LEFT_Y + BUTTON_WIDTH,
        BUTTON_TOP_LEFT_X, BUTTON_TOP_LEFT_Y + BUTTON_WIDTH);
    fill(BUTTON_LEFT_COLOUR);
    triangle(BUTTON_TOP_LEFT_X, BUTTON_TOP_LEFT_Y, BUTTON_TOP_LEFT_X +
        BUTTON_WIDTH, BUTTON_TOP_LEFT_Y, BUTTON_TOP_LEFT_X, BUTTON_TOP_LEFT_Y +
        BUTTON_WIDTH);
    line(BUTTON_TOP_LEFT_X, BUTTON_TOP_LEFT_Y, BUTTON_TOP_LEFT_X + BUTTON_WIDTH,
        BUTTON_TOP_LEFT_Y + BUTTON_WIDTH);
    // little square
    fill(BUTTON_COLOUR_TOP);
    rect(BUTTON_TOP_LEFT_X + BEVEL_WIDTH, BUTTON_TOP_LEFT_Y + BEVEL_WIDTH,
        BUTTON_WIDTH - (BEVEL_WIDTH*2), BUTTON_WIDTH - (BEVEL_WIDTH*2));
    // draw bulb
    fill(64,64,64);
    rect(93,90,15,20);
    // draw a circle for the light bulb
    if (isBulbOn) {
        fill(255, 204, 51); // an orange fill when the bulb is on
    } else {
        fill(255); // a white fill when the bulb is off
    }
    ellipseMode(CENTER);
    ellipse(100,80,30,30);
```

```
}

void mousePressed() {
    if (buttonIsInFocus()) {
        // if the button is pressed, switch the bevel colours
        if (isBulbOn) {
            BUTTON_LEFT_COLOUR = BUTTON_COLOUR_DOWN;
            BUTTON_RIGHT_COLOUR = BUTTON_COLOUR_UP;
        } else {
            BUTTON_LEFT_COLOUR = BUTTON_COLOUR_UP;
            BUTTON_RIGHT_COLOUR = BUTTON_COLOUR_DOWN;
        }
        isBulbOn = !isBulbOn;
    }
}

void mouseMoved() {
    if (buttonIsInFocus()) {
        HOVER_COLOUR = BUTTON_COLOUR_OVER;
    } else {
        HOVER_COLOUR = BACKGROUND_COLOUR;
    }
}

boolean buttonIsInFocus() {
    return (mouseX >= BUTTON_TOP_LEFT_X &&
        mouseX <= (BUTTON_TOP_LEFT_X + BUTTON_WIDTH) &&
        mouseY >= BUTTON_TOP_LEFT_Y &&
        mouseY <= (BUTTON_TOP_LEFT_Y + BUTTON_WIDTH));
}
```

As you can see, this looks much more like a button and offers the user feedback on the state of the button – in this case whether the button has been pressed or not (Figure 106)

Button Labels and Icons

Although the function of our button may be obvious at this point, it would give us a much friendlier user interface if we could put some text or images on the buttons so that people know what the buttons are for.

Adding the following few lines of code to our lightbulb sketch will add the label 'Bulb' to the button.

```
// Place text on button
```

```
textAlign(CENTER, CENTER);
fill(color(0,0,05));
text("Bulb", BUTTON_TOP_LEFT_X + (BUTTON_WIDTH/2),
BUTTON_TOP_LEFT_Y + (BUTTON_WIDTH/2));
```

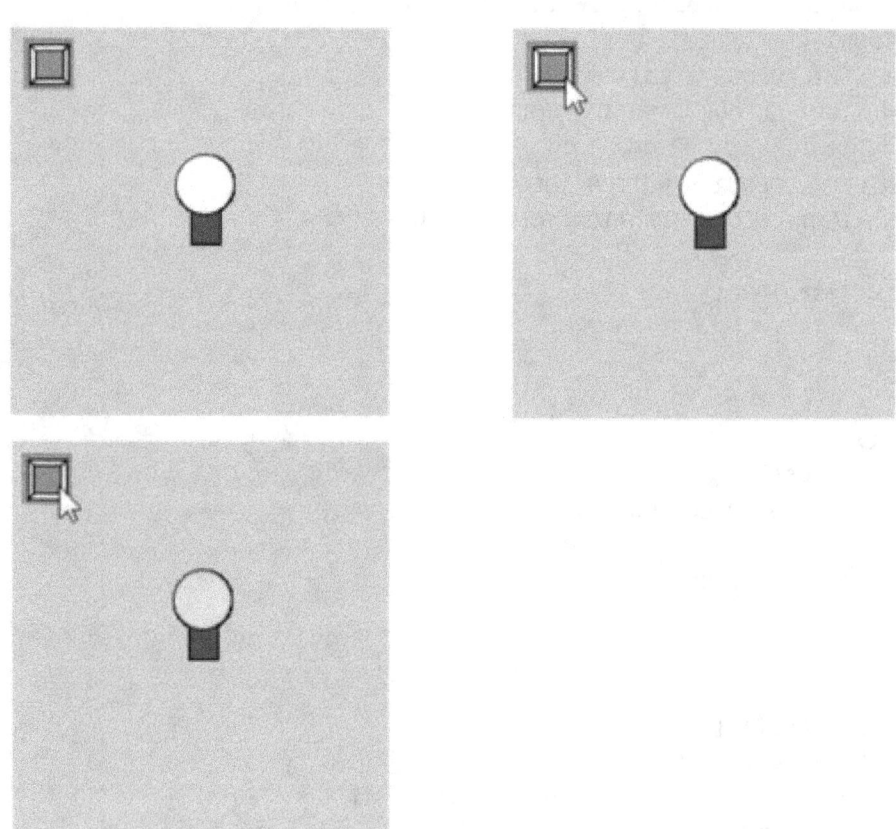

Figure 106: Lightbulb Sketch with realistic button

Of course our button will need to be larger in order to correctly display the text so we can enhance our button by using a different size height and width, creating a rectangular button

```
final int BUTTON_WIDTH = 80;
final int BUTTON_HEIGHT = 40;
```

Applying this to the rest of our button display code means that our button can be displayed with text that tells the user what the button is for (Figure 107)

We can also add an icon to the button to give a visual representation of what the button will do as shown in Figure 108

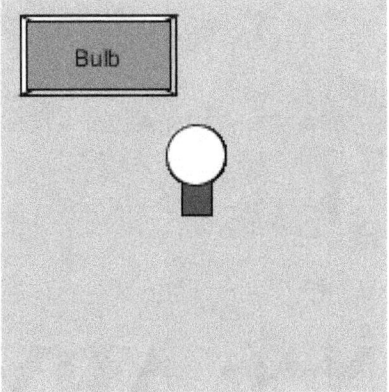

Figure 107: Button label

Text on buttons can take up a great deal of space so often it is advantageous to have a fairly small button with only an image on it

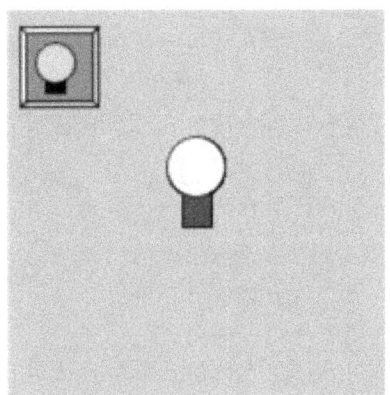 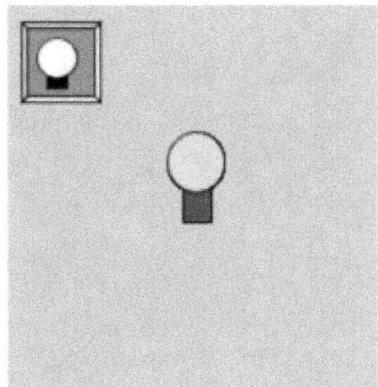

Figure 108: Button with an icon

This takes very little extra code to achieve, we can simply make the button square again and add a few lines of code to draw the icon

```
// draw icon on button
fill(0x00, 0x00, 0x00);
rect(BUTTON_TOP_LEFT_X + BEVEL_WIDTH + 10,
BUTTON_TOP_LEFT_Y + BEVEL_WIDTH + 20, 10, 10);
if (isBulbOn) {
   fill(0xFF, 0xFF, 0xFF);
} else {
   fill(0xFF, 0xCC, 0x33);
}
```

225

SECTION 3: ADVANCED PROCESSING

Chapter 17: Rendering Modes: 2D and 3D
by Antony Lees, Ben Notorianni and Boyd Stratton

So far everything you have drawn has been 2-dimensional. This Chapter introduces you to drawing rendering modes and drawing in 3-dimensions. Firstly we will introduce you to the rendering modes available in *Processing* then look at 3-dimensional space by drawing 2-dimensional shapes but introducing the third dimension. Finally we will move on to drawing 3D shapes and animating them in three dimensions

Rendering

Rendering is the process by which the geometric data and models defined within your sketch are converted to an image that you see on your screen. *Processing* provides three main rendering modes; default mode, P2D, and P3D. *Processing* uses the OpenGL graphics library within the P2D and P3D modes. In previous versions of *Processing* support for OpenGL was implemented as its own separate renderer, with all other modes being implemented in Java software.

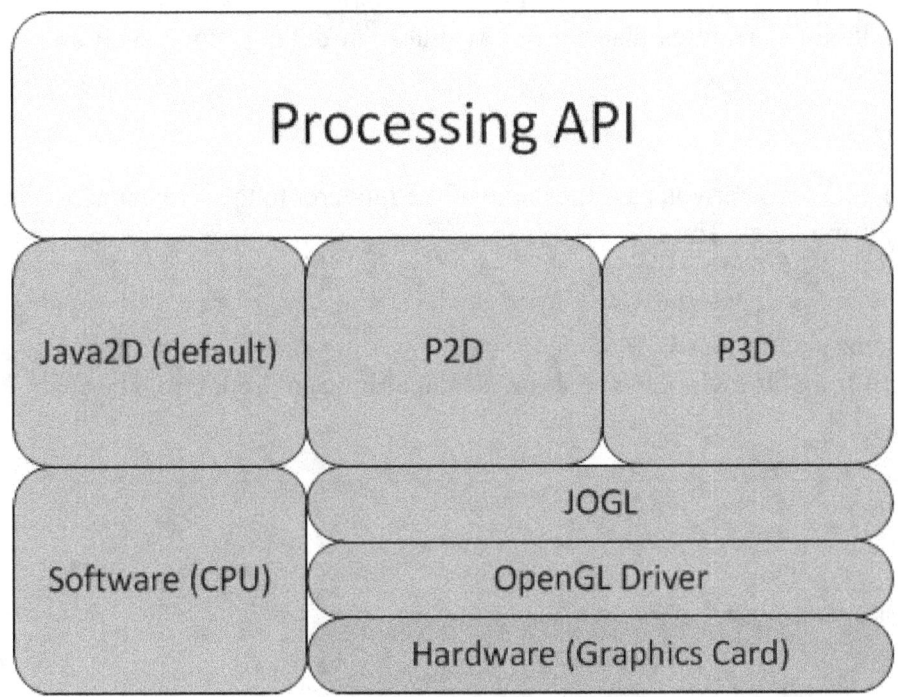

Figure 109: Processing OpenGL Stack

OpenGL is an industry standard programming interface for rendering graphics. In particular OpenGL will utilise graphics hardware acceleration to provide faster rendering of graphics than software based renderers. Depending on your sketch this will usually mean improved performance though it does require OpenGL-compatible graphics card to be enabled on your computer (you might just have to update your graphics drivers if you get an error)

In addition, and crucially important for *Processing*, OpenGL is supported in Java though the JOGL library (JOGL is short for Java OpenGL). The diagram in Figure 109 shows a simplified view of *Processing*'s drawing stack.

Rendering Modes

The renderer that you wish to run your sketch in is passed to the size function as the third parameter. We have so far used the default renderer for our sketches where you can simply omit the third parameter to the size function as shown below

```
size(800, 600);
```

This default renderer is software-based and is only capable of two-dimensional sketches. For simple sketches the default renderer is all you need. If you find that your sketches are beginning to run slowly, and OpenGL is available on your computer, then you may wish to try the P2D renderer to see if you can get the benefit of hardware acceleration. P2D also provides additional features that are not available in default mode such as lighting and textures

2D Mode

To use the P2D renderer you pass the name of the renderer to the size() function in addition to the width and height sizes

```
size(800, 600, P2D);
```

The following sketch uses P2D mode to draw a rotating square and circles (Figure 110); it may benefit from OpenGL depending on the capabilities of your computer.

```
float r=0;
int RECT_SIZE=150;
int CIRCLE_RADIUS=70;

void setup() {
   size(800, 600, P2D); // P2D mode
   noStroke();
}

void draw() {
   background(200);
   translate(width/2, height/2); // centre of screen
```

```
rotate(r); // rotate
r+=PI/128;
fill(255, 0, 0); // square dolour
rectMode(CENTER); // square
rect(0, 0, RECT_SIZE, RECT_SIZE);
fill(55, 32, 200); // circle colour
ellipseMode(RADIUS); // set radius mode
//Move to top surface of square. Translates are relative inside draw loop
//And draw circle
translate(0, -RECT_SIZE/2-CIRCLE_RADIUS);
ellipse(0, 0, CIRCLE_RADIUS, CIRCLE_RADIUS);
//Bottom surface circle
translate(0, 2*CIRCLE_RADIUS+RECT_SIZE);
ellipse(0, 0, CIRCLE_RADIUS, CIRCLE_RADIUS);
//Right surface circle
translate(RECT_SIZE/2+CIRCLE_RADIUS, -CIRCLE_RADIUS-RECT_SIZE/2);
ellipse(0, 0, CIRCLE_RADIUS, CIRCLE_RADIUS);
//Left surface circle
translate(-RECT_SIZE-2*CIRCLE_RADIUS, 0);
ellipse(0, 0, CIRCLE_RADIUS, CIRCLE_RADIUS);
}
```

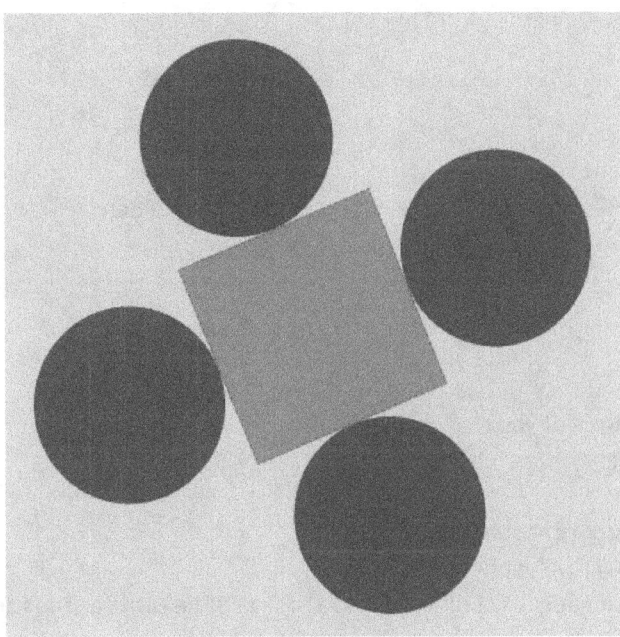

Figure 110: P2D shapes

3D Mode

The default and P2D renderers do not support the 3D features of *Processing*. To use the 3D features you need to use the P3D renderer.:

```
size(800, 600, P3D);
```

Processing's 3D features include 3D shapes such as spheres and boxes, lights and camera effects and the ability to draw in three dimensions. The P3D renderer introduces the idea of a z-axis to the 2D (x/y) coordinate system. The z-axis provides a means of specifying the third dimension, negative values of z move objects further into the distance and positive values move them closer

We can produce a three-dimensional version of the sketch to demonstrate this with the code below

```
float r=0;
int BOX_SIZE=150;
int SPHERE_RADIUS=70;

void setup() {
    size(800, 600, P3D); // P3D mode
    noStroke();
}

void draw() {
    background(200);
    lights(); // lighting
    translate(width/2, height/2, 0); // centre of screen
    // rotate all axis
    rotateX(r/4);
    rotateY(r/8);
    rotateZ(-r);
    r+=PI/96;
    //Set fill colour for box
    fill(255, 0, 0); // box colour
    box(BOX_SIZE);
    //Set fill colour for spheres
    fill(55, 32, 200); // sphere colour
    //Move to top surface of box. Translates are relative inside draw loop
    //And draw sphere
    translate(0, -BOX_SIZE/2-SPHERE_RADIUS, 0);
    sphere(SPHERE_RADIUS);
    //Bottom surface sphere
```

```
    translate(0, 2*SPHERE_RADIUS+BOX_SIZE, 0);
    sphere(SPHERE_RADIUS);
    //Right surface sphere
    translate(BOX_SIZE/2+SPHERE_RADIUS, -SPHERE_RADIUS-BOX_SIZE/2, 0);
    sphere(SPHERE_RADIUS);
    //Left surface sphere
    translate(-BOX_SIZE-2*SPHERE_RADIUS, 0, 0);
    sphere(SPHERE_RADIUS);
}
```

You should be able to see the difference between the 2D and 3D representations (Figure 111)

Choosing the renderer to use for your sketch depends on what you want your code to do. If you want to use 3D then the P3D renderer is required. For 2D sketches the default renderer is often all you need, and can be more accurate than the OpenGL based P2D renderer. For the fastest possible 2D sketches or if you want to use a couple of the features in 2D not available in the default renderer, such as textures, then the P2D renderer is a good choice

Figure 111: P3D Shapes

P3D is not limited to sketches that use 3 dimensions, you can also use it for 2D sketches. Try running sketches from other chapters in P3D or P2D mode and see how they behave.

In practice sketches running these modes will look somewhat different from the default mode. The changes may vary from no visual difference to quite dramatic changes. You may see an improvement in rendering quality and for graphic intensive sketches an increase in performance., However, if you are going to be sharing sketches with other people then you may prefer to stick with the default renderer for 2D sketches. With this mode you can be sure that your sketches will look consistent across different machines and that they will run regardless of whether OpenGL is installed or not.

In theory OpenGL mode should bring clear performance and rendering improvements to any sketch. The extent of these improvements however depends on your graphics card and the quality of the OpenGL drivers. In addition, not all graphic cards are equal. Some will be faster, much faster than others, while others may not implement every feature of OpenGL. For example, early MacBooks use integrated graphics chip sets which do not support anti-aliasing.

3D Space

To begin looking at drawing our own 3D graphics, we will start by looking at the z-coordinate and how you can draw standard 2D shapes in 3D space. Using 3D adds a third dimension, as you would expect. 3D objects are therefore drawn on three dimensions (also called *planes*) - the x-plane (left-to-right), the y-plane (top-to-bottom) and the z-plane (closer-to-further). 3D objects need to be described in terms of coordinates on all three planes

The *Processing* screen can also be thought of in terms of these three planes and objects on the screen can be manipulated across all three dimensions even if the object is 2D in nature. An example of this is rotating a 2D shape through the z-plane as well as the x- and y-planes. We can demonstrate this using our earlier hexagon example

```
float rotation = 0.1;

void setup() {
   size(200, 200);
   strokeWeight(2);
   stroke(100);
}

void draw() {
   // reset the page with a background colour
   background(0);
   // translate so rotation is around centre
   translate(100, 100);
   // rotate
```

```
    rotate(rotation);
    translate(-100, -100);
    drawHexagon(100, 100, 60);
    rotation += 0.01;
}

void drawHexagon(int x, int y, float radius) {
    beginShape() ;
    for (int i = 0 ; i < 6 ; i++) { // 6 sides
        vertex(x + radius*cos(2.0*PI*i/6), y + radius*sin(2.0*PI*i/6));
    }
    endShape(CLOSE) ;
}
```

We have added rotation into the example, but not yet added 3D. If you run this example you will see that the hexagon rotates around its centre. If we now add the P3D renderer and run it, you should see little, or no, difference since we are not yet using any aspects of 3D

```
size(200, 200);
```

In 2D there is a single rotate() function that rotates around the centre in a clockwise or anti-clockwise directions depending on the value (positive being clockwise). With only two dimensions this is the only axis that can be rotated around. However in 3D there are three ways to rotate - around the z-axis (clockwise/anti-clockwise), the x-axis (rotating over or under) and the y-axis (rotating left or right). *Processing* provides functions for these called rotateZ(), rotatex() and rotateY() respectively where rotateZ() is synonymous with rotate(). If you try using any of these functions in a 2D mode then *Processing* will display an error saying they can only be used in 3D mode

We can try these functions in our sketch by adding the letters to the function and making it rotate in different directions or you could add all of them so it rotates in all directions (Figure 112)

```
rotateX(rotation);
rotateY(rotation);
rotateZ(rotation);
```

Figure 112: Rotating hexagon

Many of the *Processing* functions we have already seen can be used with additional arguments in order to control their use in 3D. The translate() function, for example, can also be used to translate on the z-plane by adding an additional argument

```
translate(x, y, z);
```

Adding the following line to our hexagon sketch will translate the hexagon 100 pixels nearer (so making it look bigger)

```
translate(0, 0, 100);
```

Predefined 3D Shapes

Processing provides some predefined shapes specifically for 3D use; sphere and box. We saw these used in our earlier example.

Box

The box() function, as you might expect, draws a 3D box. The function is overloaded with two different versions; one assumes all sides are equal (a cube), the other allows you to specify different lengths for the sides

```
box(size);
box(width, height, depth);
```

There is not much more to it than that. You may want to rotate any box you create, as shown in Figure 113, as otherwise you only see the front face which, if using an opaque fill colour, just looks like a square

```
size(300, 300, P3D);
noFill();
background(255);
translate(width/2, height/2);
rotateY(QUARTER_PI);
box(100);
```

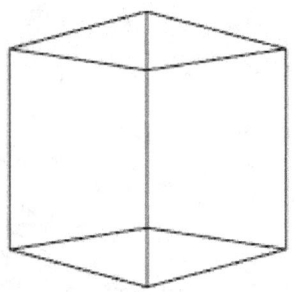

Figure 113: Rotated box

Sphere

The sphere() function draws a hollow ball of a given size (Figure 114)

```
size(300, 300, P3D);
noStroke();
background(255);
lights();
translate(width/2, height/2);
sphere(100);
```

Figure 114: Sphere

The spheres actually comprise a mesh of triangles which can be seen if you omit the noStroke() function in the code above (Figure 115)

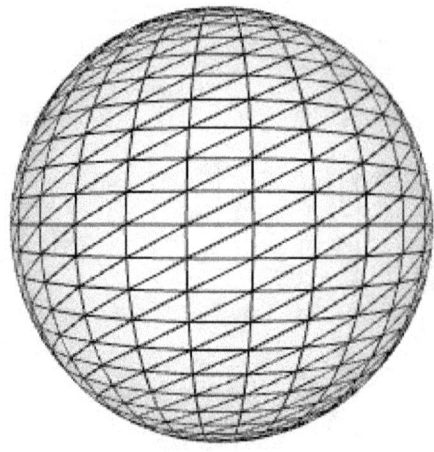

Figure 115: Sphere with visible mesh

This mesh of triangles can be controlled with the sphereDetail() function which specifies the number of vertices per revolution. The default is 30 but you can set anything from 3. Higher numbers will create a more detailed sphere, but will also use more computer power to generate, so you may need to lower it if you are creating a lot of spheres and notice that performance is affected. You can also set different numbers of vertices across the vertical and horizontal axes

```
sphereDetail(resolution);
sphereDetail(horizontalResolution, verticalResolution);
```

Some examples for comparison of different numbers of vertices can be seen in Figure 116

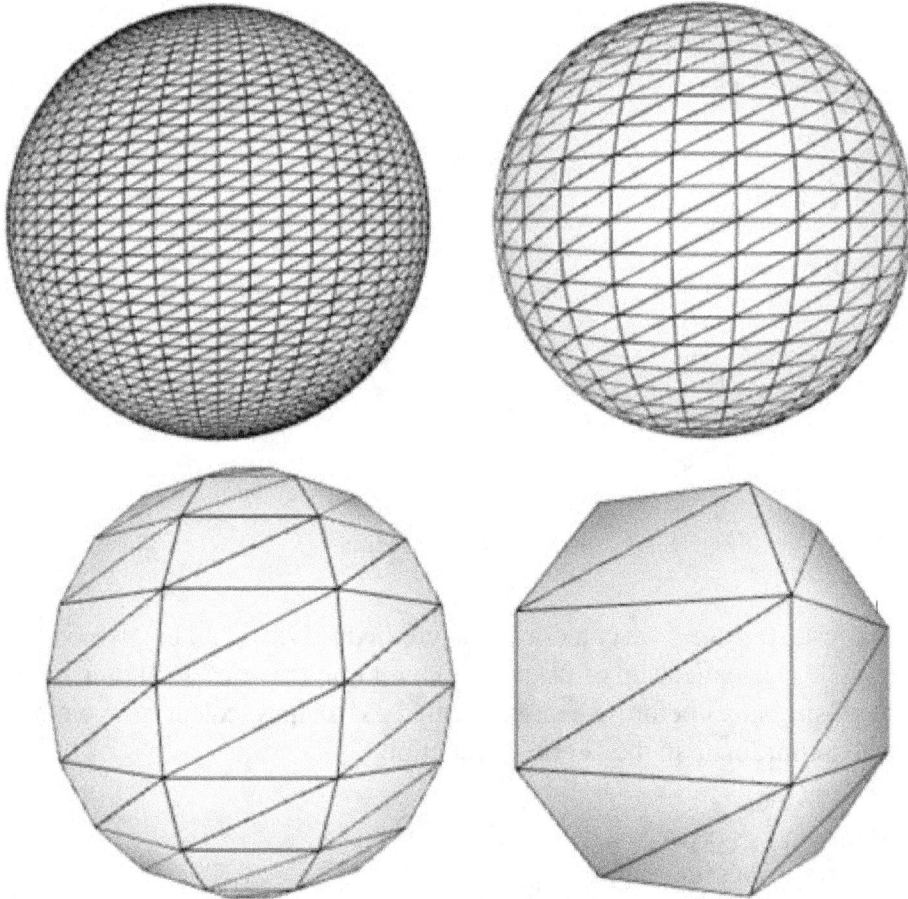

Figure 116: Sphere with sphere detail of 60 (top-left), 30 (top-right), 10 (bottom-left) and 5 (bottom-right)

Custom 3D Shapes

If we want to draw a shape not covered by spheres or boxes, we will need to draw it ourselves using vertices, as we did with the 2D shapes. This time, though, we need to specify three coordinates for each vertex to plot it in three-dimensions. *Processing*'s vertex function can have two or three arguments, so we will be using the three arguments required for 3D in the form

```
vertex(x, y, z);
```

where the x and y coordinates are the same as seen previously, and the z coordinate is the third dimension.

237

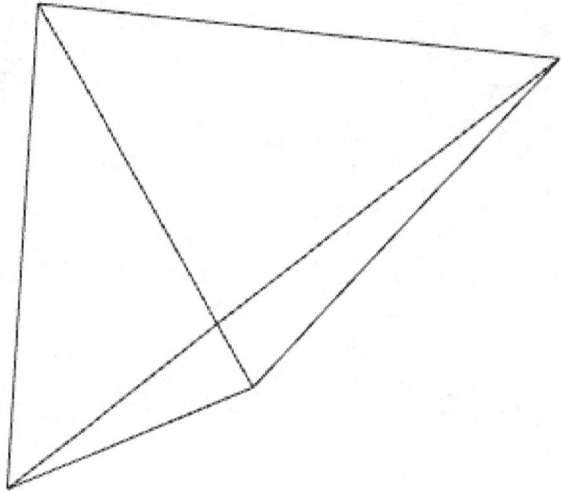

Figure 117: Tetrahedron

One of the easiest 3D shapes we can draw is a tetrahedron (Figure 117), which is a 4-sided polyhedron (a 3D shape made up of 2D shapes) with four triangles including the base. The process is very similar to before when we created 2D shapes except now we have to use the additional z-coordinate in the `vertex()` function

```
int edsgeSize = 100;
beginShape(TRIANGLE_STRIP);
vertex(edgeSize, edgeSize, edgeSize);
vertex(-edgeSize, -edgeSize, edgeSize);
vertex(-edgeSize, edgeSize, -edgeSize);
vertex(edgeSize, -edgeSize, -edgeSize);
vertex(edgeSize, edgeSize, edgeSize);
vertex(-edgeSize, -edgeSize, edgeSize);
endShape(CLOSE);
```

This will draw our tetrahedron with a given edge size. We can place some code around this to rotate it and also move it into a function called `drawTetrahedron()` so we can alter the size easily or draw more than one if we wish

```
float rotation = 0.01;

void setup() {
    size(600, 400, P3D);
    noFill();
}
```

```
void draw() {
    background(255);
    translate(width/2, height/2, 0);
    rotateY(rotation);
    rotateX(rotation);
    rotateZ(rotation);
    drawTetrahedron(100);
    rotation += 0.01;
}

void drawTetrahedron(int edgeSize) {
    beginShape(TRIANGLE_STRIP);
    vertex(edgeSize, edgeSize, edgeSize);
    vertex(-edgeSize, -edgeSize, edgeSize);
    vertex(-edgeSize, edgeSize, -edgeSize);
    vertex(edgeSize, -edgeSize, -edgeSize);
    vertex(edgeSize, edgeSize, edgeSize);
    vertex(-edgeSize, -edgeSize, edgeSize);
    endShape(CLOSE);
}
```

We can use this same idea to create any shape we wish provided we can work out the coordinates. For example, we might create a complex shape such as a cuboctahedron - a 24-sided polyhedron with faces made up of eight triangles and six squares, as shown in Figure 118

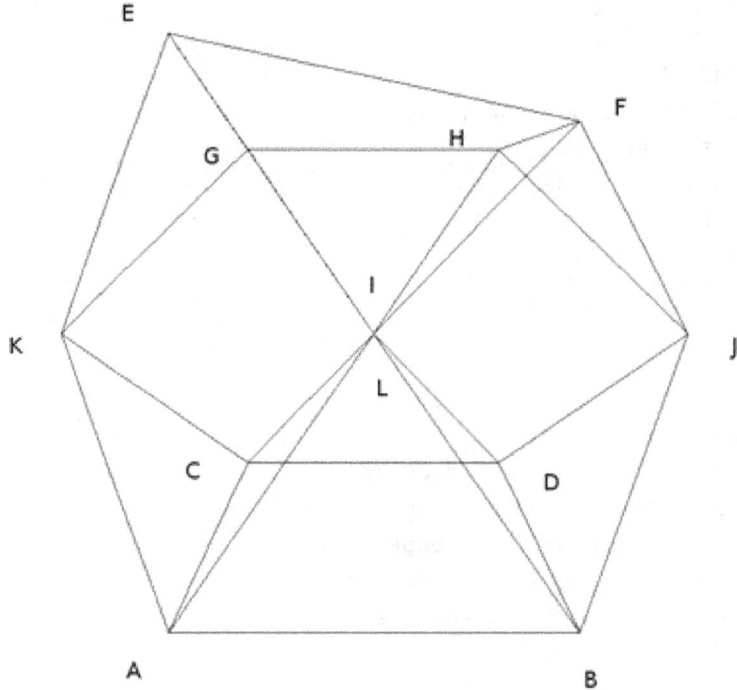

Figure 118: Cuboctahedron with vertices marked

As you can see, although there are 24 sides, there are actually only 11 vertices, to which we have assigned each a letter. To draw a shape we have to move from one vertex to another in order to make a continuous line that completes the shape. We'll create a function called drawCuboctahedron() that takes the edge size as an argument which means we can reuse our tetrahedron sketch and just call our new function

Firstly we need to calculate the size of one of the diagonals from the size of a straight edge. We won't explain this fully except to say that this is a standard calculation of the diagonal using Pythagoras theorem.

```
void drawCuboctahedron(int edgeSize) {
    // calculate the diagonal length
    float halfEdgeSize = edgeSize / 2;
    float halfDiagonalSize = (sqrt((sq(edgeSize)) + (sq(edgeSize)))) / 2;
}
```

We also need to draw the shape in relation to its centre point, so that it rotates around the centre. The centre point of our cuboctahedron is at point (0,0,-edgeSize) – that is one line-length into the screen – the halfway point between vertices I and L. If we draw our vertices in relation to these coordinates, the shape will be centred around that point and so rotate properly.

Since we need to draw a continuous line from each vertex to the next we have decided to draw them in the order A,I,E,K,A,B,J,F,I,B,D,L,H,J,D,C,K,G,L,C,A,I,E,G,H,F,E

This gives us the following function for drawing our shape

```
void drawCuboctahedron(int edgeSize) {

    int x = 0;
    int y = 0;
    int z = -edgeSize;

    // calculate the diagonal length
    float halfEdgeSize = edgeSize / 2;
    float halfDiagonalSize = (sqrt((sq(edgeSize)) + (sq(edgeSize)))) / 2;

    // draw the shape
    beginShape();
    vertex(x - halfEdgeSize, y - halfDiagonalSize, z + halfEdgeSize); // A
    vertex(x, y, z); // I
    vertex(x - halfEdgeSize, y + halfEdgeSize, z + halfEdgeSize); // E
    vertex(x - (halfEdgeSize * 2), y, z + (halfEdgeSize * 2)); // K
    vertex(x - halfEdgeSize, y - halfDiagonalSize, z + halfEdgeSize); // A
    vertex(x + halfEdgeSize, y - halfDiagonalSize, z + halfEdgeSize); // B
    vertex(x + (halfEdgeSize * 2), y, z + (halfEdgeSize * 2)); // J
    vertex(x + halfEdgeSize, y + halfEdgeSize, z + halfEdgeSize); // F
    vertex(x, y, z); // I
    vertex(x + halfEdgeSize, y - halfDiagonalSize, z + halfEdgeSize); // B
    vertex(x + halfEdgeSize, y - halfEdgeSize, z + (halfEdgeSize * 3)); // D
    vertex(x, y, z + (halfEdgeSize * 4)); // L
    vertex(x + halfEdgeSize, y + halfDiagonalSize, z + (halfEdgeSize * 3)); // H
    vertex(x + (halfEdgeSize * 2), y, z + (halfEdgeSize * 2)); // J
    vertex(x + halfEdgeSize, y - halfEdgeSize, z + (halfEdgeSize * 3)); // D
    vertex(x - halfEdgeSize, y - halfDiagonalSize, z + (halfEdgeSize * 3)); // C
    vertex(x - (halfEdgeSize * 2), y, z + (halfEdgeSize * 2)); // K
    vertex(x - halfEdgeSize, y + halfDiagonalSize, z + (halfEdgeSize * 3)); // G
    vertex(x, y, z + (halfEdgeSize * 4)); // L
    vertex(x - halfEdgeSize, y - halfDiagonalSize, z + (halfEdgeSize * 3)); // C
    vertex(x - halfEdgeSize, y - halfDiagonalSize, z + halfEdgeSize); // A
    vertex(x, y, z); // I
    vertex(x - halfEdgeSize, y + halfEdgeSize, z + halfEdgeSize); // E
    vertex(x - halfEdgeSize, y + halfDiagonalSize, z + (halfEdgeSize * 3)); // G
    vertex(x + halfEdgeSize, y + halfDiagonalSize, z + (halfEdgeSize * 3)); // H
    vertex(x + halfEdgeSize, y + halfEdgeSize, z + halfEdgeSize); // F
```

```
    vertex(x - halfEdgeSize, y + halfEdgeSize, z + halfEdgeSize); // E
    endShape(CLOSE);
}
```

Though this looks complicated it is simply drawing a line from one vertex to the next. We can plug this into our previous tetrahedron sketch and instead call our new drawCuboctahedron() function. Since we made the function reusable by providing the edge size we can even call it more than once with different sizes if we wish (Figure 119)

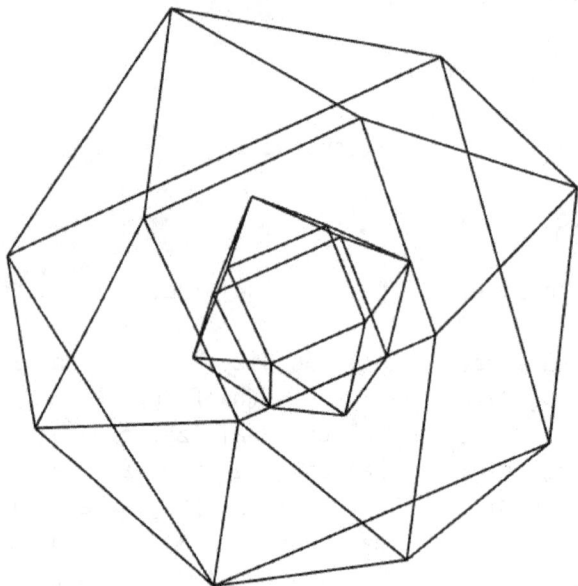

Figure 119: Cuboctahedrons of different sizes

3D Procedural Generation

Procedural generation means that the program will generate the geometry itself as opposed to drawing a 3D model designed by an artist or programmer. Procedural techniques are powerful and can generate some fascinating and amazingly beautiful images. Invariably they are rooted in mathematical methods, but don't let that put you off – the concepts involved are usually very simple and yet can produce a wide range of imagery from complex, precise geometric objects to organic, flowing animations.

In our example we will draw an icosahedron (a polyhedron with 20 triangular sides) as a fractal shape, as shown in Figure 120. Fractal shapes are those that can be subdivided into progressively smaller shapes, such as snowflakes. We will use triangles, which is known as triangular subdivision, by comprising each triangular side of smaller triangles

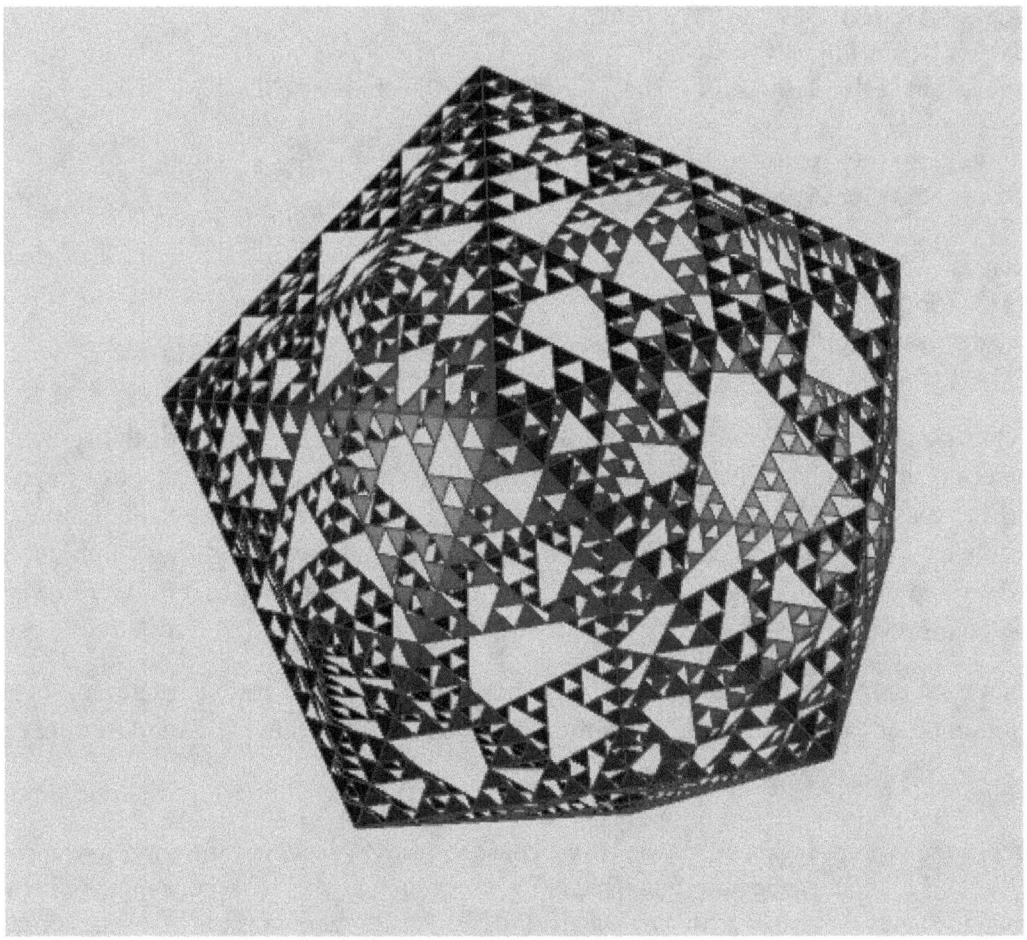

Figure 120: Fractal icosahedron

We will start by defining the setup() and draw() function, then expanding them on them as we explain what each part does

```
void setup() {
    size(1024, 768, P3D);
    colorMode(RGB, 1.0);
}


void draw() {
    background(0.75);

    // Move the origin so that the scene is centred on the screen.
    translate(width/2, height/2, 0.0);

    // Set up the lighting.
```

243

```
    ambientLight(0.025, 0.025, 0.025);
    directionalLight(0.2, 0.2, 0.2, -1, -1, -1);
    spotLight(1.0, 1.0, 1.0, -200, 0, 300, 1, 0, -1, PI/4.0, 20);

    // Rotate the local coordinate system.
    smoothRotation(5.0, 6.7, 7.3);

    stroke(0.2);
    fill(smoothColour(6.0, 9.2, 0.7));
    drawIcosahedron(5, 200);
}
```

We start by clearing the screen and translating our shape to the centre of the screen. We then set up some lights. These functions cast lighting effects onto any shapes drawn. We could have used the *Processing* function lights() to set up some default lighting, but instead we've opted for some custom lights using different types of lighting - ambient light, spotlight and directional lights. The lighting we've chosen is dark and moody but this is easily changed.

We have set up a rotating system whereby the rotation and the colour rotate in a cyclical fashion in order to give a smooth transition between the new value and the last one.

```
/**
 * Generate a vector whose components change smoothly over time in the range
 * [ 0, 1 ]. Each component uses a sin() function to map the current time in
 * milliseconds somewhere in the range [ 0, 1 ].A 'speed' factor is specified for
 * each component.
 */
PVector smoothVector(float s1, float s2, float s3) {
    float mills = 0.00003f * millis();

    float x = 0.5 * sin(mills * s1) + 0.5;
    float y = 0.5 * sin(mills * s2) + 0.5;
    float z = 0.5 * sin(mills * s3) + 0.5;

    return new PVector(x, y, z);
}

/**
 * Generate a colour which smoothly changes over time.
 * The speed of each component is controlled by the parameters s1, s2 and s3.
 */
```

```
color smoothColour(float s1, float s2, float s3) {
    PVector v = smoothVector(s1, s2, s3);

    return color(v.x, v.y, v.z);
}


/**
 * Rotate the current coordinate system.
 * Uses smoothVector() to smoothly animate the rotation.
 */
void smoothRotation(float s1, float s2, float s3) {
    PVector r1 = smoothVector(s1, s2, s3);

    rotateX(2.0 * PI * r1.x);
    rotateY(2.0 * PI * r1.y);
    rotateX(2.0 * PI * r1.z);
}
```

Both these functions animate a property over time. smoothColour() cycles through colours while smoothRotation() rotates the view in a progressive, cyclic fashion. To give these changes an element of unpredictability, the functions take parameters s1, s2, and s3. The value of these parameters determine how fast each component changes. So for example in smoothColour() s1, s2 and s3 determine how fast the red, green and blue channels change relative to each other.

Although these functions animate entirely different properties they are very similar in functionality. So much so in fact that we've broken out the common code as the separate function smoothVector(). This function takes the three parameters, s1, s2 and s3, and returns as a vector the three component values animated in the range [0, 1] (a vector is a triplet of numbers and *Processing* provides us with PVector, an extremely useful class for manipulating vectors directly).

To achieve a smooth and cyclic rhythm smoothValue() uses the sine function with the current time in milliseconds (multiplied by s1, s2 or s3) as the argument. The return value is a PVector and the x, y and z properties of this vector are used for the components of the rotation and colour.

The drawIcosahedron() function itself calculates the vertices for the 20 sides and draws them using triangles. The first few lines use three orthogonal Golden Ratio rectangles inscribed by a sphere of radius 'r' to calculate the coordinates of the twelve vertices of the icosahedron. The remaining lines draw the 20 triangular faces made from the twelve vertices. The twist in this section of code is that the drawing of the triangles is deferred to a separate function. In doing so, we open up the possibility of manipulating the triangles before actually drawing them.

```
/**
 * Draw an icosahedron defined by a radius r and recursive depth d
 */
void drawIcosahedron(int depth, float r) {
    // Calculate the vertex data for an icosahedron inscribed by a sphere radius
'r'.
    // Use 4 Golden Ratio rectangles as the basis.
    float gr = (1.0 + sqrt(5.0))/2.0;
    float h = r/sqrt(1.0 + gr * gr);

    PVector[] v = {
    new PVector(0, -h, h*gr), new PVector(0, -h, -h*gr), new PVector(0, h, -h*gr),
        new PVector(0, h, h*gr),
    new PVector(h, -h*gr, 0), new PVector(h, h*gr, 0), new PVector(-h, h*gr, 0),
        new PVector(-h, -h*gr, 0),
    new PVector(-h*gr, 0, h), new PVector(-h*gr, 0, -h), new PVector(h*gr, 0,
        -h), new PVector(h*gr, 0, h)
    };

    // reset r
    r = 0.0f;

    beginShape(TRIANGLES);
    drawTriangle(depth, r, v[0], v[7], v[4]);
    drawTriangle(depth, r, v[0], v[4], v[11]);
    drawTriangle(depth, r, v[0], v[11], v[3]);
    drawTriangle(depth, r, v[0], v[3], v[8]);
    drawTriangle(depth, r, v[0], v[8], v[7]);

    drawTriangle(depth, r, v[1], v[4], v[7]);
    drawTriangle(depth, r, v[1], v[10], v[4]);
    drawTriangle(depth, r, v[10], v[11], v[4]);
    drawTriangle(depth, r, v[11], v[5], v[10]);
    drawTriangle(depth, r, v[5], v[3], v[11]);
    drawTriangle(depth, r, v[3], v[6], v[5]);
    drawTriangle(depth, r, v[6], v[8], v[3]);
    drawTriangle(depth, r, v[8], v[9], v[6]);
    drawTriangle(depth, r, v[9], v[7], v[8]);
    drawTriangle(depth, r, v[7], v[1], v[9]);
```

```
    drawTriangle(depth, r, v[2], v[1], v[9]);
    drawTriangle(depth, r, v[2], v[10], v[1]);
    drawTriangle(depth, r, v[2], v[5], v[10]);
    drawTriangle(depth, r, v[2], v[6], v[5]);
    drawTriangle(depth, r, v[2], v[9], v[6]);
    endShape();
}
```

The drawTriangle() function does the bulk of the work by decomposing each side into smaller triangles.

```
/**
 * Draw a triangle either immediately or subdivide it first.
 * If depth is 1 then draw the triangle otherwise subdivide first.
 */
void drawTriangle(int depth, float r, PVector p1, PVector p2, PVector p3) {
    if (depth == 1) {
        vertex(p1.x, p1.y, p1.z);
        vertex(p2.x, p2.y, p2.z);
        vertex(p3.x, p3.y, p3.z);
    } else {
        // Calculate the mid points of this triangle.
        PVector v1 = PVector.mult(PVector.add(p1, p2), 0.5f);
        PVector v2 = PVector.mult(PVector.add(p2, p3), 0.5f);
        PVector v3 = PVector.mult(PVector.add(p3, p1), 0.5f);

        // Generate the next level of detail.
        depth --;

        drawTriangle(depth, r, p1, v1, v3);
        drawTriangle(depth, r, v1, p2, v2);
        drawTriangle(depth, r, v2, p3, v3);

        // Add this line to draw the central triangle
        // drawTriangle(depth, r, v1, v2, v3);
    }
}
```

The function takes five parameters, a depth, a radius r and the coordinates of the triangle's three vertices. If the value of the depth parameter is equal to one the triangle is drawn immediately. If however the depth value is not one, the triangle is subdivided into four smaller triangles. These smaller triangles are then processed using drawTriangle() but this time with a depth value one less. The process of subdivision repeats until the depth value reaches 1, at which point the resulting sequence of triangles is drawn. Figure 121 shows this process in action for an initial triangle of depth 3

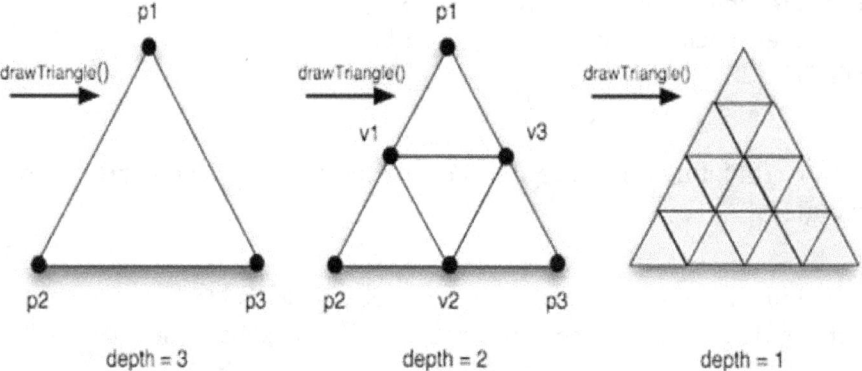

Figure 121: Procedural generation using triangles

To perform the subdivision we need to calculate the point midway along an edge of a triangle. This is accomplished by taking the average of the two vertices that define the edge. To take the average of two numbers we just add them and divide by two. For example, the average of 3 and 9 is (3+9)/2=6. The same calculation is used for vertices, for example the average of the vertices (3,6,9) and (9,4,5) is (6,5,7). We can simplify the coding of this calculation by making use of the PVector class once again.

```
PVector v1 = PVector.mult(PVector.add(p1, p2), 0.5);
```

Here we store and manipulate the vertices of the triangle as PVectors, PVector.add() adds the components of two vectors to produce another vector and PVector.mult() scales a vector by a value.

The function drawTriangle() is an example of a recursive function because it calls its own function. This is prevented from never ending by the depth argument, which prevents the recursive call when the depth reaches 1. For a bit of added interest you could try adding the last line in the drawTriangle() function which fills in the middle triangle being drawn, leaving a similar but very different effect (Figure 122)

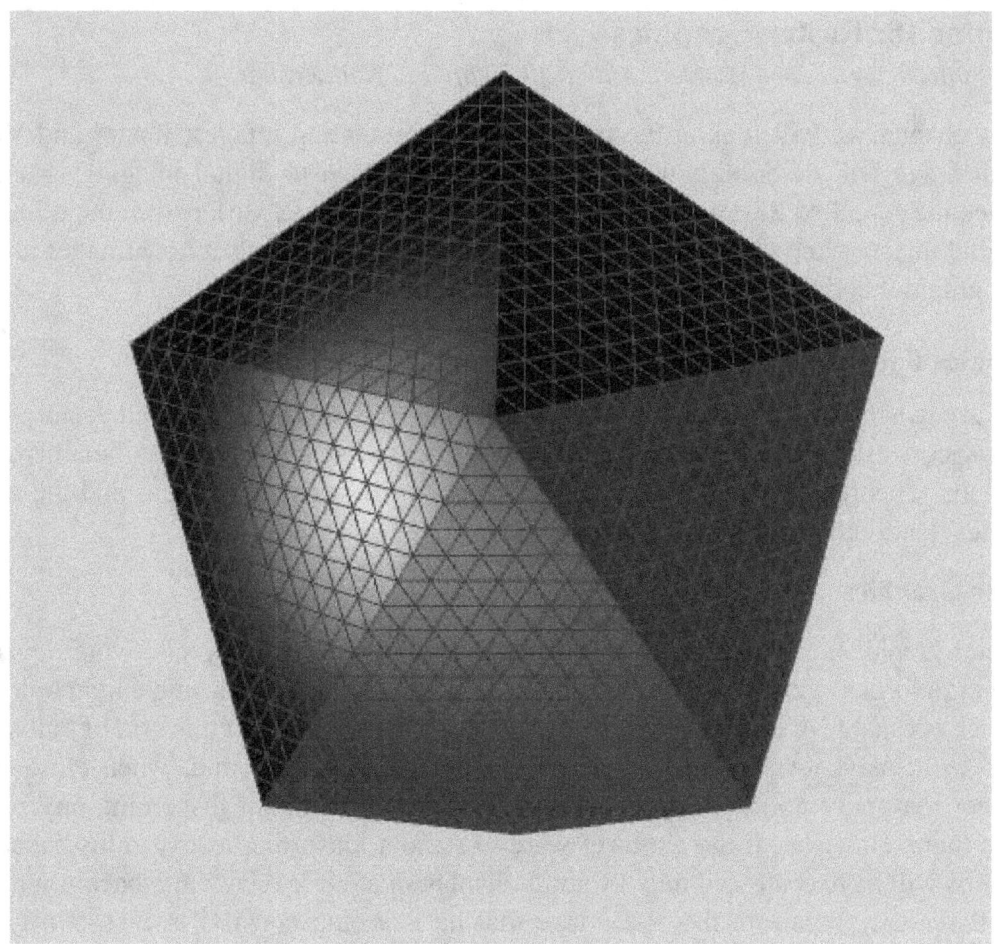

Figure 122: Fractal icosahedron with central triangle

Chapter 18: Raster Graphics

by Antonio Bruno, Liam Madden, Marshall Heap and Neil Keskar

In this chapter we will look at the two ways of representing images; Raster and Vector graphics. We will describe how the pixel-based approach to digital imaging is used to produce the so-called Raster graphics, and how Raster graphics differ from the other type of digital imagery known as Vector graphics. We finish by looking at how images are also raster graphics and they can be manipulated in the same way

Graphics Formats

There are two main types of graphics formats used to store images; raster and vector. Raster formats store image data as dots whereas vector formats use coordinates and mathematical equations. This represents the very different uses for these graphics types and the sort of graphics that might be utilised by them

Raster Graphics

In raster graphics, an image may be conceptualised as a grid of pixels. which coalesce together to form a smooth, continuous image. Imagine each pixel as a single light bulb each of which is capable of acquiring a wide range of different colours. If this grid of bulbs were set up to display, for example, a red circle on a white background, when close-up an observer may only notice different coloured light bulbs without discerning any pattern within them. However, if the observer were to stand a lot further away, to his naked eye the bulbs will have coalesced into a smooth display of a circle on a white background and he will scarcely be aware that the image that he is seeing consists in fact of a grid of individual light bulbs. A raster image formed using a matrix of pixels works in much the same way to display an image on the computer screen (or monitor).

The term 'raster' is not an innovation of computer graphics. It has been used widely in the context of the television imaging technique known as 'raster scanning' which forms the basis of television pictures. For the benefit of those interested in the etymology of the word, the term 'raster' is said to have been derived from a Latin root meaning 'rake'

Raster graphics are typically used for photographic images, or images of drawings and paintings in which there is a large variation of colour and contrast. Since, as explained above, the creation of raster graphics involves the breaking down of an image into large numbers of minute pixels, it follows that a raster graphic file is required to hold a large amount of data, such as colour, tone and position, for each individual pixel within the image. Raster graphic files therefore tend to be very large in size and consequently, data compression has become an important factor in the file formats that are prescribed for raster graphics. The formats that *Processing* supports are the Joint Photographic Experts Group

(.jpg), Truevision Graphics Adapter (.tga), Graphics Interchange Format (.gif) and Portable Network Graphics (.png) formats

Creating Raster Images

We have already created plenty of raster images so far - any time we have created images using pixels we have been creating a raster image. Instead of specifying our graphics in terms of shapes or lines, we specify each pixel, or at least each pixel we want to change.

Figure 123: Red circle on a white background using raster graphics

In order to achieve this we need to tell *Processing* to colour each pixel red inside the radius of a circular pattern in order to give the effect of a solid circle shown in Figure 123

```
void setup() {
    size(400, 400);
    background(255);
    int radius = width/2;
    drawCircle(radius);
}

void drawCircle(int radius) {
    float px = 0;
    float py = 0;
    float angle = 0;
    float angleIncrement = 0.125;//stops gaps appearing
    color c = color(255, 0, 0);
    // every pixel inside the radius
    for (int i = 0; i < radius; i++) {
        // increment around the circle
```

```
    for (float j = 0; j < 360; j += angleIncrement) {
        px = radius + cos(radians(angle)) *i;
        py = radius + sin(radians(angle)) *i;
        angle += angleIncrement;
        // set pixel colour
        set(int(px), int(py), c);
    }
  }
}
```

Vector Graphics

Vector graphics images are described by a set of mathematical expressions that plot the points (or nodes), together with the lines and the curves that form the shape of the image, using coordinates. The shape of the image thus produced, is then filled (rendered) with the required pixel detail when the image is displayed to produce the completed image.

To illustrate the difference between raster and a vector graphics, we can recreate the 'red dot on a white background'. As we explained, if this image were to be rendered as a raster graphic, the computer file that described the image would be required essentially to hold pixel data for every individual pixel that forms the pixel-grid (bitmap) for the image. Rendered as vector graphic however, the corresponding image file would merely contain six pieces of information:

- the nodes that form the four corners of the rectangle
- the node that forms the centre of the circle
- the mathematical equations that plot the four lines of the rectangle
- the mathematical equations that plot the three concentric circles
- the colour of the rectangle
- the colour of the circle

The *Processing* code for this is also notably simple

```
size(400,400);
background(255);
fill(255, 0, 0);
noStroke();
ellipse(width/2, height/2, 400, 400);
```

and the output is near-identical (Figure 124)

Figure 124: Red circle on white background Using Vector Graphics

Perhaps the most noticeable characteristic of a vector graphic, is its typically small image file. Because a vector graphic is rendered using mathematical expressions rather than large amounts of pixel data, vector graphics tend to be contained within small image files. Imagine how much easier it is to store the six pieces of information above than for every pixel in a 400 x 400 image for example (though raster graphics compression algorithms can reduce this somewhat if there are a lot of similar pixels)

Another useful characteristic of Vector graphics, is their easy scalability. Here too, the use of mathematical expressions, as opposed to bitmap data, facilitates scaling of the image to virtually any required size, since it merely requires the change of appropriate sizes within these mathematical equations to achieve the desired effect. In comparison, scaling raster graphics is not so simple - since the image is made up of pixels, the only way to scale it is to make the area covered by the pixels larger which can result in pixelated, blocky pictures or to remove them which can make the picture blurry. Scaling raster graphics often therefore results in a deterioration of the quality of the image

The choice of raster or vector graphics lies in knowing what the graphic will be used for. Where the graphic data can be more easily stored in vector format, such as graphics with bold shapes that can be easily described using mathematical formula, then the benefits of vector formats can be applied. Images with large variety, such as photographs, are usually best stored as raster graphics since each pixel needs to be described in order to show a detailed picture

Raster vs Vector Graphics

Notice how much simpler, and therefore easier to understand, this is compared to our previous code! This is partly because *Processing* is hiding the complexity from us behind the ellipse() function and partly because we don't need to specify every pixel when creating vector graphics whereas we do with raster graphics. So why use raster graphics at all? The ability to manipulate individual pixels allows us to create intricate graphics that would be difficult with vector graphics

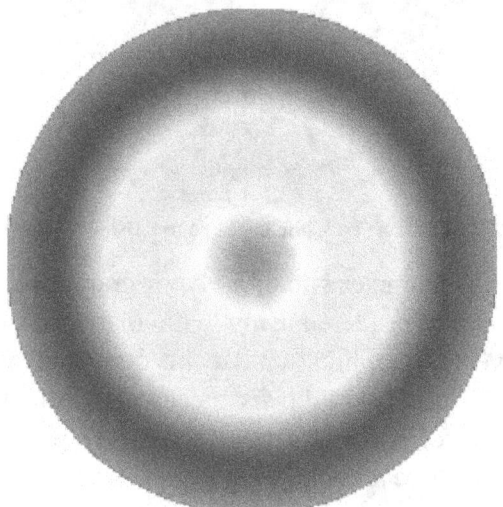

Figure 125: Graduated circular colours

Take the pattern shown in Figure 125 for example. The graduated effect shown here would be very difficult with vector graphics because the colours graduate slowly and bleed into the colours around them. Creating this with vector graphics would be extremely difficult, if not impossible, because of the stark lines it creates

```
void setup() {
    size(255, 255);
    background(255, 255, 255);
    int radius = width/2;
    int normalize = ((255/(radius))*5);//displays over spectrum range
    createGradient(radius, normalize);
}

void createGradient(int radius, int normalize) {
    float px = 0;
    float py = 0;
    float angle = 0;
    float angleIncrement = 0.125;//stops gaps appearing
```

```
color c = color(255, 0, 0);

for (int i = 0; i < radius; i++) {
  for (float j = 0; j < 360; j += angleIncrement) {
      px = radius + cos(radians(angle)) * i;
      py = radius + sin(radians(angle)) * i;
      angle += angleIncrement;
  {

          //conditional statements for each of the 5 spectral bands
          if (i < radius/5)  c = color(255, 0 + normalize * i, 0);

      }
      if (i > radius/5 && i < (2 * radius/5)) {
          int adj = radius/5;//offset to restore count value to 1 for band
          c = color(255-((i-adj)*normalize), 255, 0);
      }
      if (i > (2 * radius/5) && i < (3 * radius/5)) {
          int adj = int(2 * radius/5);
          c = color(0, 255, 0+((i - adj) * normalize));
      }
      if (i > (3 * radius/5) && i < (4 * radius/5)) {
          int adj = int(3 * radius/5);
          c = color(0, 255-((i-adj)*normalize), 255);
      }
      if (i > (4 * radius/5) && i < radius) {
          int adj = int(4 * radius/5);
          c = color(0 + ((i - adj) * normalize), 0, 255);
      }
      set(int(px), int(py), c); // set pixel colour
    }
  }
}
```

Manipulating Pixels

In addition to manipulating individual pixels using the set() and get() functions, *Processing* provides some language structures that are built to speed pixel calculations up and to access the entire set of pixels at once:

- pixels[] - array containing the current state of the pixels, each of which can be manipulated
- loadPixels() - function that loads the pixels on-screen into the pixels[] array

- updatePixels() - function that updates the pixels on-screen to represent those in the pixels[] array, which may have been changed

The pixels[] array organises the pixels of the display window as a sequence of *height* rows of *width* elements long into the array; for example a display window of 500x500 has the pixels array (width*height) of 250,000 elements long.

The following piece of code prints out on the screen the pixels array length

```
size(500,500);
loadPixels();
print(pixels.length);
```

The pixels[] array therefore contains a representation of every pixel on the screen which you can manipulate and update so that the changes are represented on-screen. If you want to change a particular pixel you can do so using the formula pixels[(y-1)*width+x-1], for example the following piece of code will set the pixel at the position (x,**y**) with the colour yellow

```
pixels[(y-1)*width+x-1] = color(255,255,0);
```

Of course, this usage isn't easier than using set(x, y). The real power of using the pixels[] array is when you want to change many pixels at once since you can change them in-memory then update them so the screen displays them. This is much faster in computing terms than setting each one individually. It is especially easy to access and change *every* pixel since all you need to do is iterate over the array. For example, the following code changes the colour of every pixel to a random colour every time, resulting in a static-like animation similar to that shown in Figure 126

```
void setup() {
   size(200, 200);
}

void draw() {
   loadPixels();
   // every pixel
   for (int i =0; i < pixels.length; i++) {
      // set a random colour
      pixels[i] = color(random(255), random(255), random(255));
   }
   updatePixels();
}
```

You should note that if you forget to call loadPixels() you will get an error since you will not have initialised the pixels[] array. If you forget to call the updatePixels() function you will not get an error but your changes to the array will have no effect

Figure 126: Static effect using pixel manipulation

Another powerful feature of using the pixels[] array is that you can access the current state of each pixel and alter it if required. When we access a pixel we are gaining access to its colour attributes. We could, for example, check the colour of a given pixel and change the colour of it. The example below uses our previous example of a red circle on white background and chooses a random pixel from a and, if the pixel is red, changes it to blue. This means that the background never changes, only the red pixels in the circle (Figure 127)

```
color red = color(255, 0, 0);
color blue = color(0, 0, 255);

void setup() {
   size(400, 400);
   background(255);
   fill(red);
   noStroke();
   ellipse(width/2, height/2, width/2, height/2);
}

void draw() {
   // choose a random pixel
   int randomPixel = int(random(width * height));
   loadPixels();
   // get the colour
   color pixel = pixels[randomPixel];
   // if it is red
```

```
    if (pixel == red) {
        // change it to blue
        pixels[randomPixel] = blue;
    }
    updatePixels();
}
```

Figure 127: Selectively changing pixel colour

We can also use the attributes of the pixels to overwrite the pixels in other places in the sketch. For example we can create a scrolling effect by setting every pixel to the attributes of the one next to it

```
void setup() {
    size(400,400);
    background(255);
    fill(255, 0, 0);
    noStroke();
    ellipse(width/2, height/2, width/2, height/2);
}

void draw() {
    loadPixels();
    // deal with the last/first pixel
    pixels[pixels.length - 1] = pixels[0];
    // set every pixel to be the one after it
    for (int i = 1; i < pixels.length; i++) {
        pixels[i - 1] = pixels[i];
    }
    updatePixels();
}
```

All that is happening here is that we are setting the colour attributes of the pixel as the one next to it. Since we are doing this for every pixel, it means that the circle appears to move to the left and wraps around the screen, reappearing on the right

Images as Pixels

Since the graphics we create in *Processing* can be manipulated as pixels, the same can be applied to images such as photographs. The four image file formats supported by *Processing* (i.e. jpg, gif, tga, png) are all raster graphics formats and so their pixels can be accessed and changed just as we did with graphics we have created

Before we can begin manipulating images, we need to load them. The image must be in one of the four formats supported by *Processing* and must be located in the same directory as the *Processing* sketch code

```
size(500, 500);
PImage img = loadImage("image.jpg");
image(img, 0, 0);
```

This code loads an image called image.jpg into a PImage variable which is then used in the image() function for display at the given coordinates. PImage stores the loaded image as an array of pixels, similar to the pixels[] array you have already seen

The pixel data in an image can be read in a number of ways. Firstly new images can be created from the data in another by using the get() or get(x, y, h, d) functions. These functions return a new PImage object containing a copy of all (in the case of get()) or some(in the case of get(x, y, h, d)) of the pixel data. The code below, for example, creates a new image from part of the original image and displays it over the top as can be seen in Figure 128

```
size(500, 500);
PImage img = loadImage("image.jpg");
image(img, 0, 0);

PImage newImage = img.get(300, 300, 200, 200);
image(newImage, 0, 0);
```

Figure 128: Creating a new image from part of another

The second method of accessing image pixel data is by accessing individual pixels, using either the familiar get(x, y) function to return the pixel colour, or accessing the pixels[] array directly. However, here only RGB colour values are returned even if the HSB colour mode was specified for the image. Similarly, pixels can be manipulated using the set(x, y,colour) function specifying the coordinates and colour value of the pixel or by setting the colour on pixels in the array.

```
size(500, 250);
PImage img = loadImage("image.jpg");
image(img, 0, 0);
// create a new blank image
PImage newImage = createImage(250, 250, RGB);

for (int i = 0; i < img.pixels.length; i++) {
   // access current pixel colour
   color currentColour = img.pixels[i];
   // access current RGB
   float red = red(currentColour);
   float blue = blue(currentColour);
   float green = green(currentColour);
   // create new colour by swapping RGB values
   color newColour = color(blue, red, green);
   newImage.pixels[i] = newColour;
}
```

```
image(newImage, 250, 0);
```

The code above creates a new image, using createImage(), and accesses the pixels from the original image by using the pixels[] array. Each pixel is then altered slightly by swapping the RGB elements and copied onto the new image. The two images can be displayed together to see the effect (Figure 129)

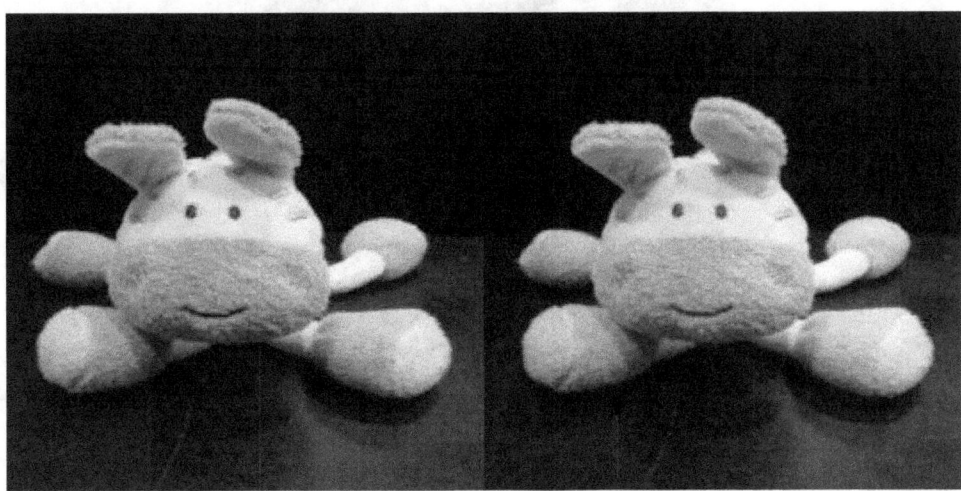

Figure 129: Altered pixels in an image

As well as altering the colour attributes of the pixels, we can also move them around, similarly to how we did the scrolling circle. We could, for example, create a reflection of an image. To do this we can use a nested pair of iteration statements to systematically access all the source pixels, for example by using get() then copying each source pixel a new image using set() with a pair of index values that (usually) differ from the source

```
size(250, 500);
PImage img = loadImage("image.jpg");
img.resize(250, 250);
image(img, 0, 0);

PImage newImage = createImage(img.width, img.height, RGB);
int w = newImage.width;
int h = newImage.height;
for (int i=0; i < w; i++) {
   for (int j=0; j < h; j++) {
      newImage.set(i, h-j-1, img.get(i, j));
   }
}
image(newImage, 0, 250);
```

The code above performs the reflection by copying pixels from one image to the other in a different order. The effect is a reflection of the original as shown in Figure 130. Note the use of the `resize()` function which can be used to alter the size of an image.

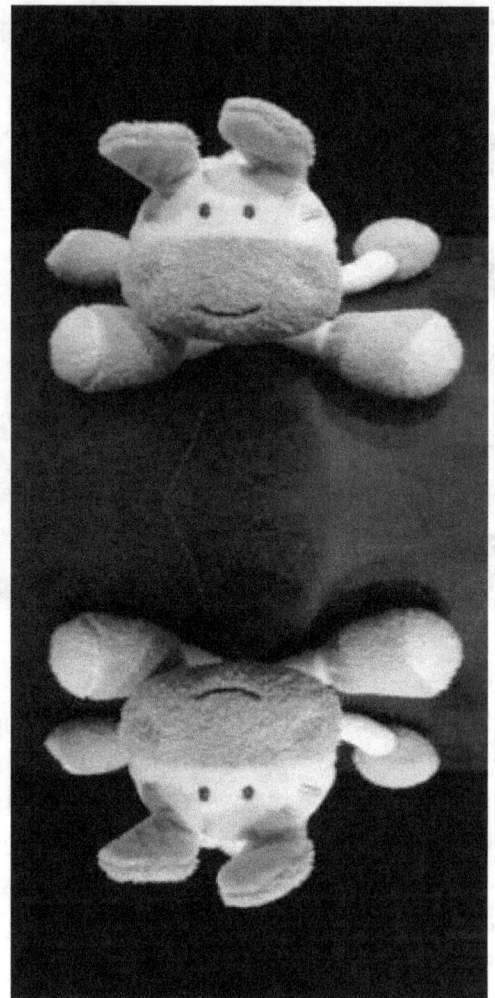

Figure 130: Image reflection

Similar techniques can be used for other image pixel manipulations, for example the following code will rotate the image by 90 degrees (Figure 131)

```
size(500, 250);
PImage img = loadImage("image.jpg");
img.resize(250, 250);
image(img, 0, 0);

PImage newImage = new PImage(img.height, img.width);//attributes transposed
int w = newImage.width;
```

```
int h = newImage.height;
for (int i = 0; i<w; i++) {
    for (int j = 0; j<h; j++) {
    newImage.set(img.height-i-1, img.width-j-1, img.get(img.width-j-1, i));
    }
}

image(newImage, 250, 0);
```

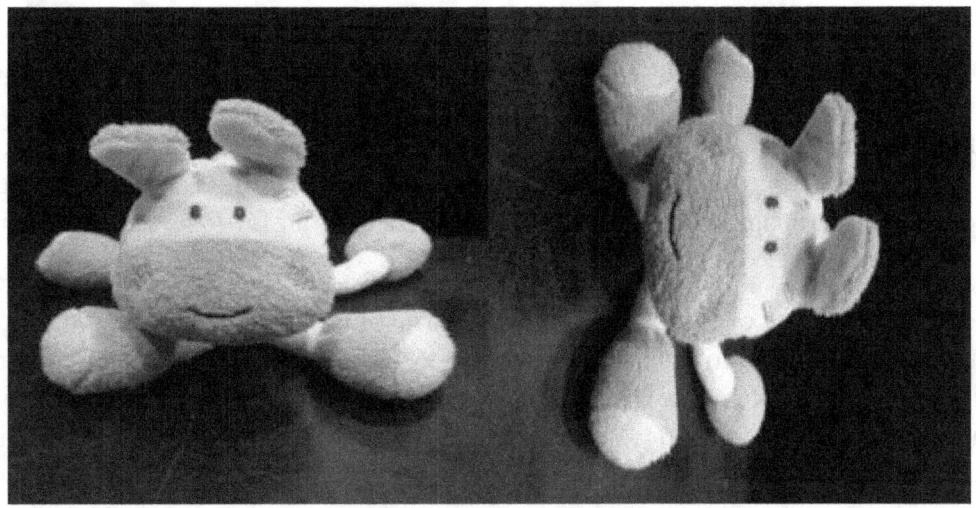

Figure 131: Image rotation

Chapter 19: Image Manipulation
by Darragh Buffini, Dušan Ličer, Jannetta Steyn and Rosie Wood

In the last chapter we looked at how images could be created and manipulated at the level of individual pixels. This chapter looks at how *Processing* makes image manipulation easier by providing functions that allow effects to be created using masking, filtering and blending techniques

Masking

The mask functionality implemented in *Processing* allows you to very simply load two images into memory and mask one with the other to alter the displayed output. The image used for masking is used to prevent display of parts of the first image and should be a grayscale image (that is, using values of 0 - 255 rather than a full RGB image). Also both the input and mask images need to be of the same size in order for *Processing* to be able to mask them.

Say you have an image of a family photo, a favourite old snapshot from years before. You want to take this image and touch it up a little, because the sky is very bright and drowns out the rest of the image a little. How would you do this? One of the simpler ways would be to import your original photo to *Processing*, and have created a gradient grayscale image that has the pixels at the top of the image set to a low value (the darker the mask colour, the more it will cover up the original input pixel), and higher values up to 255 towards the bottom. In effect, what you will get out of this operation is your original image with the sky brightness toned down.

To accomplish something like this, we could use something similar to the following code

```
size(640, 450);
PImage inputImage = loadImage("Sample.jpg");
PImage maskImage = loadImage("MaskOfSample.jpg");
inputImage.mask(maskImage);
image(inputImage);
```

In just 5 lines of code we have achieved the ability to imitate sophisticated image manipulation technology. As you can see from Figure 132 the gradient is applied to the original image by masking the darker colours more than the lighter colours giving a faded effect

Figure 132: Masking with a greyscale gradient

We don't have to use another image to create the mask however, we can use what is known as a *pixel mask*. What a pixel mask does is essentially create an image out of pixels which could be anything at all, from something as simple as a plain black image or a shaded gradient and then apply this collection of pixels as a mask to the original input image.

The following code shows an example of using a pixel mask.

```
size(640, 450);
PImage inputImage = loadImage("Sample.jpg");
background (100, 50, 50);
fill(255);
rect(random(width), random(height), 100, 100);
loadPixels();
inputImage.mask(pixels);
image(inputImage, 0, 0);
```

What is happening here is that we are applying a mask to the image using a background and a rectangle, rather than using an image as we did previously. The background is basically filling the screen with a colour - we could equally have used a large rectangle or set the colour of every pixel but the effect is the same. What this does, when applied as a mask, is dim the levels of the colours in our image. We then add a rectangle, filled with colour 255 (white). When applied as a mask this makes the rectangle transparent since darker colours are more masked as we said earlier. When this is applied as a mask the effect is that shown in Figure 133

Figure 133: Pixel mask applied to an image

You should now have an idea of what masking can do. Try examining the following code and see if you can work out what it does before running it

```
PImage inputImage;
void setup() {
    size(640, 480);
    inputImage = loadImage("Sample.jpg");
    inputImage.resize(640, 480);
    noStroke();
}

void draw() {
    fill(255);
    ellipse(mouseX, mouseY, 100, 100);
    loadPixels();
    inputImage.mask(pixels);
    background(0);
    image(inputImage, 0, 0);
}
```

What we have done here is created a pixel mask of a white circle drawn at the mouse coordinates and drawn a black background over the top of the image. When applied as a mask this will have the effect of blacking-out the image but showing a transparent circle at the mouse coordinate through which we can see the original image. The effect is like shining a torch on a dark scene and only being able to see what is currently displayed by the narrow torch beam (Figure 134).

You could also create a 'scratchcard' type effect, whereby the entire image is slowly revealed by moving your circle over all areas of the picture till it is clear, requires only one very small change - move the background(0) function call from the draw function (where it is called continually) up to the setup function where it is only called once. Since we only set the background once the circle will eventually override the darkness we have imposed.

Figure 134: Blacked-out image with circular mask

Filters

The filter function allows you to display an image with a predefined filter that will affect how the image is viewed. For example, you might display an image with a blurring effect that blurs the image. The function is very simple to use and accepts eight different constant parameters, which apply different filters to the screen content. The filters available are INVERT, GRAY, THRESHOLD, ERODE, DILATE, OPAQUE, BLUR and POSTERIZE. The effect of each of these can be seen applied to the same image in Figure 135

The signature of the filter function is

```
filter(MODE)
```

or

```
filter(MODE, level)
```

where MODE is one of the parameters listed above. Some modes can also accept a `level` parameter that specifies the intensity required.

Threshold

The threshold filter takes the most predominant colours in an image and turns them white. Colours that are less intense are turned black. Depending on the threshold level, the decision whether to change a pixel white or black varies.

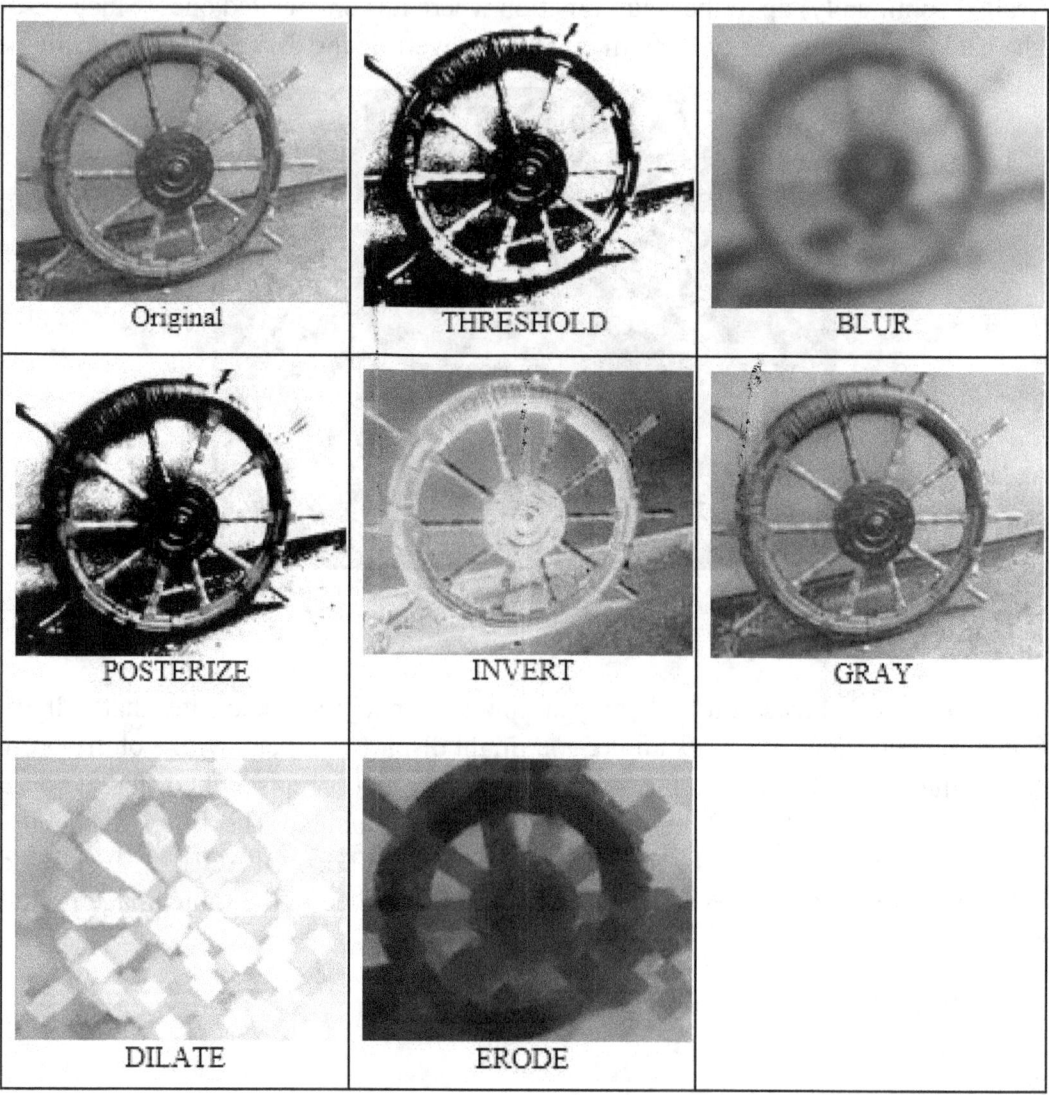

Figure 135: Image filters applied to the same image

We can demonstrate the use of the threshold filter using a few lines of code

```
PImage image = loadImage("wheel.jpg");
image(image, 0, 0);
filter(THRESHOLD);
```

When no threshold level parameter is supplied, the default value (0.5) is applied to every pixel in the display screen. Every pixel will have colour values of red, green and blue, each ranging from 0 to 255. The threshold filter examines each pixel's red, green and blue values and (using the threshold level, in this case the default 0.5) if the highest colour value is greater than half of 255 (ie 255 * 0.5), it changes the pixel to white, otherwise it is turned black

We can make an interesting effect using threshold mode by incrementally increasing the threshold level. The image therefore appears to get filled in with black as the threshold level is increased.

```
PImage image;
float thresholdLevel = 0.0;

void setup() {
    size(500, 500);
    image = loadImage("wheel.jpg");
    frameRate(10);
}

void draw() {
    thresholdLevel += 0.01;
    image(image, 0, 0, width, height);
    filter(THRESHOLD, thresholdLevel);
}
```

We can enhance this animation further by colouring the black pixels after the filter has been applied. If we divide the screen into quarters we can use for loops to change the colour of the pixels in a different quadrant of the display screen by examining the colour of each pixel and, if it is black, changing the colour. The first quadrant's pixels are not changed. The effect of this can be seen in Figure 136

Figure 136: Colourised threshold filter

```
PImage image;
float thresholdLevel = 0.0;
color c1;
color c2;
color c3;

void setup() {
   size(500, 500);
   image = loadImage("wheel.jpg");
   frameRate(10);
   c1 = getColor();
   c2 = getColor();
   c3 = getColor();
}

void draw() {
   thresholdLevel += 0.01;
   image(image, 0, 0, width, height);
   filter(THRESHOLD, thresholdLevel);
   loadPixels();
   // top-right
   for (int j = 0; j < height / 2; j++) {
      for (int i = (width / 2 + j * width); i < width + j * width; i++) {
         if (pixels[i] == color(0)) {
            pixels[i] = c1;
         }
      }
   }
 // bottom right
```

```
    for(int j = height / 2; j < height; j++) {
        for(int i = (width / 2 + j * width); i < width + j * width; i++) {
            if (pixels[i] == color(0)) {
                pixels[i] = c2;
            }
        }
    }
    // bottom left
    for(int j = height / 2; j < height; j++) {
        for(int i=(j * width); i < width + j * width; i++) {
            if (pixels[i] == color(0)) {
                pixels[i] = c3;
              }
        }
    }

    updatePixels();
}


color getColor() {
    color c = color(random(255), random(255), random(255));
    return c;
}
```

As we are using random colours, the pixel colour will vary each time the sketch is run.

Blur

The blur filter creates a blur effect on the image loaded into the display area. It can accept an integer of 100 but it is better to stick to a number under 20 unless you really want a very blurred image

```
size(640, 480);
PImage image = loadImage("wheel.jpg");
image.resize(640, 480);
image(image, 0, 0);
filter(BLUR, 15);
```

We can enhance our threshold animation by adding a blur filter which we also increment so the image has a greater level of both blur and threshold applied each time

```
PImage image;
float thresholdLevel = 0.0;
float blurLevel = 0.0;
```

```
color c1;
color c2;
color c3;

void setup() {
   size(500, 500);
   image = loadImage("wheel.jpg");
   frameRate(10);
   c1 = getColor();
   c2 = getColor();
   c3 = getColor();
}

void draw() {
   thresholdLevel += 0.01;
   blurLevel += 0.05;
   image(image, 0, 0, width, height);
   filter(THRESHOLD, thresholdLevel);
   filter(BLUR, blurLevel);
   loadPixels();
   // top-right
   for (int j = 0; j < height / 2; j++) {
      for (int i = (width / 2 + j * width); i < width + j * width; i++) {
         if (pixels[i] == color(0)) {
            pixels[i] = c1;
         }
      }
   }
   // bottom right
   for(int j = height / 2; j < height; j++) {
      for(int i = (width / 2 + j * width); i < width + j * width; i++) {
         if (pixels[i] == color(0)) {
            pixels[i] = c2;
         }
      }
   }
   // bottom left
   for(int j = height / 2; j < height; j++) {
      for(int i=(j * width); i < width + j * width; i++) {
         if (pixels[i] == color(0)) {
            pixels[i] = c3;
         }
      }
```

```
    }

    updatePixels();
}

color getColor() {
    color c = color(random(255), random(255), random(255));
    return c;
}
```

The only difference is the incremental blur filter but, as you can see from Figure 137, the result is very different due to the blurred detail of the image

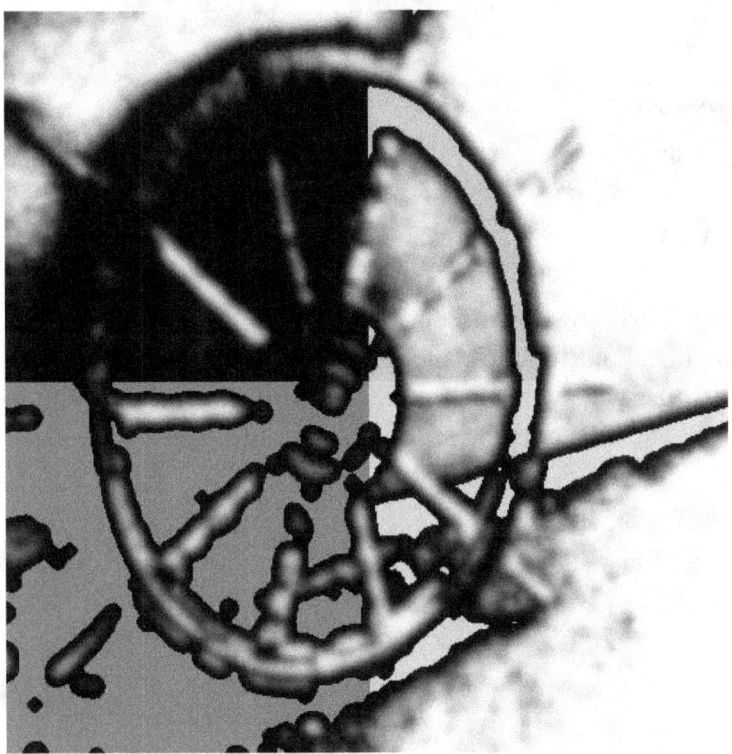

Figure 137: Image with threshold and blur filters applied

Posterize

The Posterize filter limits each colour channel (that is, red, green and blue) to the number of colours specified in the argument. The minimum value is 2, which restricts the blue, green and red channels to two colours each. Using a value of 255 would have no effect because this is the maximum number of colours in each channel and so *Processing* will show an error message if you try to. Figure 138 shows our image with a maximum of three colours per channel

Figure 138: Posterized image with 3 colours per channel

We can alter our code to show the effect of posterizing an image with different levels. We have removed the threshold function and added one for posterize instead, which restricts the value to 15 as otherwise you can't notice the difference due to the higher number of colours being used. The effect can be seen in Figure 139

```
PImage image;
int posterizeLevel = 2;
float blurLevel = 10;
color c1;
color c2;
color c3;

void setup() {
    size(500, 500);
    image = loadImage("wheel.jpg");
    frameRate(10);
    c1 = getColor();
    c2 = getColor();
    c3 = getColor();
}

void draw() {
```

```
    posterizeLevel += 1;
    if (posterizeLevel >= 15) {
      posterizeLevel = 2;
    }
    image(image, 0, 0, width, height);
     filter(BLUR, blurLevel);
    filter(POSTERIZE, posterizeLevel);
    loadPixels();
    // top-right
    for (int j = 0; j < height / 2; j++) {
        for (int i = (width / 2 + j * width); i < width + j * width; i++) {
            if (pixels[i] == color(0)) {
                pixels[i] = c1;
            }
        }
    }
    // bottom right
    for(int j = height / 2; j < height; j++) {
        for(int i = (width / 2 + j * width); i < width + j * width; i++) {
            if (pixels[i] == color(0)) {
                pixels[i] = c2;
            }
        }
    }
    // bottom left
    for(int j = height / 2; j < height; j++) {
        for(int i=(j * width); i < width + j * width; i++) {
            if (pixels[i] == color(0)) {
                pixels[i] = c3;
            }
        }
     }

    updatePixels();
}

color getColor() {
    color c = color(random(255), random(255), random(255));
    return c;
}
```

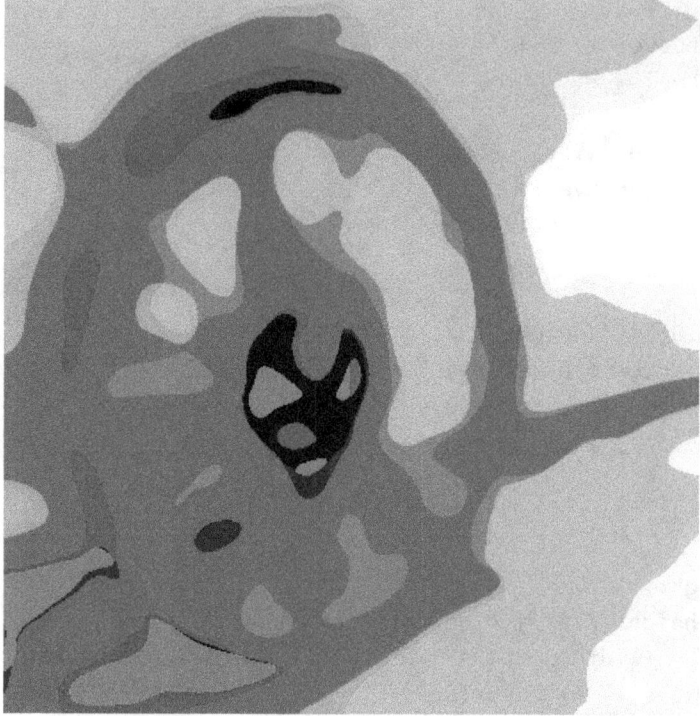

Figure 139: Image with blur and posterize filters applied

Invert

The invert filter takes an image and inverts its colours such that, for example, black is changed to white. Black has colour value 0 and white has value 255. So to invert black 255 is added to the colour value of (0,0,0) to give (255,255,255). The red, green and blue colour values set at 255 (maximum value) gives the colour white. The colour pure red has a colour value of (255,0,0), we would expect the inverse of this to be (0,255,255).

```
size(640, 480);
PImage image = loadImage("wheel.jpg");
image.resize(640, 480);
image(image, 0, 0);
filter(INVERT);
```

We can create new effects by combining filters such as combining posterize and invert. Adding a posterize to the code above creates the image shown in Figure 140

Figure 140: Image with posterize and invert filters applied

Gray

The GRAY filter turns the image to grey-scale giving a black-and-white photo effect. By simply amending the statement in the invert code we can see the gray mode filter at work (Figure 141).

```
size(640, 480);
PImage image = loadImage("wheel.jpg");
image.resize(640, 480);
image(image, 0, 0);
filter(POSTERIZE, 2);
filter(INVERT);
```

Figure 141: Image with grey and posterize filters applied

Erode and Dilate

Erosion and dilation are complex image processing effects that work to decrease (ERODE) or increase (DILATE) light areas such that the surrounding pixels are 'filled in' with dark or light colours to match those around them. The effect is minimal when applied to an image but by repeatedly applying the filters to an image, the effect becomes more noticeable.

```
PImage image;

void setup() {
   size(500, 500);
   image = loadImage("wheel.jpg");
   image(image, 0, 0, width, height);
   frameRate(10);
}

void draw() {
   filter(DILATE);
}
```

The above code repeatedly applies the DILATE filter to the image such that the light areas become larger and more prominent (Figure 142)

Figure 142: Image with dilate filter applied

We can do the same with the ERODE filter which has the opposite effect (Figure 143)

Figure 143: Image with erode filter applied

The filter function is a very easy function to work with yet gives us some fascinating effects when applied to the screen contents. As you grow more proficient in the available modes, you will be able to combine filters, producing even more amazing effects

Blending

Blending is used for image manipulation and actually involves colour mixing (blending). It is widely used, from scientific image analysis to computer games, to produce interesting visual effects that can be useful, entertaining, or in some cases just odd. Designers enjoy blending features in various graphical applications and frequently use this process. They use blending for digital photography enhancement, colouring images, and various other effects. In *Processing*, the power of blending is accessible to us through the blend() function.

The blend() function allows us to combine two images into one. For the sake of explanation, we will call the first image the destination (dst), and the second the source (src). The blend() function uses the source image, the destination image, and the blend mode as input. Its output is the resulting image (res) produced by the 'blending mode' rule. Each pixel of the source blends with the destination pixel at the same position. We can imagine that we put the source over the destination and blend pixels. There are quite a few modes of blending, the code example below uses the DODGE mode

```
size(640, 480);
PImage src = loadImage("scene1.jpg");
PImage dst = loadImage("scene2.jpg");
image(src, 0, 0);
image(dst, 0, 0);
blend(src, 0, 0, src.width, src.height,
 0, 0, dst.width, dst.height, DODGE);
```

In Figure 144 you will notice that we have displayed the destination image then blended the source image with it which displays a blended composite of both images. We distinguish between source and destination because some blend modes are not commutative, which means that the result will be different in some cases if we switch the images. The other reason is that we can also store the blended image in a PImage object.

The following code has the same effect as the code above except that we store the blended image as the destination image (using dst.blend() rather than just blend()). The resulting image replaces the destination image (not the original image file, just the reference to it in *Processing*) so the destination image is the one we want to display in order to see the blended result

```
PImage src = loadImage("scene1.jpg");
PImage dst = loadImage("scene2.jpg");
dst.blend(src, 0, 0, src.width, src.height,
 0, 0, dst.width, dst.height, DODGE);
image(dst, 0, 0);
```

Figure 144: Source, destination and blended image

The difference between these two versions of blending is that the first one blends whatever is on the screen (which may not be from an image file) with the given image, where the second blends two images together, storing the result in the destination image file which can be used like any image such as blending again or being displayed later if desired

In general, we can write the blend syntax as:

```
[dst.]blend([src,]  srcX,  scrY,  srcWidth,  srcHeight,  dstX,  dstY,  dstWidth,
dstHeight , MODE)
```

Where (variables in square brackets are optional):

- dst is the destination. If omitted, we blend on the screen (the screen becomes the destination).
- src is the source. If omitted dst is used as the source to blend with itself (dst becomes both the source and the destination). Note that if both src and dst are omitted, the screen is blended with itself (screen becomes both the source and the destination)

- srcX, srxY are the upper-left coordinates of the source image
- srxWidth, srcHeight are the width and height of the source image
- dstX, dstY are the upper-left coordinates of the destination image
- dstWidth, dstHeight are the width and height of the destination image
- MODE is the blending mode. This can be one of REPLACE, BLEND, ADD, SUBTRACT, DARKEST, LIGHTEST, DIFFERENCE, EXCLUSION, MULTIPLY, SCREEN, OVERLAY, HARD_LIGHT, SOFT_LIGHT, DODGE or BURN

When blending with the screen, this doesn't have to be an image. We can demonstrate blending the screen with an image by drawing something then blending it with an image.

```
size(500,500);
PImage src = loadImage("cat.jpg");
strokeWeight(20);
stroke(255,150,150);
fill(150,150,200);
ellipse(230, 230, 250, 250);
line(150, 310, 310, 150);
blend(src, 0, 0, src.width, src.height, 0, 0, 500, 500, OVERLAY);
```

Figure 145: Image blended with screen contents

In order to blend pixel with pixel at the same position, the image regions of the source and destination inside the blend() function should be of equal size. If we specify regions of different sizes, *Processing* automatically resizes the source to fit the size of the destination, stretching or shrinking the source to match the destination. In our example, the source image, which is much smaller than the destination image, is expanded to fit the size of the destination image, resulting in a 'no cats' effect (Figure 145)

Blend Factor

In addition to the source, destination and blend mode, we can also control how intense the blending is using the *blend factor*, which is hidden inside the alpha channel of the source. This basically means that the transparency of the source affects the result of the blend. For example, the MULTIPLY mode multiplies colours which makes them darker (more on why this happens shortly). The degree of darkness therefore depends on the factor (f) since a more transparent source will mean the source colours have less effect on the result. If we put a completely transparent source over the destination (f = 0), we don't expect changes in the destination. In the case that the source is completely opaque (f = 1), then full multiplication is in force. The same does not apply in reverse, the transparency of the destination does not have any effect on the blend result

Figure 146: Applying a Blend Factor

We can demonstrate this with an example where we apply varying transparency to the source image and blend with the destination to show how the factor changes the result (Figure 146)

```
PImage src;
```

```
PImage dst;
PImage dstBackup;
int step = 5; //granularity of progressing (1..255)
int blendFactor = 0; //value of factor (0..255)

void setup() {
    size(400, 500);
    //load images
    src = loadImage("scene1.jpg");
    dst = loadImage("scene2.jpg");
    dstBackup = loadImage("scene2.jpg"); //backup copy of destination
    src.resize(400, 500);
    dst.resize(400, 500);
    dstBackup.resize(400, 500);
}

void draw() {
    //blend dst in memory
    dst.blend(src, 0, 0, src.width, src.height, 0, 0, dst.width, dst.height,
        OVERLAY);
    //show result of blending
    image(dst, 0, 0);
    //copy original into dst from backup
    dst.copy(dstBackup, 0, 0, dstBackup.width, dstBackup.height, 0, 0, dst.width,
        dst.height);
    //increment or decrement factor, constrain for smooth transition
    blendFactor=constrain(blendFactor + step, 0, 255);
    //blendFactor=blendFactor+step
    setFactor(dst, blendFactor);
    //change the direction, if needed (up..down)
    if ((blendFactor==0)||(blendFactor==255)) {
        step*=-1;
    }
}

void setFactor (PImage img, int factor) {
    int f = factor << 24; //shift factor to place for alpha
    img.loadPixels();
    for (int i=0; i <= img.width * img.height - 1; i++) {
        img.pixels[i]= (img.pixels[i] & 0xFFFFFF)|f; //alpha = factor
    }
    img.format=ARGB; //be sure that transparency is supported
    img.updatePixels();
```

}

You needn't understand all of this except to know that we apply an alpha (transparent) factor to the source image before blending with the destination. You might note the use of the copy() function which can be very useful when manipulating images. This function basically copies pixels from one place to another so we can copy all, or part of, an image to another. In this instance we are using it to obtain a 'fresh' copy of the destination image without having to reload it from the image file each time which is more intensive

Blend Modes

Blend modes are the heart of blending and to use them most effectively it is a good idea to understand them. The easiest way to begin to understand how blending works is to understand the simple maths behind blend modes and then gradually progress through experimentation.

Blend modes have names like MULTIPLY or ADD, so you might assume that multiplication and addition are involved, and actually they are. MULTIPLY, for example, produces the resulting image by the multiplication of colours. We could say that resulting image equals source multiplied by destination and write it like this:

```
res = src * dst
```

This means that each source pixel is multiplied by the corresponding destination pixel. For proper understanding we should note two things. The first is that each RGB channel is multiplied and that the formula above should be read as:

```
resRED = srcRED * dstRED
resGREEN = srcGREEN * dstGREEN
resBLUE = srcBLUE * dstBLUE
```

The second is that all blend maths are between 0 and 1. This makes blend maths universal regardless of the internal representation of colours. *Processing* uses values of 0-255 to represent each RGB channel where lower values mean darker colours and higher values mean brighter colours.

To represent these low and high values, blend maths represents the lowest value (0) with 0 and the highest value (255) with 1, with all other values lying in between. For example, the value 1 is represented by 1/255, 2 by 2/255 and so on. The transformation is then simple as shown in Table 12.

We can now start to work out how blending works. When we multiply two bright colours, for example as represented by the value 200, we end up with a darker colour represented by 157.

Processing	Blend maths
0	0/255 = 0
1	1/255 = 0.004
2	2/255 = 0.008
...	...
254	254/255 = 0.996
255	255/255 = 1.000

Table 12: Blend maths representations of colour values

The multiplication is first done in blend math as

$(200/255)*(200/255) = 40000/65025 = 0.615$

and then converted to *Processing* representation as

$0.615*255 = 157$

This is why MULTIPLY makes colours darker and the term 'multiply' could be misleading. We might assume that by multiplying we get larger values (brighter colours), but the multiplication of two numbers higher than 0 and lower than 1 will always produce a lower value than either multiplier.

We can most easily see the effect of blend modes in greyscale. Figure 147 shows a comparison of all the available modes

For an easier overview we will place them in five groups as shown below. The first group has only two modes and they are there just because we could not categorise them with the other four.

All modes except REPLACE use a factor (alpha channel of source) to control the intensity of the effect.

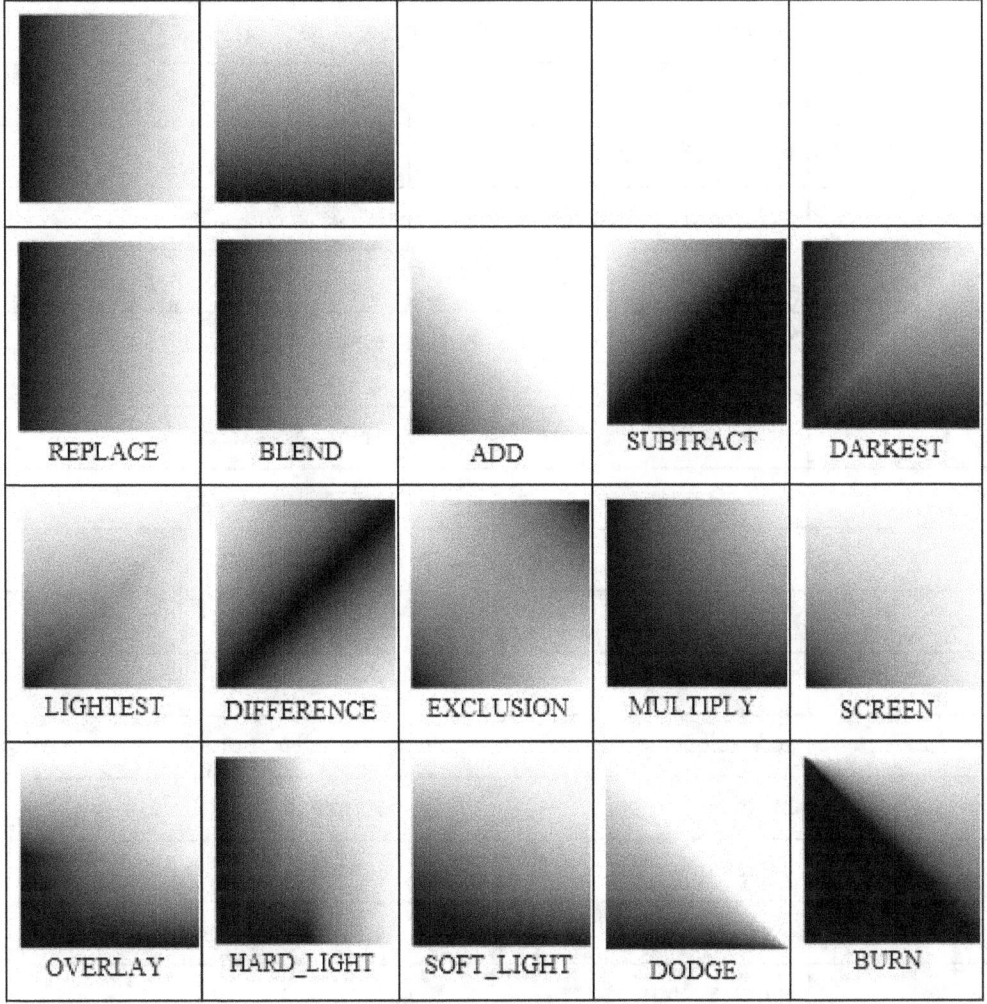

Figure 147: Greyscale comparison of available blend modes

In Table 13 we omit the factor in some modes to simplify the formulas and clearly describe the basic behaviour of a particular mode.

Mode	Description	Formula
General modes		
REPLACE	trivial mode, result equals source	res=src
BLEND	linear interpolation of colours	res= dst + (src-dst)*f,
Darken modes		
MULTIPLY	white pixel preserve and black absorbs values	res=dst*src
SUBTRACT	lighter src darkens more	res= max(dst-src*f, 0)
DARKEST	darkest pixels prevail	res= min(dst, src*f)
BURN	darken and intensify with src colour	res=1-(1-dst)/src
Lighten modes		
SCREEN	black preserve white absorbs	res=1-((1-src)*(1-dst))
ADD	adds colours to brighten	res=min(src*f+dst, 1)
LIGHTEN	lightest pixels prevail	res=max(dst, src*f)
DODGE	lighten and intensify with src colour	res=dst/(1-src)
Contrast modes		
OVERLAY	enhance contrast	res= dst<.5 ? 2*src*dst : 1 - 2 * (1 - src) * (1 - dst)
HARD_LIGHT	contra-overlay	res= src<.5 ? 2*src*dst : 1 - 2 * (1 - src) * (1 - dst)
SOFT_LIGHT	like overlay but not as harsh	res= src <.5 ?"darken" : "lighten"
Comparative modes		
DIFFERENCE	image comparison	res=abs(dst-src)
EXCLUSION	similar to DIFFERENCE, but softer	res=dst+src-2*src*dst

Table 13: Blend modes

General Blend Modes (REPLACE and BLEND)

REPLACE Mode

REPLACE mode just copies source image over destination area and performs similarly to the copy() function. The blend factor has no effect at all since we are just replacing one image with another

BLEND Mode

BLEND mode is described as the 'linear interpolation of colours' which is just the slow continuous progression from one colour to another. This mode is widely used in computer games and other situations. For example, suppose we have a cartoon character who is embarrassed and starts to blush. We can produce this effect by first showing the normal face (destination) and then blending it with a blushing face (source) many times, while slowly increasing the blending factor from 0 to 255. At the beginning the normal face is shown (f=0), this face will then blush slowly, and at the end only the blushing face will dominate (f=255). This means that with a full blend (f=255) the source image will dominate and the destination image will not be visible. This mode can also be used for a smooth transition from one slide to another.

```
PImage src;
PImage dst;
int blendFactor = 120;

void setup() {
   src = loadImage("scene1.jpg");
   dst = loadImage("scene2.jpg");
   src.resize(640, 480);
   dst.resize(640, 480);
   size(dst.width, dst.height);
   setFactor(src, blendFactor);
   dst.blend(src, 0, 0, src.width, src.height,
      0, 0, dst.width, dst.height, BLEND);
   image(dst, 0, 0);
}

void setFactor(PImage img, int factor) {
   int f = factor << 24; //shift factor to place for alpha
   img.loadPixels();
   for (int i=0; i <= img.width * img.height - 1; i++) {
      img.pixels[i]= (img.pixels[i] & 0xFFFFFF)|f; //alpha = factor
   }
```

```
    img.format=ARGB; //be sure that transparency is supported
    img.updatePixels();
}
```

Our example above blends two images together, with a blend factor applied to the source so that you can see them blended (Figure 148)

Figure 148: Images blended using BLEND mode

Darken modes

The darken modes typically favour darker pixels and will result in a darker image than the original

MULTIPLY Mode

MULTIPLY mode results in an image where the colour is a multiplication of source and destination, which makes the resulting image darker. How much the destination will be darkened by the source is defined by the factor. It works the same way as mixing colours: the more you mix, the darker it becomes. The formula `res = dst * src` shows us that:

0*x=0, which means that black pixels (0) will absorb colours or will stay black, and

1*x=x, which means that white pixels (1) will preserve colours.

However, for speedy calculations, *Processing* takes a shortcut which results in a slightly different outcome than we might expect. If we try to MULTIPLY two white areas in *Processing*, we should get a white area as result. However, in reality we get something grey. The reason behind this is that there is a compromise between fast blending and correct blending. Blend operations are very time consuming so, for speed, *Processing* speeds them by using bitwise operations (shifting bit values). We saw earlier in converting colours to blend math that we must divide colour values by 255. These divisions are slow, and there are a lot of them. However, division by 256 (28) is fast and can be done by shifting a value by 8 bits to the right. Dividing values by 256 instead of 255 produces an error of approximately 0.4%. This is insignificant for practical use and only affects higher values. The point here is that we must be aware of the inconsistency

```
PImage src=loadImage("cat2.jpg");
PImage dst=loadImage("catr.jpg");
dst.blend(src, 0,0,src.width,src.height,0,0,
 dst.width,dst.height,MULTIPLY);
image(dst, 0,0);
```

This example multiplies two images together. As you can see in Figure 149, the darker pixels are more prevalent than the lighter pixels of the original image.

Source   Destination

Result

Figure 149: Image source, destination and result using MULTIPLY mode

SUBTRACT Mode

SUBTRACT mode is similar to MULTIPLY except that source pixels are subtracted from the destination image, making the resulting image darker. The key point here is that lighter source pixels darken more than dark pixels so white source pixels make the result black and black source preserves destination

```
PImage src=loadImage("cat6.jpg");
PImage dst=loadImage("scene3.jpg");
dst.blend(src, 0,0,src.width,src.height,0,0,
 dst.width,dst.height,SUBTRACT);
image(dst, 0,0);
```

As you can see from this example the lighter pixels in the source image are darkened by the destination image resulting in a negative-looking image (Figure 150)

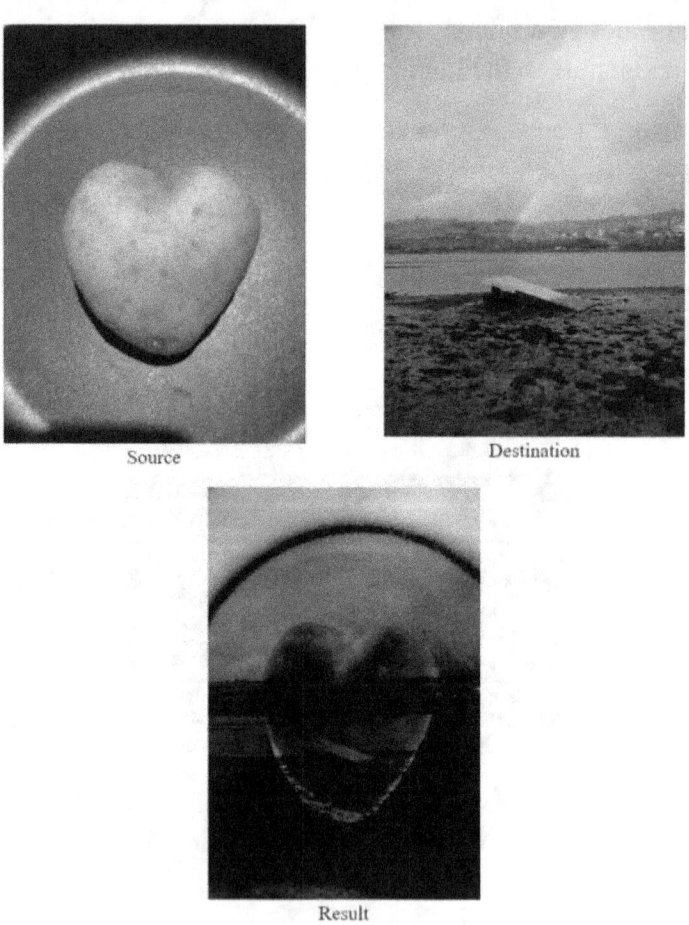

Figure 150: Image source, destination and result using SUBTRACT mode

DARKEST Mode

DARKEST mode is used to make the darker pixels in both images stand out. Only the darkest pixels remain in the result. This mode has many uses including placing lighter images behind darker ones and colouring images since black pixels absorb colours and white preserves them. Also, an interesting effect is that darkening an image with its blurred copy produces an interesting effect as seen in the example below (Figure 151)

```
PImage src=loadImage("wheelblurred.jpg");
PImage dst=loadImage("wheel.jpg");
dst.blend(src, 0,0,src.width,src.height,0,0,
 dst.width,dst.height,DARKEST);
image(dst, 0,0);
```

Source

Destination

Result

Figure 151: Image source, destination and result using DARKEST mode

BURN Mode

BURN mode intensifies colours by first darkening the destination and, when the destination is darker, more source colour is used in the result. We can thus adjust the colours of the destination by using the source. For example, we can make colours warmer with the appropriate selection of source and destination. BURN will tend to intensify colours

```
PImage src=loadImage("scene3.jpg");
PImage dst=loadImage("flowers.jpg");
dst.blend(src, 0,0,src.width,src.height,0,0,
 dst.width,dst.height,BURN);
image(dst, 0,0);
```

As you can see from this example, BURN provides the darkest images and the darker destination dominates but incorporates the colour from the source image (Figure 152)

Source

Destination

Result

Figure 152: Image source, destination and result using BURN mode

In order to provide a comparison of darken modes, the example below shows what happens when you blend a smiley face image source using each mode to show how the result differs

294

Figure 153: Image source, destination and result using different modes

You should be able to see in Figure 153 how MULTIPLY mixes the smiley face image with the background, SUBTRACT produces a negative image, DARKEST favours the colours from the destination, and BURN intensifies the colours.

Lighten Modes

Lighten modes represent the opposite to darken modes and result in lighter images than the original

SCREEN Mode

SCREEN mode can be used for lightening images by inverting the values of the colours, ; multiplying them, and inverting the result to get the SCREEN effect. Inverse colours are those which are symmetrically on the opposite side. For example, if we look at a single RGB channel, the inverse of black is white and the inverse of pretty bright is pretty dark. If we have colour x, its inverse value is 1-x in blend maths and if we invert it twice, we get the original colour back.

We previously saw that multiplying colours results in darker images. If we invert an image after multiplying it, we get a brighter image but the colours will be inversed. The trick here is to invert the colours first, multiply them to darken the inversed image, and invert the image again to get the original lightened image. SCREEN has the same effect as projecting two images onto the same spot on a wall. It can be used to add shine or reflections of light to an image. Also note that black pixels don't change value (preserves) and white pixels make the result white (absorbs). We can control the amount of lightening using a factor.

One practical use for lightening is to lighten underexposed photographs as seen in the example below of a scene taken in the dark

```
PImage src=loadImage("london2.jpg");
image(src,0,0);
blend(src,0,0,src.width,src.height,0,0,src.width,src.height,SCREEN);
```

Here we are applying SCREEN to the same image in order to lighten it allowing the detail of the photograph to be seen. The more times we apply it the lighter the image gets (Figure 154)

Figure 154: Applying SCREEN multiple times to lighten an image

ADD Mode

ADD mode is simple addition of values, which makes the result brighter. The difference to SCREEN, and potential problem, here is that the result may become too bright and the values quickly exceed 1 (or 255) as they are added together resulting in an image that is too light

Source   Destination

Result

Figure 155: Using ADD to display lighter pixels

In the example below we add two images together in order to display the lighter of the colours from each image

```
PImage dst = loadImage("lions2.jpg");
PImage src = loadImage("london2.jpg");
dst.blend(src,0,0,src.width,src.height,0,src.height/2,src.width,src.height,SCRE
EN);
image(dst,0,0);
```

As you can see in Figure 155 the lighter pixels from the building are displayed but the darker background is not in favour of the lighter background from the source, making it look like the building is inside the lion enclosure

LIGHTEST Mode

LIGHTEST is used to make the lightest pixels from both images stand out. Only the lightest pixels remain in the result. As opposed to DARKEST it can be used to hide the darker part of an image behind the lightest part. Its applicability is the same as DARKEST, though in the opposite fashion. White pixels absorb colours and black pixels preserve them.

In the example below we use a black colour to change the colour of our smiley face image. We fill the screen with a single colour, purple, and blend it with the image

```
PImage src = loadImage("smiley face.jpg");
background(139,0,255);
blend(src, 0,0,src.width,src.height,0,0,src.width,src.height,LIGHTEST);
```

As you can see from Figure 156, the darker pixels absorb more of the purple colour than the lighter ones

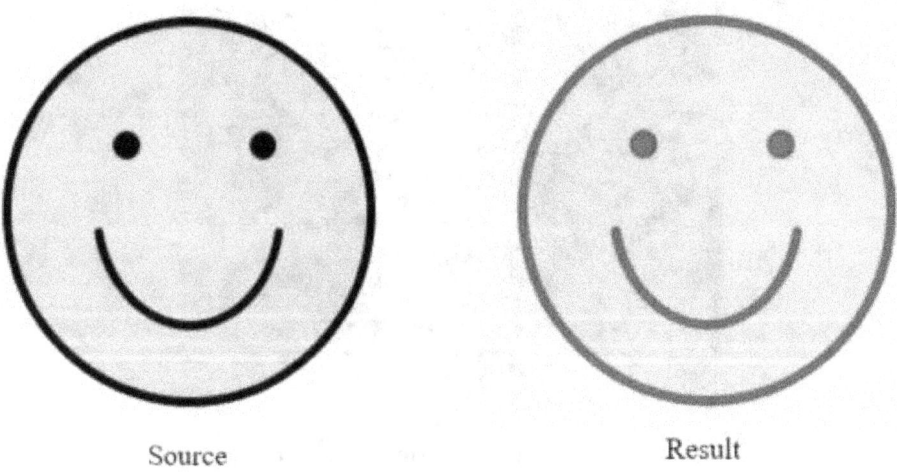

Source   Result

Figure 156: Applying colour using LIGHTEST

DODGE Mode

DODGE does the opposite of BURN. It first lightens the destination and then the lighter the destination is, the more source colour is used. It is used for colour adjustments, glowing, and some special effects. In contrast to BURN, darker destination colours absorb source colours while a darker source preserves the destination. On the other hand, a lighter source absorbs the destination

The example below demonstrates using DODGE to make an image warmer using a brown background colour and a dark image (Figure 157)

```
PImage dst = loadImage("penguin.jpg");
background(204,78,92);
dst.blend(g,0,0,dst.width,dst.height,0,0,dst.width,dst.height,DODGE);
image(dst,0,0);
```

Figure 157: Applying colour using DODGE

As a comparison of the lighten modes, Figure 158 shows what happens when we blend a tree texture with a an image with a light foreground and a dark background

Although subtle, you should be able to see that the modes have a different effect on the destination image

Contrast Modes

The contrast modes manipulate images by altering contrast - that is the relationship between dark and light colours

Source   Destination

SCREEN   ADD   LIGHTEST   DODGE

Figure 158: Comparing lighten modes

OVERLAY Mode

OVERLAY has a fairly basic function of increasing contrast. This mode determines whether pixels are on the bright or dark side, brightening the bright pixels and darkening the dark pixels. If MULTIPLY tries to eliminate bright pixels and SCREEN tries to eliminate dark pixels, then OVERLAY is about eliminating grey pixels. In general we can say that OVERLAY MULTIPLIES dark pixels and SCREENS light pixels. This mode can be used for special effects such as sharpening, dream scenes, glowing, and others

The following example overlays a picture of a dull day with itself

```
PImage dst=loadImage("scene3.jpg");
dst.blend(0,0,dst.width,dst.height,0,0,dst.width,dst.height,OVERLAY);
image(dst,0,0);
```

Notice in Figure 159 how the resulting image is much brighter with less grey, though dark colours are now darker than before

Source   Result

Figure 159: Increasing contrast with OVERLAY mode

HARD_LIGHT Mode

HARD_LIGHT has a similar effect as OVERLAY except that the effect is like SCREEN if there is greater than 50% grey, else the effect is like MULTIPLY (Figure 160)

```
PImage dst=loadImage("car2.jpg");
dst.blend(0,0,dst.width,dst.height,0,0,dst.width,dst.height,HARD_LIGHT);
image(dst,0,0);
```

Source   Result

Figure 160: Using HARD_LIGHT on an image with lots of grey

SOFT_LIGHT Mode

SOFT_LIGHT does the same as OVERLAY but not as harshly (Figure 161). It can be used similarly to OVERLAY and especially for effects like soft glamour look and correction of overexposed photos. The formula is complex and it is enough to remember that source pixels are used to decide whether darker areas will become darker or bright areas brighter.

```
PImage dst=loadImage("cat11.jpg");
dst.blend(0,0,dst.width,dst.height,0,0,dst.width,dst.height,SOFT_LIGHT);
image(dst,0,0);
```

Source   Result

Figure 161: Using SOFT_LIGHT to enhance contrast

The contrast modes are subtly different so the effects may not be immediately obvious so the example below shows the difference modes applied to the same picture.

```
PImage src = loadImage("car2.jpg");
PImage dst = loadImage("../images/car2.jpg");
src.filter(BLUR, 10);
dst.blend(src,0,0,dst.width,dst.height,0,0,dst.width,dst.height,SOFT_LIGHT);
dst.blend(src,0,0,dst.width,dst.height,0,0,dst.width,dst.height,SOFT_LIGHT);
image(dst,0,0);
```

To highlight the differences we have increased the effect by blurring the source and applying the contrast mode twice (Figure 162)

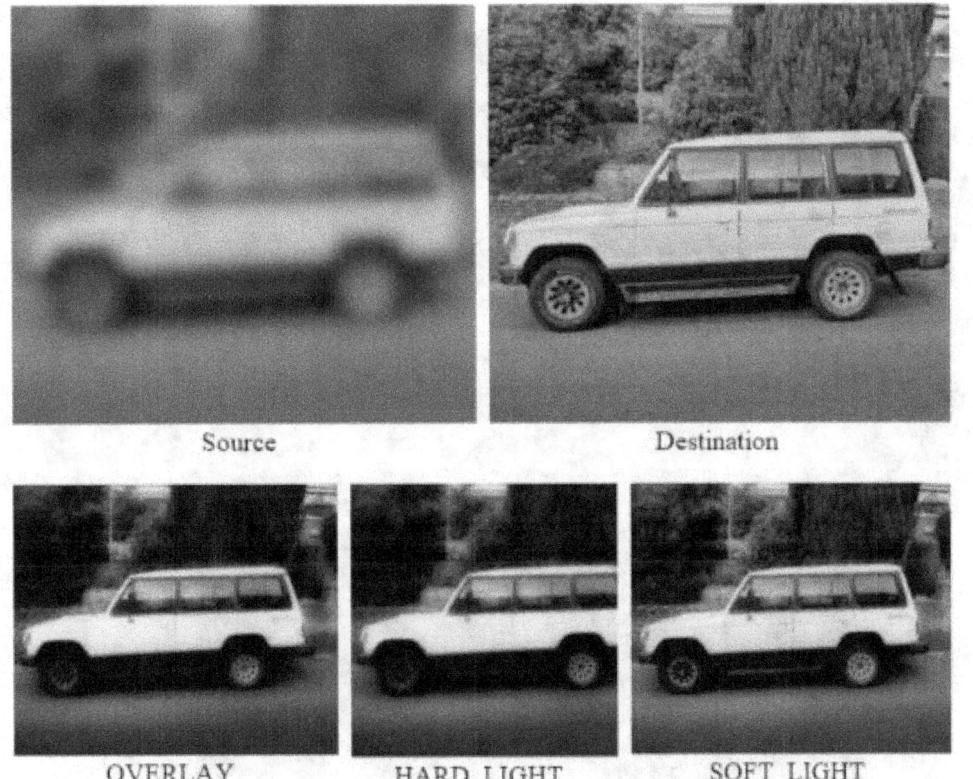

Source   Destination

OVERLAY   HARD_LIGHT   SOFT_LIGHT

Figure

162: Comparing contrast modes

Comparative Modes

The comparative modes focus on comparing pixel colours between the source and destination

DIFFERENCE Mode

DIFFERENCE is used to determine how far away the pixels are by subtracting them. If the pixels are equal, we get a black result. This mode could be used for image comparison, image alignment, and simple motion detection in surveillance cameras.

The example below detects the difference in two similar photographs

```
PImage dst=loadImage("cat2.jpg");
Image src=loadImage("cat5.jpg");
dst.blend(src,0,0,dst.width,dst.height,0,0,dst.width,dst.height,DIFFERENCE);
image(dst,0,0);
```

Since similar pixel colours will show darker and pixels less similar show lighter, you should be able to see the differences between the two images - largely that the cat moved its head slightly (Figure 163)

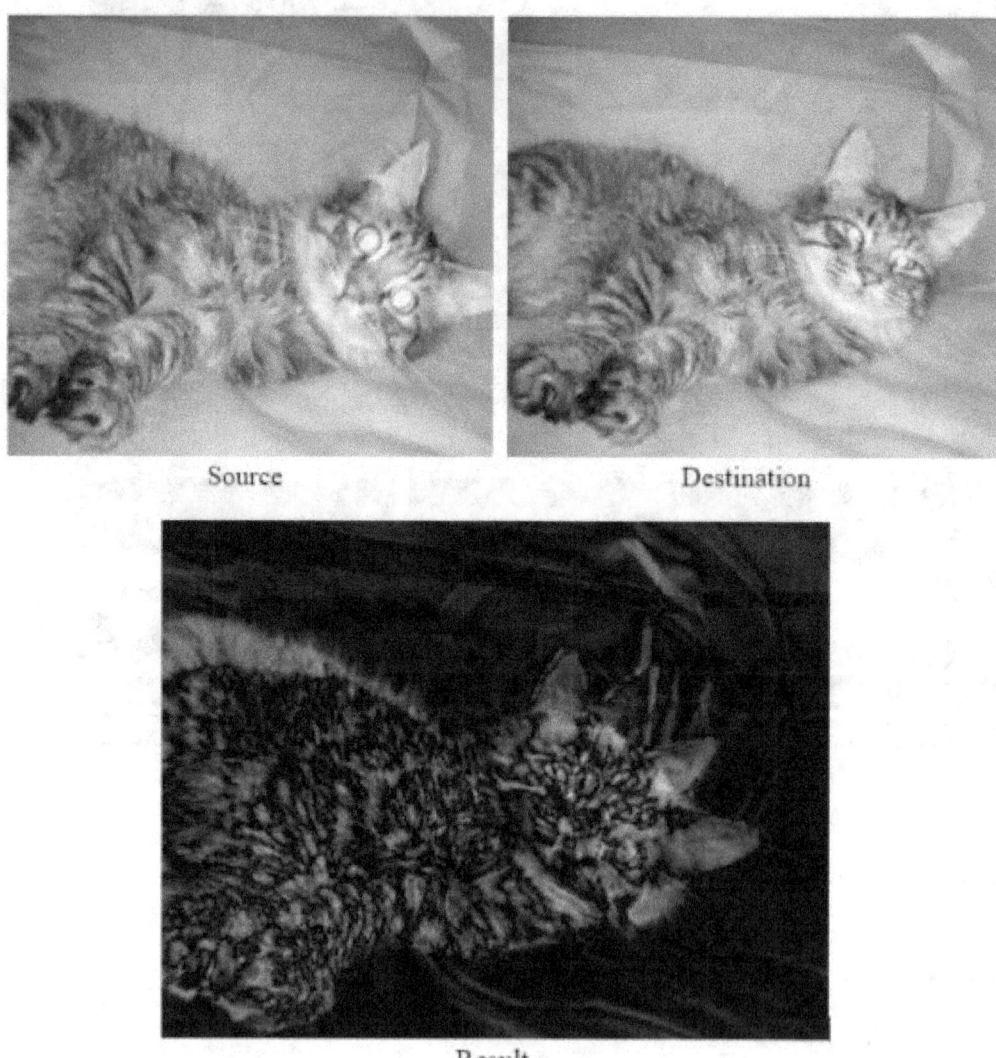

Source   Destination

Result

Figure 163: Visualising differences between images using DIFFERENCE

EXCLUSION Mode

EXCLUSION has similar, but less extreme, behaviour as DIFFERENCE . In this case black preserves and white inverts colours. Grey (50%) also absorbs. The example below demonstrates the behaviour

```
PImage dst=loadImage("cat3.jpg");
Image src=loadImage("cat4.jpg");
dst.blend(src,0,0,dst.width,dst.height,0,0,dst.width,dst.height,DIFFERENCE);
image(dst,0,0);
```

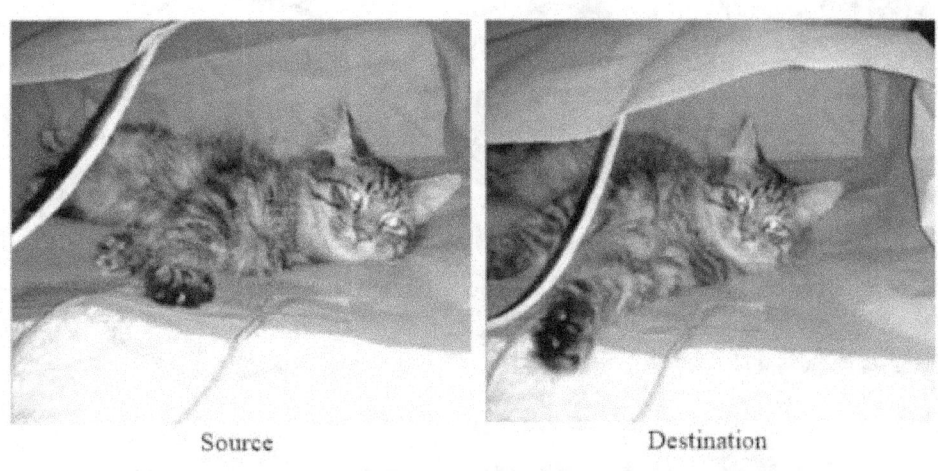

Source   Destination

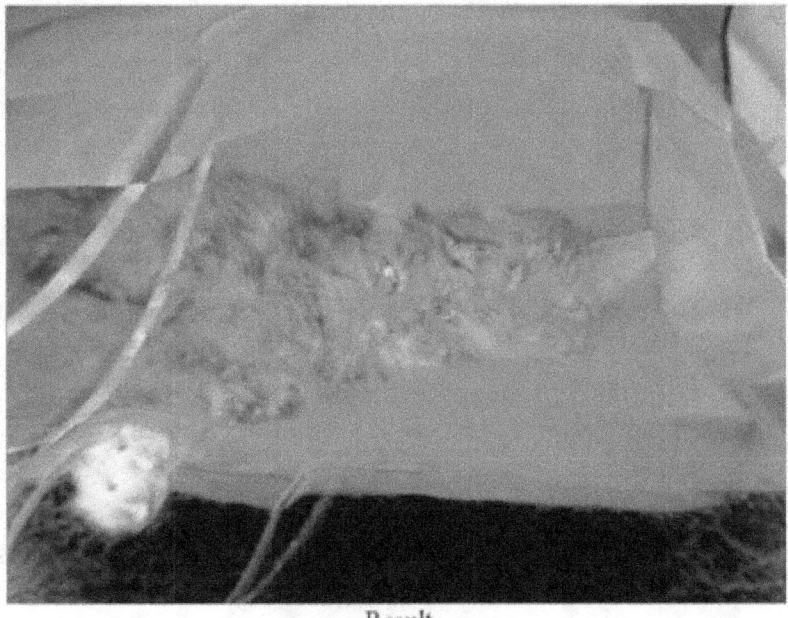

Result

Figure 164: Visualising differences between images using EXCLUSION

As you can see the difference in Figure 164 is not as marked as when using DIFFERENCE and the resulting image retains more of the original colours

In order to demonstrate the differences between the comparative modes we broke out the smiley face again. You should be able to see in Figure 165 that both exhibit similar behaviour but EXCLUSION retains more of the original image colours whereas DIFFERENCE has a more extreme effect

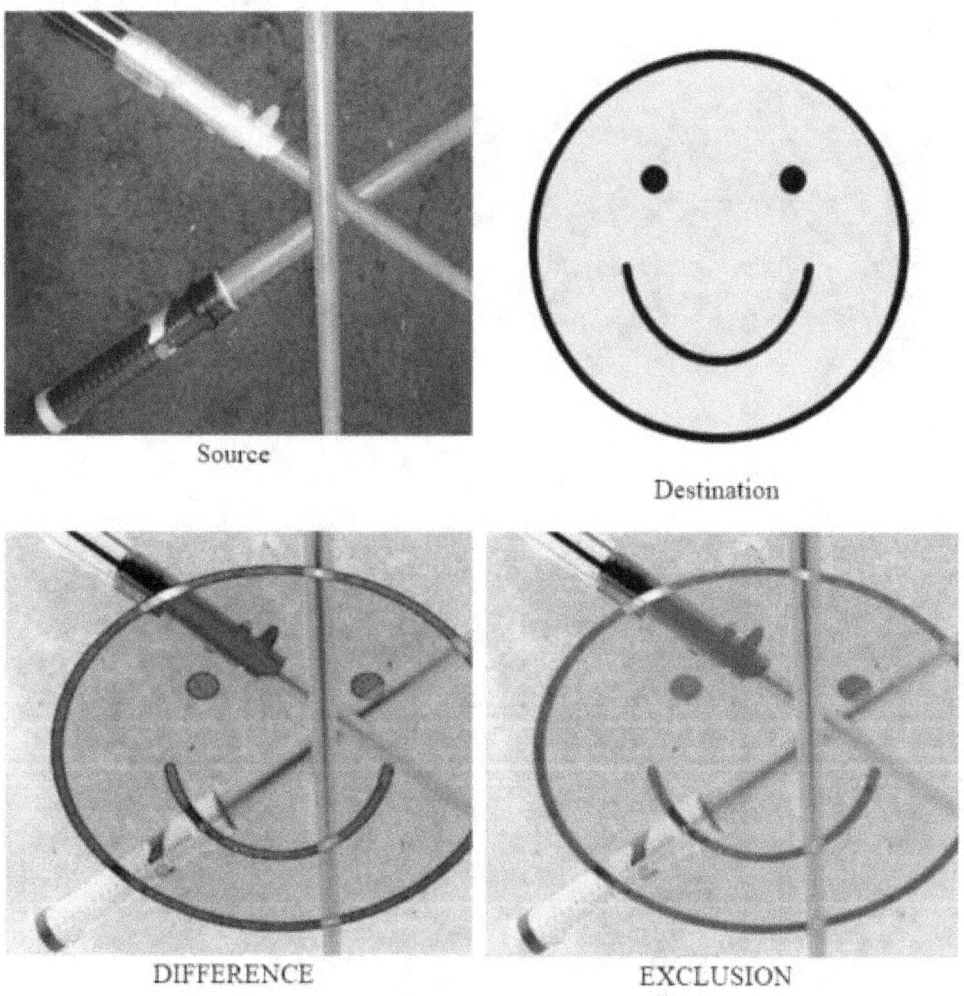

Figure 165: Comparative mode comparison

We have demonstrated that the blend() function in *Processing* allows us to combine images in various ways. We put the source image over the destination image and blend corresponding pixels according to a blending mode rule. The blend mode selected is crucial and defines the result. Blend modes can be grouped by their basic behaviour but their actual deployment depends primarily on the blender's imagination and experience. The blending factor allows us to control the intensity of blending. And that's it, let's start blending . . .

Images and Buttons

When we last looked at buttons we showed how an icon could be drawn in order to give visual feedback on what the button will do. An easier alternative would be to use a pre-prepared image for the icon (Figure 166). There is nothing new here, you already know how to do this using images and events with the button dimensions adjusted to conform to that of the images we are using

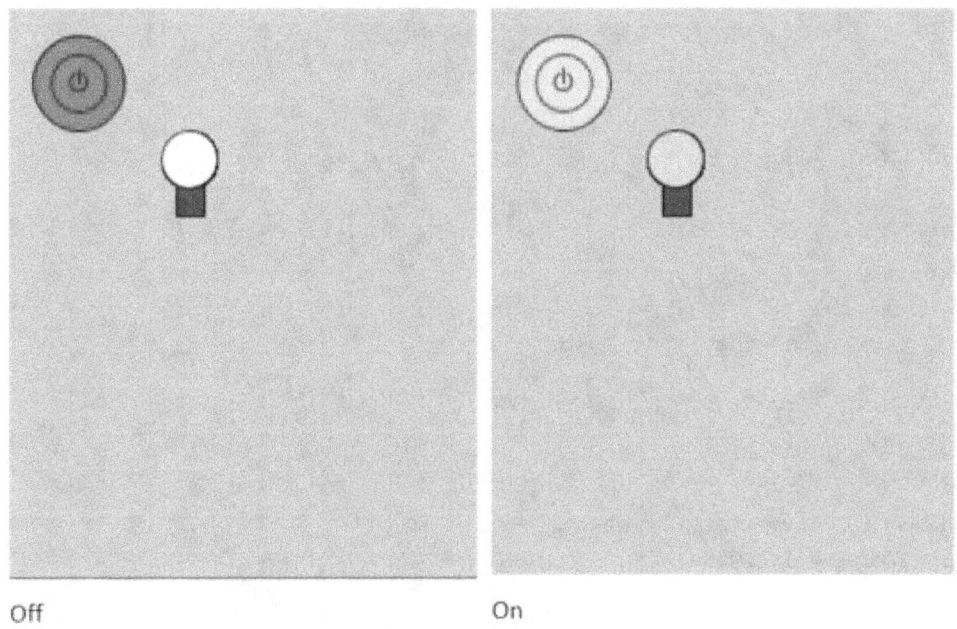

Off   On

Figure 166: Images for Buttons

This involves very little code to achieve and simply displays the relevant image

```
final int BUTTON_TOP_LEFT_X = 10;
final int BUTTON_TOP_LEFT_Y = 10;
int buttonWidth;
int buttonHeight;
PImage offImage;
PImage onImage;
PImage currentImage;
int BACKGROUND_COLOUR = color(192);

boolean isBulbOn = false;
```

```
void setup() {
    size(300,300);
    background(BACKGROUND_COLOUR);
    offImage = loadImage("../images/off.png");
    onImage = loadImage("../images/on.png");
    currentImage = offImage;
    // Make sure both images have the same width and height when creating them
    buttonWidth = currentImage.width;
    buttonHeight = currentImage.height;
}

void draw() {
    //button
    imageMode(CORNERS);
    image(currentImage, BUTTON_TOP_LEFT_X + 5, BUTTON_TOP_LEFT_Y + 5);

    // draw bulb
    fill(64,64,64);
    rect(93,90,15,20);
    // draw a circle for the light bulb
    if (isBulbOn) {
        fill(255, 204, 51); // an orange fill when the bulb is on
    currentImage = onImage;
    } else {
        fill(255); // a white fill when the bulb is off
        currentImage = offImage;
    }
    ellipseMode(CENTER);
    ellipse(100,80,30,30);
}

void mousePressed() {
    isBulbOn = !isBulbOn;
}
```

Chapter 20: Trigonometry

by Anabela Greene, Boyd Stratton, Neil Petrie and Rebecca Ewen

Trigonometry is the mathematics of angles. This chapter introduces the main aspects of trigonometry that will enable you to understand angles in *Processing* and will be useful when looking at curves in the next chapters

Trigonometric functions

Trigonometric functions are basically the function of an angle in relation to a right triangle. We will describe the trigonometric functions in terms of their drawing capabilities and demonstrate their use within *Processing*

The trigonometric functions are:

- Sine
- Cosine
- Tangent

The Sine Function

To help us visualize these functions it is useful to define them with the help of the 'unit circle'. A unit circle is a circle, which has a radius (**r**), of 1 unit in length

Angles can be measured in radians or in degrees:

Radians = degrees * π / 180°

Degrees = radians * 180° / π

As shown in Figure 167 let's think of the circle as being a wheel, with centre **C**= 0, 0. The point **P** is the intersection of the line, with length **r**, traced from the centre to the edge (the circumference) of the wheel. Also note that the point **P** is following the circumference of the wheel in an anti-clockwise movement

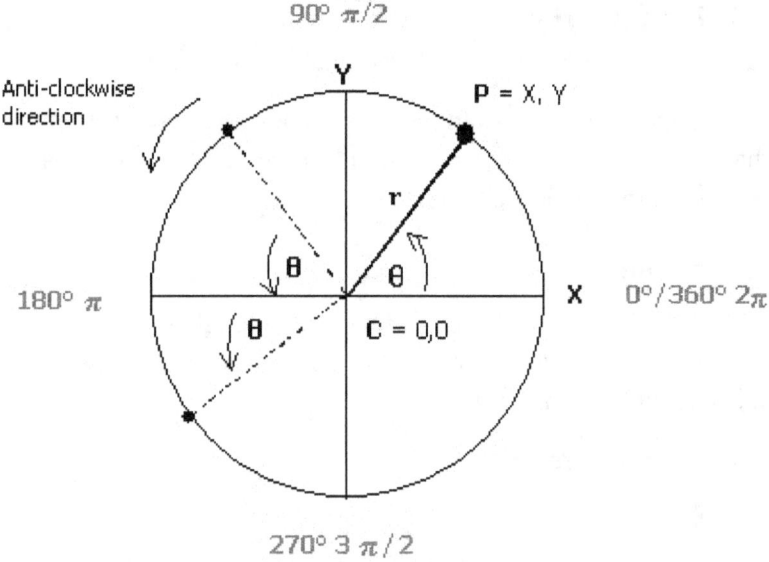

Figure 167: The Unit Circle

We can trace a perpendicular line from point P ending on the horizontal axis, X, and we do this for every point P on the circumference, as in Figure 168

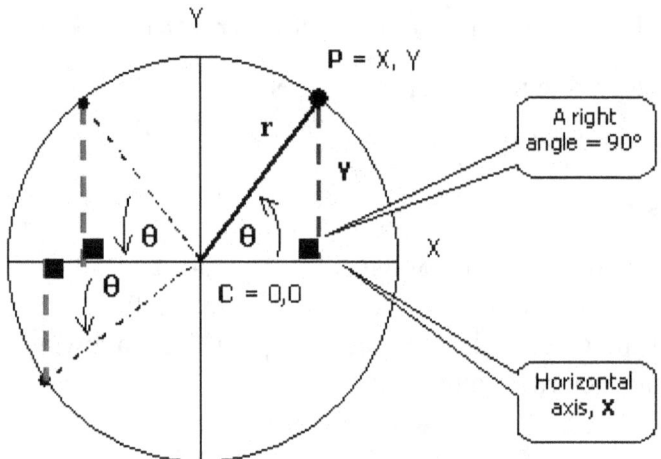

Figure 168: The Unit Circle Circumference

We can easily see that for every point on the circumference we end up with an infinite number of perpendicular lines on the X-axis, **Y**. It is this line that we are interested in, as it corresponds to the function sine of the angle theta, sin (θ).

If you are mathematically minded or want to understand why this is, it can be explained using trigonometric functions of an angle (θ) in relation to a righted-triangle; that is, as ratios of the lengths of the triangle sides, as shown below

Sine facts

The trigonometric functions of angle theta, **θ**, in relation to a righted-angle are equal to the ratios of the triangle sides

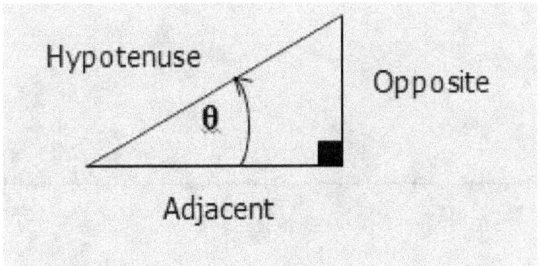

- ➲ sin (θ) = Opposite/Hypotenuse
- ➲ cos (θ) = Adjacent/Hypotenuse
- ➲ tan (θ) = Opposite/Adjacent

In our figure of the unit circle, figure 1.2, the corresponding values are:

- Hypotenuse equals to 1 unit, **r**.
- Opposite side is the perpendicular line **Y**

Therefore sine of theta is:

Sin(θ) = Y/1 = Y (expression 1)

If theta is:

0° then sin(θ) = Y = 0

90° then sin(θ) = Y = 1, the radius

180° then sin(θ) = Y = 0

270° then sin(θ) = Y = -1

360° then sin(θ) = Y = 0

We can now move on to see how sin (θ) provides us with the power to graphics programming.

We can draw the movement of the point **P** in a x-y coordinates plane (the Cartesian plane), with horizontal axis X and vertical axis Y, as it circles around the wheel.

We need to plot on the axis **Y** the positive and negative value of 1 unit and on axis **X** the value of the angle theta that **P** has travel along the wheel, against time, in this example 1 second.

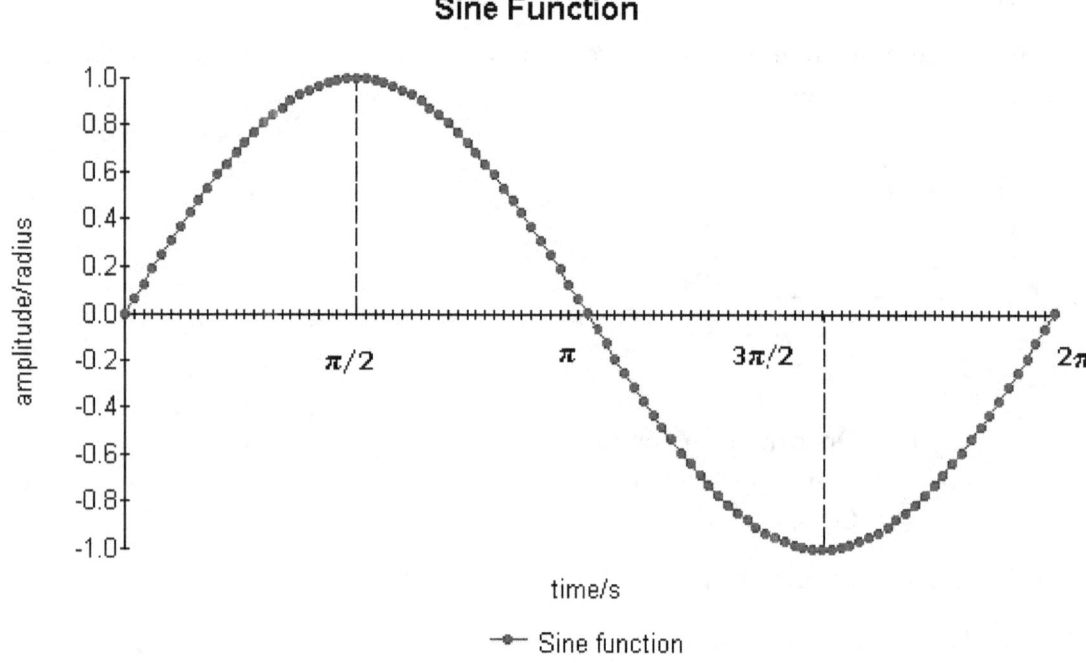

Figure 169: Sine Function

Here Figure 169 shows the graphic characteristics of a sine function, a sine wave. Point **P** has travelled 360 degrees (or 2π radians); in other words one revolution.

If **P** were to carry on rotating along the circumference of the wheel more than 1 revolution, then we will have a periodic sine function. This means that in the graph the wiggly line will continue towards infinity.

The amplitude, that is, the magnitude of the radius of the wheel on our example can have any other value, making the wheel smaller or bigger.

The trigonometric function for sin therefore looks like

```
f(θ) = sin(amplitude * θ) * amplitude
```

In *Processing* this is

```
float y = sin(radians(angle)) * radius
```

Please note the difference between using degrees and radians for measuring the angle theta. Here the function **radians(angle)** is used to give the angle in radians.

The maximum value of the sine function is equal to the amplitude, and the minimum value is equal to minus the amplitude. The function varies smoothly between these values during the period of the wave.

The frequency affects the number of repetitions of the wave within the period radians; such that if then the wave repeats once over the period and if then the wave repeats n times.

We can demonstrate the sine function in *Processing* with a simple example which draws two sine waves differing in colour as shown in Figure 170

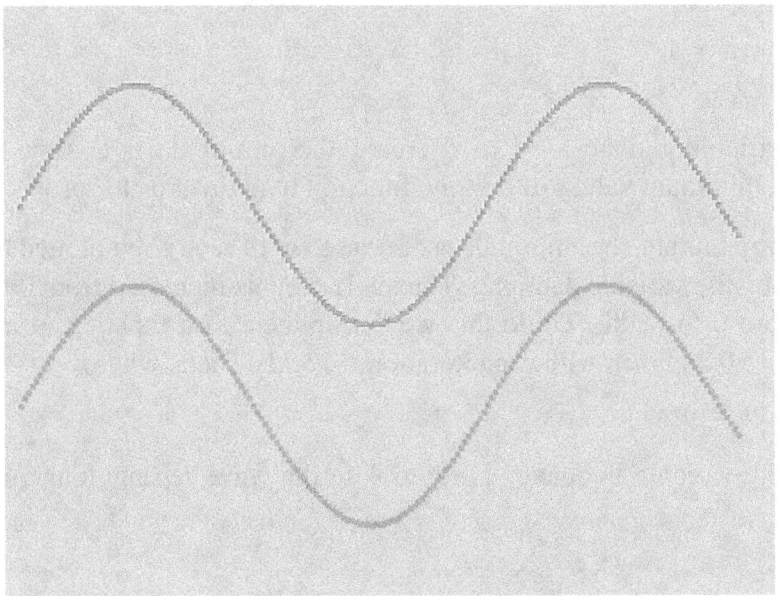

Figure 170: Coloured Sine Waves

```
// initialising variables
int y = 100; // the screen vertical coordinate
float S = 0; // sine value/y coordinate
float theta = 0; // angle
float amplitude = 60; // radius

// set up window
size (400, 300);
strokeWeight(3);// thickness of point

// draw the first wave of green colour
stroke(0, 190, 0); // green
```

```
for (int i = 10; i <= 380; i=i + 2) {
    S = sin(radians(theta))*amplitude;
    point (i, y - S);
    theta = theta + 3;
}

// draw a second wave of orange colour
stroke(255, 128, 0); // orange
theta =0;
y = 200;
for (int i = 10; i <= 380; i=i + 2) {
    S = sin(radians(theta))*amplitude;
    point (i, y - S);
    theta = theta + 3;
}
```

A damping variable can be used to decrease the amplitude over time such that the maximum and minimum values of the sine function tend towards to zero

In the following example, the amplitude is decreased with each point plotted by multiplying the amplitude by the variable damping. The angle theta is increased from 0 to TWO_PI as x increases from 0 to width. To do this we define theta as a function of and width. We initialise theta to 0 and then with each iteration we add dTheta, where

```
dTheta = TWO_PI/width;
```

Additionally the variable frequency is set to 4 so the wave repeats four times within the period.

```
size(600, 300);
background(0);
stroke(255);
smooth();
float y = 0;
float theta = 0.0;
float amplitude = height/2 ;
float damping = 0.994;
float dTheta= TWO_PI/width;
float position = height/2;
float frequency = 4;
color strokeColor = 255;

for(int x=0; x < width; x++) {
    y = position + amplitude*sin(frequency*theta);
```

```
  // map red y coord values onto red range
  float red = map(y, 72, 270, 0, 255);
  float blue = 255 - red;
  strokeColor = color(red, 0, blue);
  stroke(strokeColor);
  point (x, y);
  amplitude *= damping;
  theta += dTheta;
}
```

We have applied some colouring to the wave to make it more interesting. The result of this can be seen in Figure 171

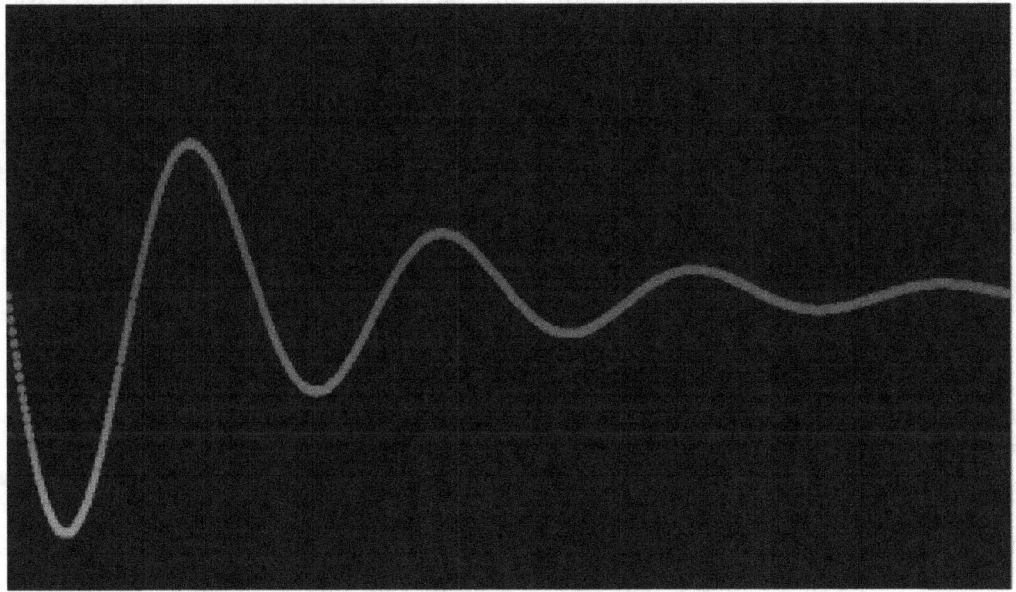

Figure 171: Sine Wave with Damping Effect

To make the colours make more sense, we can colour it in relation to how close the line is to the calculated sine function. We will attempt a smooth colour shift from blue to red through green. To achieve this, we scale the range of possible value to keep it in the range of colours, namely 0 to 255.

```
float adjVal = y - (-amplitude + position);
float adjMaxVal = (amplitude + position) - (-amplitude + position);
float scaledVal = adjVal * (255/adjMaxVal);
scaledColourValue = scaledVal;
```

To scale the value we first need to ensure that the minimum value returned will be 0. This is achieved by subtracting the argument the minimum possible value . Hence if the value is greater than 0 it is reduced to 0, and conversely if the value is less than 0 then it is increased to 0. This new adjusted value is adjVal.

Next we need to ensure that the maximum value returned is 255. In order to do this we create a scale factor which we will multiply by adjVal to give us the required results.

We begin by adjusting the maximum value in the same way as before - subtracting the minimum value. Then we divide 255 by this new adjusted maximum value adjMax to create a scale factor. This scale factor is multiplied by adjVal to produce a number in the range 0 to 255 proportional to the maximum and minimum values

This scaled value is then used to determine the colour, divided into four equal sections. In each section two of the RGB values were kept constant whilst the other was increased or decreased to give a smooth transition.

For example, in the first section we use colour values 0 and 63 - to get from blue to cyan. We keep the red component of the colour as 0 and the blue value constant at 255. We then increase the amount of green proportional to the current value. We need to ensure the green value increases from 0 to 255 (approximately), which ranges from 0 to 63; hence we multiply by 4

```
if (scaledColourValue >= 0 && scaledColourValue <= 63) {
    redVal = 0;
    greenVal = 4 * scaledColourValue;
    blueVal = 255;
}
```

Similarly in the other sections we subtract the start of the range before multiplying by 4 to give a value between 0 and 255 that can be used to vary one of the colours red, green or blue.

With all four sections this gives us the colour scale in Figure 172

Figure 172: The Colour Scale

Putting this all together means that we can colour each part of the sine wave according to its relativity to the calculated sine function (Figure 173)

```
strokeWeight(5);
```

```
size(600, 300);
background(0);
stroke(255);
smooth();
float y = 0;
float theta = 0.0;
float amplitude = height/2 ;
float damping = 0.994;
float dTheta= TWO_PI/width;
float position = height/2;
float frequency = 4;
color strokeColour = 255;
float scaledColourValue = 0;

for (int x=0; x < width; x++) {
    y = position + amplitude*sin(frequency*theta);

    //Scale values to ensure new max equals 255
    float adjval = y - (-amplitude + position);
    float adjMaxVal = (amplitude + position) - (-amplitude + position);
    float scaledval = adjval * (255/adjMaxVal);
    scaledColourValue = scaledval;

    float redVal = 0;
    float greenVal =0;
    float blueVal =0;

    //subdivide colour selection based on range of values
    if (scaledColourValue >= 0 && scaledColourValue <= 63) {
        redVal = 0;
        greenVal = 4 * scaledColourValue;
        blueVal = 255;
    } else if (scaledColourValue > 63 && scaledColourValue <= 127) {
        redVal = 0;
        greenVal = 255;
        blueVal = 255 - 4 * (scaledColourValue - 64);
    } else if (scaledColourValue > 127 && scaledColourValue <= 191) {
        redVal = 4 * (scaledColourValue - 128);
        greenVal = 255;
        blueVal = 0;
    } else if (scaledColourValue > 191 && scaledColourValue <= 255) {
        redVal = 255;
        greenVal = 255 - (4 * (scaledColourValue - 192));
```

```
      blueVal = 0;
  }

  strokeColour = color(redVal, greenVal, blueVal);

  stroke(strokeColour);
  point (x, y);
  amplitude *= damping;
  theta += dTheta;
}
```

Note that the minimum and maximum values change as the function is plotted, so that each peak and trough is plotted in the same colour. This is because the amplitude is passed to scale the value after each iteration so the damping is taken into account when determining the maximum and plotting each point.

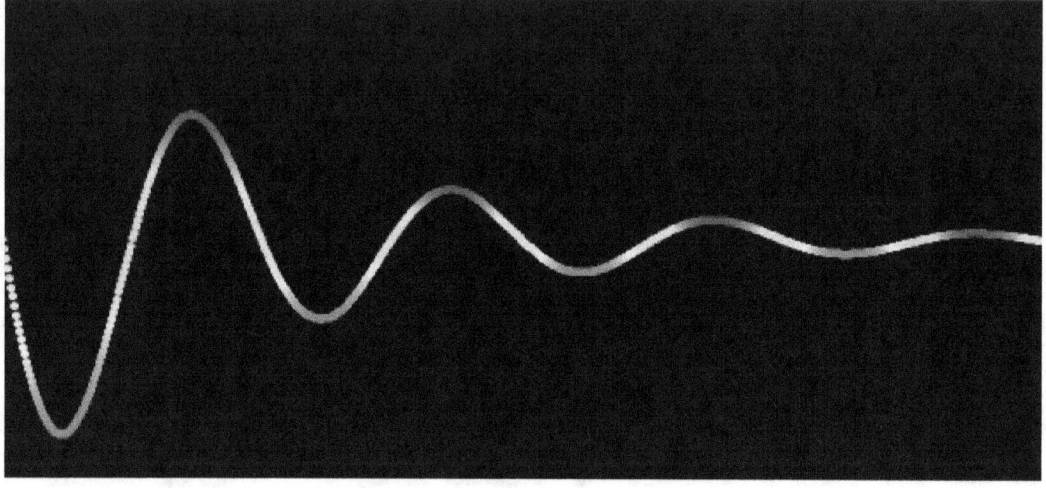

Figure 173: Sine Wave with Sine Colouring

The Cosine Function

As with the sine function the cosine function can be demonstrated to possess graphics properties. This time, however, we are concerned with the adjacent side of the angle theta, **X** (Figure 174)

318

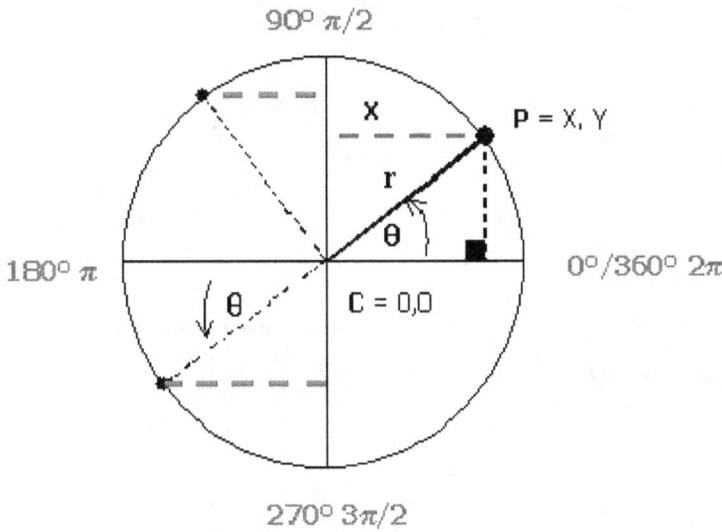

Figure 174: The Unit Circle Showing Cosine Function

Cosine facts

cos(θ) = adjacent/hypotenuse

cos(θ) = X/1 = X (expression 2)

Therefore, when theta, θ, is:

0° then cos(θ) = X = 1, the radius.

90° then cos(θ) = X = 0

Figure 175 illustrates the cosine function graphed on the Cartesian plane, in which we can note another kind of wave

We can compare the two functions by graphing them together as shown in Figure 176 The sine wave can be considered identical to a cosine wave, but they are separated by one quarter of a cycle; that is $\pi/2$ radians. In other words, the cosine leads the sine wave by 90 degrees.

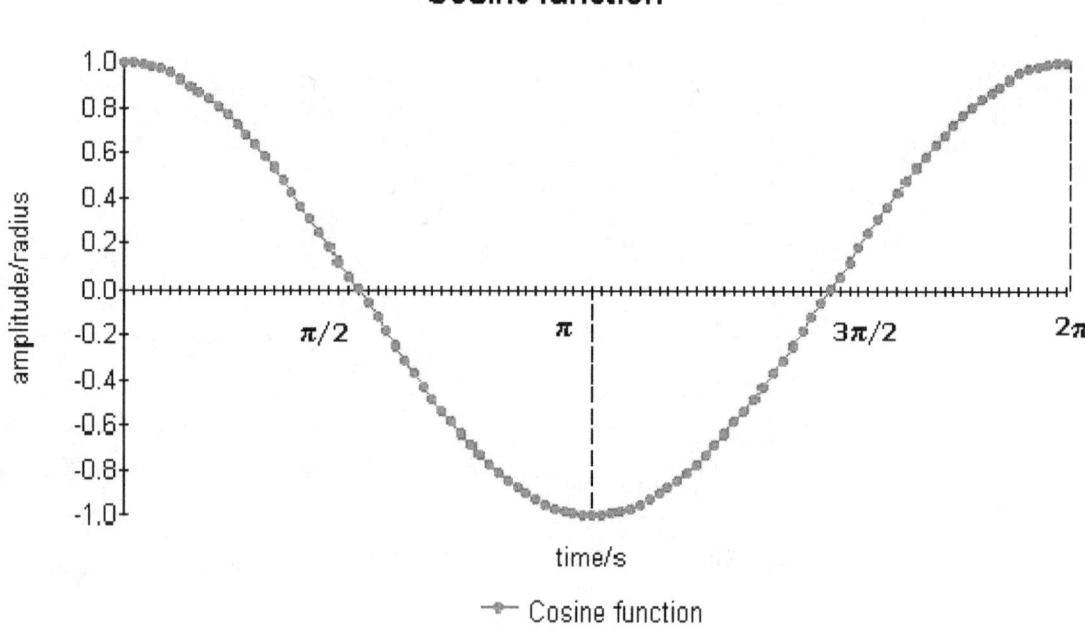

Figure 175: Cosine Function Graphed on the Cartesian Plane

As we have seen, the sine and cosine functions are translated into the Cartesian plane by:

```
X = cos(θ) * radius  (expression 3)
Y = sin(θ) * radius  (expression 4)
```

Note that these expressions are deducted from expression2 and expression 1 respectively.

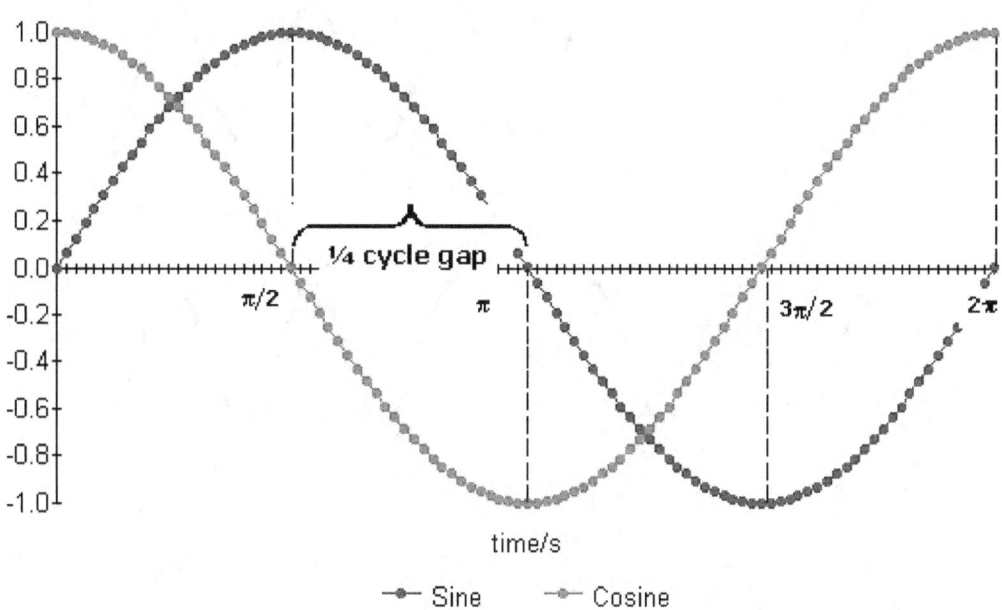

Figure 176: Cosine and Sine Functions Graphed on the Cartesian Plane

The trigonometric function in *Processing* is

```
float x = cos(radians(angle)) * radius
```

Again note that the function uses radians to calculate the angle

Similarly to the sine example, we can demonstrate this with a simple sketch that draws a series of cosines waves with its directions alternated. The effect of this can be seen in Figure 177. The waves in black colour can be seen as mirrored by the waves in purple

321

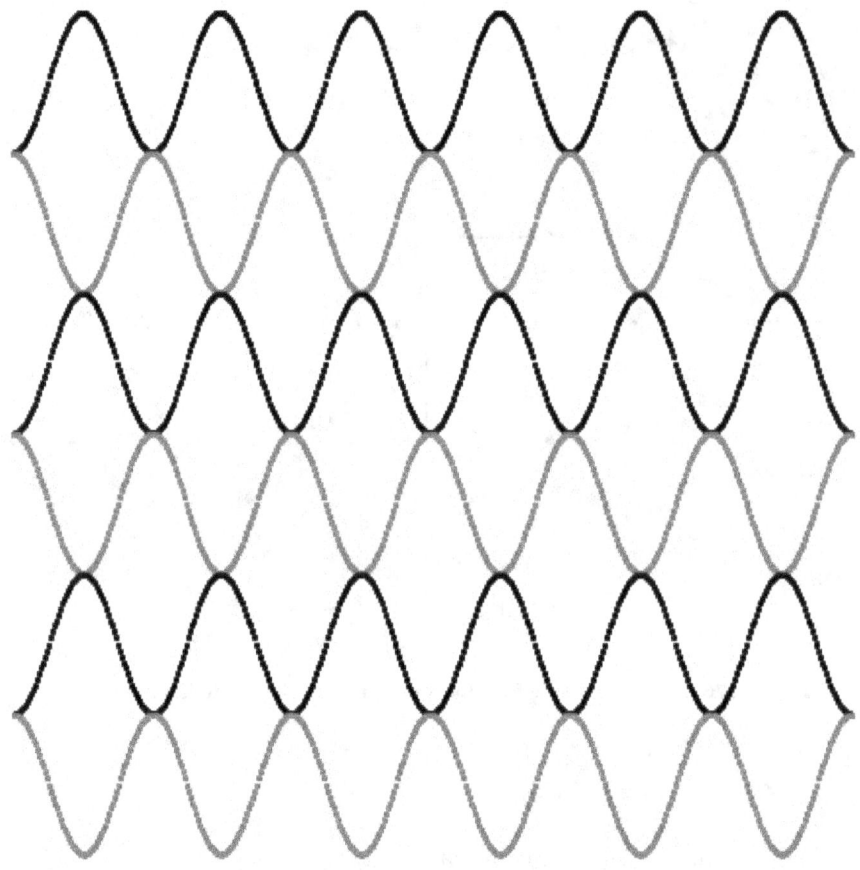

Figure 177: Alternating Cosine Waves

```
// var initialising
int y = 75;
float theta = 0;

void setup() {
   size(500, 500);
   background(255);
   strokeWeight(3);
}

void draw() {
   float cosine = 0;
   if (y < 425) {
```

```
    // j represents times cosine function will draw in screen
    for (int j = 1; j <= 6; j++) {
        theta = 0;
        // i is the length of the cosine wave across the screen
        for (int i = 20; i < 453; i++) {
            if ((j+1)%2 == 0) {
                stroke(0);
                cosine = cos(radians(theta))*(35);
                point(i, cosine + y);
                theta = theta + 5;}
            else {
                stroke(180, 35, 255); // purple
                cosine = cos(radians(theta))*(35);
                point(i, y - cosine);
                theta = theta + 5;
            }
        }
        y = y + 70;
    }
  }
}
```

The Tangent Function

The tangent function can be derived from the sine and cosine functions. You may recall from earlier that

```
tan(θ) = Opposite/Adjacent
```

Let's repeat our figure of the unit circle but this time showing both sine and cosine functions, shown in Figure 178. Here we can see the line, highlighted in green (**Z**), which corresponds to the tangent function forming a perpendicular with the radius on point **P**. We could say that the tangent just touches the unit circle at point **P**.

Also recall that the expressions for sine and cosine are:

```
sin(θ) = Y/1 = Y
cos(θ) = X/1 = X
```

Therefore we can conclude that:

```
tan(θ) = sin(θ) / cos(θ)
```

We can calculate values of tangent when theta, **θ**, equals:

```
0° then tan(θ) = Y/X = 0/1 = 0
```

```
90°  then tan(θ) = Y/X = 1/0 = undefined
180° then tan(θ) = Y/X = 0/-1 = 0
270° then tan(θ) = Y/X = -1/0 = undefined
360° then tan(θ) = Y/X = 0/1 = 0
```

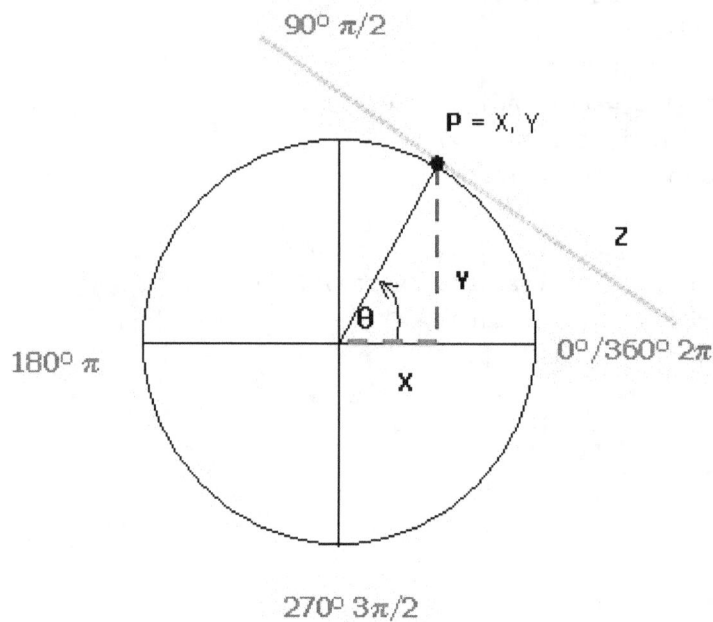

Figure 178: Unit Circle Showing Sine and Cosine

The *Processing* expression to create the tangent function is:

```
float z = tan(radians(angle)) * radius
```

The following code draws the tangent for one revolution on the Cartesian plane

```
// initialising variables
float tang = 0;
float Y = 0;
float X = 0;
float Cx = 100;
float Cy = 350;
float radius = 75;
float theta = 0;
int i = 188;
PFont font;
String label = "π/2     π     3π/2     2π";
boolean last = false;
```

324

```
// set up frame, circle and coordinates plane
void setup() {
   size (600, 700);
   frameRate(5);
   fill(255);
   strokeWeight(1);
   ellipse(Cx, Cy, 150, 150);

   // draw cartesian plane
   strokeWeight(1);
   line(Cx, Cy, Cx+465, Cy);
   line(191, 250, 191, 500);
   stroke(185);
   line(270, 50, 270, 660);
   line(450, 50, 450, 660);
   // write labels
   fill(0);
   font = createFont("Helvetica", 32);
   textFont(font, 15);
   text(label, 271, 370);
}

//draw the tangent function in the cartesian plane
void draw() {
   if (theta <= 360) {
      // when the last horizontal line has been drawn
      // then change to grey, so that leading line is black
      if (last) {
         stroke(185); // grey
         strokeWeight(1);
         line(Cx + X, Cy - tang, i, Cy - tang);
         if (theta == 185) {
            stroke(0);
            line(191, Cy - tang, i, Cy - tang);
          }
      }
      // axis x and y
      strokeWeight(1);
      tang = tan(radians(theta))*radius;
      Y = sin(radians(theta))*radius;
      X = cos(radians(theta))*radius;

      // draw the angle line, radius
```

```
        stroke(185); // grey radius
        line(Cx, Cy, Cx + X, Cy - Y);

        // draw the point that follows the tangent
        strokeWeight(3); // dot thickness
        stroke(20, 180, 250); // blue
        point(Cx + X, Cy - tang);

        // draw sine wave in axis coordinates, a series of green dots
        strokeWeight(6); // thick dot
        stroke(30, 200, 175); // green
        i = i + 5;
        point (i, Cy - tang);

        // draw a line to joint tangent point with tangent wave
        stroke(0);
        strokeWeight(1);
        line(Cx + X, Cy - tang, i, Cy - tang);
        theta = theta + 5; // increment angle
    }
    last = true; // last line drew
}
```

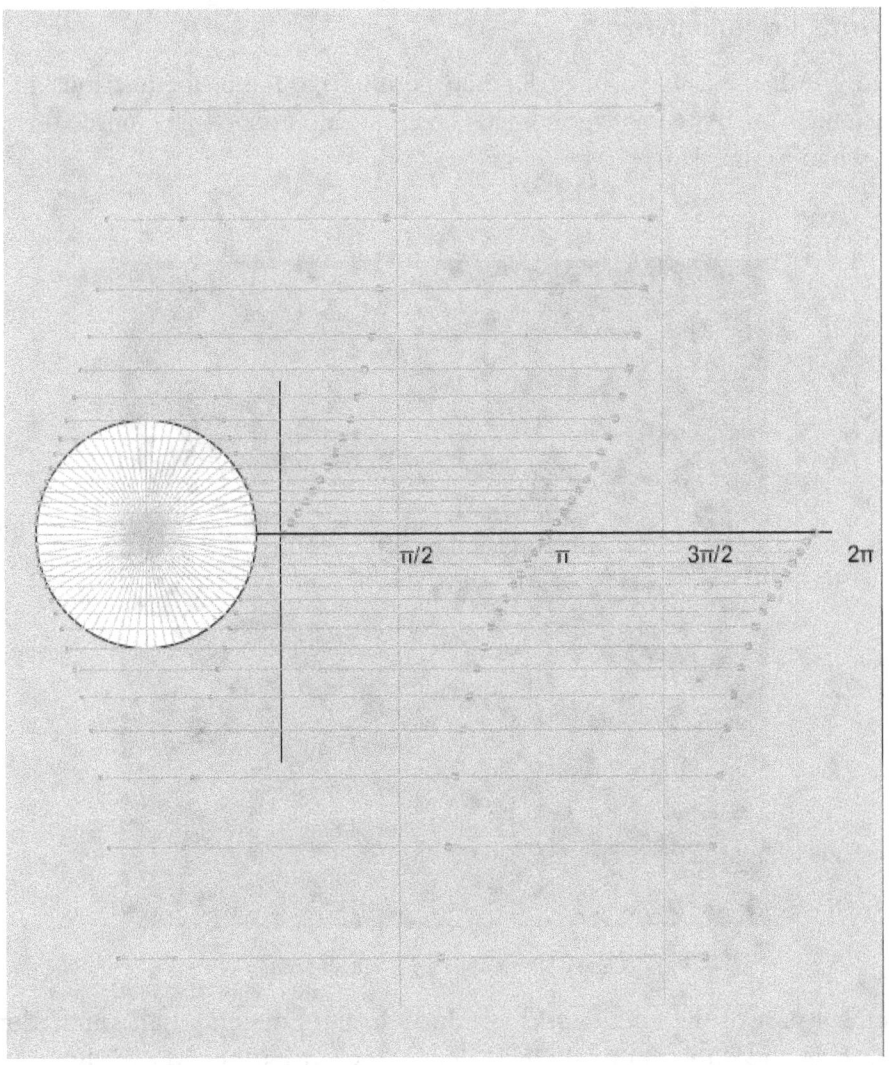

Figure 179: Tangent Function Drawn in the Cartesian Plane

Figure 179 above illustrates a different curve altogether from those of the sine and cosine functions. We can see that at 90 and 270 degrees ($\pi/2$ and $3\pi/2$ radians respectively) the curve is undefined, going upwards towards positive infinity (+ Y) at 90 degrees and reappearing on the negative coordinate Y at 91 degrees. The same can be said when theta is at 270, 450, etc.

Again, if we can carry on further than one revolution, we will be able to see that there is a repeating pattern at every 180 degrees. For example we can see a curve formed between angles 90 ($\pi/2$) and 270 ($3\pi/2$) degrees, this shape of curve will repeat at angles between 270 and 450, and between 450 and 630 degrees and so on

327

Drawing with Trigonometry

We can now utilise what we have learned about trigonometric functions to create an interesting animation by using trigonometry to create a realistic light source for a bouncing ball as shown in Figure 180

Figure 180: Animated Bouncing Ball

The movement part of the code works similarly to the bouncing ball simulation we saw earlier. We alter the direction of the ball depending on its location so that it appears to bounce off the sides of the screen

```
//move ball across screen by changing X-coordinate of centre
xPosition += ySpeed;
yPosition += xSpeed;

//detect collision with top or bottom of screen and 'bounce' if required
if ((yPosition + ballRadius >= height) || (yPosition <= ballRadius)) {
   xSpeed *= -1;
}
//detect collision with left or right of screen and 'bounce' if required
if ((xPosition + ballRadius >= width) || (xPosition <= ballRadius)) {
   ySpeed *= -1;
```

```
}
```

The ball is made to have a 3D effect by drawing a series of concentric ellipses in slightly varying colours. However, it is in the highlighting that trigonometry is used in order to make it focus on the ball as it moves, as if a fixed light source was in the room and reflected on the ball

```
// calculate the position of the light source relative to the ball
float lightsourceAngle = atan(lightSourceHeight/(lightSourcePosition
    - ballPosition));
float lightsourcePosition = (ballRadius * cos(lightsourceAngle));
```

Here we use the atan() function, which produces the inverse of tan() to calculate the angle of the light source in relation to the ball's position. This is then used, along with the cos() function, to calculate the position of the light source

We have reused these calculations in a function we have called calculateHighlightPosition() so that we can reuse it for both the vertical and horizontal positioning

```
// size of ball
float ballRadius = 50;

// initial position
float xPosition = ballRadius + 1;
float yPosition = 200;

// horizontal and vertical movement of the ball;
int ySpeed = 3;
int xSpeed = 3;

// colour of ball
float red = 60;
float blue = 10;
float green = 10;

// to draw the highlight relative to the centre of the ball
float highlightSize = ballRadius / 3;

// to define the position of the light source
float lightSourceX = 200;
float lightSourceY = 200;
float lightSourceHeight;
```

```
void setup() {
    size(400, 400);
    background(40, 10, 10);
    noStroke();
    frameRate(25);
    lightSourceHeight = width/2;
}

void draw() {
    background(0);

    //move ball across screen by changing X-coordinate of centre
    xPosition += ySpeed;
    yPosition += xSpeed;

    //detect collision with top or bottom of screen and 'bounce' if required
    if ((yPosition + ballRadius >= height) || (yPosition <= ballRadius)) {
        xSpeed *= -1;
    }

    //detect collision with left or right of screen and 'bounce' if required
    if ((xPosition + ballRadius >= width) || (xPosition <= ballRadius)) {
        ySpeed *= -1;
    }

    //position the highlight
    float highlightCentreX = xPosition;
    float highlightCentreY = yPosition;
    float highlightRadius = ballRadius;

    //re-set colours
    red = 60;
    green = 0;
    blue = 0;

    //draw the ball
    while (highlightRadius > 0) {
        // calculate colour of ellipse
        red += 255/ballRadius;
        if (highlightRadius <= highlightSize) {
            green += 255/highlightSize;
            blue += 255/highlightSize;
        }
```

```
      fill(red, green, blue);
      // calculate highlighting of ellipse
      highlightRadius --;
      highlightCentreX += calculateHighlightPosition(lightSourceHeight,
          lightSourceX, xPosition);
      highlightCentreY += calculateHighlightPosition(lightSourceHeight,
          lightSourceY, yPosition);
      // draw ellipse
      ellipse(highlightCentreX, highlightCentreY, highlightRadius * 2,
          highlightRadius * 2);
  }
}


/**
 * Uses trigonometry to calculate the position of the highlight
 * relative to the positions of the ball and the light source.
 */
float calculateHighlightPosition(float lightSourceHeight, float
    lightSourcePosition, float ballPosition) {

  // calculate the position of the light source relative to the ball
  float lightsourceAngle = atan(lightSourceHeight/(lightSourcePosition
      - ballPosition));
  float lightsourcePosition = (ballRadius * cos(lightsourceAngle));

  // calculate the position of the highlight
  float highlightPosition;
  if (ballPosition < lightSourcePosition) {
    highlightPosition = ballPosition + lightsourcePosition;
  } else {
    highlightPosition = ballPosition - lightsourcePosition;
  }
  // return the calculated position
  return (highlightPosition - ballPosition)/ballRadius;
}
```

Drawing Shapes with Trigonometry

We can utilise trigonometric functions to draw useful shapes that are not available as general *Processing* shapes, such as drawing a trigonometric arc as seen in Figure 181

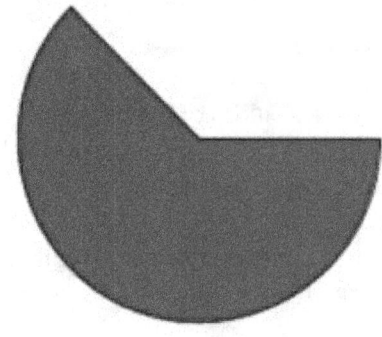

Figure 181: Arc Drawn Using Trigonometry   Figure 182: Standard Processing Arc

There is an inbuilt arc function within *Processing*, but it does not provide us with the shape type we want as it produces a pie wedge shape (Figure 182) rather than the arc shape we are looking for.

We will create a new class for this that allows us to draw arcs of any size. The basic structure of our class, which we will call SimpleArc, looks like the below

```
class SimpleArc {

    // Set the colour of the arc
    public void setColour(color c)

    // Set the rotation 'speed'
    public void setRotation(float va)

    // Render the arc
    public void render()

}
```

The class will include functions for drawing the arc. Before we code the class we need to just look at a little mathematics to understand one way of describing an arc that we can use in *Processing*.

There are a number of ways to draw an arc shape in *Processing*, in this example we have used the capability of *Processing* to draw strips of quadrilateral between different vertices (points) to provide our arc shape. We look into this in more detail now.

Figure 183 shows that we can calculate the x and y co-ordinates of any point on a circle if we know the radius and the angle of that radius from the x-axis. The x co-ordinate is given by:

Radius * cos(angle to x-axis)

And the y co-ordinate by:

Radius * sin(angle to x-axis)

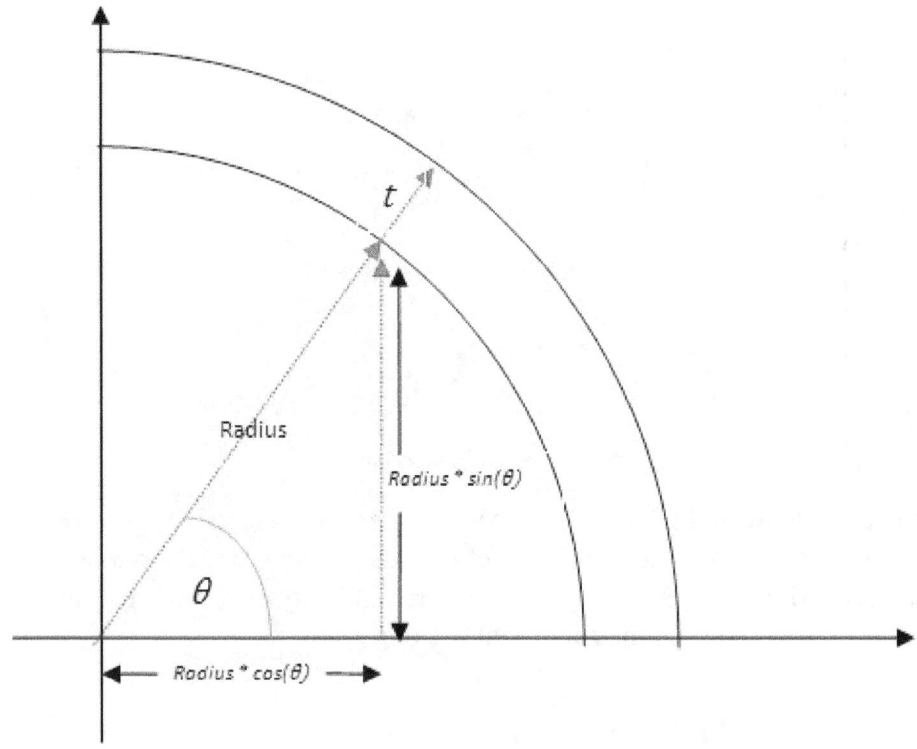

Figure 183: Points on a Circle

In Figure 184 you see that we will create an arc by calculating various points along both the inner and outer curved edge of the arc and then drawing quadrilateral at these points to approximate an arc. Fortunately *Processing* makes it very easy to do this with the *beginShape(QUAD_STRIP)* and *endShape()* functions

333

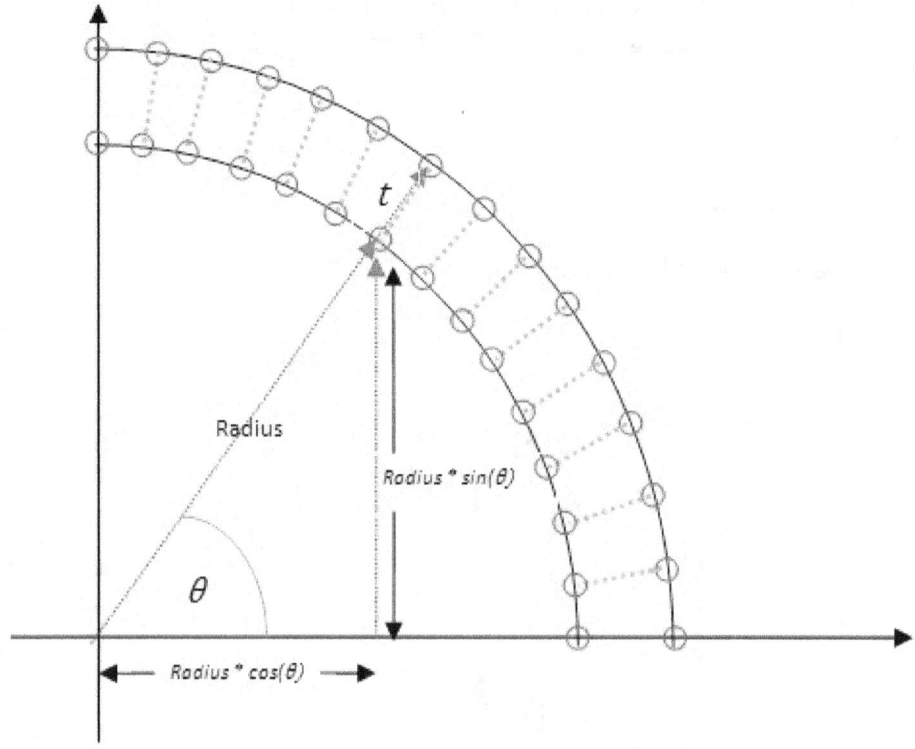

Figure 184: Arc Made from Quadrilaterals

Below is the code showing the class instance variables and the constructor used to define our SimpleArc. The code outside the constructor is just class instance variable declarations . These are declared to give us space inside our arc object to store data relating to our arc that we may want to use during the life of our arc object.

```
class SimpleArc {

    float cx;  //Centre x co-ordinate of the circle the arc lies on
    float cy;  //Centre y co-ordinate of the circle the arc lies on
    float acx;  //The x-coord 'midpoint' of the arc.
    float acy;  //The y-coord 'midpoint' of the arc.

    float radius; //The radius of the circle the arc lies on
    float thick;  //The 'width' of the arc

    float startAngle; //The angle around a circle where this arc starts
    float endAngle;   //The angle around a circle where this arc ends
    float angleRange; //This holds the angle the arc sweeps through
    float anglePad = 0; // overlap arcs by this amount say PI/200
```

```
int  curvePoints; // number of points spread along curve of the arc where we
                  // draw a QUAD

color colour; // The colour of this arc

float vr = 0;
// The rotational 'speed' of the arc, used if the arc is moving across the
// screen
float vrStep = 0;
// The amount to increase the rotation speed by on each render
float vx = 0;
// The amount to increase the x-coord of centre of arc if arc is moving
float vy = 0;    // The amount to increase the y-coord as above

// cx is the circle centre x-coord that this arc lies on
// cy is the circle centre y-coord that this arc lies on
// r is the radius we want
// t is the thickness we want
// startAng is the angle we start at
// endAng is the angle we end at
public SimpleArc(float cx, float cy, float r, float t, float startAng, float
    endAng) {
    //Store the parameters we need
    this.radius = r;
    this.thick = t;
    this.startAngle = startAng-anglePad;
    this.endAngle = endAng+anglePad;

    // flip the angles if the end is less than the start
    if (this.startAngle > this.endAngle) {
        float tmp = this.endAngle;
        this.endAngle = this.startAngle;
        this.startAngle = tmp;
    }

    this.angleRange = this.endAngle - this.startAngle;
    this.cx = cx;
    this.cy = cy;

    //Choose a random colour for the arc
    this.colour = color(random(255), random(255), random(255), 255);

    // A rough calculation to determine the number of
```

```
    //vertex points for each arc
    this.curvePoints = 1 + round(49*angleRange/TWO_PI) ;

    //Calculate and store the 'centre' of the arc
    float cr = r + t/2;
    this.acx = cr*cos(this.startAngle+this.angleRange/2);
    this.acy = cr*sin(this.startAngle+this.angleRange/2);
  }
}
```

There are a few items here that it is worth delving into a little more.

The **angleRange** variable is the angle that the arc we want makes if you draw two radius lines to the arc we want as shown in Figure 185

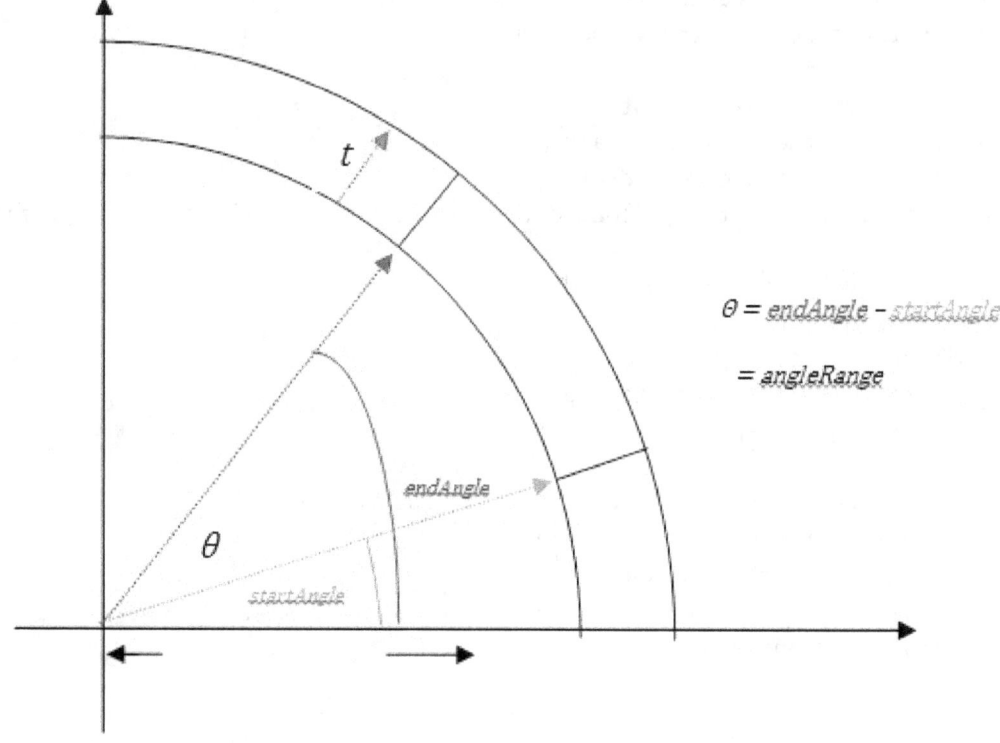

Figure 185: Calculating the Angle of an Arc

The *acx* and *acy* variables may seem unnecessary and for drawing an arc this is true. However, it is useful to calculate this value in case we want to rotate an arc around its 'midpoint', so we calculate its value in the constructor and store in class instance variables.

The *anglePad* variable is not required to draw our arc but is included as a little hack used to slightly increase the size of the arc we ask for at both ends to remove some of the rendering glitches that occur when you are manipulating shapes that are very close to each other. For example, later in the chapter we position arcs next to each other to produce a ring, and slightly overlapping the arcs reduces these glitches.

The *curvePoints* variable is calculated by what looks like some 'magic' maths to determine how many vertex points (the red dots in Figure 186) that we will calculate for a given arc. A larger arc requires more quadrilaterals to be drawn to still look like an arc. If you reduce this number too much for larger arcs you will find that you no longer gain the illusion of a curve. On the other hand smaller arcs require very few quadrilaterals and if we can adjust the number we require (just enough to still create the illusion of a curve) we can improve on performance. Through some experimentation this calculation works reasonably well.

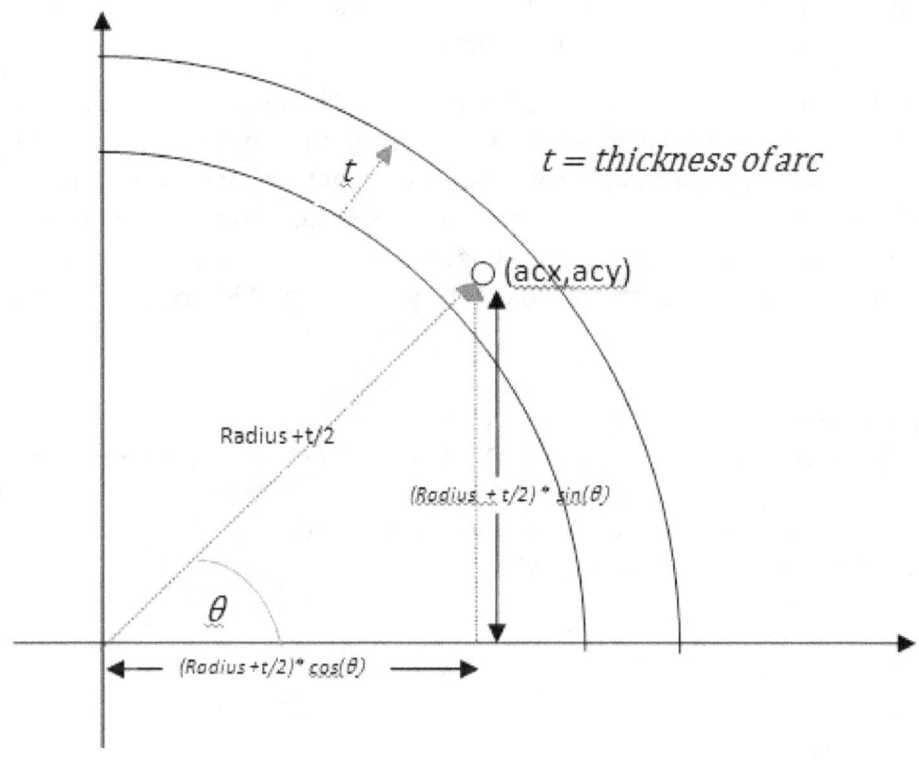

Figure 186: Calculating the Midpoint of an Arc

To make the class usable we need to add some additional functions. The first of these functions is *setColour(color c)* a very simple function to just change the colour of our arc to one we specify. This is helpful if we want to produce effects by altering the colour of the arc as *Processing* loops . The *setRotation(float va)* is very similar for setting the rotation speed.

```
// Set the colour of the arc
public void setColour(color c) {
    this.colour = c;
}

// Set the rotation 'speed'
public void setRotation(float va) {
    this.vrStep = va;
}
```

The *render()* function has two main tasks. The first of these tasks is to position the arc where we want it, and this is achieved by the potentially unfamiliar *Processing* functions *pushMatrix(); translate()* and *popMatrix()*. The second task is to define a shape in *Processing* made up of the quadrilaterals to produce our arc.

As we have previously seen, the *translate()* function in *Processing* moves the co-ordinate origin (i.e. x=0, y=0) to somewhere else on the screen from its default position of top-left. In effect we are always drawing our arc at location (0,0) but we are moving the co-ordinate origin to where ever we want our arc to appear on the screen. This may seem like an overly complicated way of drawing a shape, but this means we can control the placement and rotation of multiple arcs on the screen at one time using the pushMatrix() and popMatrix() functions

```
// Render the arc
public void render() {
    //push the Matrix so rotations/translations etc only apply to this arc
    pushMatrix();
    //Move the co-ordinate system origin to be the midpoint of the arc
    translate(this.cx+acx, this.cy+acy);

    // perform the rotation if set
    if (abs(vrStep)>0) {
      rotate(vr);
      vr += vrStep;
    }

    //Set the fill colour
    fill(this.colour);
    stroke(this.colour);
```

```
// Perform the maths to draw the vertices we need to define
// something reasonably arc shaped
float stepSize = this.angleRange/this.curvePoints;
// We chop our arc into smaller quads
float vAngle = this.startAngle; // The start angle of the current QUAD

beginShape(QUAD_STRIP); // start to define shape
for (int i=0; i < this.curvePoints+1; i++) {
// Calculate vertex on the 'inside' curve of the arc
vertex(cos(vAngle)*radius-acx, sin(vAngle)*radius-acy);
// Calculate vertex on the 'outside' curve of the arc.
vertex(cos(vAngle)*(radius+thick)-acx, sin(vAngle)*(radius+thick)-acy);
vAngle += stepSize; // Move around the arc ready for next point
}
endShape();

// Pop the matrix back as we have finished translation/rotation for this shape
popMatrix();

// Move the arc according to any vx or vy speed ready for next render
this.cx+=vx;
this.cy+=vy;
}
```

Now all we need do is tell *Processing* to draw some of our SimpleArc objects.

```
void setup() {
   background(255);
   size(600, 300);
}

void draw() {
   SimpleArc arc = new SimpleArc(random(0, width), random(0, height),
      random(40, 150), random(5, 50), random(0, TWO_PI), random(0, TWO_PI));
   arc.render();
}
```

This will repeatedly create new SimpleArc objects at random and draw them on the screen. If you run the sketch you should get something similar to that shown in Figure 187

Figure 187: Random SimpleArc Objects on Screen

Chapter 21: Curves

by Graham Hall, John Wilson, Mark Miller, Neil Singh, Martin Prout and Rosie Wood

So far we have looked at how lines and shapes made up of lines are generated. This chapter looks at how curves are drawn using lines. We will look at polynomials and also at how life-like effects can be created using acceleration. Note that some basic maths and physics are used which you needn't fully understand, though it will enhance your understanding of curve-drawing if you do

Polynomial Curves

Graphics applications often make use of different shapes of curve in creating images. Smooth and pleasing curves are produced by various mathematical functions. In this section we will look at the simplest of these, polynomials. Later you will meet other mathematical curves, such as trigonometric functions.

A polynomial is a function involving powers of a number. The number is often represented by the variable x. Powers include x^2 (which means 'x times x') and x^3 (which means 'x times x times x').

 We will begin by looking at a function involving x^2. This is called a quadratic equation:

`y = Ax² + Bx`

The letters A and B represent any numbers which we choose. A graph can be plotted by selecting a series of values for x, then calculating the equivalent results for y. Whichever values of A and B we use, the graph always has the shape of a hill or valley (Figure 188). The code below produces a quadratic curve with the equation

`y = 0.01 x² + x`

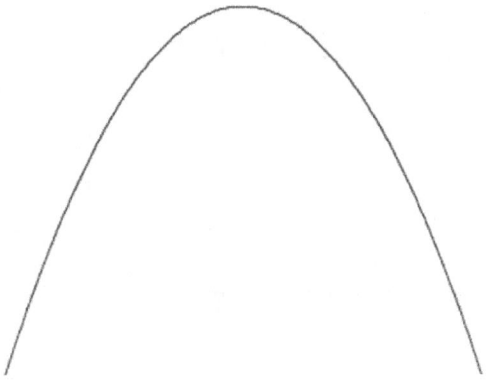

Figure 188: Polynomial Curve

The code uses the power function pow(x,2) to calculate x^2. A series of values for y are produced as x is varied from -200 to +200 in a loop. At each step, a small line is drawn to connect the previous end of the curve to the newly calculated point. The current values of x and y are then stored as oldX and oldY, ready to form the starting point of the next line segment (Figure 189).

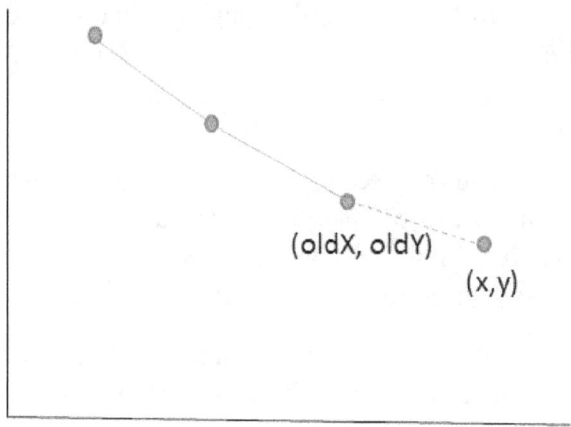

Figure 189: Polynomial x and y

```
float x;
float y;
float A = 0.01;
float B = 1;

int xOffset=250;
int yOffset=200;
float oldX;
float oldY;

void setup() {
   size(400,400);
   background(255);
   stroke(0,0,0);

   //loop to plot each segment of the curve
   for (int x=-200;x<=200; x++) {
      //calculate each point along the curve
      y=A*pow(x,2)+B*x;

      //don't draw a line segment if this is the first point
      if (x>-200) {
```

```
    //draw a line between this point and the previous point
    line(x+xOffset,y+yOffset,oldX+xOffset,oldY+yOffset);
  }

  //remember the previous point
  oldX=x;
  oldY=y;
  }
}
```

Notice the two variables xOffset and yOffset. These just allow the curve to be moved vertically or sideways, so that it can be positioned where required on the screen. You might like to experiment by slightly changing the values of A, B, xOffset and yOffset to see the effect on the curve.

Polynomial Maths

Each component of a polynomial expression is called a term, and they are usually ordered from the highest exponent to the lowest. Polynomial expressions do not contain negative or fractional exponents. A typical polynomial expression would have an ordered syntax

$6x^3+5x^2+7x-12$

In this expression the leading term which has the largest exponent is $6x^3$ with a degree of 3. ie 6x*6x*6x meaning 6x to the power of 3.

The leading term has a coefficient of 6, the second term coefficient is 5, the third term has a coefficient of 7 and the final term, which is a constant, doesn't have a coefficient. Monomial expressions have only one term, binomials have 2 and trinomials 3.

When working with polynomials it is usual to name them for their leading degree (largest exponent). The expression $6x^3 + 5x^2 + 7x - 12$ would therefore be a 3rd degree polynomial or cubic

- Polynomials of 2 degrees are called quadratics
- Polynomials of 3 degrees are called cubics
- Polynomials of 4 degrees are called quartics
- Polynomials of 5 degrees are called quintics

Quadratic Curves

Polynomials with an even numbered degree in their leading term, always enter and leave in the same direction. ie up or down. Therefore, quadratic polynomials are always

343

parabolas, as shown in the figure above. If the coefficient is even, then the curve will enter and leave at the top of the graph and if the coefficient is odd, it will enter and leave at the bottom

Polynomials with an odd numbered degree in their leading term, however, have curves that start and end in opposite directions. An odd numbered leading degree with a positive coefficient, will have a curve that starts at the bottom and exits at the top, while a negative coefficient, will have its starting curve coming in from the top and exiting at the bottom

We can use both types to create an interesting pattern of different colour curves as shown in Figure 190

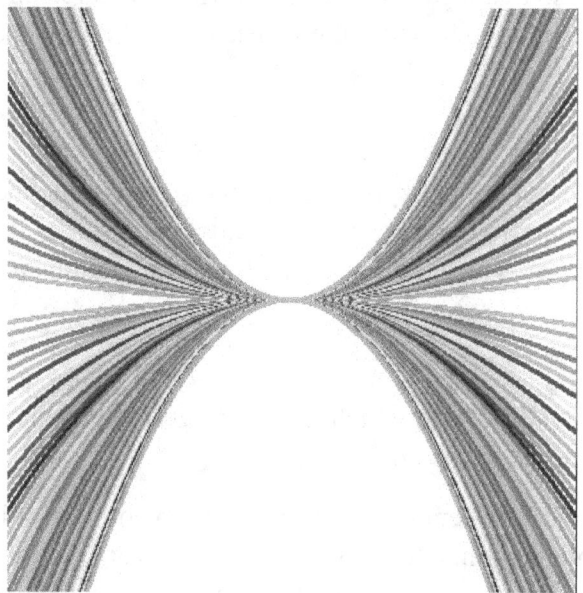

Figure 190: Quadratic Curves

To plot quadratic polynomials, we need to be able to place the x and y coordinates from 0 to the size of the window. We do this by using an offset of half the width/height of the window. The width of the parabola is shifted right by adding half the width of the window to the x coordinate and this variable has been named xShift

```
size(400, 400);
background(255);
strokeWeight(3);
float x = 0;
float y = 0;
int loopLimit = 200;
//shifts curve to the right
int xShift = width/2;
```

```
int yShift = height/2;
//ensure loops do not leave the screen
float ratio = height/(50*pow(loopLimit-1, 2)-50*loopLimit-1 + 100);
for (int coEfficient=2; coEfficient<50; coEfficient++) {
    stroke(random(255), random(255), random(255));
    for (int i=-xShift; i<loopLimit; i++) {
        x = i;
        /*Here the coefficient of the leading term is positive so the parabola
        should enter and leave at the top*/
        y = coEfficient* pow(x, 2)-7*x + 1;
        point(x+xShift, yShift-y*ratio);
        /*Here the coefficient of the leading term is negative so the parabola
        should enter and leave at the bottom*/
        y = -coEfficient* pow(x, 2)-7*x + 1;
        point(x+xShift, yShift-y*ratio);
    }
}
```

The height of the parabola is shifted down by subtracting half the height of the window from the y coordinate and this variable has been named yShift. This allows both up facing and down facing curves to be displayed together, at the same time in the window

An example quadratic such as

$y = 6x^2 - 7x + 10$

In *Processing* is written as

```
y= 6* pow(x, 2)-7*x + 10;
```

Since *Processing* uses screen coordinates that start at the upper-left corner, we need to shift the x and y coordinates

```
x+xShift, yShift-y*ratio
```

We also want to be able to display positive and negative versions of a quadratic expression at the same time so we must use the yShift variable to place the curves centrally in our display window. The ratio uses our maximum coEfficient to calculate the spacing for our plots. As our maximum coEfficient is 50 we work out the scale with the statement

```
float ratio = height/(50*pow(loopLimit-1, 2)-50*loopLimit-1 + 100);
```

The statements inside the loop then draw one curve with plots of x and y for our chosen quadratic expression. We replace the leading term's coEfficient, with a variable between 2 and 50, in a for next loop, each time the loop is executed, the stroke colour is randomly changed. This will give us a graph of nested parabolas with a variable coEfficient. As the exponent is an even number, we know our curves will all enter and leave in the same direction, also because our equation is quadratic we will have a parabola and because the coefficient is even its opening will be at the top.

Cubic Curves

Cubic curves have an additional bend in the middle as shown in Figure 191, producing a trough and peak within the line of the curve. The equation this time is

```
y = 0.00015 x³ + 0.02 x² + 0.1x
```

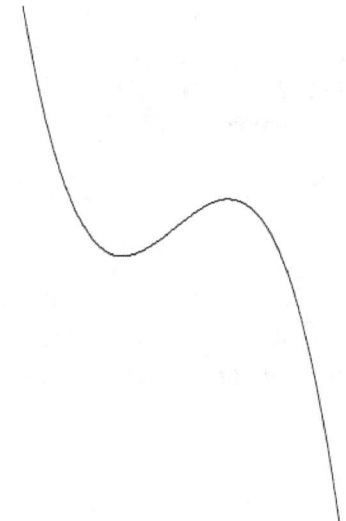

Figure 191: Cubic Curve

Notice how the power function pow(x,3) is used to obtain the value of x^3.

```
float x,y;
float A = 0.00015;
float B = 0.02;
float C = 0.1;

int xOffset=250;
int yOffset=150;
float oldX, oldY;


void setup() {
   size(400,400);
   background(255);
   stroke(0,0,0);
```

346

```
for (int x=-200;x<=200; x++) {
    y=A*pow(x,3)+ B*pow(x,2) + C*x;
    if (x>-200) {
        line(x+xOffset,y+yOffset,oldX+xOffset,oldY+yOffset);
    }
    oldX=x;
    oldY=y;
    }
}
```

To make this more interesting, we can write a small animation to represent a roller coaster. We will begin with a simple cubic curve which extends across a window of width 800 pixels. We can then animate a circle so that it travels down the curve to represent the roller coaster car (Figure 192).

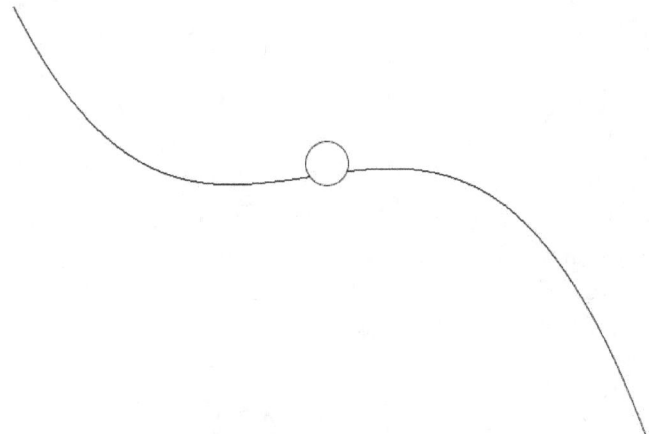

Figure 192: Simple Rollercoaster Using a Cubic Curve

Enter the code given below. We will use a curve with the formula

$$y = 0.000009\ x^3 + 0.002\ x^2$$

Two new variables **xCar** and **yCar** are needed to keep track of the position of the circle as it moves along the curve. We have also added a timber framework to support the track to make the scene more realistic (Figure 193)

```
float x;
float y;
float A = 0.000009;
float B = 0.002;
int xOffset=450;
int yOffset=150;
float oldX;
```

```
float oldY;
int xCar = -600;
float yCar;

//variables to record the position of the timber supports
float oldXtimber;
float oldYtimber;
float r=9;

void setup() {
    size(800,400);
    frameRate(30);
}

void draw() {
    background(255);
    xCar=xCar+10;

    if (xCar>400) {
        xCar= -600;
        //each time the car completes its trip across the window,
        //generate a random number and use this to produce a
        //different value for A. This will change the shape
        //of the track for the next animation sequence
        r=random(9);
        A = 0.000001*r;
    }
    stroke(0,0,0);
    for (int x=-800;x<=800; x++) {
        y=A*pow(x,3)+ B*pow(x,2);
        if (xCar==x) {
            yCar=y;
        }
        stroke(255,165,00);
        strokeWeight(10);

        //draw timber supports at intervals of 40 pixels
        if (x % 40 == 0) {
            line(x+xOffset, 410, x+xOffset, y+yOffset);
            //create the diagonal struts which connect this vertical
            //timber support to the previous one.
            //Only add struts which would be below the level of the track
            for (int top=360; top>0; top=top-40) {
```

```
            if(oldYtimber<top-yOffset && y<top-yOffset) {
                line(x+xOffset, top, oldXtimber+xOffset, top+40);
                line(x+xOffset, top+40, oldXtimber+xOffset, top);
            }
        }
        //record the position of the previous vertical support
        oldXtimber=x;
        oldYtimber=y;
    }
    stroke(0,0,0);
    strokeWeight(10);
    if (x>-800) {
        line(x+xOffset,y+yOffset,oldX+xOffset,oldY+yOffset);
    }
    oldX=x;
    oldY=y;
}
strokeWeight(1);
ellipse(xCar+xOffset,yCar+yOffset-10,40,40);
}
```

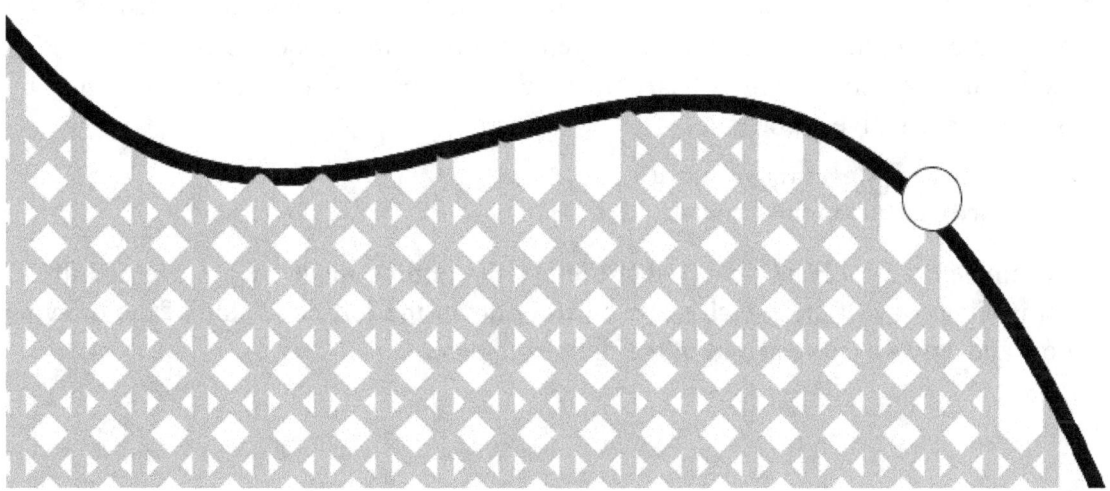

Figure 193: Completed Rollercoaster Using a Cubic Curve

You might try enhancing the code by varying the value of **A**, which multiplies x^3 in the equation; so that different shapes of curve are produced each time the car crosses the screen.

349

Acceleration and Deceleration

In nature, acceleration and deceleration are forces that cause objects to change their speed. Acceleration causes objects to move faster and faster as time goes by, whereas deceleration causes objects to move progressively slower. Acceleration is made up of two components: its size and its direction. When a car driver presses her foot down on the accelerator pedal the car is subjected to acceleration whose size is proportional to how far down the pedal is pressed and whose direction is forward as viewed by the driver. Also, if the same driver engages the car's reverse gear and presses the accelerator then the car is accelerated backwards.

Mathematically, it makes sense to use positive numbers to represent accelerations in the forward direction then negative numbers represent accelerations in the backward direction. For example if an acceleration of 10 represents that a car accelerates forward by ten miles per hour for each second that passes, then a value of -2 will denote that the car accelerates backwards, or decelerates, by two miles per hour per second.

Considering that both acceleration's size and direction are important and that *Processing*'s coordinate system results in *higher* y-axis values representing positions *lower* down the drawing window, we need to agree on terminology that will help us avoid confusion. We will stick to using the terms *upward acceleration* and *downward acceleration* to describe acceleration towards the top and bottom of the screen respectively.

The examples we will use need to generate upward and downward accelerations that have randomly chosen sizes. To do this the examples use the code similar to that which is shown below. In this case, the `random()` function returns a random number between 0.2 and 0.8 inclusive and the minus sign (-) is used to convert the positive number returned by `random()` to a negative number.

```
float downwardAcceleration=random(0.2,0.8);
float upwardAcceleration=-random(0.2,0.8);
```

This example draws a bendy curve that mimics the outline made by a range of hills as shown in Figure 194. The sketch starts halfway down the left-hand side of the drawing window and draws a curve across to the right hand-side.

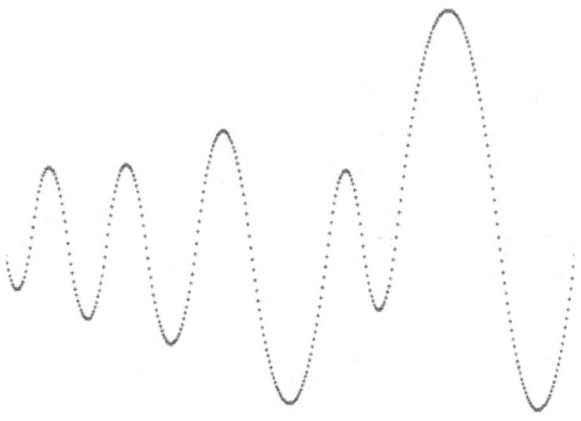

Figure 194: Acceleration Hills

The sketch applies a constant speed to the x-axis and a varying acceleration to the y-axis. The y-axis acceleration is changed each time the y value passes the y-axis centre-line – an imaginary horizontal line halfway down the drawing window. Each time the y value passes the centre-line the sketch changes the direction of the acceleration so that it is always towards the centre-line – when the y value is above the centre-line the acceleration is set to be downward and vice-versa.

```
// Setup the drawing window
size(400,400);
background(255);
smooth();
strokeWeight(2);
stroke(0,0,255);

// Set initial values for variables
int yCentre=height/2;
int y=yCentre;
float ySpeed=8;
float yAcceleration=-random(0.2,0.8);

// Main loop: Increment x from left-hand side of window to right-hand side.
for(int x=0;x<width;x++) {
    // When y passes up through the y-axis centre-line,
    // randomly choose a new downward acceleration.
```

```
  if(y<yCentre && yAcceleration<0) {
    yAcceleration=random(0.2,0.8);
  }
  // When y passes down through the y-axis centre-line,
  // randomly choose a new upward acceleration.
  if(y>yCentre && yAcceleration>0) {
    yAcceleration=-random(0.2,0.8);
  }
  // Update y value and draw point
  ySpeed+=yAcceleration;
  y+=ySpeed;
  point(x,y);
}
```

The bulk of the work here is done inside the loop. The acceleration is varied by selecting a random number which updates the y coordinate and speed variables, which are then used to plot points to draw the curves

We can alter this to become more chaotic, a little like the path an insect may make whilst flying around a room. Instead of applying a varying acceleration to the y-axis, we can apply varying accelerations to both the x- and y- axes. The result is a bendy curve that looks somewhat like the path of a fly trying to escape a room (Figure 195)

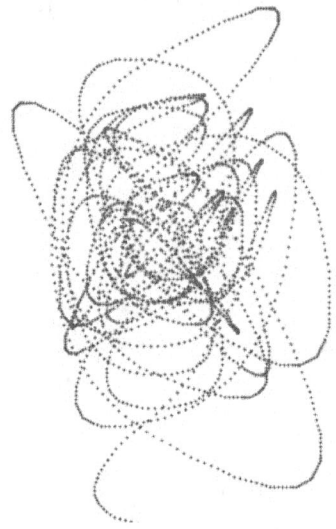

Figure 195: Fly in a Room

Like the 'hills' example, this example considers each axis has a centre-line and varies accelerations so that they point towards the centre-lines. The x-axis acceleration will always be in the direction of the x-axis centre-line and likewise with the y-axis acceleration pointing to the y-axis centre-line. The sum of the x- and y-axis accelerations result in an acceleration that always points to the centre of the display window. This time, however, we start drawing from the centre

So how does the fly escape the room? Well, even though the accelerations are always pointing towards the centre of the display window sometimes strong accelerations will cause the x, y position to shoot past the centre point and end up outside of the display window. When that happens the sketch is configured to stop drawing and to show the display window to the viewer.

```
// Setup the drawing window
size(400,400);
background(255);
smooth();
strokeWeight(2);
stroke(0,0,255);

// Set initial values for variables
int yCentre=height/2,xCentre=width/2;
int y=yCentre,x=xCentre;
float ySpeed=4,xSpeed=4;
float yAcceleration=-random(0.1,0.4),xAcceleration=-random(0.1,0.4);

// Main loop: Continue drawing until either the x or y value becomes outside the
// drawing window.
while(y>0 && y<height && x>0 && x<width) {
  // Vary y-axis acceleration when y-axis centre-line passed.
  if(y<yCentre && yAcceleration<0) {
    yAcceleration=random(0.1,0.4);
  } else if(y>yCentre && yAcceleration>0) {
    yAcceleration=-random(0.1,0.4);
  }
  // Vary x-axis acceleration when x-axis centre-line passed.
  if(x<xCentre && xAcceleration<0) {
    xAcceleration=random(0.1,0.4);
  } else if(x>xCentre && xAcceleration>0) {
  xAcceleration=-random(0.1,0.4);
  }
  // Update x and y values and draw point
  ySpeed+=yAcceleration;
  y+=ySpeed;
  xSpeed+=xAcceleration;
  x+=xSpeed;
```

```
    point(x,y);
}
```

In theory, because the x and y values depend on random numbers it is possible that the main `while` loop (see Chapter X) will continue forever. Although, in practice when the sketch is run it has always terminated and displayed the drawing window to the user. If we wanted to ensure that the sketch does always terminate within a reasonable amount of time, we can introduce a time clause to the sketch's central loop. The below code shows how the `while` loop can be changed to ensure that the loop does not continue for more than one second (1000 milliseconds).

```
int startTime=millis();
while(y>0 && y<height && x>0 && x<width && millis()-startTime<1000){
...
}
```

Curve Physics

This example looks at some basic physics using a simple fireworks simulation. Fireworks will give us a chance to use curves with trajectories and will allow us to display some pretty colours. When a firework explodes, it throws out a multitude of particles, each of which are acted on from the force of the explosion and gravity. This should provide us with an interesting algorithm to show some rather pretty patterns as can be seen in Figure 196

There are some extremely complicated formulas for working out projectile trajectories which take into account wind resistance and all sorts of other variables. In order to keep the simulation simple, the fireworks code below uses a very simple algorithm for working out the x and y coordinates of a particle at a given time. We will not delve into the mathematics behind this formula or the sin and cos functions as there is plenty of material on the web available and this demo is not intended to be a maths lesson.

```
x = (velocity * cos(angle) * time)
y = (velocity * sin(angle) * time) - (½ gravity * time²)
```

The x and y coordinates given from this formula assume that the projectile was initially at 0, 0 though the explosion particles will have their initial position set by a random number

Figure 196: Firework Effect using Curves

The fireworks sketch makes use of a couple of OO design principals in order to reduce the amount of code through reuse. The code contains a 'Firework' class, with an array of 'Particle' objects. Using this model means each particle can contain its own information on colour and location, and be animated separately.

Analysing the code

As this is a fairly large sketch in comparison to some of the other examples, we will not analyse the code line for line but rather give an overview of how the code reaches its objectives. The code itself is commented and should be fairly self-explanatory.

The sketch sets up a single firework using the Firework constructor. This in turn creates a firework with a random number of particles for the explosion. Processing calls the main draw() function which delegates to the firework. Each particle is then drawn in a loop in order to animate the firework particles

One important point to note is that both *Processing* and Java expect the value for the cos and sin functions to be given in radians.

```
// Setup the gravity constant.
float gravity = 9;

// Create the initial firework.
Firework firework = new Firework();

void setup() {
```

```
   // Setup the canvas.
   background(255);
   smooth();
   size(400,400);
   frameRate(30);
}

void draw() {
   // Draw the firework
   firework.draw();
}

/**
 * Represent a rocket together with its explosion particles.
 **/
class Firework {
   Particle[] particles;

   Firework() {

      // Setup the explosion particles
      particles = new Particle[(int) random(80, 200)];
      // random explosion point
      float explosionStartX = random(100, 300);
      float explosionStartY = random(100, 300);

      for (int i = 0; i < particles.length; i++) {
         particles[i] = new Particle(
         explosionStartX, explosionStartY,
         random(20, 40), random(0.5, 2.5),
         random(200, 255), random(100, 200), random(0, 255));
      }

   }

   void draw() {
      strokeWeight(2);

      for (int i = 0; i < particles.length; i++) {
         // Increase the colour values of the particles, should give the effect
         // of the particle fading out.
         particles[i].fadeOut();
```

```
            // Draw the particle.
            particles[i].draw();
        }
    }
}


/**
 * Represent a particle which has a trajectory.
 **/
class Particle {
    float dy = 0;
    float dx = 0;
    float particleTime = 0;
    float velocity;
    float angle;
    float initialX;
    float initialY;
    float initialisationTime;
    float colourRed;
    float colourGreen;
    float colourBlue;

    Particle(float x, float y, float v, float a, float r, float g, float b) {
        velocity = v;
        angle = a;
        initialX = x;
        initialY = y;
        colourRed = r;
        colourGreen = g;
        colourBlue = b;
    }

    /**
     * Cause the colours to tend towards white (255, 255, 255).
     **/
    void fadeOut() {
    colourRed++;
    colourGreen++;
    colourBlue++;
    }

    void draw() {
```

```
    // Here we use the trajectory formula. Note that the cos and sin functions
expect angles in radians.
    dx = velocity * cos(angle) * particleTime;
    dy = (velocity * sin(angle) * particleTime) - (0.5 * gravity * particleTime
* particleTime);

    stroke(colourRed, colourGreen, colourBlue);
    point(initialX + dx, initialY - dy);

    particleTime = particleTime + 0.1;
  }
}
```

Curved Vertices

Another method for drawing curves in *Processing* is to use vertices to define the point we want to draw between. There is a special function for this called curveVertex() which tells *Processing* to draw a curve between the vertices, rather than a straight line as we have previously seen with the vertex() function

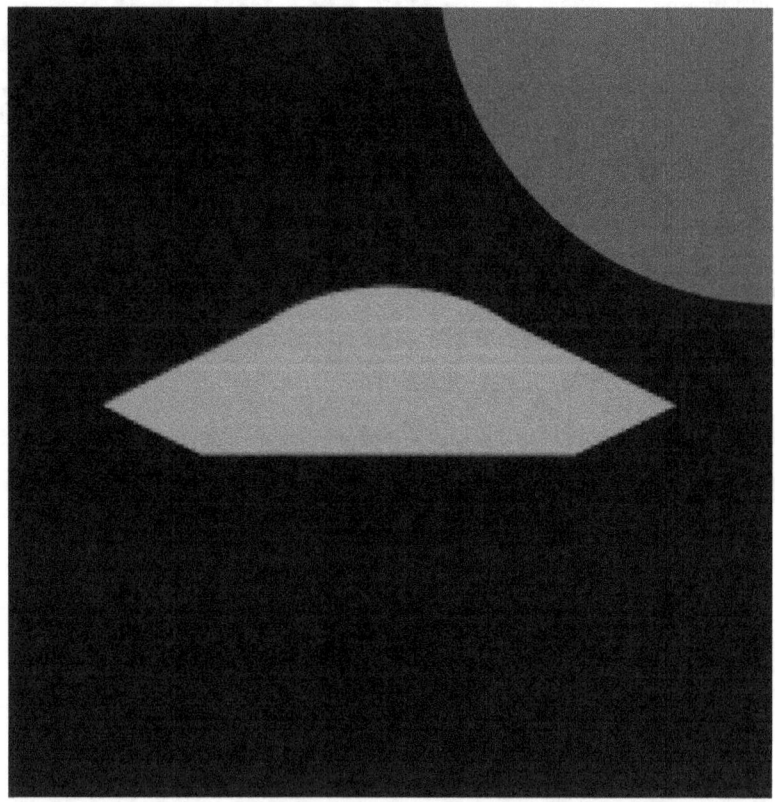

Figure 197: Flying Saucer Made From Curved Vertices

In our example, shown in Figure 197, we have combined the curveVertex and vertex elements to define a classic flying saucer shape. The curved 'saucer dome' is defined using curveVertex (the planet is drawn using an ellipse off the side of the viewable area)

```
size(400, 400);
background(0);
stroke(0);
strokeWeight(1);
smooth();
// planet
fill(116, 39, 39); // set planet color
ellipseMode(CENTER);
ellipse(400, -25, 350, 350); // create planet at center positon
fill(255, 0, 0);
// flying saucer
curveTightness(-0.05f);
beginShape();
curveVertex(332, 292); // defines curve
curveVertex(262, 158);
curveVertex(138, 158);
curveVertex(68, 292); // defines curve
vertex(138, 158);
vertex(50, 200);
vertex(50, 200);
vertex(103, 225);
vertex(103, 225);
vertex(297, 225);
vertex(297, 225);
vertex(350, 200);
endShape(CLOSE);
```

Here you can see that there are 4 curveVertex()points, the inner points are part of the saucer whilst the outer points are needed to define the curve (shown in Figure 198). These points are used to define the shape of the curve

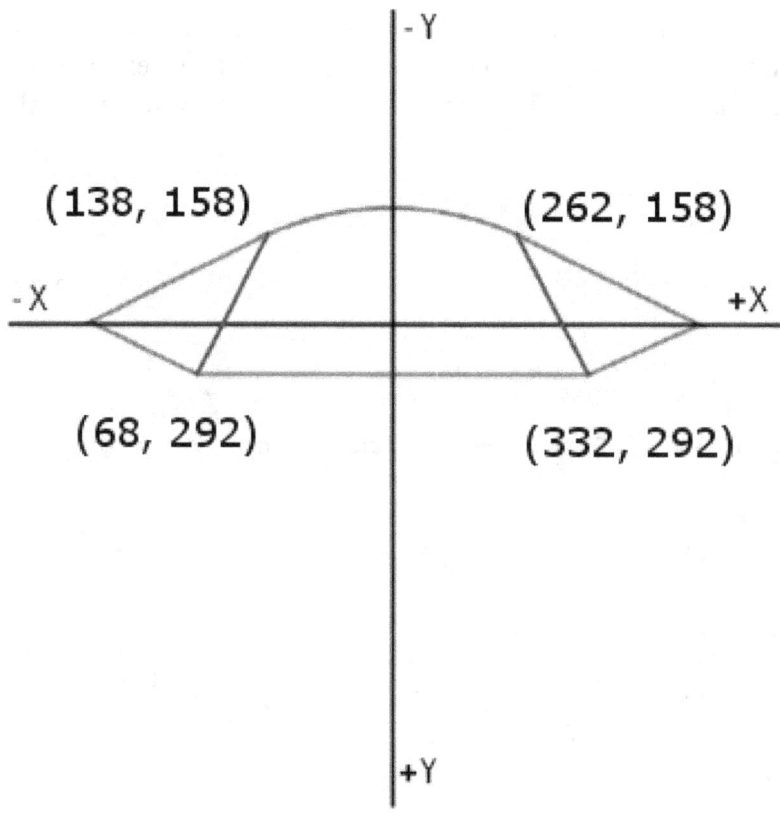

Figure 198: Flying Saucer Curve Coordinates

Another parameter that is used to control the shape of the curve is the argument of the curveTightness() function, this function should be placed prior to the beginShape() function, and the best value to use can be determined experimentally. The default beginShape() mode produces a fillable shape, note that you may omit the line that 'closes' the shape when set the endShape() mode is set as CLOSE. The fill and stroke color of the saucer object is inherited from the current fill and stroke color as with the standard library shapes such as rect and ellipse

Bézier Curves

Bézier curves are a particular type of curve made popular half a century ago by the work of two French car engineers Pierre Bézier and Paul de Casteljau, though the mathematics behind these curves has been known for over 100 years. Back in the 1960s the curves were originally used to aid the design of the car chassis but today in the 21st century they are also used in defining such things as font shapes, paths for computer-generated image rendering or movement of 'flying nasties' in computer arcade games.

The Mathematics

The Bézier curve is describe by a parametric function - with constants defined by a set of points (2 Dimensional or 3 Dimensional) and a variable (usually defined by the symbol t) which defines the shape as you vary the value between 0.0 and 1.0.

The set of points is defined by start and end points of the curve (sometimes referred to as the anchor points) , along with a series of control points. Strictly speaking, we don't need to have any control points. A *linear* Bézier 'curve' can be defined with just the start and end points forming a simple straight line (Figure 199).

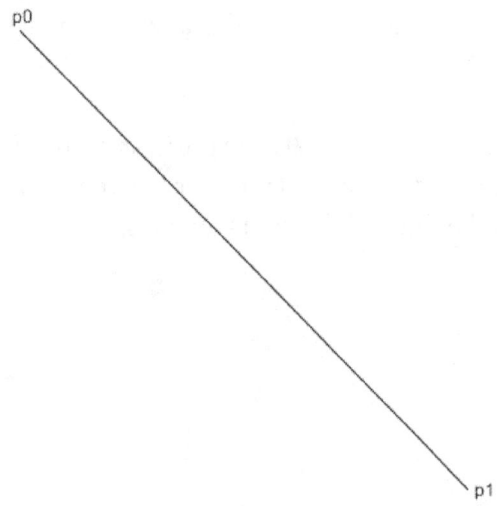

Figure 199: Linear Bézier Curve

The equation for linear Bézier is defined by :

```
B(t)= (1-t)P₀ + t P₁
```

The formula describes the position in 2D or 3D space, $B(t)$ from the start point P_0 to the end point P_1 at the time where t is defined between 0 and 1.

For the sake of simplicity let's go through an example in 2 dimensional space with a start position (P_0) of [2,3] to an end position (P_1) of [5,7]. For this linear Bézier our equation would be :

$$B(t) = (1 - t)[2,3] + t[5,7]$$

If we focus on just 3 possible values of t (0.0, 0.5 and 1.0) - we get the 3 points

$$B(0) = (1 - 0)[2,3] + 0[5,7] = [2,3]$$

$B(0.5) = (1 - 0.5)[2,3] + 0.5[5,7] = [3.5,5]$

$B(1) = (1 - 1)[2,3] + 1[5,7] = [5,7]$

You can see from above that at t = 0 and t = 1 we get the start and end points respectively and that at t = 0.5 we get a point which just so happens, for the linear Bezier - to be the midpoint of our line.

Quadratic Bézier

The above curve is just a mathematical curiosity and pretty useless to us in our quest for drawing complex curves. Let's move on to the next level of the Bézier set of curves - the quadratic Bézier - which is defined by 3 points, 2 anchor points and 1 control point.

$B(t) = (1 - t)^2 P_0 + 2t(1 - t)\ P_1 + t^2 P_2$

The above quadratic formula describes a 2D/3D position on our Bézier curve at a particular value for t. Again, the range of t is any real number between 0 and 1. For this equation, P_0 is our start point, P_2 the end point and P_1 here is our single control point as shown in Figure 200

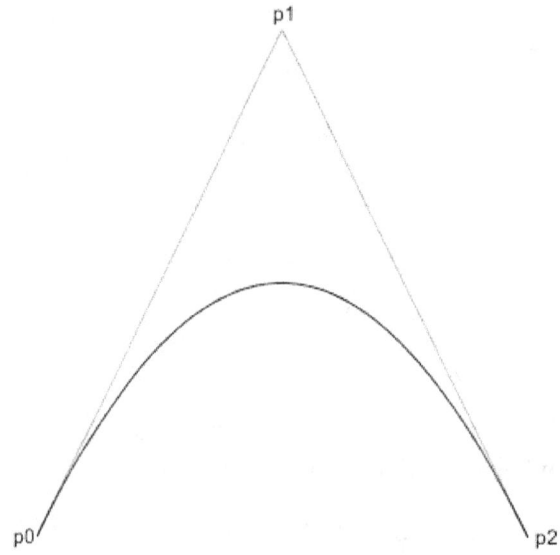

Figure 200: Quadratic Bézier

It should be simple to verify that $B(0)$ and $B(1)$ come up with our start and end points. $B(0.5)$ comes up with some other point on our Bézier curve - and for non-linear curves - this may not be halfway along our curve

Processing does have the ability to draw quadratic Bézier curves, though does not provide a single, simple, function for it. Instead a shape has to be drawn in combination with vertex functions in the form

```
beginShape();
vertex();
quadraticVertex();
endShape();
```

Where the vertex() function specifies the first anchor point (P_0 in our example above) and the quadraticVertex() function specifies the anchor point (P_1) and the second control point (P_2) respectively. The code below will draw the quadratic curve shown in Figure 200

```
size(600, 600);
background(255);
// text
fill(0);
text("p0", 35, 355); // anchor point 1
text("p1", 195, 45); // control point
text("p2", 355, 355); // anchor point 2
// lines
stroke(150);
line(50, 350, 200, 50);
line(200, 50, 350, 350);
// quadratic bezier
stroke(0);
noFill();
beginShape();
vertex(50, 350);
quadraticVertex(200, 50, 350, 350);
endShape();
```

Cubic Bézier

$$B(t) = (1-t)^3 P_0 + 3t (1-t)^2 P_1 + 3t^2 (1-t) P_2 + t^3 P_3$$

We have finally arrived at the equation which is implemented in the *Processing* language - the cubic Bézier. You may see from the formula above that there are 4 points needed to define our Bézier curve, the two anchor points (P_0 and P_3) and two control points (P_1 and P_2)

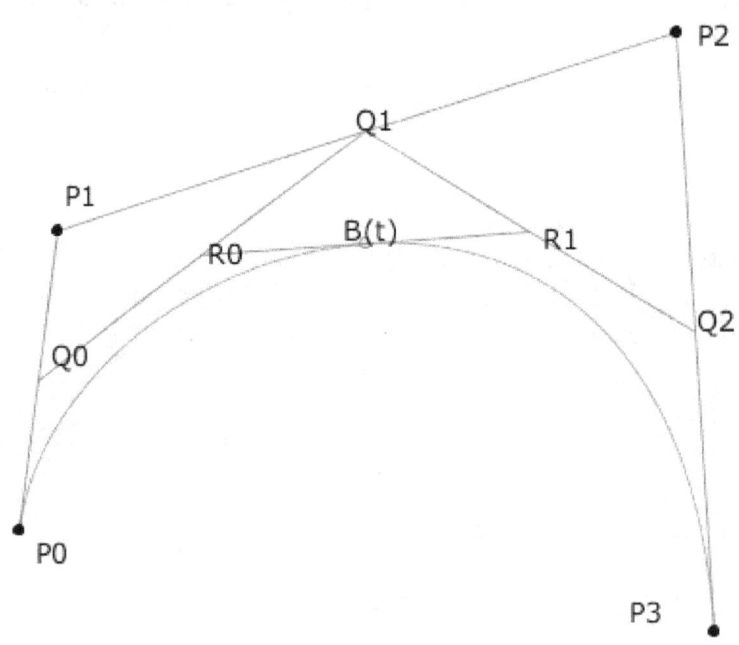

Figure 201: Cubic Bézier Curve

Figure 201 goes some way to explaining how a Bézier curve is plotted. You can see from the diagram that the curve has the property that the function is contained within the 'convex hull' defined by our four points (P_0, P_1, P_2 and P_3).

To calculate *B(t)* we have to calculate Q_0, Q_1 and Q_2. Q_0 is the point on the line P_0 to P_1 defined by the fraction value *t*. So if **t** was equal to 0.5 then Q_0 would be half way on the line P_0 to P_1. Likewise Q_1 and Q_2 are similar distances on the lines defined by P_1 to P_2 and P_2 to P_3 respectively. We do a similar process on these new lines, Q_0 to Q_1 and Q_1 to Q_2 using the same value *t* to make a single line R_0 to R_1. Finally on our final line R_0 to R_1 we use *t* to place the plot point, B(**t**). In our example with *t* being equal to 0.5, this would be half way across the line R_0 to R_1. If we were to have higher orders of Bézier curves - the plot position could be calculated in a similar way but with more recursive steps to reduce our plotting point to be placed on a single line

There are two *Processing* functions defined to allow us to draw a cubic Bézier :

```
bezier(x1, y1, x2, y2, x3, y3, x4, y4)
bezier(x1, y1, z1, x2, y2, z2, x3, y3,z3, x4, y4, z4)
```

The first one which we will go into using in more detail is used to draw 2D curves. The second function which involves the extra 'z' parameters used to create 3D objects

Processing does not support higher degree curves since it is possible to define more complex shapes by drawing a series of cubic Bézier curves

We can demonstrate the use of Bézier curves in *Processing* with a small sketch

```
void setup() {
    size(600, 600);
    smooth();
    colorMode(HSB,width);
}

void draw() {
    background(0);
    noFill();
    for (int i = 0; i < width; i++) {
        stroke(i, 600, 600);
        bezier(i, 0, width, 0, width, 0, i, height);
    }
}
```

The above code simply draws a number of curves in a loop, using the place in the loop and the height and width of the screen as its anchor and control points. The colour of the curve is altered slightly each time to create an interesting rainbow effect as shown in Figure 202

Figure 202: Rainbow Made From Bézier Curves

We can make this a bit more interesting by introducing some animation and rotation. To do this we have altered the code only a little, adding in some variables for the curve, moving the start point to the middle of the screen and introducing some rotation. Here we are simply drawing the rainbow curves as before, but rotating them each time, resulting in the swirl shown in Figure 203

```
void draw() {
    translate(width/2, height/2);
    for (int i = 0; i < width; i++) {
        float offSet = PI/width*i;
        pushMatrix();
        // rotate a single curve
        rotate(offSet);
        stroke(i, width, width);
        bezier(i, y1, x2, y2, x3, y3, i, y4);
        popMatrix();
    }
}
```

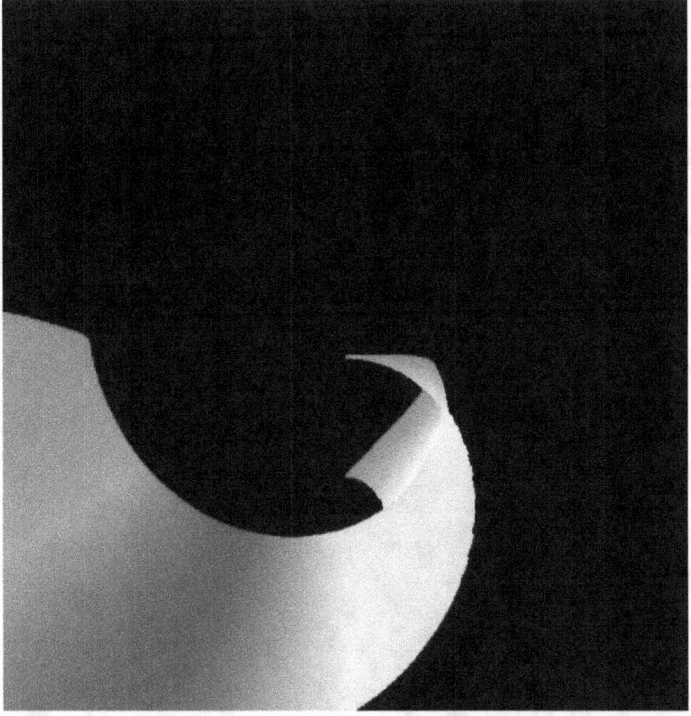

Figure 203: Rotated Rainbow Bézier Curves

We can then rotate the entire thing to produce a circular rotating pattern, shown in Figure 204

Figure 204: Rotating Ranbow Béziers

```
int x1; // anchor point 1
int y1 = 0; // anchor point 1
int x2 = 100; // control point 1
int y2 = 0; // control point 1
int x3 = 100; // control point 2
int y3 = 0; // control point 2
int x4; // anchor point 2
int y4 = 100; // anchor point 2
float rotation;

void setup() {
   size(600, 600);
   smooth();
   colorMode(HSB, width);
   strokeWeight(3);
   background(0);
   noFill();
}
```

```
void draw() {
    translate(width/2, height/2);
    // rotate the whole thing
    rotate(rotation);
    for (int i = 0; i < width; i++) {
        float offSet = PI/width*i;
        pushMatrix();
        // rotate a single curve
        rotate(offSet);
        stroke(i, width, width);
        bezier(i, y1, x2, y2, x3, y3, i, y4);
        popMatrix();
    }
    rotation += 1;
}
```

As you have seen, drawing curves can be quite complex but very powerful in drawing sketches containing curved structures or adding realism to a drawing

Chapter 22: Programming Modes

by Antony Lees, Richard Brown and Sheep Dalton

This Chapter introduces the concept of programming modes in processing. We will explore the modes available and explain, with examples, 3 of the major programming modes available: Java, JavaScript and Android

Programming Modes

Although we have previously mentioned programming modes in *Processing*, you have likely been unaware of it. You may recall Figure 205 from an earlier chapter – here we told you that the button on the right represent the 'Mode'. This is the programming mode being used by *Processing*

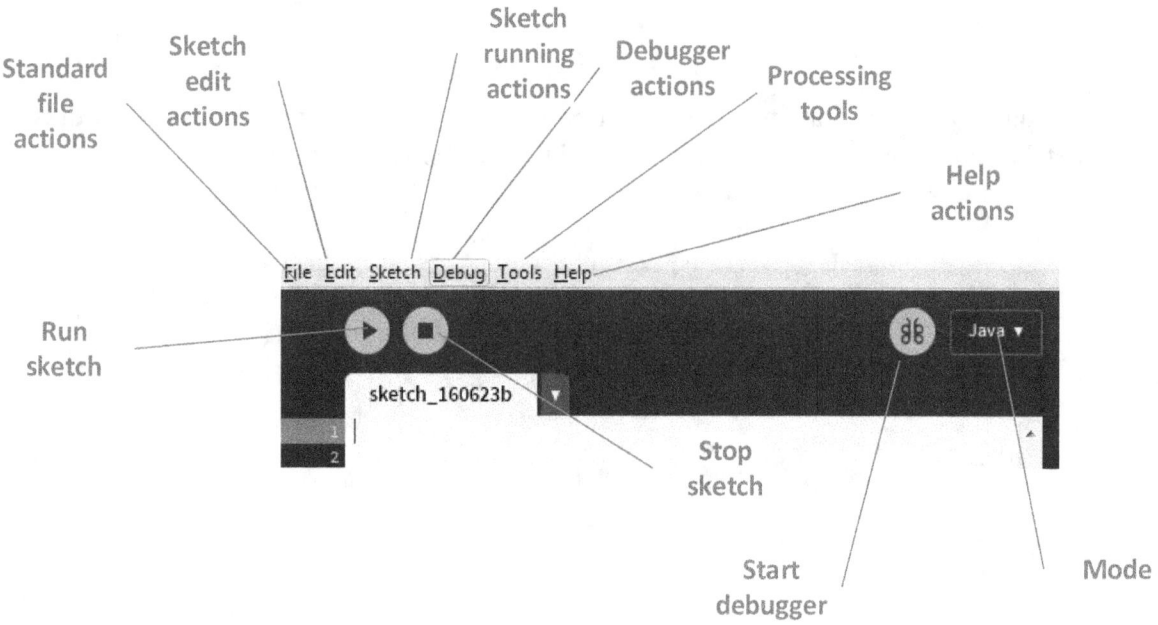

Figure 205: Processing Environment Toolbar

If you now click on the button, you will see a list of the available modes, which should look similar to that shown in Figure 206

Figure 206: *Processing* **Mode Button**

You can add additional modes by clicking 'Add Mode' and choosing the one(s) you want to install. The default programming mode, and the one we have used throughout the book, is Java mode

Java Programming Mode

As we have previously explained, *Processing* is a graphics-oriented programming language based on the Java programming language, an extremely popular programming language used for all manner of software, from cars and refrigerators to websites and mobile phones. All of the code you have written so far has been written in Java mode.

If you are already a Java programmer, or just interested in advancing your knowledge in this area, you can integrate *Processing* with any Java code, including Java libraries, since they are compatible. Libraries can be added via the Sketch > Import Library menu. You can also, if you wish, use *Processing* in your favourite Java IDE by importing the core.jar library and having your sketch extend PApplet from the *Processing* library. These are advanced topics however that we don't cover here on the assumption that you will know what you are doing if you are this way inclined

We won't provide any further examples of Java mode as you have been using it thus far

Javascript Programming Mode

In 2008, John Resig, famed creator of the JavaScript library jQuery, noticed that *Processing*'s Applet technology, which permits a sketch to be embedded in web pages, looked endangered. It was also impossible to view webpage Applets on new smartphones and tablet devices. To solve this he began an Open source project to port *Processing* to JavaScript. This became known as the *Processing*.js project. More recently a rival project, p5.js, has been developed and accepted as the official JavaScript version of *Processing*. Both *Processing*.js and p5.js are still available as competing JavaScript implementations of *Processing*. The objective of these projects are to provide a way to convert and run *Processing* sketches almost untouched on the web

The upside of this is you can take a processing project and quickly embed it into a web page and have access to one of the fastest growing web browser markets (tablets and smartphones). This is possible because of the new Canvas element which became part of the HTML 5 standard. Basically, the Canvas element provides a procedural drawing area, much like the window in standard processing that allows routines like *Processing*'s draw() function which do the actual drawing. The original intent was to provide interactive elements like charts but it's capable of much, much more.

In its depths, classic *Processing*, running in Java programming mode, takes the *Processing* source code and outputs java byte code. This can be run on any machine with a Java interpreter. *Processing*.js and p5.js are both runtime engines that convert processing to JavaScript which is then combined with a large library of routines to provide the *Processing* Core. The result of this is that the web browser the user is running downloads the JavaScript code then runs the code in the browser. This can result in smooth, fast animations and fluid interactivity. The key weakness is that the *Processing*.js and p5.js libraries had to reimplement every feature of *Processing* and do this while smoothing over the differences between types of browsers which often have different JavaScript engines

It is important to remember that although the JavaScript projects implement the *Processing* features, they do not replicate the Java language itself. If you have code that relies on Java classes, rather than *Processing* classes, they will likely not work. This also means that that the large and highly desirable set of external libraries is no longer simply available. If you want to port a project to the web which relies on the functionality of some external library you are going to have to think about how to implement that functionality yourself. On the positive side there are a number of JavaScript libraries for *Processing* available as well as a vast range of general JavaScript libraries that you could use in your sketches

There are also other small differences that may crop up as you create code for JavaScript mode such as the need to be more careful when naming variables and functions which may conflict with existing JavaScript or *Processing* functions. In particular, p5.js expects some parts of your code to be closer to JavaScript (for example, using *function* to define functions) whereas *Processing*.js goes further in allowing *Processing* code to be run unchanged

JavaScript mode can be used with no knowledge of the JavaScript language but it is a good way to get started with JavaScript if you wanted to learn it and isolate yourself from the individual complexities of different browsers

Installation

At the time of writing, there is more than one method of getting started with JavaScript mode depending on how comfortable you are with new software or with developing web pages. We will describe 3 methods of getting starting; using the familiar *Processing* environment, using the p5.js environment, and adding the *Processing* JavaScript file to a web page manually

We will demonstrate the differences in the code in our examples to give you a flavour of how they differ and so that you don't get confused with whichever method you choose

Using the Processing Environment

Before you can run in JavaScript mode you will need to download and install the JavaScript mode. To do this you need to be connected to the internet. Open a processing window and on the top right hand corner click on 'Java' and select the 'add mode' menu.

Select 'JavaScript mode' and click Install. This might take a fair amount of time depending upon your internet connection. The download instructions will walk you through the process and you *might* have to restart (quit and reopen or relaunch) processing.

Once completed, you should see JavaScript mode with a tick against it, as shown in Figure 207

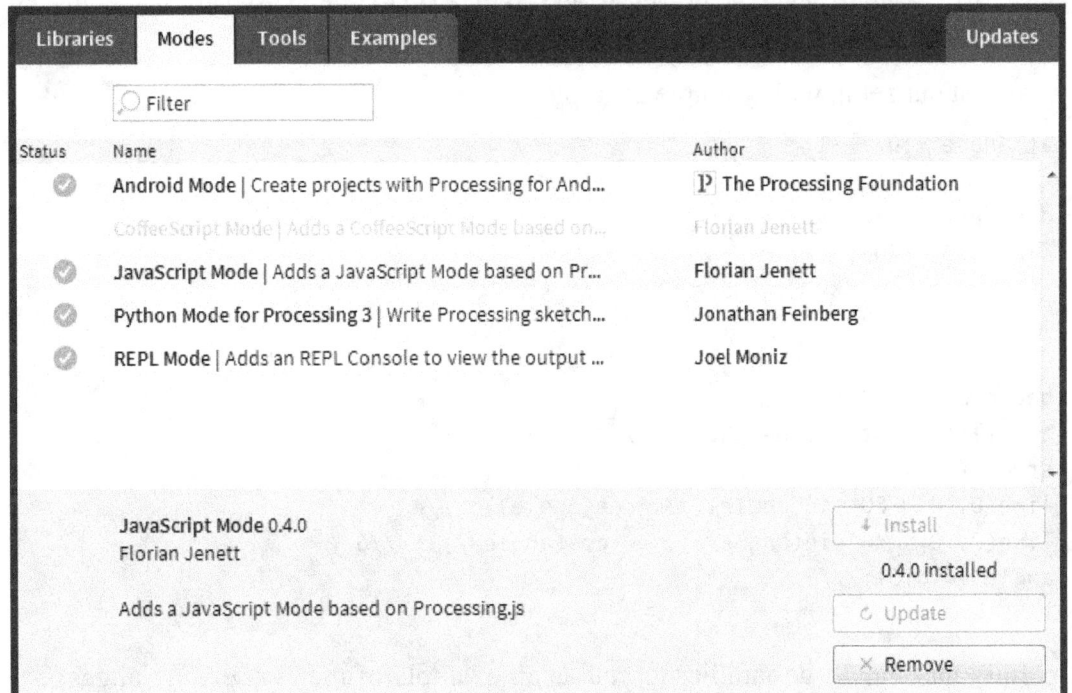

Figure 207: Processing with Javascript Mode Installed

You can close this window and you should now see JavaScript mode available as an option (Figure 208). Choosing this will launch your *Processing* environment in JavaScript mode

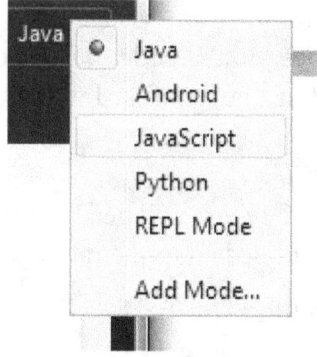

Figure 208: Choosing Javascript Mode

You should now be able to write some *Processing* code and run it in JavaScript mode. This will launch a browser window running your sketch. *Processing*.js goes a long way to allowing 'pure' *Processing* code to be created and run using JavaScript. In general your sketch code will not require any alteration, though there are a few instances (such as loading images) where small changes are necessary. The *Processing*.js website has some good information on the differences so we will not list them here

We can test our setup with a simple example

```
float angle = 0; //1

void setup() { //2
   size(320, 240);
}

void draw() {
   background(127);
   translate(width/2, height/2); //3
   stroke(255);
   line(0, 0, -80*sin(angle), 80*cos(angle)); //4
   line(0, 0, -40*sin(angle/2), 40*cos(angle/2)); //5
   angle += 0.01; //6
}
```

Hopefully this should be familiar to you as an example of the *Processing* language you have seen up to this point. Here is an explanation of the key parts of the example:

1. Creates an angle variable which we will use to store the angle of the line we will draw

2. setup()creates a small window (the canvas) of 320 pixels by 240 pixels. You're free to use any size you like but web pages typically have other content.
3. translate() moves the center of drawing to the center of the canvas.
4. Draw a line 80 pixels long from the center at the angle specified by angle
5. Draw a shorter line 40 pixels long with half the angle
6. Increments angle by 0.01 radians. You can make this larger to move faster (try 0.15) or smaller to go slower(try 0.002)

If you run this example it should fire up whichever default browser you have on your computer and run the JavaScript code. You should see that we have created a clock-like animation running that will run in your browser similar to that shown in Figure 209

Figure 209: Clock Built in Processing.js

Using the p5.js Environment

Another way to access JavaScript mode for *Processing* is to use the p5.js environment. This is a separate environment installation to the *Processing* environment you have been using so far, but is designed to be easy to use and should have familiar features. The p5.js

JavaScript library has been adopted as the official *Processing* JavaScript implementation, so you may prefer to use it for this reason

To install it, simply head over to https://p5js.org/ and download the Editor environment for your operating system. You should be able to extract it and run it as you have done with the *Processing* environment. Once running you should see a screen similar to that shown in Figure 210

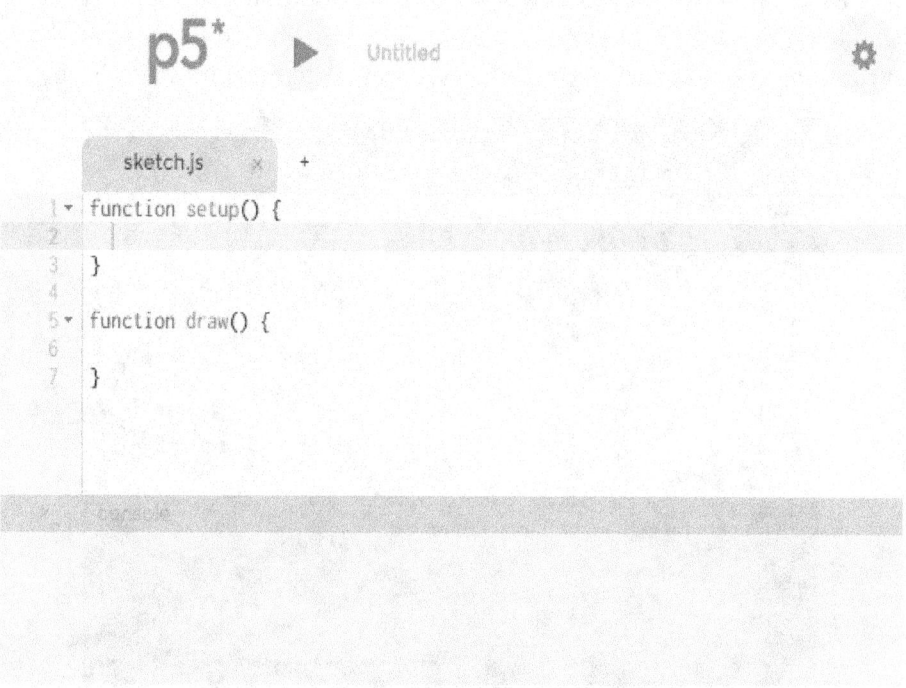

Figure 210: p5 Environment Window

You may notice a slight difference is the template code given, namely that the setup() and draw() functions start with *function* rather than void(). This is simply a JavaScript notation and otherwise the setup() and draw() functions work the same as we have already seen. You can run your sketches by clicking on the large 'play' arrow button

If you choose to use p5.js you should note that it does not play well with 'pure' *Processing* code and expects some changes to reflect JavaScript notation, as well as renaming some of the functions. The p5.js website has a good list of the difference between p5.js and the *Processing* language aimed at *Processing* programmers, but most notable are:

- Functions have to be prefixed with *function*
- Variables in JavaScript do not have types and are just prefixed *var*

- *size()* has been replaced with *createCanvas()*
- *popMatrix()* and *pushMatrix()* have been replaced with *pop()* and *push()* respectively

We can test out our environment by adapting our clock animation example to the language expected by p5.js

```
var angle = 0 ; //1

function setup() { //2
   createCanvas(320, 240);
}

function draw() {
   background(127);
   translate(width/2, height/2); //3
   stroke(255);
   line(0, 0, -80*sin(angle), 80*cos(angle)); //4
   line(0, 0, -40*sin(angle/2), 40*cos(angle/2)); //5
   angle += 0.01; // 5.
}
```

Here you should see that the language is slightly different to the *Processing* language you have used this far. We have altered the size() function to createCanvas() as expected by p5.js

Also notice that the setup() and draw() functions now state they are JavaScript functions and have no return type (void) specified since JavaScript functions do not specify types. In addition we have changed the *angle* declaration to be a 'var' rather than specifying the variable type for the same reason

Running this sketch will load up a browser window and display the same clock animation we saw previously (Figure 211)

Figure 211: Clock Animation Built in p5.js

Using Javascript Files

If you are familiar with web development, or are adventurous and just want to know how it works, you can use the manual route of creating a web page and adding the *Processing* JavaScript files yourself, using whatever IDE or text editor you have handy

This is more advanced than using the environments provided by *Processing* or p5.js, so if you are unsure it might be wise to use one of those methods for now

The steps to do this are:

1. Download the JavaScript file required to run *Processing* in a browser
2. Create an HTML file
3. Add tags to your downloaded *Processing* JavaScript file
4. Create your sketch
5. Link your sketch to the HTML file

We will walk through the steps

Step 1: Download the javascript file required to run Processing in a browser

To do this you first need to download the relevant JavaScript files from your chosen provider (either *Processing*.js or p5.js). This is the JavaScript implementation of *Processing* that will be used to render your sketch code. Both also offer a 'minimised' version, which is simply the same JavaScript code but with the spaces removed to make the file smaller

Step 2: Create an HTML file

This is as simple as creating a new file with a .html extension, for example processingExample.html

If you were going to follow good form for HTML, you should add some HTML tags to your file, using your favourite editor. However, these are not necessary to make your *Processing* sketch work

```html
<!DOCTYPE html>
<html lang="en">
   <head>
      <meta charset="utf-8">
      <title>title</title>
      <!-- source files here -->
   </head>
   <body>
      <!-- page content -->
      </body>
</html>
```

Step 3: Add tags to your downloaded Processing javascript file

You now need to link your HTML file to the *Processing* JavaScript file you downloaded. We have assumed you have placed them both in the same directory on your computer

This simply involves placing a <source> tag into your HTML file referencing the *Processing* JavaScript file you downloaded where it says <source files here> in the HTML above. This will be *one* of the following depending on which *Processing* library you are using

```html
<script src="processing.js" type="text/javascript">
</script>
<!-- processing.js -->
<script src="p5.js" type="text/javascript">
</script>
<!--p5.js -->
```

This tells your HTML page where the *Processing* libraries are located and that they are JavaScript files

Step 4: Create your sketch

You can now go ahead and create your sketch code. You have some options here on how you want to write your code. We will demonstrate with some simple code that will draw a series of rotating rectangles. The *Processing*.js code can be used exactly as below

```
float rotate1 = 0;
float rotate2 = 0;

void setup() {
    size(400, 400);
}

void draw() {
    translate(width/2, height/2);
    rotate(rotate1);
    fill(10, 10, 120);
    rect(0, 0, 100, 100);
    rotate1 += 1;
    rotate(rotate2);
    fill(120, 10, 10);
    rect(0, 0, 100, 100);
    rotate2 += 0.01;
}
```

If you are using *Processing*.js, you can write your sketch code in the *Processing* environment and save your sketch code to a file. The saved file (with the .pde) extension can be used as the source for your sketch. We will assume you have called it rectangle.pde

As an additional option, you can write *Processing* using *only* JavaScript, utilising the JavaScript *Processing* library. However, since this would require a good knowledge of JavaScript, we will not delve any further into this. If this is something that interests you there is information on the *Processing*.js website

If you are using p5.js, you can write your code in a new JavaScript file, with a .js extension, and place your *Processing* code in there. We will assume you have called it rectangle.js. This will be linked to your HTML page in the next step

The p5.js equivalent for our code would be as follows

```
var rotate1 = 0;
var rotate2 = 0;

function setup() {
    createCanvas(400, 400);
}

function draw() {
    translate(width/2, height/2);
    rotate(rotate1);
```

```
fill(10, 10, 120);
rect(0, 0, 100, 100);
rotate1 += 1;
rotate(rotate2);
fill(120, 10, 10);
rect(0, 0, 100, 100);
rotate2 += 0.01;
}
```

In either case, your code can optionally also be placed directly inside your HTML file within a *<script>* tag. This removes the need to create a separate JavaScript file though we don't recommend it as it makes your code harder to control and it is best practice to keep the HTML and JavaScript separated

An example of this is shown below. You should be able to see the *Processing* code for drawing a rectangle inside the *<script>* tag. Note the need to specify the canvas as we must tell the JavaScript engine where to draw the resulting sketch

```
<!DOCTYPE html>
<html lang="en">
    <head>
        <meta charset="utf-8">
        <title>title</title>
        <!-- source files here -->
        <script src="processing.js" type="text/javascript">
        </script>
        <!-- processing.js -->
        <!-- rectangle -->
        <script type="application/processing" data-processing-target="canvas1">
            var rotate1 = 0;
            var rotate2 = 0;

            function setup() {
                createCanvas(400, 400);
            }

            function draw() {
                translate(width/2, height/2);
                rotate(rotate1);
                fill(10, 10, 120);
                rect(0, 0, 100, 100);
                rotate1 += 1;
                rotate(rotate2);
```

```
        fill(120, 10, 10);
        rect(0, 0, 100, 100);
        rotate2 += 0.01;
      }
    </script>
  </head>
  <body>
    <!-- page content -->
    <canvas id="canvas1"> </canvas>
  </body>
</html>
```

Step 5: Link your sketch to the HTML file

If you have chosen to write your sketch code directly into the HTML file in a *<script>* tag, you need do nothing more here

If you have created your code using p5.js in a JavaScript file, rectangle.js, then you need to specify this file as a JavaScript source

```
<script src="rectangle.js" type="text/javascript"></script>
```

This tells the page to use the p5.js and rectangle.js source files to render the page. In this instance it will draw a rectangle

```
<!DOCTYPE html>
<html lang="en">
  <head>
    <meta charset="utf-8">
    <title>title</title>
    <!-- source files here -->
    <script src="p5.js" type="text/javascript"></script>
    <script src="rectangle.js" type="text/javascript"></script>
  </head>
  <body>
  <!-- page content -->
  </body>
</html>
```

We think you might agree that this is much neater than the previous example where we placed our *Processing* code inside the HTML page itself. In this case the code is quite small, but it would get very unwieldy with a large sketch

If you have created your code and saved it using the *Processing* environment, rectangle.pde, then you need to specify this as the canvas content

```
<!DOCTYPE html>
<html lang="en">
    <head>
        <meta charset="utf-8">
        <title>title</title>
        <!-- source files here -->
        <script src="processing.js" type="text/javascript">
        </script>
        <!-- processing.js -->
    </head>
    <body>
        <!-- page content -->
            <canvas data-processing-sources="rectangle.pde"></canvas>
    </body>
</html>
```

You can now run your code by opening the page in your favourite browser. Either by opening the file (clicking, or double-clicking) or by using the menu in your browser to browse to the location of your file and opening it. You should see your *Processing* code running in the browser using JavaScript, similar to that shown in Figure 212

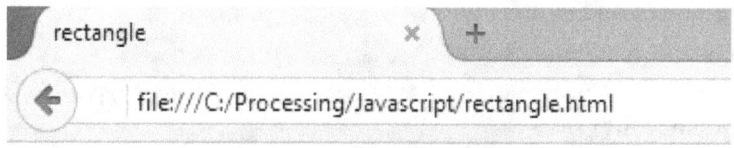

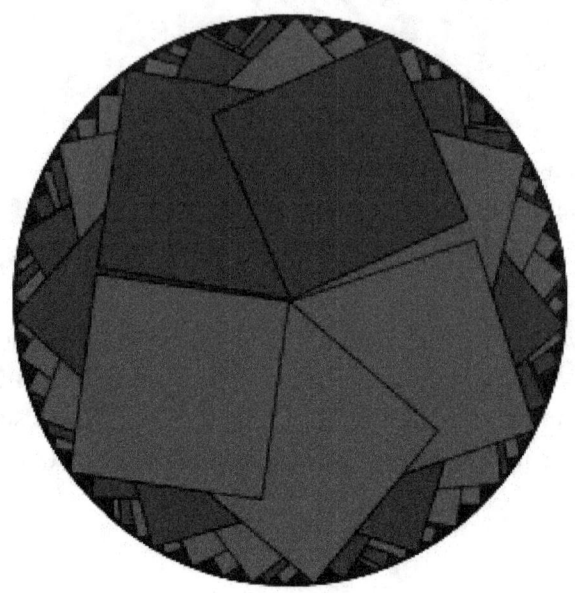

Figure 212: Javascript Rectangle Animation Running in a Browser

A Javascript Animation

We can now move on to writing an interesting animation in JavaScript mode. You can use whichever environment you wish, we will highlight the code differences between *Processing*.js and p5.js as we go

For our example we will create a JavaScript animation that interacts with the mouse pointer by drawing a pulse effect that begins wherever you click the mouse and expands until it leaves the screen as shown in Figure 213

You might, for example, use this to create a website that generates expanding pulses when the user clicks something with the mouse, which would be a pretty neat effect

Since we don't know where the mouse may be clicked, or how many times, we will need a mechanism for creating new pulses on each mouse click and storing the current state of the pulse so that we can draw it expanding. To do this, we will create a Pulse class and an array to store them in

Figure 213: Javascript Pulses

In *Processing* language, as used in *Processing*.js, our class might look like the one below

```
// class for holding pulse details
class Pulse {

   int x;
   int y;
   int diameter;

   Pulse(int x, int y, int diameter) {
      this.x = x;
      this.y = y;
      this.diameter = diameter;
   }
}
```

```
}
```

We have deliberately simplified this in order to demonstrate the use of the class. Best practice would indicate that you should create functions for setting and retrieving the variables x, y and diameter, but we will simply use a constructor and access them directly for simplicity. Note the use of the keyword *this* which shows that we are using variables local to the object we are creating

The class is even simpler in p5.js, using JavaScript as we do not need to explicitly create a constructor or variables, but can simply create a function to hold them

```
// class for holding pulse details
function Pulse(x, y, diameter) {
    this.x = x;
    this.y = y;
    this.diameter = diameter;
}
```

We will hold the Pulse objects we create in an array so we can loop through them and draw them at the relevant location

```
ArrayList<Pulse> pulses = new ArrayList(); // projessing.js
var pulses = new Array(); // p5.js
```

Since we want to draw our pulses at the location where the mouse is clicked, we need to use a mouse event function. The mouse event functions are available in JavaScript mode so you should recognise the mousePressed() function

```
// processing.js
void mousePressed() {
    // add a new pulse at the mouse coordinates
    Pulse pulse = new Pulse(mouseX, mouseY, 0);
    pulses.add(pulse);
    println("Added, size is now " + pulses.size());
}
```

Here we are creating a new Pulse object when the mouse is pressed, using the mouse coordinates, and adding it to the array we have created. The 0 indicates the initial diameter of the pulse. We have deliberately left a println() statement in here as it provides useful feedback about the size of the array. You would likely want to remove this if you used it in a real website, but it is interesting when developing our sketch to see that the array is changing size and objects are being added and removed as expected.

The p5.js version of the function is very similar. We have highlighted the differences

```
function mousePressed() {
    // add a new pulse at the mouse coordinates
    pulse = new Pulse(mouseX, mouseY, 0);
    pulses.push(pulse);
    print("Added, size is now " + pulses.length);
}
```

As you can see, there is very little difference between this and the processing.js version. We have already discussed how we need to declare functions with the keyword *function*. The only other differences are:

- we have to use *push* instead of *add* to add an object to the array
- we need to use *print* instead of *println*

We can now go on to define our draw() function which will draw the pulses. We will need to do this in a loop in order to draw each pulse added to the array

```
void draw() {
    background(255);
    // draw each pulse in the list
    for (int i = 0; i < pulses.size(); i++) {
        Pulse pulse = pulses.get(i);
        ellipse(pulse.x, pulse.y, pulse.diameter, pulse.diameter);
        pulse.diameter += 2;
    }
}
```

You should be able to decipher this code by now. Here we are setting the background colour, in order to clear the screen, and looping through our array of Pulse objects. For each Pulse found we are using the coordinates and diameter contained to draw an ellipse, then increasing the diameter for the next time we draw it. Note that, if there are no Pulse objects in the array, the loop will simply be skipped because its size will be 0

Again, the p5.js version of this is extremely similar

```
function draw() {
    background(255);
    // draw each pulse in the list
    for (i = 0; i < pulses.length; i++) {
        pulse = pulses[i];
        ellipse(pulse.x, pulse.y, pulse.diameter, pulse.diameter);
        pulse.diameter += 2;
    }
}
```

The only differences, highlighted, are:

- declared as a function
- we need to use *length* instead of *size()* to find how large the array is
- we don't specify the variable type for the Pulse object and access it using square brackets [] rather than using the get() function

With the addition of a pulseWidth variable, this code will work now and you can try it if you wish

```
int pulseWidth = 3; // processing.js
var pulseWidth = 3; // p5.js
```

However, there are a couple more things we should do; we should add a setup() function to make our sketch look a bit nicer, and we should consider cleaning up our array a bit as otherwise it will get very full of Pulse objects that are no longer being displayed as they have left the screen

Our setup() function simply sets a size, stops filling the ellipses and sets the stroke parameters to give a blue colour to the ellipse

```
// processing.js
void setup() {
    size(600, 600);
    noFill();
    stroke(0, 150, 255);
    strokeWeight(pulseWidth);
}
```

We have already seen how this would differ in p5.js using the createCanvas() function instead of size()

```
// p5.js
function setup() {
    createCanvas(600, 600);
    noFill();
    stroke(0, 150, 255);
    strokeWeight(pulseWidth);
}
```

To clean up our array, we will check to see if the current diameter of each Pulse has left the screen and, if it has, remove it from the array

```
// remove pulse if off screen
if (pulse.diameter + pulseWidth > (2 * height)) {
    pulses.remove(pulse);
```

```
    println("Removed, size is now " + pulses.size());
}
```

This should be fairly self-explanatory. We should add this to the bottom of the draw() function. The p5.js version of this is very similar, the only difference being the use of the splice() function to remove the object, rather than using remove()

```
// p5.js
// remove pulse if off screen
if (pulse.diameter + pulseWidth > (2 * height)) {
    pulses.splice(i, 1);
    print("Removed, size is now " + pulses.length);
}
```

If you put this all together you should now be able to run this and click around, seeing the pulses being created where you click. If you look at the console you will see the print/println statements telling you that pulses are being added and removed from the array

Embedding Processing in a Web Page

For some realism, we can integrate our sketch into a web page as a small demonstration of the kind of thing that is now possible since web browsers utilise JavaScript and we have a JavaScript version of *Processing*

We will focus our efforts here on demonstrating how to achieve this amalgamation of *Processing* and web pages and will not focus too much on the *Processing* code

For our example we are going to integrate our pulse sketch with an interactive pie chart, running on a web page. The chart will highlight the section selected and, using our pulse animation, show the user where they clicked. The page we are aiming to create looks like the one shown in Figure 214. Here we have a mix of *Processing* JavaScript, HTML and CSS (Cascading Style Sheets) to achieve an interactive web page. We will demonstrate with p5.js code, but this could easily be altered to *Processing*.js language if required

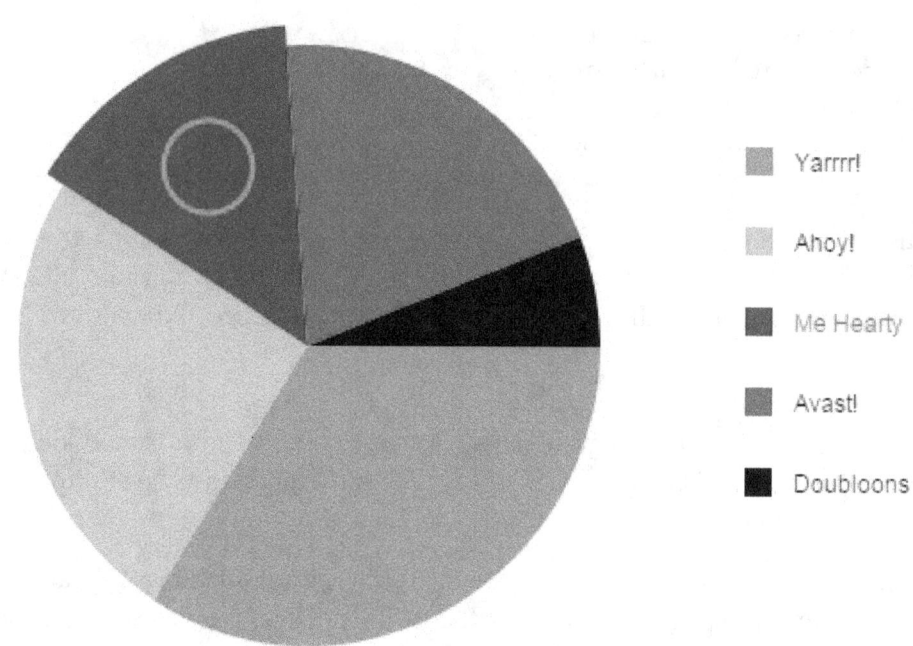

Figure 214: Pirate Saying Web Page

To achieve this we can simply start with creating a *Processing* sketch that we want to use on our web page. As we have seen with the p5.js createCanvas() function, the *Processing* sketch is drawn in a canvas, which is a graphics area in an HTML page. We can use this canvas to add additional web page features, as shown in our new setup() function and declarations below

```
var canvas;
var pulseWidth = 3;
var pulses = new Array();
var pieData = [57, 42, 25, 34, 10];
var pieDataTitles = ["Yarrrr!", "Ahoy!", "Me Hearty", "Avast!", "Doubloons"];
var pieSlices = new Array();
var pieCentralX;
var pieCentralY;
```

```
function setup() {
   canvas = createCanvas(600, 600);
   canvas.position(100, 150);
   titleText = createP("Frequency Of Pirate Sayings");
   titleText.position(100, 50);
   titleText.class("title"); // css class for title
   // initialise chart
   angle1 = 0;
   angle2 = pieData[0];
   totalData = 0;
   pieCentralX = width / 2 - 100;
   pieCentralY = height / 2 - 100;
   // get total data
   for (i = 0; i < pieData.length; i++) {
      totalData += pieData[i];
   }
   piePortion = 360 / totalData;
   // each pie slice
   for (i = 0; i < pieData.length; i++) {
      fillColour = color(int(random(255)), int(random(255)), int(random(255)));
      angle2 = angle1;
      angle1 += pieData[i] * piePortion;
      pieSlice = new PieSlice(pieData[i], pieDataTitles[i], fillColour,
         angle1, angle2, false);
      pieSlices.push(pieSlice);
   }
}
```

Here we are setting up some arrays and objects for holding the pie chart pieces. However the important points for our web page are the canvas interactions that we have highlighted.

You may notice that we are now storing the canvas in a variable called *canvas* that we can use to manipulate it. We can change the position on the page using canvas.position() and add other aspects to it such as our title text. The titleText.class("title") line is a reference to a CSS style that will be used to change the appearance of the title text

Cascading Style Sheets, if you have not used them before, is a method of changing the appearance of items on a page using 'classes' – definitions of an appearance. We have created a style called 'title' which we are telling *Processing* to apply to our title text. The style, saved in a file called a stylesheet that we have named style.css, looks like the one below

```
title {
```

```
    font-family: monospace;
    background-color: #000000;
    color: #FFFFFF;
    font-size: 18pt;
    padding: 10px;
}
```

We are telling the browser that we want anything with the class 'title' to have the appearance we have specified: 18pt font size, monospace font, 10 pixel padding, white text and black background

We will need to link our sketch and stylesheet together, but before we do, lets finish the sketch code. We need to extend our draw() function to draw all of the pie chart pieces as well as the pulses that we previously drew

```
function draw() {
    background(255);
    noStroke();
    // pie chart
    y = pieCentralY - 100;
    for (i = 0; i < pieSlices.length; i++) {
        fillColour = pieSlices[i].colour;
        angle1 = pieSlices[i].angle1;
        angle2 = pieSlices[i].angle2;
        title = pieSlices[i].title;
        selected = pieSlices[i].selected;
        sliceData = pieSlices[i].data
        // set properties for selected slice (if any)
        textColour = 0;
        sliceRadius = 300;
        if (selected) {
            textColour = color(255, 0, 0);
            sliceRadius = 320;
        }
        // draw pie slice
        fill(fillColour);
        arc(pieCentralX, pieCentralY, sliceRadius, sliceRadius,
            radians(angle2), radians(angle1));
        // draw legend
        fill(fillColour);
        rect(pieCentralX + 225, y, 14, 14);
        fill(textColour);
        text(title, pieCentralX + 250, y + 12);
```

```
    y += 40;
}

// draw each pulse in the list
stroke(0, 150, 255);
strokeWeight(pulseWidth);
noFill();
for (i = 0; i < pulses.length; i++) {
    pulse = pulses[i];
    ellipse(pulse.x, pulse.y, pulse.diameter, pulse.diameter);
    pulse.diameter += 2;
    // remove pulse if off screen
    if (pulse.diameter + pulseWidth > 100) {
        pulses.splice(i, 1);
        print("Removed, size is now " + pulses.length);
    }
}
}
```

You will see that we are also using objects to store and fetch the values for the pie chart as well as the pulses

```
// class for holding pulse details
function Pulse(x, y, diameter) {
    this.x = x;
    this.y = y;
    this.diameter = diameter;
}

// class for holding pie chart slice details
function PieSlice(data, title, colour, angle1, angle2, selected) {
    this.data = data;
    this.title = title;
    this.colour = colour;
    this.angle1 = angle1;
    this.angle2 = angle2;
    this.selected = selected;
}
```

All that remains for our sketch is to make it interactive. We can extend our mousePressed() function to detect which piece of the pie chart we have clicked and set a property that we have selected it. This will enable us, in our draw() function, to determine which one was last selected. We are using the colour of the pie chart piece to determine which one we have clicked

```
function mousePressed() {
    // add a new pulse at the mouse coordinates
    pulse = new Pulse(mouseX, mouseY, 0);
    pulses.push(pulse);
    print("Added, size is now " + pulses.length);
    // work out colour of where mouse pressed
    mouseColour = get(mouseX, mouseY);
    mouseRed = red(mouseColour);
    mouseBlue = blue(mouseColour);
    mouseGreen = green(mouseColour);
    // find if we clicked on this colour slice
    for (i = 0; i < pieSlices.length; i++) {
        intRed = int(red(pieSlices[i].colour));
        intBlue = int(blue(pieSlices[i].colour));
        intGreen = int(green(pieSlices[i].colour));
        // set selected property
        if (intRed == mouseRed && intGreen == mouseGreen &&
            intBlue == mouseBlue) {
            pieSlices[i].selected = true;
        } else {
            pieSlices[i].selected = false;
        }
    }
}
```

If you have gotten this far, you should now have a working *Processing* animation that allows you to click any part of the pie chart and have the chart react by highlighting the description of that piece and making the piece larger. You should also see that the pulse is generated as before. We changed the pulse slightly to fade out earlier, rather than fill the entire screen as before

Frequency Of Pirate Sayings

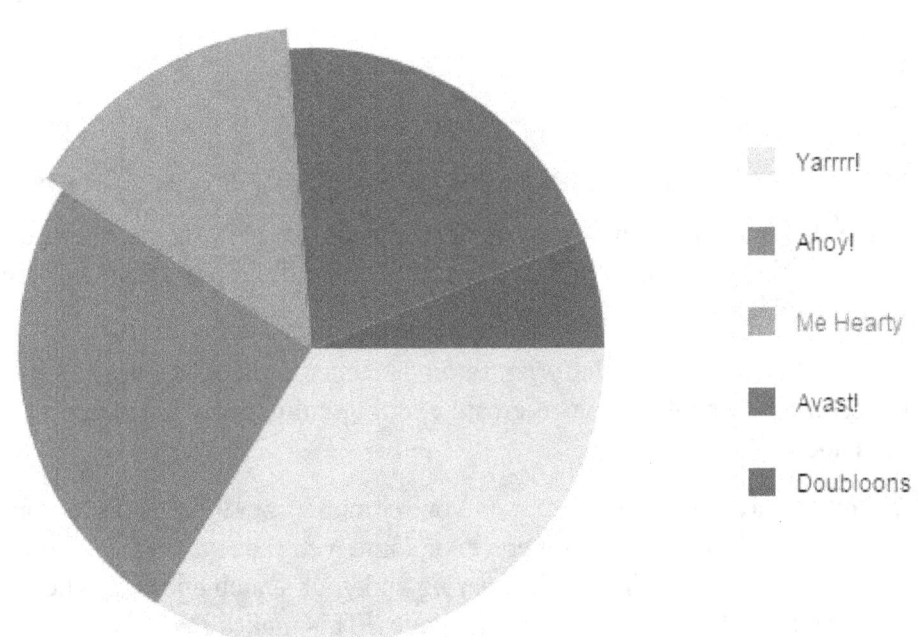

Figure 215: Unstyled Pirate Chart

If you run this you might see that there is something amiss. The styling we created has not been applied to the title (Figure 215). This is because we haven't linked the stylesheet to the page. Notice that nothing fails, it just doesn't look like we anticipated

To link a stylesheet to a web page, you need to tell the page to load the stylesheet files. In our case we called it style.css, so we need to add

```
<link rel="stylesheet" type="text/css" href="style.css">
```

This tells the web page where the stylesheets are. Since we are using p5.js, we should already have an index.html file created for us which we can alter. Adding the above line should result in an HTML page with the following code

```
<!DOCTYPE html>
<html>
    <head>
        <meta charset="UTF-8">
```

```
        <title>Pirate Sayings</title>
        <script src="libraries/p5.js" type="text/javascript"></script>
        <script src="libraries/p5.dom.js" type="text/javascript"></script>
        <script src="libraries/p5.sound.js" type="text/javascript"></script>
        <script src="sketch.js" type="text/javascript"></script>
        <link rel="stylesheet" type="text/css" href="style.css">
        <style> body {padding: 0; margin: 0;} canvas {vertical-align: top;}
        </style>
    </head>
    <body>
    </body>
</html>
```

If you save this and run your sketch again (or open the HTML page in a browser) you should see that the title is now styled correctly. Congratulations, you have created a web page with embedded *Processing* graphics!

You can probably see by now that *Processing* sketches embedded into web pages can be a very powerful tool, enabling you to create exciting animations and graphics on any web page you choose

These examples have all been running on your computer but there is no reason you cannot run them on the web if you have a website or some web space available. You simply need to copy the required files (HTML, *Processing* and your sketch code) to wherever you host them and treat them like any other website pages. This makes *Processing* a very powerful graphics tool for the web, especially for creating exciting animations. You might want to try some of the sketches you have already created and practice converting them to JavaScript, or create some of your own. Have fun with it!

Android Programming Mode

Processing Android mode makes it very easy to run your sketches on an Android phone or tablet. Since both Android and *Processing* are based on the Java language, many basic sketches will run without changes. This makes *Processing* a very exciting prospect for creating Android graphics and animations and opens up the world of mobile application development to anyone with knowledge of the *Processing* language

Installation

In order to use Android mode you need to add the Android mode to processing, and install the Android SDK (Software Development Kit) which is required to build and run Android applications

Install The Android SDK

If you haven't developed anything with Android before, you will need to install the Android SDK. To install this head over to the official site: https://developer.android.com/studio/

The website encourages you to download Android Studio, the official IDE for Android development. You can choose to do this if you wish, or you can download only the SDK (usually labelled 'command line tools'. Once downloaded, install into a suitable place on your computer and take note of the installation directory

Install Android Mode

The process for installing Android Mode is similar to installing JavaScript mode. Open a processing window and on the Mode button (top right hand corner) and select the 'add mode' menu.

Select 'Android Mode' and click Install. This might take a fair amount of time depending upon your internet connection. The download instructions will walk you through the process and you *might* have to restart (quit and reopen or relaunch) processing.

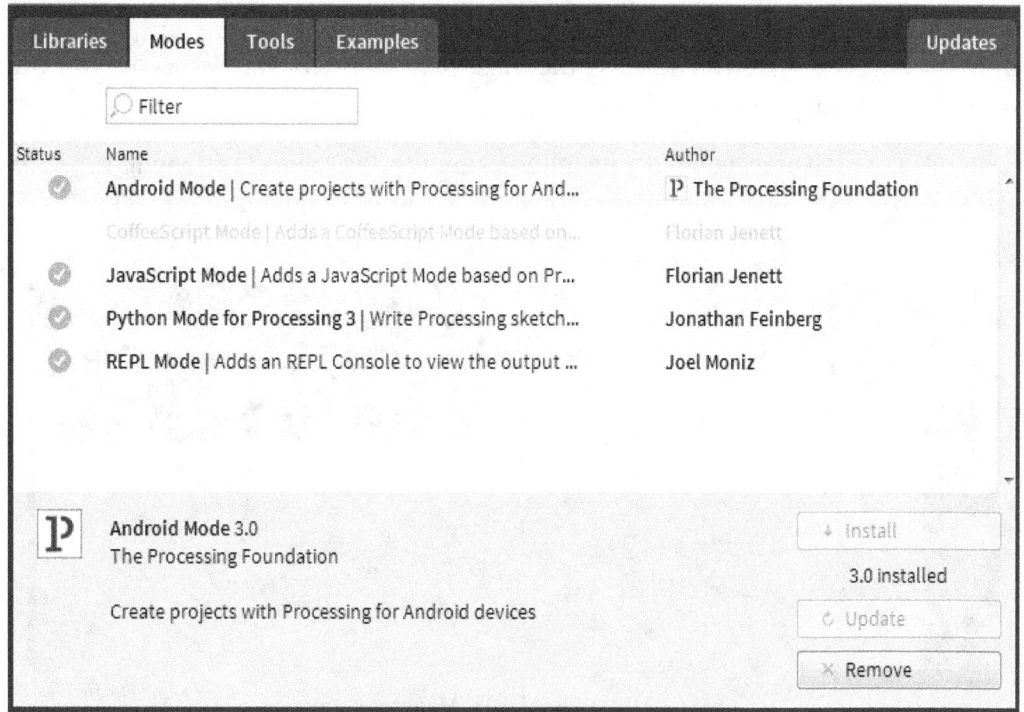

Figure 216: Processing with Android Mode Installed

Once completed, you should see Android mode with a tick against it, as shown in Figure 216

You can close this window and can now select Android from the mode button to launch *Processing* into Android mode (Figure 217). *Processing* may ask you for the location of your Android SDK which you installed in the previous step – it is the top-level directory that is required where the SDK was installed

Figure 217: Processing in Android Mode

Check Android SDK Details

When you downloaded the Android SDK it will have installed the most recent Android version. At the time of writing this is Android 7.0 Nougat (API version 24). *Processing* supports anything above Android 3.0 Honeycomb (API version 11), but the recommendation is to use whichever is the most recent one for the device(s) you want to run your sketches on

You can check which ones you have installed using the Android SDK manager, which can be accessed from the *Processing* environment in the Android menu Figure 218

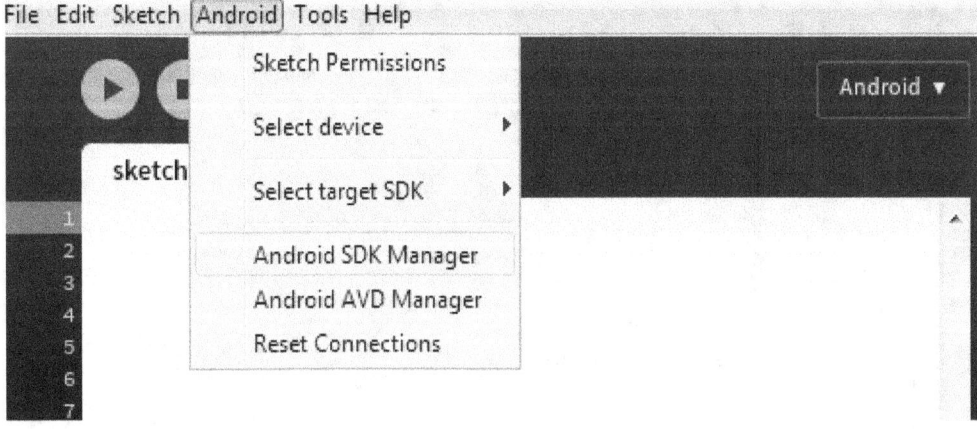

Figure 218: Android SDK Manager Menu

Clicking on this will launch the Android SDK Manager which will show you the SDK versions you have installed. As you can see from Figure 219, we have Android N (API 24) and Android 5.1.1 (API 22) installed

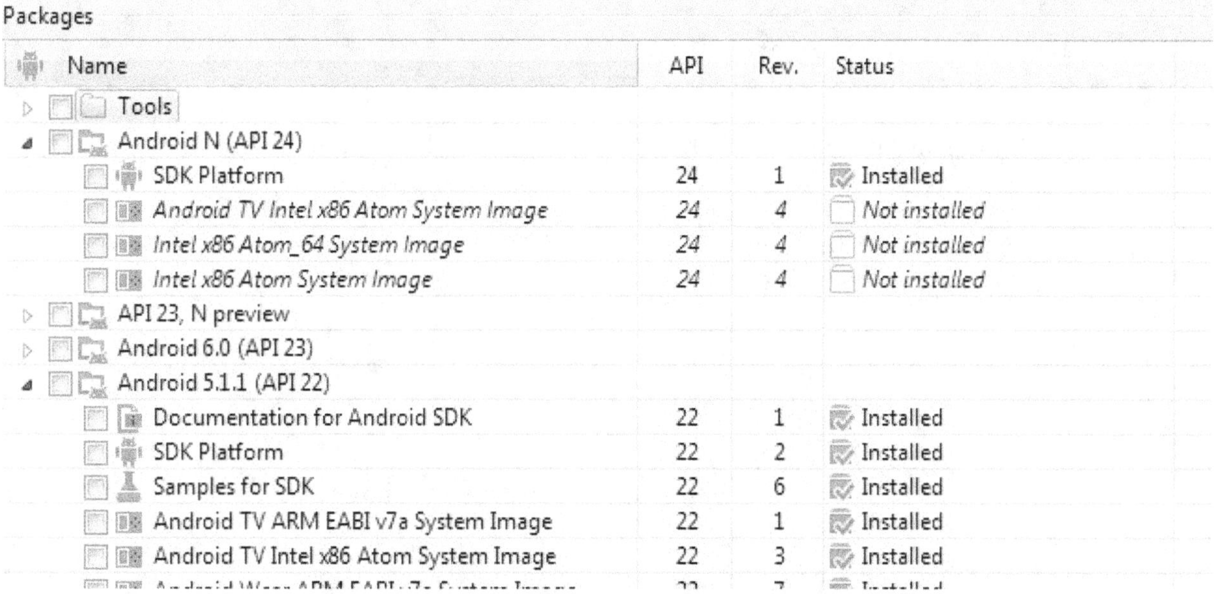

Packages

Name	API	Rev.	Status
▷ ☐ 🗀 Tools			
◢ ☐ 🗀 Android N (API 24)			
☐ 🤖 SDK Platform	24	1	✅ Installed
☐ 🗔 Android TV Intel x86 Atom System Image	24	4	☐ Not installed
☐ 🗔 Intel x86 Atom_64 System Image	24	4	☐ Not installed
☐ 🗔 Intel x86 Atom System Image	24	4	☐ Not installed
▷ ☐ 🗀 API 23, N preview			
▷ ☐ 🗀 Android 6.0 (API 23)			
◢ ☐ 🗀 Android 5.1.1 (API 22)			
☐ 📄 Documentation for Android SDK	22	1	✅ Installed
☐ 🤖 SDK Platform	22	2	✅ Installed
☐ ⚒ Samples for SDK	22	6	✅ Installed
☐ 🗔 Android TV ARM EABI v7a System Image	22	1	✅ Installed
☐ 🗔 Android TV Intel x86 Atom System Image	22	3	✅ Installed
☐ 🗔 Android Wear ARM EABI v7a System Image	22	7	✅ Installed

Figure 219: Android SDK Manager

You can, if you wish, install other versions from here as needed. For example, if you needed Android 4.4.2 (API 17) installed, you can choose this and install it from here. We recommend you just use the most recent unless you have a reason not to

You can close this window when you are done

Your First Android Sketch

Let's create a really simple sketch to show how Android mode works. It is often simpler to develop your sketch code in Java mode before switching to Android due to the simplicity and speed of running the sketch

```
void setup() {
  size(400, 400);
  smooth();
  noStroke();
  rectMode(CENTER);
}

void draw() {
  background(234, 201, 190);
```

```
    fill(243, 224, 184);
    rect(width/2, height/3, 200, 70);
    rect(width/2, 2*(height/3), 200, 70);

    fill(172, 165, 194);
    ellipse(width/2, height/2, 150, 150);
}
```

If you run this in Java mode you should see something like that in Figure 220

Figure 220: Simple Android Sketch

Now that we know this works, we can try it in Android mode. There are 2 ways of doing this; using the Android emulator, or on a physical Android device (phone or tablet)

Running in the Android Emulator

Android comes with an emulator that allows you to set up Android Virtual Devices (AVDs) that look and act like a real Android device on your computer. You can 'swipe' using your mouse pointer and there are buttons to represent buttons on the device such as the Menu or Home buttons.

An Android Virtual Device should have been set up for you when you installed the Android SDK. You can check which AVDs you have created using the Android AVD Manager option in the Android menu in the *Processing* window (only visible in Android mode). Clicking on this will launch the Android AVD Manager which will show you the virtual devices available. As you can see in Figure 221 we have one AVD that has been created to mimic a Nexus 5 device running Android 5.1.1 with an ARM CPU.

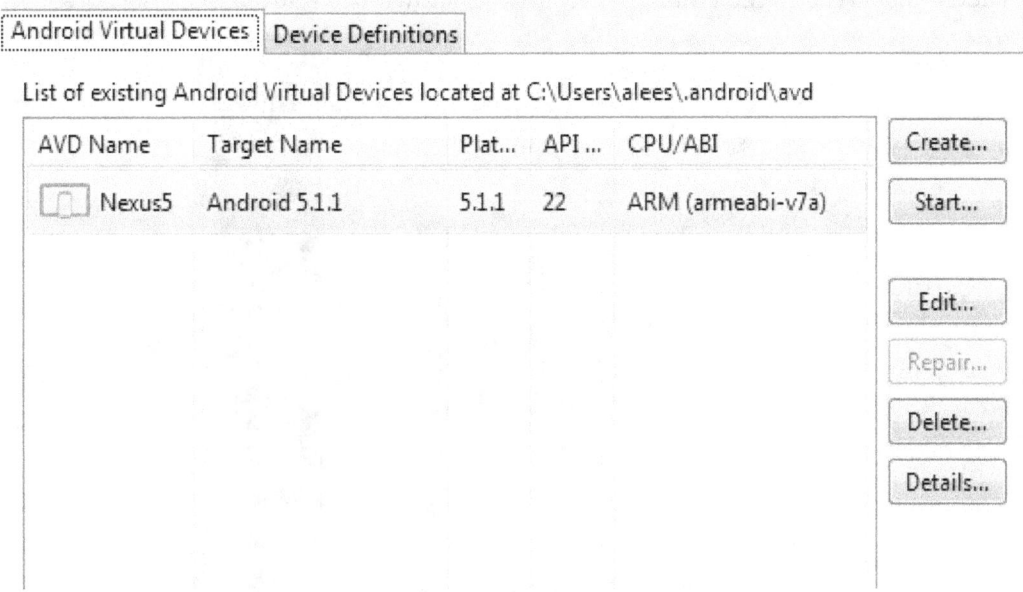

Figure 221: Android AVD Manager

You can simply use the default one created for you if you wish, or create new configurations here if you would like to.

To run your sketch in the Android Emulator, switch to Android mode and select the 'Run in Emulator' option in the Sketch menu (Figure 222) rather than using the 'Play' button

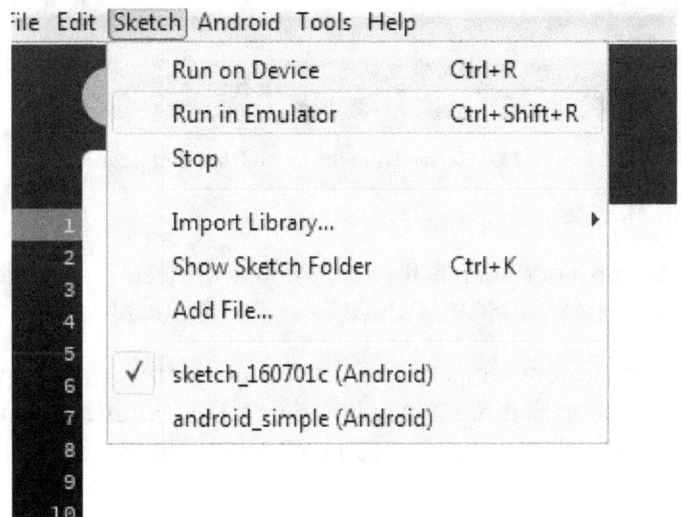

Figure 222: Run In Emulator Option

The emulator is sloooow … so expect to wait a while for it to load up. Once loaded you will need to swipe to unlock like you would on a real phone or tablet. You should then see your sketch displayed in the emulator window as shown in Figure 223

Figure 223: Sketch Running in Android Emulator

Running on a Real Device

Now you're ready to run your sketch for real. You will need a suitable Android device (phone, tablet or even an Android Wear device) and a USB cable

You first need to prepare it for connecting to your computer by turning on USB debugging. This can usually be found in Settings > Applications > Development menu on your device. If you can't find it then a quick Internet search should yield some instructions on how to do it.

Now plug your device in to your computer using the USB cable. Hopefully you will have a suitable driver installed or one can be installed automatically. If you're using Windows, you may also need to install a USB driver. Details can be found here: https://developer.android.com/studio/run/oem-usb.html

Once that's done, it's simply a matter of pressing the normal Run button, or choosing Run on Device from the menu. Your sketch should be installed on your device and be displayed on the screen (Figure 224)

Figure 224: Sketch Running on a Real Device

An Android Animation

Now that we have Android mode working we can look at creating an animation and utilising some of the features that Android provides. To begin with we will create a simple animation of a sphere that responds to screen touches by drawing the sphere wherever you touch the screen as shown in Figure 225

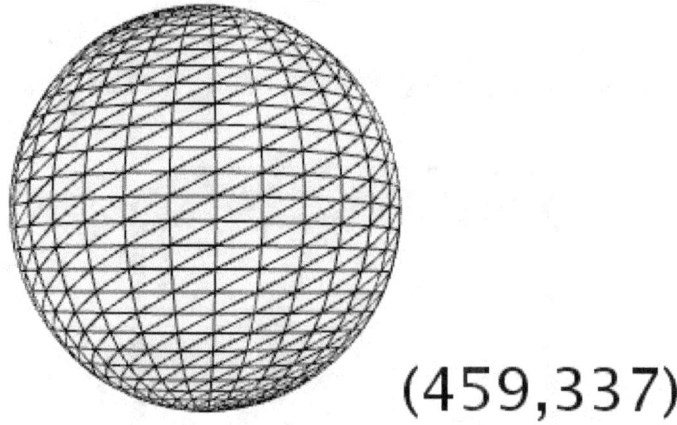

(459,337)

Figure 225: Touch Screen Sphere

In the first instance we can try this out using Java mode since there is no specific Android code involved (we will add this later). This provides you with an easy way to develop your sketches and test them on your computer before trying to run them on an Android device or emulator. Since there is no mouse pointer on Android, Android mode will simply translate the mouse pointer into screen touches so there is no code change required to enable this

```
void setup() {
    fullScreen(P3D);
}

void draw() {
    background(255);
    translate(mouseX, mouseY);
    fill(0, 255, 0, 50);
    sphere(100);
    fill(0);
    textSize(30);
    text("("+mouseX+","+mouseY+")", 100, 100);
}
```

This should all be familiar to you. You can immediately try this sketch on an Android emulator or device in order to see that a Java Mode sketch can be converted to an Android sketch extremely easily. All you need do is switch between the two modes and run them accordingly. You should see that the cat is drawn wherever you touch the screen. This highlights the beauty of *Processing* modes since you can create sketches for different uses very easily using the same code

Adding Android Features

We can now think about adding some Android-specific code to our sketch to take advantage of some of the features it provides.

Firstly, we can force the sketch to run in a given orientation using the orientation() function. The parameter for this can either be LANDSCAPE or PORTRAIT and will force your sketch to displayed in that orientation. For example, adding

```
orientation(PORTRAIT);
```

to the setup() function in our code will mean our cat sketch is always displayed in landscape orientation, even if we turn the device. Note that you still add this in Java mode and it will simply be ignored

To really take advantage of the features of Android, we can tap into the sensors on the device such as the accelerometer. The accelerometer sensor detects movement of the device either by tilting side-to-side (x-axis), forward and backward (y-axis) or up and down (z-axis). If we alter our sphere sketch to use two variables for coordinates, we can utilise the accelerometer to update the location based on screen tilt

We first need to create a listener class that will be accessed when the accelerometer sensor detects a change

```
class AccelerometerListener implements SensorEventListener {
    public void onSensorChanged(SensorEvent event) {
        ax = event.values[0];
        ay = event.values[1];
        az = event.values[2];

        sphereX -= ax;
        sphereY += ay;

    }
    public void onAccuracyChanged(Sensor sensor, int accuracy) {
        // do nothing
    }
}
```

The ax, ay and az variables hold the sensor data provided by the accelerometer. We can use these to update two variables that we will now use to draw our sphere at sphereX and sphereY coordinates. We need to register our listener class in the setup() function so that Android can pass data to it

```
context = getActivity();
manager = (SensorManager)context.getSystemService(Context.SENSOR_SERVICE);
sensor = manager.getDefaultSensor(Sensor.TYPE_ACCELEROMETER);
listener = new AccelerometerListener();
manager.registerListener(listener, sensor, SensorManager.SENSOR_DELAY_NORMAL);
```

This code tells Android to inform our AccelerometerListener class when the accelerometer sensor detects a change.

There are two more things we need to do to make our sketch work. We will need to import the Android classes we require – this tells our sketch code where to find the Android classes. We also need to add two functions that tell Android to pause listening to the sensor when the sketch is not being used. This is best practise in order to reduce drain on the battery

```
public void onResume() {
    super.onResume();
    if (manager != null) {
        manager.registerListener(listener,
            sensor, SensorManager.SENSOR_DELAY_NORMAL);
    }
}

public void onPause() {
    super.onPause();
    if (manager != null) {
        manager.unregisterListener(listener);
    }
}
```

You should now have all the code you need to try this on an Android device. Note that this code will not work in Java mode, since it contains Android-specific code. Indeed *Processing* will complain that it doesn't understand the Android code if you are still in Java mode. The complete code is shown below

```
import android.content.Context;
import android.hardware.Sensor;
import android.hardware.SensorManager;
import android.hardware.SensorEvent;
```

```
import android.hardware.SensorEventListener;

Context context;
SensorManager manager;
Sensor sensor;
AccelerometerListener listener;
float ax;
float ay;
float az;

int sphereX;
int sphereY;

static final int SPHERE_SIZE = 100;

void setup() {
    fullScreen(P3D);
    orientation(PORTRAIT);
    // initialise location
    sphereX = width/2;
    sphereY = height/2;

    context = getActivity();
    manager = (SensorManager)context.getSystemService(Context.SENSOR_SERVICE);
    sensor = manager.getDefaultSensor(Sensor.TYPE_ACCELEROMETER);
    listener = new AccelerometerListener();
    manager.registerListener(listener,
        sensor, SensorManager.SENSOR_DELAY_NORMAL);

    }

void draw() {
    background(255);

    translate(sphereX, sphereY);
    fill(0, 255, 0, 50);
    sphere(SPHERE_SIZE);
    fill(0);
    textSize(30);
    text("("+sphereX+","+sphereY+")", 100, 100); }

public void onResume() {
    super.onResume();
```

```
    if (manager != null) {
       manager.registerListener(listener,
          sensor, SensorManager.SENSOR_DELAY_NORMAL);
    }
}

public void onPause() {
    super.onPause();
    if (manager != null) {
       manager.unregisterListener(listener);
    }
}

class AccelerometerListener implements SensorEventListener {
    public void onSensorChanged(SensorEvent event) {
       ax = event.values[0];
       ay = event.values[1];
       az = event.values[2];

       sphereX -= ax;
       sphereY += ay;

    }
    public void onAccuracyChanged(Sensor sensor, int accuracy) {
       // do nothing
    }
}
```

If you try this code you should see that tilting the device side-to-side or forward and backward will move the sphere. The current coordinates are displayed as text (Figure 226)

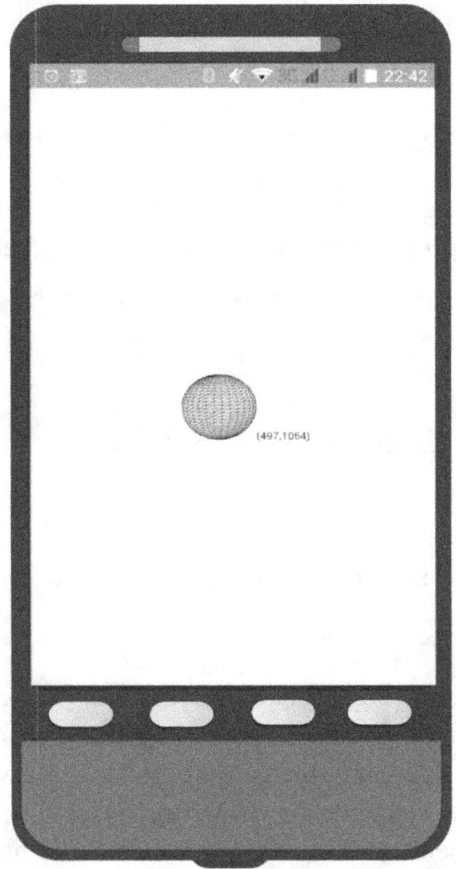

Figure 226: 3D Sphere Running On Android

Depending on the specifications of your device, you may notice some jerkiness in the movement of the sphere. If you do, it is likely due to the frequency at which the accelerometer tilt is recognised by the listener. In our sketch we used the 'normal' frequency (the slowest)

```
SensorManager.SENSOR_DELAY_NORMAL
```

You can opt to receive more frequent sensor data by using faster values of sensor delay, in order of speed from lowest to greatest

- SENSOR_DELAY_NORMAL
- SENSOR_DELAY_UI (designed for User Interface elements)
- SENSOR_DELAY_GAME (designed for games)
- SENSOR_DELAY_FASTEST (fast)

Increasing the rate of the sensor data will increase the speed, and so reduce the jerkiness effect, though at the expense of using the battery more

One enhancement we might make at this point is to stop the sphere from leaving the screen. We can simply place conditions around the

```
sphereX -= ax;
sphereY += ay;
```

lines to only update them if the sphere would not leave the screen

```
if (sphereX - ax > SPHERE_SIZE && sphereX - ax < width - SPHERE_SIZE) {
    sphereX -= ax;
}

if (sphereY + ay > SPHERE_SIZE && sphereY + ay < height - SPHERE_SIZE) {
    sphereY += ay;
}
```

You should now see that the sphere stops at the edges of the screen.

Creating An Android Game

We can now think about applying what we have learned to create a more realistic and interesting animation by creating an Android game that you can run on a real Android device. Our game will involve using the accelerometer to move a 3D cat over a moving board, collecting the gold squares and avoiding the holes. We will concentrate on explaining the Android aspects of the game, so won't explain every aspect of the sketch, but a full code listing can be found in Appendix A. First let's draw our cat as shown in Figure 227

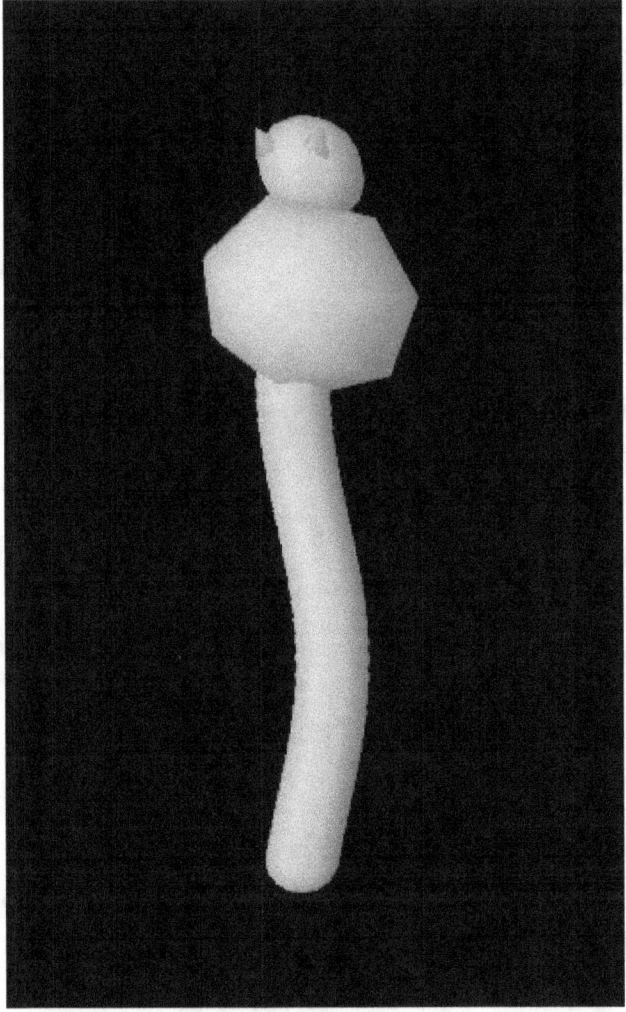

Figure 227: 3D Cat

The code for this sketch is listed below. You should have seen everything here before – we have used a class to define the cat which we draw at the mouse pointer location. The cat itself is made up of spheres which are drawn in separate locations using translate(), pushMatrix() and popMatrix() in order to achieve different transformations that do not affect the others. The body sphere is rotated separately to give the illusion of movement and we have used sphereDetail() to create a pyramid-type shape for the ears. The tail, also made of spheres, is drawn using trigonometry which changes over time (using frameCount) to make it curve and move

```
Cat cat;
int catSize;
```

```
void setup() {
   fullScreen(P3D);
   orientation(PORTRAIT);
   catSize = width/10;
   cat = new Cat(catSize);
   // initial position
   cat.x = width/2;
   cat.y = height - catSize;
   // set bounds
   cat.minX = cat.size;
   cat.maxX = width - cat.size;
   cat.minY = cat.size;
   cat.maxY = height - cat.size;
}

void draw() {
   background(0);
   lights();
   //rotateX(radians(50));
   cat.draw();
}

class Cat {

   final int tailLength;
   final int tailThickness;
   final color CAT_COLOUR = color(255, 200, 0);
   final int size;
   // tail segments
   PVector[] tail;
   // location
   int x;
   int y;
   // bounds
   int minX;
   int maxX;
   int minY;
   int maxY;

   Cat(int size) {
      this.size = size;
      this.tailLength = size/4;
      this.tailThickness = size/7;
```

```
    tail = new PVector[tailLength];
    for (int i = 0; i < tailLength; i++) {
        tail[i] = new PVector(0, 0);
    }
}

void draw() {
    // draw body in separate matrix so can rotate
    pushMatrix();
    noStroke();
    translate(x, y);
    rotateX(frameCount/20.0); // roll
    sphereDetail(7);
    fill(CAT_COLOUR);
    sphere(size * 0.4);
    popMatrix();

    pushMatrix();
    noStroke();
    // draw head
    translate(x, y - (size/2));
    sphereDetail(8);
    sphere(size * 0.2);
    // draw ears
    // left
    pushMatrix();
    //fill(0, 0, 255);
    translate(-size*0.1, -size*0.05, size*0.15);
    rotateY(0.5);
    rotateX(4);
    sphereDetail(1);
    sphere(size*0.1);
    popMatrix();
    // right
    pushMatrix();
    translate(size*0.1, -size*0.05, size*0.15);
    rotateY(3);
    rotateX(2);
    sphereDetail(1);
    sphere(size*0.1);
    popMatrix();
    // draw tail
    sphereDetail(8);
```

```
tail[tailLength-1].x = (sin(frameCount * 0.2) * 10);
tail[tailLength-1].y = size/2;
for (int i = 0; i < tailLength-1; i++) {
    tail[i].x = tail[i+1].x;
    tail[i].y = tail[i+1].y + (tailThickness/2);
    pushMatrix();
    translate(tail[i].x, tail[i].y);
    sphere(tailThickness);
    popMatrix();
}
popMatrix();


  }
}
```

Notice that we have created maximum and minimum coordinates for the cat so that we can use them to contain the cat within the bounds of the screen

We can immediately try this on an Android device and, for fun, we could change the x and y coordinates to be mouseX and mouseY to draw the cat wherever we touch the screen by adding the following lines to the draw() function

```
cat.x = mouseX;
cat.y = mouseY;
```

Running this will display our 3D cat wherever we touch the screen (Figure 228)

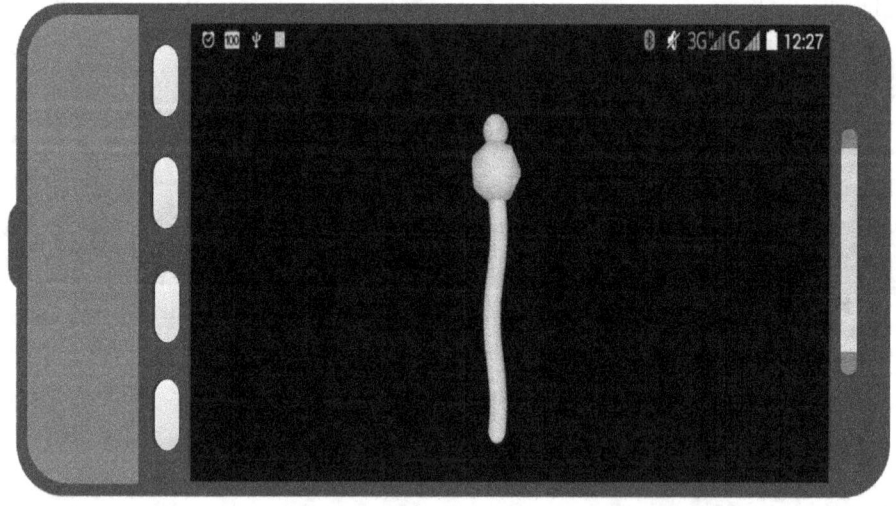

Figure 228: 3D Cat On An Android Device

We can now include our accelerometer Android code in order to move the cat using tilting of the device. This is very similar to the code we used before to move the sphere. To avoid confusion with the axes, we will force our game into PORTRAIT mode. The code for this is exactly the same as before apart from we want to update our cat's location based on the accelerometer and not the mouse/touch location. We can simply remove the two lines we added above and add in our previous code for using the accelerometer, replacing the sphere coordinates with our cat.x, and cat.y coordinates and using our newly-created maximum bounds values to keep the cat on the screen

```
class AccelerometerListener implements SensorEventListener {
    public void onSensorChanged(SensorEvent event) {
        ax = event.values[0];
        ay = event.values[1];
        az = event.values[2];

        if (cat.x - ax > cat.minX && cat.x - ax < cat.maxX) {
            cat.x -= ax;
        }

        if (cat.y + ay > cat.minY && cat.y + ay < cat.maxY) {
            cat.y += ay;
        }
    }

    public void onAccuracyChanged(Sensor sensor, int accuracy) {
        // do nothing
    }
}
```

You should now see that the cat moves in the direction the screen is tilted and does not leave the screen as we saw with the sphere. We now have the basis for our game

The game board will comprise a series of tiles, drawn as squares, some of which we will designate as gold, point-scoring, squares and others as holes that will mean a life is lost. Similarly to our Cat, we will create a class to hold the state of each tile since we will need to remember the location and type of tile each time the screen is drawn

```
// class for tiles
class Tile {
    int x;
    int y;
    int type;
```

```
    Tile(int x, int y, int type) {
        this.x = x;
        this.y = y;
        this.type = type;
    }
}
```

We can hold these in an array and assign locations and types to them as needed which we can then use to display each tile. The tile types are randomised so they appear interspersed and are not the same each time. We will recycle the tiles as they leave the screen so that we can have a relatively small array size, so we will need to randomise the tiles each time a row is no longer visible

```
// initialise tiles
tiles = new ArrayList<Tile>();
for (int i = 0; i < numberOfRows; i++) {
    // set y coordinates (-y so scrolls downwards)
    int y = -i * tileSize;
    for (int j = 0; j < NUMBER_OF_COLUMNS; j++) {
        // set x coordinate
        int x = j * tileSize + offsetX;
        int tileType = STANDARD_TILE;
        // allow grace period of normal tiles
        if (i > GRACE_PERIOD) {
            // random tile types
            tileType = generateRandomTileType();
        }
        tiles.add(new Tile(x, y, tileType));
    }
}


// generate a random type of tile
int generateRandomTileType() {
    int tileType = STANDARD_TILE;
    // randomised tile chances
    if (random(0, 5) > 4) {
        tileType = HOLE_TILE;
    }
    if (random(0, 50) > 45) {
        tileType = SPECIAL_TILE;
    }
    return tileType;
}
```

Displaying the tiles is then as simple as looping through each one, drawing a rectangle at the specified location and changing the colour for specific tiles (Figure 229). Adding a value to the y coordinate for each tile will give the impression of movement, leaving the cat its own position but advancing the tiles for each loop iteration

```
// draw tiles
stroke(0);
for (Tile tile : tiles) {
  // move tiles
  tile.y = tile.y + speed;
  if (tile.type == HOLE_TILE) {
    fill(0);
    // check location of kitty
    if (hitTile(tile.x, tile.y, cat.x, cat.y)) {
      // hit a hole, do something
      lives--;
      tile.type = SEALED_HOLE_TILE;
    }
  } else if (tile.type == SPECIAL_TILE) {
    fill(255, 255, 0);
    // check location of kitty
    if (hitTile(tile.x, tile.y, cat.x, cat.y)) {
      // hit a special tile, do something
      score++;
      tile.type = STANDARD_TILE;
    }
  } else if (tile.type == SEALED_HOLE_TILE) {
    fill(255, 0, 0);
  } else {
    fill(255);
  }
  rect(tile.x, tile.y, tileSize, tileSize);
}
```

We will need to add other functions, such as the ability to check which tile the cat is currently touching, increment scores, lose lives when a hole is hit and recycle the tiles when they leave the screen. These are all shown in the code listing in Appendix A. We now have a functioning game!

Figure 229: Cat Game in 2D

There are some niceties we might now add to make the game more appealing. A title screen and game over screen would make the game more fun for the player. We can just display some text and use the score we have stored to tell the user how well they did. Rotating the display also gives a nice 3D effect (Figure 230)

```
// rotate for 3D
rotateX(radians(45));
```

Figure 230: Cat Game in 3D

As a last piece of nice functionality we might add something to utilise the features of the Android device. To give the player additional feedback we could use the device's vibrate function to provide haptic (that is, felt by touch) feedback that they have hit a hole and therefore lost a life. This is accessed via the android.os.Vibrator class

We will define a Vibrator object called vibe

```
Vibrator vibe;
```

and call the vibrate function when a hole tile is hit

```
vibe.vibrate(100);
```

This is specified in milliseconds, so we will vibrate the device for 100 milliseconds. We also need to register the vibe object in a similar way to the accelerometer

```
// register vibrator
vibe = (Vibrator) getActivity().getSystemService(Context.VIBRATOR_SERVICE);
```

You will also need to set the VIBRATE permission which you can do using the Processing menu option for managing permissions. This is all that is required to utilise the vibrate function of the device. We can also use the same object to vibrate for longer when the game is over

You can find the complete source code in Appendix A if you would like to try it out, or perhaps you might want to work through the code and create a game yourself, maybe making some changes that you would like to see

The source code is also downloadable from the accompanying website as well as a link to the complete game if you would like to try it

https://devoniant.com/apps/kitty-hero-app/

You may also like to investigate other Android features such as accessing the camera, sound or physical device buttons, either to enhance the game we have created here, or create your own Android games or applications using *Processing*!

Other Programming Modes

Now that you have seen how *Processing*'s programming modes work and had a chance to try Java, JavaScript and Android modes you should be able to see how powerful *Processing* can be in creating graphic-rich applications and computer graphics for a wide variety of uses

If you are interested in other programming modes available, there are others available including Python, Ruby and Scala which allow you to create *Processing* graphics using those languages. It is likely that others will be added as interest peaks and wanes in particular programming languages

Summary

Having reached this point in the book you should now have everything you need to go and create all manner of graphics, sketches, programmes and applications using the *Processing* language. We encourage you to experiment, try out new features or mix features to see what effect you get which can often be surprising! But most of all, have fun

APPENDICES

Appendix A: Android Game Code

This appendix contains all of the course code for the cat game

```java
import android.content.Context;
import android.hardware.Sensor;
import android.hardware.SensorManager;
import android.hardware.SensorEvent;
import android.hardware.SensorEventListener;
import android.view.WindowManager;
import android.os.Bundle;
import android.os.Vibrator;

static final int NUMBER_OF_COLUMNS = 5;
static final int GRACE_PERIOD = 1;

static final int STANDARD_TILE = 0;
static final int HOLE_TILE = 1;
static final int SEALED_HOLE_TILE = 2;
static final int SPECIAL_TILE = 3;

static final int INITIAL_SCORE = 0;
static final int INITIAL_LIVES = 9;
static final int LOWEST_SPEED = 5;
static final int GREATEST_SPEED = 20;

static final String SCORE_TEXT = "Score: ";
static final String LIVES_TEXT = "Lives: ";
static final String GAME_OVER_TEXT = "GAME OVER";
static final String END_SCORE_TEXT = "You scored: ";
static final String RESTART_TEXT = "Press To Restart";
static final String START_TEXT = "Press To Start";
static final String GAME_TITLE_1 = "Kitty Hero:";
static final String GAME_TITLE_2 = "The Adventures of";
static final String GAME_TITLE_3 = "Mr Kittenson";


Context context;
SensorManager manager;
Sensor sensor;
AccelerometerListener listener;
Vibrator vibe;
```

```
float ax;
float ay;
float az;

int numberOfRows;
int tileSize;
int offsetX;

Cat cat;

int lives;
int score;
int speed;

boolean started;
boolean gameOver;

ArrayList<Tile> tiles;

void setup() {
    //size(600, 600, P3D);
    fullScreen(P3D);
    orientation(PORTRAIT);
    tileSize = width/NUMBER_OF_COLUMNS/2;
    numberOfRows = (height/tileSize) * 2;
    // set gap at sides
    offsetX = (width-tileSize * NUMBER_OF_COLUMNS)/2;
    // initialise game
    initialise();
    // setup accelerometer
    context = getActivity();
    manager = (SensorManager)context.getSystemService(Context.SENSOR_SERVICE);
    sensor = manager.getDefaultSensor(Sensor.TYPE_ACCELEROMETER);
    listener = new AccelerometerListener();
    // SENSOR_DELAY_FASTEST
    // SENSOR_DELAY_GAME
    manager.registerListener(listener,
        sensor, SensorManager.SENSOR_DELAY_FASTEST);
    // register vibrator
    vibe = (Vibrator) getActivity().getSystemService(Context.VIBRATOR_SERVICE);
}

void draw() {
```

```
   background(0);

   if (!started) {
      showStartScreen();
   } else if (gameOver) {
      showGameOver();
   } else {
      play();
   }
}

void initialise() {
   lives = INITIAL_LIVES;
   score = INITIAL_SCORE;
   speed = LOWEST_SPEED;
   cat = new Cat(tileSize);
   // initial position
   cat.x = width/2;
   cat.y = height - (height/4);
   // set bounds
   cat.minX = offsetX;
   cat.maxX = width - offsetX;
   cat.minY = tileSize;
   cat.maxY = height-(height/8);
   // initialise tiles
   tiles = new ArrayList<Tile>();
   for (int i = 0; i < numberOfRows; i++) {
      // set y coordinates (-y so scrolls downwards)
      int y = -i * tileSize;
      for (int j = 0; j < NUMBER_OF_COLUMNS; j++) {
         // set x coordinate
         int x = j * tileSize + offsetX;
         int tileType = STANDARD_TILE;
         // allow grace period of normal tiles
         if (i > GRACE_PERIOD) {
            // random tile types
            tileType = generateRandomTileType();
         }
         tiles.add(new Tile(x, y, tileType));
      }
   }
}
```

```
void startGame() {
   started = true;
   gameOver = false;
}

void play() {
   if (lives < 1) {
      gameOver = true;
      vibe.vibrate(500);
   }

   lights();
   // scoreboard
   textAlign(LEFT);
   fill(255);
   textSize(tileSize/2.5);
   text(SCORE_TEXT + score, 10, tileSize/2);
   text(LIVES_TEXT + lives, width-(tileSize*1.5), tileSize/2);

   // set speed but keep within limits
   speed = constrain(score/2, LOWEST_SPEED, GREATEST_SPEED);

   pushMatrix();
   // rotate for 3D
   rotateX(radians(45));

   // draw tiles
   stroke(0);
   for (Tile tile : tiles) {
      // move tiles
      tile.y = tile.y + speed;
      if (tile.type == HOLE_TILE) {
         fill(0);
         // check location of kitty
         if (hitTile(tile.x, tile.y, cat.x, cat.y)) {
            // hit a hole, do something
            lives--;
            vibe.vibrate(100);
            tile.type = SEALED_HOLE_TILE;
         }
      } else if (tile.type == SPECIAL_TILE) {
         fill(255, 255, 0);
```

```
            // check location of kitty
            if (hitTile(tile.x, tile.y, cat.x, cat.y)) {
                // hit a special tile, do something
                score++;
                tile.type = STANDARD_TILE;
            }
        } else if (tile.type == SEALED_HOLE_TILE) {
            fill(255, 0, 0);
        } else {
            fill(255);
        }
        rect(tile.x, tile.y, tileSize, tileSize);
    }
    // draw kitty
    cat.draw();
    popMatrix();
    // recycle tiles
    recycleTiles();
}

// show game over screen
void showGameOver() {
    fill(167, 0, 174);
    int offset = width/10;
    rect(offset, offset, width-offset*2, height-offset*2);
    fill(0);
    textAlign(CENTER);
    int fontSize = textToFontSize(GAME_OVER_TEXT);
    textSize(fontSize);
    text(GAME_OVER_TEXT, width/2, offset + fontSize);
    fontSize = textToFontSize(END_SCORE_TEXT + score);
    textSize(fontSize);
    text(END_SCORE_TEXT + score, width/2, height/2);
    fontSize = textToFontSize(RESTART_TEXT);
    textSize(fontSize);
    text(RESTART_TEXT, width/2, height - offset - fontSize);
    cat.draw();
}

// show start screen
void showStartScreen() {
    fill(167, 0, 174);
    int offset = width/10;
```

```
   rect(offset, offset, width-offset*2, height-offset*2);
   fill(0);
   textAlign(CENTER);
   int fontSize = textToFontSize(GAME_TITLE_2);
   textSize(fontSize);
   text(GAME_TITLE_1, width/2, offset + fontSize);
   text(GAME_TITLE_2, width/2, offset + fontSize * 2);
   text(GAME_TITLE_3, width/2, offset + fontSize * 3);
   textSize(textToFontSize(START_TEXT));
   text(START_TEXT, width/2, height - offset - fontSize);
   cat.draw();
}


// calculates the font size for a piece of text
int textToFontSize(String text) {
   // work out space per character
   int chars = text.length();
   int availableSpace = width;
   int characterSpace = availableSpace / chars;
   // convert pixels to font size
   int size = (int) (characterSpace * 1.3);
   return size;
}


// generate a random type of tile
int generateRandomTileType() {
   int tileType = STANDARD_TILE;
   // randomised tile chances
   if (random(0, 5) > 4) {
      tileType = HOLE_TILE;
   }
   if (random(0, 50) > 45) {
      tileType = SPECIAL_TILE;
   }
   return tileType;
}


// recycle tiles off the screen
void recycleTiles() {
   // get y coord of last tile
   int y = 0;
   for (Tile tile : tiles) {
      if (tile.y < y) {
```

```
            y = tile.y;
        }
    }
    // moves tiles to the end (x coord can stay the same)
    int newY = y - tileSize;
    for (Tile tile : tiles) {
        // if off the screen
        if (tile.y > height) {
            tile.y = newY;
            tile.type = generateRandomTileType();
        }
    }
}

// check if we hit a tile
boolean hitTile(int tileX, int tileY, int locationX, int locationY) {
    return (locationY >= tileY && locationY <= tileY + tileSize
        && locationX >= tileX && locationX <= tileX + tileSize);
}

// class for tiles
class Tile {
    int x;
    int y;
    int type;

    Tile(int x, int y, int type) {
        this.x = x;
        this.y = y;
        this.type = type;
    }
}

// class for drawing kitty
class Cat {

    final int tailLength;
    final int tailThickness;
    final color CAT_COLOUR = color(255, 200, 0);
    final int size;
    // tail segments
    PVector[] tail;
    // location
```

```
int x;
int y;
// bounds
int minX;
int maxX;
int minY;
int maxY;

Cat(int size) {
   this.size = size;
   this.tailLength = size/4;
   this.tailThickness = size/7;
   tail = new PVector[tailLength];
   for (int i = 0; i < tailLength; i++) {
      tail[i] = new PVector(0, 0);
   }
}

void draw() {
   // draw body in separate matrix so can rotate
   pushMatrix();
   noStroke();
   translate(x, y);
   rotateX(frameCount/20.0); // roll
   sphereDetail(7);
   fill(CAT_COLOUR);
   sphere(size * 0.4);
   popMatrix();

   pushMatrix();
   noStroke();
   // draw head
   translate(x, y - (size/2));
   sphereDetail(8);
   sphere(size * 0.2);
   // draw ears
   // left
   pushMatrix();
   //fill(0, 0, 255);
   translate(-size*0.1, -size*0.05, size*0.15);
   rotateY(0.5);
   rotateX(4);
   sphereDetail(1);
```

```
        sphere(size*0.1);
        popMatrix();
        // right
        pushMatrix();
        translate(size*0.1, -size*0.05, size*0.15);
        rotateY(3);
        rotateX(2);
        sphereDetail(1);
        sphere(size*0.1);
        popMatrix();
        // draw tail
        sphereDetail(8);
        tail[tailLength-1].x = (sin(frameCount * 0.2) * 10);
        tail[tailLength-1].y = size/2;
        for (int i = 0; i < tailLength-1; i++) {
            tail[i].x = tail[i+1].x;
            tail[i].y = tail[i+1].y + (tailThickness/2);
            pushMatrix();
            translate(tail[i].x, tail[i].y);
            sphere(tailThickness);
            popMatrix();
        }
        popMatrix();
    }
}

void mousePressed() {
    // ignore if game is playing
    if (gameOver || !started) {
        initialise();
        startGame();
    }
}

public void onCreate(Bundle bundle) {
    super.onCreate(bundle);
    // keep the screen on
    getActivity().getWindow().addFlags(
        WindowManager.LayoutParams.FLAG_KEEP_SCREEN_ON);
}

public void onResume() {
    super.onResume();
```

```
    if (manager != null) {
       manager.registerListener(listener,
           sensor, SensorManager.SENSOR_DELAY_FASTEST);
    }
}

public void onPause() {
    super.onPause();
    if (manager != null) {
       manager.unregisterListener(listener);
    }
}

class AccelerometerListener implements SensorEventListener {
    public void onSensorChanged(SensorEvent event) {
        ax = event.values[0];
        ay = event.values[1];
        az = event.values[2];

        if (cat.x - ax > cat.minX && cat.x - ax < cat.maxX) {
           cat.x -= ax;
        }

        if (cat.y + ay > cat.minY && cat.y + ay < cat.maxY) {
           cat.y += ay;
        }
    }

    public void onAccuracyChanged(Sensor sensor, int accuracy) {
       // do nothing
    }
}
```

INDEX